ENDO⟨

I wish every church had this book years ago! Most churches desire better worship but lack the knowledge and expertise to create a culture that produces an excellent spiritual, corporate, and creative worship experience. Through personal stories and life experience, Jeff unpacks how to create this culture in a very practical way.

—JONATHAN STOCKSTILL
Lead Pastor, Bethany Church

Here's a book on worship that's both inspiring and practical, both visionary and nitty-gritty. And it comes from someone who has arisen as a father in the worship movement. Decades of experience are distilled into succinct, helpful instruction. Learn how to ignite the body of Christ with your passion for Jesus, and how to steward your calling to lead worship in these last days.

—BOB SORGE
Author, Exploring Worship:
A Practical Guide to Praise and Worship

Jeff Deyo has given us all a gift with his new book, *SPARK: A Comprehensive Worship Leadership Handbook.* Jeff has wonderfully woven together personal and relatable stories with practical and proven worship techniques, all encompassed within a framework of the importance of building culture. His emphasis on building culture is paramount throughout this marvelously written book.

I've known Jeff for years, and what he has built at North Central University has proven that with the right culture, the sky is the limit. This is a joyful read for anyone with a heart to worship, but to a worship leader, it's God's heart and mind all wrapped in a book. It will change the culture in your heart, thereby forever changing the culture of your church and your community.

—CHRIS DuPRÉ
Speaker, pastor, and author of The Wild Love of God

Jeff Deyo is far from the typical worship leader and songsmith; he is a pure worshiper. I've not only seen it from afar through his music, but up close as his friend. In this much-needed message to the Church, Jeff opens up and shares his life experiences as well as practical ways to create the same culture he daily lives by. If you're looking for a worship reboot to ignite the flames of revival in your life (and church), look no further than *SPARK*.

—Brian Ming
Co-Founder, Unveiled Worship,
Author of the Secret Heart Series

In this book, Jeff Deyo provides a profound, cogent road map to develop and enlighten both the individual worship leader and the community he/she serves. *SPARK* will provoke thought, challenge the paradigm, and help transcend the barriers we have all faced within our spiritual community.

—Elisha St. James
Worship Pastor, Faith Community Fellowship

Jeff is a gifted worship leader and teacher, and the practical lessons I learned from his coaching of our worship team have been incredibly empowering to me as a leader. Our team has grown closer together, and deeper with the Lord as we patiently implemented His vision for our church. If you desire to seek God with your team and grow the Kingdom culture of worship in your church and life, Jeff's new book *SPARK* is what you are looking for!

—Kathi Garner
Worship Leader, Rolla First Assembly of God

The principles in this book, if applied, will do exactly what they are designed to do: ignite a *SPARK* in the Kingdom of God. Jeff's ability to speak directly to your heart by sharing his heart for worship will inspire you to "offer in public what you have cultivated in private," a heart for pure worship. As you dive into this resource, ask God to show you areas of your ministry that need to be fully surrendered to Him.

—Mark Overturf
Worship Leader, Trinity Temple Assembly of God

Leading worship half empty? Looking for a push to keep going? Jeff Deyo shares a passionate message from his heart in his new book *SPARK*. As you read these pages, you will feel inspired and encouraged while being able to explore Scripture and gather tips. Jeff captures the power of worship for you as an individual and as a leader in corporate settings. It's a great read for both leaders and teams!

—MATT HIGGS
Music & Young Adult Pastor, Sunset Avenue Church of God

Jeff gets it. He's learned it. He lives it. He's leading it. Jeff is a guiding voice in a new reformation that we desperately need. I invite you to lend your ear to his voice and join him on the journey!

—TODD MARSHALL
Worship is Life Ministries/Author of Worship Is Life

Speed and activity can have a negative impact on ministry. Jeff Deyo's latest book release, *SPARK*, provides direction and inspiration to help you step back and rediscover how to grow in worship, both in your life and in the life of your church. *SPARK* is a field manual for leaders who are building a worship culture that helps believers grow deeper in their relationship with Jesus.

—TOM JACOBS
Lead Pastor, Family Life Assembly of God

In the day and time we live, Jeff Deyo's wisdom and insight into worship leadership is absolutely needed in the body of Christ. Worship and the power it holds is something Jeff knows and communicates exceptionally well. The purity of heart and dedication in surrender found in this book will absolutely revitalize your approach to worship.

—DANIEL ERIC GROVES
Worship Evangelist/DEGM Teaching Pastor,
Hope City Church

Jeff Deyo's new book, *SPARK*, is a breath of fresh air for all who serve Jesus in worship ministry. It will not only help transform the way leaders think about worship, but more importantly, it will establish true Kingdom culture by encouraging them to utilize the many unsung techniques found in Scripture to build up their teams and congregants. May it be used to bring many closer to Jesus.

—ERIK BURKLIN
President, China Partner/WCM Board Member

Culture is continually created, whether good or bad. And *this* is the book to help you create the Kingdom culture of pure worship in your church! I have watched Jeff Deyo live this message as he leads our worship ministry at Celebration Church in these principles, and I highly recommend this resource to you.

—DERRICK ROSS
Lead Pastor, CelebrationChurch.net

I've had the honor of knowing Jeff for years, and he embodies the ethos of this book. For that reason, I know this was done with authenticity and passion, for not only building a culture of worship, but to be a practical and powerful tool to build the Kingdom.

—CLINTON ALLEN
Worship Leader, River Valley Worship

SPARK is a must-read for every worship pastor/leader! Jeff exposes the many subtle lies we've often believed as leaders and also dives into practical, biblical strategies designed to help us lead our church from having a good experience on Sunday to having a God encounter every day. You will be challenged, encouraged, and inspired to lead with new passion and purpose!

—JOSH BREWER
Worship Pastor, Pinelake Church

Over the years, I have had the privilege of hearing firsthand many of the God-given revelations Jeff writes about in his new book. Yet even as I read it, I see so much more. God has given Jeff fresh revelation that will help us humble ourselves before Him in a time when we struggle greatly between building our kingdom and building God's Kingdom. Trust me, this book will help your soul rediscover the *spark* it needs to unite with Jesus and to lead others to do the same.

—JONATHAN LEE
Songwriter/Creative Pastor,
Cedar Rapids First Assembly of God

SPARK

IGNITING THE CULTURE OF PURE WORSHIP
IN YOUR TEAMS AND YOUR CONGREGATION

SPARK

A COMPREHENSIVE WORSHIP LEADERSHIP HANDBOOK

JEFF DEYO

SPARK: A Comprehensive Worship Leadership Handbook
Igniting the Culture of Pure Worship In Your Teams and Your Congregation

Cover design by Brendan Hollis
"Spark" image by Jez Tims/Unsplash.com
Interior design and typeset by Katherine Lloyd

Printed in the United States of America
20 21 22 23 24 25 5 4 3 2 1

DEDICATION

For all the Franks out there who are knowingly or unknowingly in desperate need of a God-spark that only an authentic, Kingdom-minded worship leader can help facilitate.

In honor of Gordon Anderson, Larry Bach, Scott Hagan, Doug Graham, and Derrick Ross for affording me the incredible freedom to implement Spirit-led, biblical strategies at North Central University and Celebration Church in order to cultivate the culture of the Kingdom in our worship spaces.

CONTENTS

Section One
IT ALL BEGINS WITH AUTHENTICITY

Section Two
ACTIVATING TEAMS FOR PURE WORSHIP LEADERSHIP

Chapter 13

THE PERFECT UNION: A MARVELOUS MARRIAGE OF THE SCRIPTED AND THE UNSCRIPTED

THE DAY IT ALL BEGAN

UP CAME A SHOOT

WHAT IS SPONTANEOUS WORSHIP?

CREATING SPACE FOR GOD

DRAWN TO THE SCRIBBLES

THE BIG QUESTION

PLANNING GOD OUT OF THE SERVICE

NAVY SEALS, BORN TO ADAPT

THE BIBLICAL PRECEDENT FOR SPONTANEOUS WORSHIP

PLANNING FOR THE UNPLANNED

REHEARSING SPONTANEOUS WORSHIP WITH YOUR TEAMS

INTRODUCING SPONTANEOUS WORSHIP TO YOUR CONGREGATION

CRITICAL STRATEGIES

A HOLY SPIRIT REBUKE

KEEPING YOUR CONGREGATION ZONED IN

A JOYFUL NOISE

CAUTIONS CONNECTED TO SPONTANEOUS WORSHIP

CATCHING THE CURRENT

Chapter 14

BONA FIDE BABIES AND BRACKISH BURNOUT

WORSHIP LEADERS, CLIMATE SETTERS

WHOSE JOB IS IT, ANYWAY?

FRIENDSHIP SUNDAY

SHEPHERDS VS. TROUBADOURS

WHEN WE COME TOGETHER

THE ACTIVATION OF ALL

EXPECT GREAT THINGS

WHAT IF SOMETHING GOES WRONG?

HOLDING LOOSELY TO YOUR SET LIST

A KINGDOM MODEL

EVERYONE BRINGS SOMETHING

FOREWORD

Eric Liddell, the Scottish Olympic gold-medalist runner portrayed so well in the 1981 movie *Chariots of Fire*, said, "God made me fast. And when I run, I feel His pleasure."[1] I remember when I heard him say that in the movie. It struck a chord. In the years that followed, as I began my journey into worship ministry, I've often been reminded of Eric's powerful statement.

When I step up to a microphone, about to lead believers in musical worship, I often begin from a place of slight trepidation and anxiety. And yet, after singing the first few lines, I always transition to a place of peace and confidence. It never fails, even after having done this for over thirty years. And when I'm in the middle of a worship song, singing together with other believers, I also "feel His pleasure." May the day never come when leading worship becomes routine or void of the anticipation of the Lord's presence.

Getting to a place of peace is something I desire in the other parts of my life too. It doesn't come automatically, though; I have to actively pursue it. The variety of social media channels vying for my attention are invariably filled with vitriol. Truth is being replaced with opinion, peace replaced by angst.

I'll be honest. The last thing I want in a book on igniting biblical worship culture is someone's opinion. That's why this new narrative by Jeff Deyo is so refreshing and timely. Drawing from over two decades of leading worship around the world, from large venues to small churches, Jeff champions the ideals of how to build the "culture of the Kingdom"

---

1   Eric Liddell, *Chariots of Fire* movie (Warner Bros., 1981).

into local church worship teams and congregations. Thankfully, *SPARK* is rich with biblical insight that will challenge and inspire every person who has been called into worship ministry.

The life of every believer is filled with extraordinary pitfalls and temptations, but I dare say, those whose ministry is often in front of people—through speaking, teaching, or leading worship—face higher scrutiny. The apostle Paul even speaks to a greater level of responsibility in James 3:1: *"Not many of you should become teachers, my fellow believers, because you know that we who teach will be judged more strictly"* (NIV). For those who are serving in public ministry, extra vigilance is clearly required, especially if we aspire to maintain a walk of humility, something these chapters explore so vigilantly.

You will likely find yourself referencing the truths in this book regularly with your worship team(s) and your congregation. In fact, I would strongly encourage you to get copies for everyone on the team and go through it together. Laboring with others on your team is like working out in a spiritual gym. Rather than working on abs and pecs and getting your physical body in shape, working together with other believers affords you the constant challenge of forgiving, submitting, practicing patience, encouraging, and serving each other, which in turn gets you all into healthy spiritual shape, as iron sharpens iron. Your worship team community becomes an environment that offers the potential for everyone in the group to grow incrementally in Kingdom maturity.

In the years since I started leading worship in our small East Texas congregation with a simple guitar/vocal, modern worship music has grown to become a major component of the local church experience. For better or worse, an entire industry has sprung up to support this movement. Much of it is to be applauded, and I am tempted to call it "progress"—most of the time. But occasionally the pendulum swings too far, and a return to balance is required. My friend and occasional co-writer, Matt Redman, so beautifully described this tension and our need to continually recalibrate when he wrote the inspiring lyrics for his song, Heart of Worship.

SPARK takes us on a journey of what Spirit-led worship should be *and* what it can be, both in your heart and soul, and as it pertains to the members of your team and local church body. Because of our tendency to get out of balance, the insightful analogies, stories, and scriptural underpinnings Jeff uses become a fresh inspirational focus regarding our highest pursuit—one I have dedicated my life to.

May the chapters that follow serve as a spark to guide you, and may you always "feel His pleasure" as you worship Him.

Paul Baloche
Worship Pastor/Songwriter

A KINGDOM CULTURE BUILDING GUIDE

I don't want to help you lead worship. I want to help you spark culture. Kingdom worship culture, to be exact. In your teams and in your congregation. Funny thing is, you're already doing it, whether you realize it or not. As leaders, we must understand that everything we do—and don't do—is establishing culture. Either culture we desire or culture we despise. It's happening right under our noses, so we might as well be intentional about it.

Imagine if you could deeply graft the culture of *Awakening Pure Worship* (my first book) into your worship teams and congregation. A culture of authenticity, passion, and hunger for God. Not as a result of human ingenuity, the latest marketing trends, or learned psych ological manip- ulation, but as a result of God's true unadulterated power and presence. True faith in His Kingdom process. The kind that brings tangible and lasting change to all men and women. Black and White. Young and old. Families. Singles. Students. Elderly. Everyone.

Could it be? Yes.

A PICTURE OF A PREFERRED FUTURE

Question: If you woke up and discovered you were leading your church in ways (big or small) that are contrary to Scripture or that

you were unintentionally disregarding some of the more important biblical directives in your services—even after years of church
ministry—would you be willing to change? I believe you would. And
that's exactly why I wrote this book. To help each one of us become
increasingly aware of our current culture as well as increasingly empowered as leaders.

I believe we're going to revolutionize the landscape of your worship
teams and your church family. By God's grace, I'm going to paint a picture of a preferred leadership future. Not one I dreamed up, but one God
dreamed up. One He lays out in His Word and confirms with His Spirit.
Simple yet powerful, all unfolding poignantly in the pages ahead as we
concentrate on three vital culture-building strategies:

1. **Worship Leadership: It All Begins with Authenticity**
2. **Activating Your Teams for Pure Worship Leadership**
3. **Instilling the Heart of Pure Worship in Your Congregation**

We're going to discover and rediscover the mysteries of true Kingdom culture—as woven mysteriously throughout God's Word—with
the singular purpose of serving our teams and our congregations much
more effectively. Remember: as leaders in God's Church, we will be held
accountable for the choices we make with every passing week—choices
that either move us farther from or closer to God's Kingdom culture.

This is our calling. This is our assignment. This is our joy!

BUCKLE YOUR SEATBELTS

Fittingly, this book was written for worship pastors, musicians, and singers, as well as all pastors, who have one thing in common: *they're not
satisfied with the status quo.* Don't hear me wrong. They're not judgmen-
tal or negative toward the body of Christ, but they do believe things
could be—and probably should be—flying at a much higher altitude.

Ask yourself: What is *my* vision for our congregation? What is *God's*
vision for our congregation? Are they congruent?

Again. This is *not* primarily a "How to Lead Worship" book. But don't worry. I do provide a boat load of practical ideas on just about every topic regarding leading worship and building teams—almost anything you might want to know. But it is still much, much more than that. This is a "How to Build Kingdom Culture" book. A book that will help you encourage, instill, and impart the ways of God's Kingdom—according to His Word—into your church.

Thankfully, you don't have to sit by and hope your church grows into all that God wants it to be. You can be a part of its genuine Spirit-led transformation. Slowly. Intentionally. Over time. You can undoubtedly create a healthy culture within your church (even if it's currently one where people seem largely apathetic). With the biblical principles I share, and the help of God's Spirit, you'll be able to spark a culture where the congregation worships with genuine freedom and wholehearted abandon with their songs *and* with their lives.

"But Jeff, we're already experiencing the profound move of God in our church." Okay, are you sure? Maybe there's still more.

"But Jeff, our people are too set in their ways to change."

Fair, but this is where we need a monumental paradigm shift. Whatever our congregants are feeling, however they're responding during the musical worship, whatever their natural tendencies have become during any part of our services, it's mostly a result of the culture we—the leaders in our church—have built.

For example, if you find yourself frustrated when your church family becomes restless and ready to leave at noon—or hesitates to linger genuinely at the altar—it's because they're anticipating the close of the service. Why? Because of us. As a result of the culture *we* have built. Because we have strongly conditioned them to know when the service is ending. As a result of *our* leadership. Hundreds and hundreds of services have come and gone, and we've nearly always left the building three to four minutes after the sermon is complete.

Why should we think our congregation would expect anything different? They simply exist within the world we've created. A world we've handed them. An order of service. A liturgy.

And they respond—as they should—in like manner.

Not surprisingly, attempting to deviate from our typical order of service on the fifty-first Sunday of the year—after not doing so for fifty Sundays in a row—could be shocking or, even worse, downright offensive.

It's simple. You and I have clearly communicated our plan over and over again—mostly without saying it, but by modeling it and by establishing (in this particular instance) that leaving immediately after the sermon is over is simply what we do. It's our *culture*.

You may have surmised that the majority of the goings-on in your church are simply beyond your control—and some of this may be true. But don't overlook the obvious. Together, the leaders in our churches have largely created or affirmed the current culture in our church. This is a fact.

Indeed, our congregants have simply responded to the culture we have built; they have either embraced it (enthusiastically or begrudgingly) or they have changed churches. Plain and simple. For those who've stayed, *our* plans have now become *their* plans. *Our* patterns have become *their* patterns. *Our* culture has become *their* culture. All of us simply exist together within a cultural bubble we have created called "church." Sometimes for better, but often for worse.

This is the very definition of culture: *patterns walked out by a group of people, again and again, over a long period of time.*

WHAT LEADERS DO

Culture is not inherently good or bad. It just is. It's not the cause. It's the effect. The effect of countless hours, days, weeks, months, and years of human doings. Human habits. Human decisions. All adding up to the thing that is our culture.

Of course, I'm not suggesting it's a bad idea to build a culture. Just the opposite. Creating culture is what leaders do. Not as a tool of control, but as an act of service.

It's in everything we do—24/7/365—whether we grasp it or not. Whether we want it or not. Culture is being carefully crafted with every word we say and every action we take. With every set list and service order we build. With every prayer and message we craft. With every announcement and every baby dedication. Every baptism and every altar response. Every PowerPoint slide and every video.

We've conditioned our congregations to respond in certain ways, as a result of our decisions, our planning, our phraseology, and our programming. And yet, paradoxically, we often find ourselves genuinely bewildered by their passion and participation, or lack thereof. Of course, this is completely unreasonable. Why? Because they are behaving, for the most part, exactly the way we've shown them to behave. In the way we've encouraged them to behave. In the way we've allowed them to behave.

> It is not that the people in our churches are closed to the deeper things of God; it's that we must boldly encourage our congregants in the deeper things of God by becoming devoted instigators of this type of culture.

Contrary to popular opinion, it is not that people in our churches are closed to the deeper things of God; it's that we must boldly encourage our congregants in the deeper things of God by becoming devoted instigators of this type of culture—with generous guidance from the Spirit of God. That is, if we want the deeper things of God to become our norm. Our culture.

A CULTURAL EXPERIMENT

In this book, I share countless stories from an eleven-year (ongoing) experiment—one where I and many others have invested considerable blood, sweat, and tears into sparking the culture of pure worship at North Central University (NCU)—and in my home church, Celebration Church. Admittedly, part of my journey has involved perpetuating the passionate culture I inherited from those who came before me, but large portions of it has involved decisively spurring things on—against the grain—in order to align or realign our culture with Kingdom culture.

It's ironic. We all make excuses for why some churches can't make the necessary adjustments. For example, some people believe megachurches are incapable of implementing the techniques I lay out in this book. But this is not true. These principles apply whether your church is large or small, rural or urban, evangelical or Pentecostal.

Kingdom identity transformation is God's specialty. Yet, as always, if we believe God's ideas cannot become a part of our church culture, we're probably right, and we have effectively placed a lid on a potent future while holding tightly to an impotent past.

Granted, the vision for change must be introduced to our congregations slowly and intentionally over time with the support of every leader. This is the nature of true leadership. And this is what I'm going to help you with.

Are you going to build the perfect church? No. Will yours look exactly like mine? Nope. But God is equipping you to present to Him *"a glorious church without a spot or wrinkle or any other blemish"* (Ephesians 5:27), and the principles in *this* book—compiled directly from *The* Book—are going to give you the best chance of sparking a church like this.

WHY *SPARK*?

Here's the story. On June 30, 2018, in Janesville, Wisconsin, I met a man named Frank who was extraordinarily "sparked" by the presence of God during our set. We were leading worship at Freedom Fest, a family festival where several thousand people gather each summer to listen to some of the most inspiring bands in the nation, to enjoy a plethora of legit carnival rides, and—as important as anything—to eat giant corn dogs, loaded cheese fries, and sugar-sprinkled elephant ears.

This particular day was hot, even for June. The temperature hovered near one hundred, with not a cloud in the sky and peanut-butter-like humidity. The bands were hot too. Bands like Manic Drive, We Are Messengers, and Plumb dotted the lineup along with, of course, yours truly.

I had a stellar band playing with me that day. Sam Rodriquez on drums. Johnny Q on bass. Caleb Ballew on keys. And Justin Jacobs on electric. I couldn't ask for more. Of course, I was scheduled to hit the stage at 4:30 p.m., right at the most sweltering point of the day. On a giant black stage, facing the gradually setting sun. With no shade.

The trampled yellow grass was littered with colorful lawn chairs and blankets. Tiny Chihuahuas and little children ran freely, chasing moths and butterflies. Older folks, many of whom were there for the seventeenth time, sat under faded umbrellas fanning themselves with empty nachos containers. The smell of cotton candy was in the air.

The MC encouraged the enthusiastic crowd as the sweat-drenched Manic Drive fled the stage, eager for shade and water. He prayed zealously and then said, "Okay, everybody. Let's get on our feet and welcome Jeeeeeeff DAY-OOOOOH!"

Oh, shoot. I thought we covered that. "It's DEE-YO (not DAY-oh)," I had clarified just minutes before he introduced me. "Remember the letters D and O, and you've got it."

Oh well, no time to be petty. The track for "Glorious Day" was already rolling.

With a classic set that included songs like NCU's "Hearts on Fire," "Unstoppable God," "Reckless Love," "Always Remain," "What a Beautiful Name," and "Surrounded (Fight My Battles)," we were off and running.

Finally, as we came to the end of the last song and exploded into the final chord, I boldly exhorted everyone to lift their voices—under the clear skies of their Creator—one last time. They did, and I said a prayer and skipped off the stage.

Now. Just to sit. Just to drink. Just to rest.

I searched for a spot. For a towel. For my breath. Then I shuffled over to the merchandise area. Thankfully, it was shaded.

Several people came over to talk. Others went to get seconds on fried chicken. Then Frank walked up, and everything changed.

Frank is the reason I've *finally* written this book.

See, I'm just not satisfied with the typical wasn't-that-a-nice-worship service response. There's just got to be more. And I believe there is. More. Undoubtedly there is. I've tasted it. And so have you. That's why you're reading this book.

What if we could create an environment where what happened to Frank happens to everyone? Or most everyone? Or even a lot of everyone.

Now we're talking.

But what did happen to Frank?

God happened.

When Frank walked up to me, I was beyond exhausted. I was ready to go back to the green room for some AC and some good eats. But he stopped me in my tracks.

He shook my hand, and then he stood there. Shaken. He tried to speak, but his eyes welled up. He uttered a profoundly heartfelt thank-you, and again attempted to tell me his story. But he struggled.

For a second, I honestly wondered if he was mentally challenged in some way. Turns out he was. Not for natural reasons but for supernatural reasons. He said something like this: "Jeff, I came to this festival to have a good time. I brought the fam like every year. We rode the rides, ate the food, and listened to the bands. But then you and your band started singing. And everything disappeared. Everything except the knowledge of God, my Creator, invading my life. It was like the whole world stopped and it was just me and Jesus. Standing there on the limp grass. I was not looking for this. I was not hoping for this. I was not ready for this. I couldn't have imagined the punch of God's presence that was about to knock me off my spiritual feet."

He continued with juddered speech, "I don't know how to thank you. I stood there in the Wisconsin heat, with my hands lifted to God, unaware. Without a care. Lost in God's love. And now the world has an entirely new feel. It's like my heart has been reopened. Rehabilitated. Regenerated. My mind's been reborn. My vision is turning clear. For the first time in a long time. Thank you, Jeff. Thank you. Something is different. You were different. I am different. Thank you."

I didn't know what to say. But it sparked something special in me, too. It genuinely moved me and spurred me onward. To refuse to focus on past successes (or the lack thereof). To not give up. To keep fighting for God's presence. To keep growing in my ability to move in the power of the Spirit. To keep believing for an anointing that can accelerate people's hunger for God. To keep expecting more. To keep contending for breakthrough. To keep praying for…the "R" word.

Yes. Revival.

So, that's it. This book is called *SPARK* because I believe in something. I believe I've been called to serve you. To encourage you. To *spark* you— after twenty-nine plus years of ministry. In churches all over the world.

After years and years of failures and victories. I'm still burning bright with a rich passion to help you help your church family ignite a wildfire in their connection with God—so together we can stoke the flames of God's life-giving Kingdom culture across the earth.

Section One

WORSHIP LEADERSHIP: IT ALL BEGINS WITH AUTHENTICITY

Chapter 1

DIGGING THE WELL

Lie #1

*"I just don't have time to spend regular time
alone with the God who created time."*

CHAPTER NOTE: *You may be tempted to skip past this chapter to get to the more "practical" stuff of leading teams and congregations, but I beg you not to do so. These first five chapters will lay a critical foundation for you as a leader that will not crumble no matter the storms that come your way.*

AS THE DEER

I'll never forget the summer of 1994. My family was on vacation at beautiful Lake Powell in sun-beat Utah. We were docking our little houseboat on the sandy beach below the canyon cliffs when we saw a sight I will never forget.

Beyond the burnt-orange rocks, a scrawny, malnourished deer staggered toward the beach. He stood statue still, eyeing the waters below—about one hundred feet away. A rocky slope lay between him and salvation.

Suddenly, he began to walk.

With each determined stride, the bones beneath his skin strained to maintain balance. Marching slowly but steadily toward the glistening lake—unwavering in his focus—he considered the water his one hope for survival. Every few steps, he glanced at us to make sure we didn't mean any real harm, weighing which was the greater threat—us or death by dehydration.

He traipsed on. Tirelessly. Hopeful.

When he finally reached the shallow shore, he paused. For what seemed like an eternity. He gathered himself, lowered his shriveled head, and stole a taste. We stood motionless as his eyes and ears twitched nervously in our direction.

Then he did the unthinkable. In desperation, he dropped slowly, intentionally, trembling, to his knees—seemingly now oblivious to the potential perils all around—if only to fully revitalize his parched carcass.

FRUITLESSNESS

The image of that deer on his knees, drinking from the deep-blue waters of Lake Powell, will remain in my mind forever, as if it happened yesterday—in slow motion. Nothing would keep him from reaching the refreshment he required. Not the rocks or the rough terrain, not the onlookers or the threat of their attack, not the cruel sun or the violent heat. Not even his own exhaustion.

> We would never dream of going more than a few hours without a meal or a snack, but we manage to press on for days, months, or even years without proper relational God-nourishment for our souls.

In that moment, I was disheartened by an augmented revelation regarding leadership. Namely, the way many of us attempt to lead from a place of near exhaustion. Near emptiness. *As the deer longs for streams of water, so I long for you, O God*" (Psalms 42:1). Oh, that God's leaders would return daily to the thirst-quenching 'Rivers of living water.'

There are times, in response to physical hunger, that we may announce dramatically, "I'm starving to death." But truth be told, most of us have never been *that* depleted—so hungry or thirsty that we truly dangle on the edge of life. Even so, just as the shriveled deer was desperately malnourished physically, many church leaders are desperately malnourished spiritually.

We may have a sense that something isn't quite right—as we wrestle with near burnout, depression, or anxiety—yet we walk around smiling and looking good on the outside, one step away from total collapse. We engage in our religious duties and continue posting inspirational Scripture verses, yet when all is said and done, our spirit is nothing more than a sack of skin and bones.

And we wonder why. Why we aren't producing lasting fruit? As leaders. As ministers.

Clearly, our spiritual need for God is analogous to our physical need for food. One provides nourishment for our bodies, while the other provides essential nourishment for our withered souls. We would never dream of going more than a few hours without a meal or a snack, but we manage to press on for days, months, or even years without proper relational God-nourishment for our souls. Without drinking in real, intimate time alone with God—in His Word, in prayer, in musical worship, in fellowship—in His presence.

We fool ourselves, believing we can indirectly absorb God's good vibes while simply working at church. Doing God's work. Ministry. Or, even worse, we attempt to *survive* on the leftovers from last year's midweek revival, worship conference, or couples' retreat. Or on the passion we had for God a few years back, when things were less…complicated. We do the very thing we tell our congregants not to do: live from Sunday to Sunday, as if one small regurgitated meal each week is enough.

HALF-FULL LEADERS

Ask yourself: Have I lost my spark? What would it take for me to be sparked again? Sparked by the relational things of God? Unnumbed to the true joy of my First Love? Again?

Maybe you're a worship singer or musician, and you'd be satisfied just to wake up without feeling guilty while leading worship on Sunday, void of authentic connection with God. Maybe you're a pastor and you've become entangled in the business of church politics and finances and have honestly lost sight of why you became a Kingdom shepherd in the first place. Maybe you're a board member or a volunteer, and your heart aches for the many who attend church and yet seem adrift just beyond meaningful relationship with God.

Life is hard. Ministry is hard. And many of us are driven to focus more on survival than revival. Maybe it's enough just to work a church job and take care of our family. To keep our heads down and embrace the daily grind. Maybe we're living oblivious to the grand possibilities. Or maybe we've simply given up—having experienced one disappointment after another.

The devil has us right where he wants us. We genuinely desire to be anointed. To lead with passion. To live in the authority of Christ. We genuinely want to help hurting people. To set the captives free. To move in the supernatural power of God. But how can we share the nourishing things of the Kingdom with others when we ourselves have too often pursued the *work* of God over the *love* of God?

As leaders, we face a serious conflict. We long to be used powerfully by God in public ministry settings, yet this captivating desire can easily eclipse our hunger for establishing a deeper friendship with God for ourselves. We must embrace this staggering irony: When we neglect to cultivate a private walk with God in favor of polishing our public ministry, we fail to acquire the life-giving relationship with God we need as well as the enduring, impactful ministry we seek. The latter is always dependent on the former. But the latter is more intriguing and more rewarding in the short term.

We must realize that it all begins with authenticity. And authenticity begins with the cultivation of a genuine relationship with God. In the secret place. I call it "digging the well."

Evangelist Lowell Lundstrom used to remind believers that there's nothing worse than a *half full* Christian trying to overflow. I suppose that is true, unless we happen upon a half-full Christian *leader* trying to overflow.

THE TOUR GUIDE ANALOGY

Imagine you decide to throw caution to the wind and move to Arizona. You've never told anyone, but you've always dreamed of moving out West. To the Grand Canyon. One of your bucket-list locations. Yep. There's nothing quite like those magnificent rust-colored rocks. They stir you. The epic scenes of the Colorado River zig-zagging through the sunbaked formations of the Arizona desert. That gigantic fracture in the earth whose width spans more than 316 football fields. It's more than you can fathom. And it's absolutely breathtaking.

So you quit your job, pack your things, and move there. All with the glorious hope of landing a job as a tour guide. You arrive, and it happens. The job is yours! They immediately assign you your first tour. With only one problem. You've never actually *been* to the Grand Canyon.

You've seen pictures of the Grand Canyon. You've heard stories about the Grand Canyon. You've dreamed dreams about the Grand Canyon. But in your entire life, you've never actually stepped out on the rocky cliffs, tasted the dry air, or walked the dusty paths meandering down into the heart of this gorgeous gorge.

You blurt out, "So when do we start my training?"

The manager quips, "Training? What training? We don't have time for training. Head straight over there, make two lefts and a right, and you'll find your group waiting just ahead. Grab your pack, your map, and your mule, and take them out on the ride of their lives, Captain!"

Apprehension fills your chest as you consider guiding a tour you've never toured yourself. Truth is, many of the voyagers will be taking the journey for the second, third, or even twentieth time. And they'll know it like the back of their hand.

Isn't this how some of us approach worship leadership?

Clearly exposed is a fundamental flaw in our thinking. Somehow, we've come to believe the number one goal in successful worship leadership is to focus primarily on God while leading from a stage. However, though it's imperative we worship God while leading worship, surprising as it may be, this is not our chief aim as worship leaders.

In fact, dare I say, when we allow ourselves to place our personal connection with God as a top priority in worship leadership, we might as well argue that the tour guide's primary objective is to be seen enjoying the tour for himself. But *this* would make for a terrible tour guide.

Think about it. What is the top priority of the tour guide? To be seen enjoying the exquisite sights for himself? Certainly not. The top priority of the tour guide is to put every effort into serving the tourists by facilitating the best possible encounter for them.

If the tour guide wants to enjoy the trip for himself, he certainly may join a tour led by another guide. Likewise, if he wants to increase his knowledge of the tour to bolster his effectiveness as a tour guide, he should venture out on his own, regularly, that he might re-encounter the fullness of every sight and sound, twist and turn, soaking in each and every unique aspect of the tour. For himself. Alone. This is the path to becoming the best tour guide possible. He must explore the tour on his own, vigilantly, and then and only then will he truly be effective in guiding other sojourners.

> In leadership, we just can't take people where we haven't been.

Bottom line: In leadership, we just can't take people where we haven't been. It's impossible. Ironically, the leader's main role on the stage is not to seek the Lord for himself. This must take place in secret in order to bear fruit in public. Then the leader is free to minister from a place of authenticity with the goal of serving the congregation in achieving an ever-increasing, authentic God encounter for themselves. With each and every expedition.

Of course, like many analogies, this one breaks down a bit in the sense that once the Grand Canyon guide perfects his script, he rarely finds reason to embark on the tour alone again. (I suppose this is a real danger for ministers of the gospel as well.) For pastors and worship leaders, the tour must be revisited daily in order to keep the fires of authentic relationship with God burning—with each and every solo voyage.

SOFTENING THE HARD PLACES

As we set aside time with God in the secret place, it's like He's handing us a shovel to dig a well—specifically the well of relationship with the Father. Not in a "works" kind of way, but in the way that all healthy relationships require investment to flourish. The act of digging equates to nurturing our personal relationship with God through singing, prayer, dancing, reading the Word, repenting, listening, shouting, being still, etc. Each time we engage in these activities in private, we cultivate the soil of our heart for a richer connection with God in our life.

But dirt can be hard. Hard like our hearts. Digging can be hard. Especially when hearts are hard.

Yet, if we dig long enough and deep enough over time—not cutting short the often-arduous process—we will strike water. Spiritual water. Water, referred to by Jesus in John 7:37-39, as the 'Rivers of living water,' which He likens to the Holy Spirit.

"On the last day, the climax of the festival, Jesus stood and shouted to the crowds, "Anyone who is thirsty may come to me! Anyone who believes in me may come and drink! For the Scriptures declare, 'Rivers of living water will flow from his heart.'" (When he said "living water," he was speaking of the Spirit, who would be given to everyone believing in him. But the Spirit had not yet been given, because Jesus had not yet entered into his glory.)

It's simple. When we dig the well, we make way for a fresh outpouring of the Spirit's cleansing water to fill our hearts, soften the hard places, break up the cynical clods, and wash away our overwhelming filth. All the while fostering pure and genuine connection—communion—with the Lover of our souls.

Beautiful.

As stated, many leaders overlook this deeply satisfying private pursuit of God (or they have moved beyond it), believing it all happens simultaneously as they lead from the stage. Or as they prepare their messages. But this isn't the case. Great leadership is built on the idea that leaders lead in public out of the sweet overflow of fellowship with God that has been fostered in private.

TODAY'S SPECIALS

Interestingly, the shovel itself is taken away as we move from the secret place to the public stage. It is replaced by another tool—a pitcher. As we established with the Grand Canyon tour guide, worship leaders don't step onto a platform primarily to enjoy their own personal time with God—to experience the tour for themselves. They've already been enjoying it by themselves all week—in the secret place. Now, fully filled, they step onto the platform with one main goal in mind: to overflow in sincere service to others—to help facilitate, by God's grace, a supernatural encounter between creation and Creator.

Like a server in an exclusive restaurant, the leader inquires, "Ma'am, can I offer you more of our famous Bread of Heaven?" Or, "How about a refill on our choicest 'Rivers of living waters,' sir?" Or, "Would you care to taste and see a little more of the goodness of God this evening?"

Corny, I know. But poignant. This is our role.

Yet, sorrowfully, we've begun to see talented worship leaders and popular pastors as rock stars. Still, our true calling is clear: to be chief servants. Our task is not to point people to how amazing we are, but to how amazing God is. We are not attempting to wow people but to wait on people. Don't miss this. The only way to effectively describe the "specials of the day" is to sample them before attempting to sell them.

> In reality, we can only offer in public what we've cultivated in private.

Unlike the shovel, the pitcher cannot be used to dig our well; it can only be used to draw from whatever is already in our well. With every song we lead and every message we preach in public, it's as if we're continually plunging the pitcher down into the reservoir of our souls to dish out to our congregation whatever has filled us up.

In reality, we can only offer in public what we've cultivated in private.

Maybe it's been an eternity since our last genuine secret-place God-encounter, and the well has dried up. Maybe it's been a few weeks and there's only a little water left. Water that's stagnant and swampy, with bacteria, moss, and even a few lovely lily pads flourishing on the surface.

Oh, well.

With reluctance—and a somewhat-religious grin—we scoop the murky contents of our deficient well into our pitchers, as any well-meaning leader might, and sling it out into the unsuspecting congregation. We double down on that hyped-up Sunday morning church lingo with hopes of distracting the nice church folks. Why? Because when there is little water in our well, we have no choice but to offer up a shadow of the real in an attempt to cover up the shallows of our heart.

Please don't misunderstand. I'm not saying if we miss a day with God, we can't lead in church. There is certainly some grace for this. Even so, it becomes awesomely apparent that digging the well in private each day is the only way to keep the soil of our hearts pliable, soft, and filled to overflowing with the invigorating waters of the Spirit.

CLEANING THE INSIDE OF THE CUP

Jesus provides this eye-widening caveat: *"You are so careful to clean the outside of the cup and the dish, but inside you are filthy—full of greed and self-indulgence"* (Matthew 23:25).

It's true. Jesus has the same issue with us that He had with the Pharisees. Like them, we're often more driven to beautify the part of our ministry that everyone sees—the outside of the cup—rather than to purify the heart of our ministry, the part very few will ever see. While the outside of the cup clearly represents the *us* everyone knows—my public face and ministry—the inside of the cup represents the real me, off the stage. The part only God and my family sees.

Why do we mix this up? It's simple enough.

Sadly, it comes down to an issue of time management. We've wrongly convinced ourselves that there's no time to clean both the inside of the cup *and* the outside of the cup. So we default to cleaning the outside of our cup. For the same old reasons. For the sake of a good impression. To save face.

We do it all backwards. We reason, *It'll be okay just this once. I know I haven't made much time for God of late, but I've got all these responsibilities to lead God's people. Lord knows, they're a handful. And I want to continue to encourage them to stay close with God. I'll have to make time for seeking God later.* Meanwhile, Jesus whispers, "Do it my way, and you'll have it all. You'll be clean inside and out. And you'll experience lasting peace. You'll grow in personal godliness. *And* you'll be perpetually effective in ministry."

He pleads, *"You blind Pharisee! First wash the inside of the cup, and then the outside will become clean, too"* (Matthew 23:26).

Did you see that? Jesus just revolutionized your calendar. It's so easy. Almost too easy.

After working tirelessly to save face—trying to roll the boulder of ministry up the steep side of a cliff—we suddenly discover it never was our job to clean the outside of our cup after all. Nope. That's God's job. And, to our benefit, He will do the supernatural work of keeping our outsides clean *if* we will do the natural work of keeping our insides clean by digging the well of relationship with Him.

Not only is this the *best* way to keep both the inside and the outside of our cup clean, but it is the *only* way. Relying on God to keep the outside of our cup—our public ministry—clean while we focus on the inside of our cup—our hearts—is ultimately the key to an authentic walk with Christ. Not surprisingly, this is also what increases our anointing and keeps us from believing we need to put on a religious face.

DRINK FREELY

Remember, the 'Rivers of living water' are meant for leaders to drink, too. In order to purify, to refresh, and to cleanse. This is the only way we can establish—or re-establish—a taste for the things of God. For ourselves. And for our congregations. It's the only way we can ever grow close to God and also be fully effective in authentic, God-sanctioned ministry. It's time we stop attempting to increase an authentic thirst for God in others without first increasing an authentic thirst for God in ourselves. It's time we once again make our way back to the water. Toward God. Like the deer on the craggy rocks.

As I asked in my first book, *Awakening Pure Worship*, "Surely we didn't think we would grow closer to God by spending less time with him, right?"[1] Truth be told, our thirst for God will only increase in proportion to the amount we seek Him.

The invitation stands: *"The Spirit and the bride say, 'Come.' Let anyone who hears this say, 'Come.' Let anyone who is thirsty come. Let anyone who desires drink freely from the water of life"* (Revelation 22:17).

---

1   Jeff Deyo, *Awakening Pure Worship* (Shippensburg, PA: Destiny Image, 2018), page 228.

Chapter Highlights

1. Many leaders unknowingly attempt to lead others into fulfillment in Christ while walking around like zombies—empty and malnourished—themselves. This cannot be. We must not place our love of ministry over our pursuit of the Father.

2. As leaders, we face a serious conflict. We long to be used powerfully by God in public ministry settings, but this alluring desire often overshadows our hunger for establishing a deeper friendship with God for ourselves. But if we neglect cultivating a private walk with God in favor of polishing our public ministry, we will fail every time to acquire the life-giving relationship with God we need as well as the enduring, impactful ministry we seek.

3. As believers in Christ, the most important thing we can do is to spend time with God. Alone. "Digging the well." Nothing can grant us the level of passion, authenticity, and anointing we desire more than spending time with God in the secret place. Of course, we don't spend time alone with God for the sole purpose of becoming better leaders, but it is a fact that nothing else we do can bolster our leadership more than sparking our own personal friendship with God.

4. We just can't take people where we haven't been. As a worship leader—or "tour guide"—we must never attempt to take people on a tour we ourselves are unfamiliar with. The most effective tour guides "practice" going on the tour with the Father alone countless times before attempting to lead others into His presence. This is an ongoing practice that should never cease. Our passion for the tour must take precedence over our desire to lead the tour. Only then will we be authentic and fruitful.

5. Resist the temptation to "clean the outside of the cup" rather than focusing on the biblical mandate to "clean the inside of the cup" through daily fellowship with God. Cleaning the outside of our cup is equivalent to putting on a spiritual face, while cleaning the inside of our cup is equivalent to strengthening our personal walk with God.

Chapter 2

WHEN OUR PRAISE
IS A RACKET

Lie #2

*"In His mercy, God understands when the songs
of our lips don't jive with the songs of our lives."*

Ever sit down, put pen to paper, and draw up a detailed strategy to become a 100 percent complete phony? I mean, we all have audacious goals, right?

How about this: Ever made a New Year's resolution to become lukewarm? You know, for real this time?

Ever decide to focus anew in your life on avoiding—at all costs—practicing what you preach? With the desperate hope of fooling everyone around you into believing you are genuinely spiritual?

Uno mas. Just before being wed, did you ever sit down and concoct a dastardly plan to stay hitched for twenty-five years, have 3.5 kids, a dog, and a white picket fence, and then leave them all for a young lover? Spurred on, in all likelihood, by a grandiose midlife crisis? You know, just when your family needs you most?

Ever set out to be a Pharisee?

A fake?

A traitor?

An unbeliever?

Not likely. Nobody sets out to be any of these things. To be unauthentic, to be counterfeit, to be legalistic, to fall away from God, to embezzle money, to become an addict, to betray a friend, or to walk away from their faith. Yet somehow, many leaders still arrive at these places.

Frustrating, right? The challenges of leadership.

Of course, the question is not, "What can we do about *those* people?" The question is, "Is there anything I can do to guard against these plagues in *my* life—in *my* family, in *my* leadership?"

I say, "Yes, absolutely."

But, since few of us seem to be intentionally strategizing against these common failures, it should behoove us to do so now. That is, if we—and those under our leadership—hope to avoid falling victim to the same old traps of the enemy.

FAKING THE FUNK

It should come as no surprise that we are not the only ones disgusted by the human propensity to talk the talk without walking the walk. Our Maker is in full agreement. Like us, He is eagerly searching for those who would cherish and obey Him completely. With actions *and* with words. With heart, soul, mind, *and* strength.

John 4:23 is a prime example: *"But the time is coming—indeed it's here now—when true worshipers will worship the Father in spirit and in truth. The Father is looking for those who will worship him that way."*

That little four-letter word just before the word *worshipers* says it all.

Realize, Jesus wasn't obligated to use the word *true* in this sentence. He could have simply said, *"But the time is coming—indeed it's here now—when worshipers will worship the Father in spirit and in truth."* But He recognized something that is still true today. People are prone to adopting a skewed understanding of worship.

In Jesus' opinion, the word *worship* wasn't enough. He was compelled to add a qualifier to keep His listeners—and us—from missing the point.

SPELLING CONUNDRUM

Side note. Can we go ahead and establish here and now that, as worship leaders, we need to know the correct spelling of the word *worshiper?* Truth is, one "p" in the words *worshiper, worshiping,* and *worshiped* is greatly preferred over two. The good news is, there's actually a simple grammatical rule we can learn to help us avoid confusion moving forward.

Rong-Chang.com puts it simply: "If the last syllable is not stressed, do not double the final consonant letter."[1] This means words like *focus, travel, cancel,* and *worship* don't need to double the final consonant when adding a suffix. Even though spell check allows for a double or single consonant for these words (which pointlessly confuses the issue), a single consonant is actually correct.

Think about it. In the USA, we never write *benefitting* or *counselling.* We never write *listenning* or *offerred.* Why? Because the syllable closest to the suffix is unaccented. Consequently, there is no need to double the ending consonant (as is typically required with words like *beginning, acquitting,* and *controlling*). The very reason we double the consonant in these words is because the syllable closest to the suffix is accented.

Fact is, a double "p" in the word *worshipper* is at best redundant and at worst grammatically incorrect. It should always be written *worshiped, worshiper, worshiping.* This keeps everything looking cleaner and keeps us all on the same page.

Nevertheless, if for some reason these commonsensical findings don't satisfy (I know, some habits do die hard), just pick up any Bible. Turn to John 4:23 or any other passage with the word *worshiper* or *worshiping,* and you will find it spelled with one "p." (That is, any translation besides the King James Version. Language and grammar have modernized so much since then, right?)

Additionally, most authors agree. From Louie Giglio to Paul Baloche to Bob Sorge, it's always one "p." Why? Because that's the rule.

Anyway... where were we?

When Jesus adds the qualifier *true* to the word *worshipers,* it upgrades the meaning entirely—or at least gives it more precision.

---

1 www.rong-chang.com/double_rule.htm.

First, it is immensely important to God—being true, that is. Jesus underscores this in the second half of John 4:23 as something the Father is actively "looking for." Something He is actively seeking. Something foundational, tied to the health of all His kids.

Second, it reminds us that more than one type of worshiper exists. We can easily read between the lines—as Jesus speaks of His Father's passionate pursuit of *true* worshipers. He hints at an altogether different sort of worshiper. One that is *not* true. One that is *not* genuine. A *false* worshiper.

Here again, as always, Jesus is pushing our buttons. In no way is He giving us the easy way out. He purposefully chooses to make us uncomfortable. We squirm. "Surely He isn't saying *we* are false worshipers? Surely He isn't saying *we* are a bunch of fakes? Surely He isn't questioning *our* integrity? Is He?"

Hmm. Isn't that what Jesus does? I mean, maybe this is *exactly* His point. Maybe He really is asking us to reconsider ourselves. To look in the mirror.

I know. It's easy to get riled up when people start looking under our hood. As soon as someone starts poking around below the surface, we start squawking, "Who died and made you judge?"

Even so, Jesus is, of course, our ultimate judge (see John 5:27). And yet He certainly isn't pushing our buttons for fun. He's engaging in the all-important work of helping us grow into matured sons and daughters. As part of His Kingdom. To Him, becoming an authentic worshiper—an authentic believer, both in and out of the public eye—is one of the most foundational aspects of the Kingdom. Not only is it high on the list, but it's so high that God is scanning the entire earth to see if there are indeed any authentic worshipers—anyone, anywhere—who are truly seeking Him, as evidenced not only by church attendance or ministry prowess, but through each and every word, thought, and action of their lives. Sunday to Sunday.

Sadly, we regularly run across those who enjoy music more than those who enjoy worship. Those who love applause more than those who walk in genuine fellowship with the King. Those who love the stage, the spotlight, and the recognition far more than those who love the Kingdom.

MUSIC TO GOD'S EARS

To this point, Amos 5:21–23 burns like fire: *"I hate all your show and pretense—the hypocrisy of your religious festivals and solemn assemblies. I will not accept your burnt offerings and grain offerings. I won't even notice all your choice peace offerings."* (Sounds very Old Testament-ish so far, right? Wait for it…) He continues, *"Away with your noisy hymns of praise! I will not listen to the music of your harps."*

Okay. God's getting a little feisty with us here. But let's ask a dumb question or two. Does God hate music? Does God hate hymns of praise? Does God hate religious festivals? Does God hate solemn assemblies? What about youth retreats? Church services? Worship nights? Women's Bible studies? Campfire singalongs? Hmmm, maybe. (Just kidding.)

Of course He doesn't hate these things. He is the *initiator* of these gatherings. So what's He getting at? Why does He say, "Away with your noisy hymns of praise" if He doesn't actually hate hymns of praise? Was He concerned about the instrumentation? Or the volume? Hardly. (We'll get to that in chapter 8.) Were the singers hitting too many sour notes? Unlikely. Does Jesus have something against hymns or songs of the old-fashioned type? Nah. That can't be it.

Then what? Why in the world does He suggest that these lovely refrains—hymns, even—have suddenly become noise to His ears?

I wonder, is it possible God hears things very differently than we do? Is it possible He's not listening to our Sunday morning services in the same way we are? Is it possible He isn't blown away by the drummer's bombastic drum fill or the guitarist's insane guitar lick—as wonderful as they may be? Is it possible He's not nearly as enamored by the incredible vocal skills of the singers and their mellifluous harmonies (since He's the One who created them, after all)? Is it possible there's more at play, when it comes to what God hears on Sunday's, than we realize?

What if God isn't really listening to our music? What if, instead, He is listening to our hearts? What if He's listening to our authenticity? Our integrity? Our faithfulness? Our obedience? Or lack thereof?

What do those things sound like—to God?

Maybe we should go ahead and ask the one-hundred-million-dollar question: *After all is said and done, what really is music to God's ears?* I mean, if our music can be *noise* to His ears, and, as a result, can cease to be music to His ears, what, then, *is* music to His ears? What makes God tip His head back, close his eyes, tap His toes, and smile really big? When it comes to music? When it comes to worship?

The prophet Amos wasted no time in clarifying these things: *"Instead, I want to see a mighty flood of justice, an endless river of righteous living"* (Amos 5:24).

I love those words. *Flood of justice. River of righteous living.* Words painting pictures. Lives painting pictures.

THE SONG OF OUR LIVES

What if we could go back to the day each of us was born and take every thought, word, and deed, and position them neatly as notes on a page? Joined together into a singular song. A life symphony of sorts. The spiritual "sound" of our lives.

What would yours sound like? What would mine sound like?

To speak musically, there'd likely be healthy portions of dissonance. Notes flying here and there. Some out of tune. Some out of rhythm. Some completely in the wrong key. Even atonal. Some way too soft and some way too loud. Some moving at the wrong tempo and some in an opposing genre. A cacophonous mess.

But isn't it possible that this is exactly what God hears? Isn't this the melody we're trumpeting? Each and every day? The song of our lives? The sound of us? Who we are? How we speak? How we think? How we live?

It's like we get it all backwards—again. We shout what God is whispering and whisper what He is shouting. We're completely caught up in songs and music, while God is listening to the tune of our hearts.

E. M. Bounds comments daringly on the subject, "Preaching is not the performance of an hour. It is the outflow of a life."[2] We might simply change it to read, "Worship leading is not the performance of an hour. It is the outflow of a life." Here we see the rub. Worship leading isn't a

---

2   E. M. Bounds, *Power Through Prayer* (Chicago, IL: Moody Publishers, 2009), page 19.

skill that's developed where people gather to observe and applaud. It's a bubbling spring that bursts forth from the overflow of a life lived in God's presence.

We can be sure: The song that flows from our lives sings much louder than the song that flows from our lips. Therefore, the goal of any authentic worship leader must be to marry the life we live with the songs we sing—to let the songs we sing with our mouths flow out of the song we're singing with our lives.

> The song that flows from our lives sings much louder than the song that flows from our lips.

David had it right concerning the importance of prioritizing our life song over our worship "sacrifices" when he suggested in Psalm 51:16–19:

You do not desire a sacrifice, or I would offer one. You do not want a burnt offering. The sacrifice you desire is a broken spirit. You will not reject a broken and repentant heart, O God. Look with favor on Zion and help her; rebuild the walls of Jerusalem. Then you will be pleased with sacrifices offered in the right spirit—with burnt offerings and whole burnt offerings. Then bulls will again be sacrificed on your altar.

He's saying, "Don't you see? God isn't as interested in our religious sacrifices (our songs, our musical worship, and our other offerings) as He is in our humility and obedience, as exhibited by lives completely surrendered to Him. It's only when we've engaged in rewriting our life song (in the power of God's Holy Spirit) that it truly blesses God to hear our worship songs."

In fact, that's the best time to strike up the band—when justice rolls on like a river. When righteousness flows like a mighty stream. When our praise songs mirror our life songs.

MINDLESS OFFERINGS

In Ecclesiastes 5:1, Solomon chimes in, *"As you enter the house of God, keep your ears open and your mouth shut. Don't be a fool who doesn't realize that mindless offerings to God are evil."*

Mindless offerings? Whoa.

Do we do this? Do we offer worship to God without thought—without care, without true meaning? Do we lift our songs to Him rashly, without contemplating their ultimate significance? Or flippantly, in the tradition of men rather than in the pursuit of the King?

Sometimes.

More than we'd like to admit.

In fact, one of the great frustrations of Jesus concerning His own people is that we would honor Him with our lips while dishonoring Him with our lives: *"These people honor me with their lips, but their hearts are far away. Their worship is a farce, for they teach man-made ideas as commands from God"* (Matthew 15:8–9).

I once heard someone say, "Christians don't tell lies. They sing them." Ouch.

This is a little scary, honestly. How often do we sing, "You're all I need," or "No one compares to you, Lord"? But all the while, we cozy up to our little vices with hopes that they will satisfy.

Honestly, we're not so unlike the Israelites. In fact, in many ways, we're *exactly* like them. Their stories. Their idolatry. Their unfaithfulness. Those passages of Scripture are about us too. They aren't tales of some far-off rebellious people group we can't relate to. They're the tales of our people. Our families. Our friends. Our rebellion. And they reveal once again our incredibly desperate need for a Savior.

It's not just Israel that needed saving. *Those* people. The ones in the ancient Bible stories. No. We *all* need saving. For without God, we, like the Israelites, are destined to repeat many corrupt and unrighteous acts. Over and over again. We need God to save us from ourselves. From *our* rebellion. From *our* traitorous hearts.

Too harsh?

How is it that seemingly five minutes after Moses led the people of Israel out of Egypt—delivering them from the most hellish bondage—they were already melting down gold jewelry and molding it into a calf to worship, declaring it to be the god who delivered them (see Exodus 32)?

How is it that five minutes after a powerful Sunday church service—where we wear our very best and smile our grandest smiles—we find ourselves engulfed in gluttony or sin-filled rage toward our children or parents, or we're found ignoring God's kind command to take a Sabbath rest? Are we so different when left to ourselves?

Psalm 78:36–37 sums it up: *"But all they gave him was lip service; they lied to him with their tongues. Their hearts were not loyal to him. They did not keep his covenant."*

In his book *The Air I Breathe*, Louie Giglio reminds us that the words we speak are very important to God. He reasons, "But God isn't honored by words alone. Like any of us, He's moved by words that are authenticated by actions. When it comes to worship, it's the total package that matters—what you say, how you say it, and whether you mean it. And our words mean most when they're amplified by the way we choose to live our lives."[3]

WORSHIP IS OBEDIENCE

This is the essence of authenticity. And the opposite of hypocrisy. Doing what we say we will do. Anything else, quite frankly, causes God to want to vomit us out of His mouth. Authenticity is proven through obedience. But, of course, obedience does not produce godliness. It simply reveals whether our hearts are truly submitted to God or not. Obedience is not the *way to* righteousness. It is the *fruit* of righteousness, through faith.

Just a few chapters before the Israelites chose to bow down to a man-fashioned golden calf—Exodus 24:3—they promised this: *"We will do everything the LORD has commanded."* But they didn't. And so often, *we* do not. Why? Because when left to ourselves, we tend to choose rebellion over submission. Sin over holiness. Death over life. Our way over God's way.

No doubt, God recognizes our inability—in our own capacity—to become the authentic worshipers He intends us to be. Yet He has now made a way for us to become that which we cannot be in our own power. All through the supernatural power and work of His Spirit. He knows what we often miss. Singing lovely songs won't produce in us the godly lives we were meant to live, but living godly lives—in the power of the Spirit—will bring forth the most beautiful songs we could ever sing.

---

3   Louie Giglio, *The Air I Breathe* (Colorado Springs, CO: Multnomah Books, 2003), page 78.

Chapter Highlights

1. No one sets out to be fake. Every leader desires to be authentic. But many of us teeter on the edge of works-driven spirituality, increasing the likelihood of moral failures, burnout, and major employee- or family-relational breakdowns. We must keep our guard up so we don't become one of those all-too-familiar front-page stories—the ones the world continues to need to provide an excuse to reject Jesus.

2. It is an agonizing consideration to imagine a time when God would place His hands over His ears in disgust as we sing our songs of praise on Sunday morning. We must remember He always hears our worship first through the filter of how we are living our lives.

3. Our life song always sings louder than the songs we sing in church. No matter how talented or charismatic we are in our worship leadership, God is always listening to our life worship over our beautiful harmonies, our slick transitions, or our creative arrangements. The songs we sing in church should always and only be a reflection of the life we're living in the power of His Spirit.

4. God is looking for worship that comes from *both* our lips and our lives. Just as in our earthly relationships, both are important. None of us wants to be referred to as God often did to the Israelites: as people who honor Him with their lips but not their hearts.

5. Always remember to resist bringing "mindless offerings" to God. It is easy to go through the motions, leading our congregations to do the same. Recognizing this common struggle goes a long way toward helping us remain aware so we can stay engaged relationally in worship.

6. When adding suffixes to the word *worship*, we never need to double the "p." Words with unaccented second syllables, like "WOR-ship," look strange with a doubled ending consonant. We should simply write it like this: *worshiper, worshiping, worshiped.*

Chapter 3

ACCELERATING TRUE FRIENDSHIP WITH GOD

Lie #3

*"What our teams and congregants do
in their time alone with God is something
with which we shouldn't concern ourselves."*

Carving out time alone with God isn't easy. But neither is it hard. In pinpointing the strategy for personal revival, renowned, best-selling author, A. W. Tozer affirms, "It is simply the old and ever-new counsel: *Acquaint thyself with God*."[1] He continues: "To know God is at once the easiest and the most difficult thing in the world."[2] And the cherry on top? "To the soul that is athirst for God, nothing could be more delightful."[3] Simple but profound. And yet, how does this shake out for us as leaders, from day to day?

In my book *Awakening Pure Worship*, you wouldn't be surprised to find that I expound on the necessity of growing in intimacy with God, setting aside daily time in the secret place, and cultivating a closer friendship with our heavenly Father. But I never actually divulge the practical things

---

1   A. W. Tozer, *Knowledge of the Holy* (New York, NY: HarperCollins Publishers, 1961), page 114.
2   Ibid., page 115.
3   Ibid., page 12.

I practice in my own personal time with God—the techniques I employ to help foster and maintain a vibrant friendship with my God. My Father. My Friend.

So what about it? I see no reason we can't pull back the curtain on some of these foundational strategies, as a source of inspiration for you and your team. Of course, you don't need to spend your time alone with God in the same manner I do, but I'm hoping to spark some ideas that will inspire you to push the refresh button on what it means to hang out with your Creator.

THE START OF SOMETHING

In the spring of 2011, I received a phone call from my good friend and mentor James Goll, who is a father figure to me. He told me he was writing a new book. No surprise there. But this time he decided to invite several like-DNA authors to contribute a chapter, me included. Wow. This was something I had always wanted to do. It was going to be a *real* book. Published by a *real* publishing company. Found in *real* book stores!

Awesome.

The title was *The Lost Art of Pure Worship*, which was perfectly fitting, since the phrase "pure worship" had become synonymous with my passion to help people grow closer to God—*and* because it was the name of the worship conference I started in 2008, the Pure Worship Institute (pureworship.org).

After titling my chapter "The Authentic Worshiper," and going through the extensive writing and editing process, my chapter was finally complete.

I was beaming.

A few months later, a large pallet of books arrived on my doorstep. Just then, a strange thought crossed my mind: *I have never read this book.* I mean, I had read *my* chapter, but, as you might imagine, the publisher didn't see fit to send me everyone else's chapters for my approval.

Suddenly I wondered, *What is this book really about? Oh no. I hope it's as good as I've imagined. Certainly, with authors like James Goll, Chris DuPré, Sean Feucht, Julie Meyer, and James's daughter, Rachel Tucker, I needn't worry.*

So guess what I did?

I began reading. And consuming. And highlighting and circling and folding down corners. Wow. What I read in those God-drenched pages moved me in ways I find difficult to describe. And that was only *my* chapter! (Kidding.)

Seriously, chapter after chapter had me in tears, sitting on the edge of my seat, and saying *amen* aloud over and over again. Especially when I came to chapter three—Julie Meyer's chapter, "Oil for Pure Worship." This one sparked me so intensely that it has continued to shape me ever since. (Side note: I appeal to you to order this book from Amazon. Read it. Devour it. Even if it's only for Julie's chapter.)

I NEED MORE OIL

I already knew the importance of spending time alone with God. It was something I had heard discussed many times. But Julie Meyer's chapter emphasized our need for fellowship with God in ways I hadn't considered.

She spoke of a dream she had. In the dream, it was as if she had been inserted directly into the parable of the ten virgins in Mathew 25:1–10. In real time. She was actually *in* the story.

She describes herself watching scores of people engaging with one another—all carrying different lanterns. Lanterns of all sizes, shapes, qualities, and worth. Of course, she noticed the most remarkable ones first. The ones that would catch anyone's eye.

But then—much like you do when you suddenly discover an unforeseen nuance of a beloved, annual vacation spot—her eyes turned to the contents of the lanterns. To the lustrous, translucent liquid cradled inside. The oil. Interestingly, some of the most splendid lanterns housed the least oil. And some of the most run-of-the-mill lanterns were generously spilling over.

She describes the hour as growing late. Everyone slept. Lamps burned into the night. Yet, just as the quiet set in, a loud announcement erupted like a geyser from the mouth of the Bridegroom, who had suddenly and without warning arrived on the scene. Julie identifies the tremendous struggle that ensued. Many of the loveliest lanterns had gone out. Burned out. They contained no more oil. And produced no more light.

Through the Spirit of God, she understood that the oil inside symbolized each individual's time spent alone with the Father. Time spent cultivating real relationship. Privately. Faithfully. Intentionally. Or not. She also realized the lanterns themselves—the outsides—symbolized each person's public ministry.

Many had built prestigious ministries with great effort, but also at great cost. They had prized ministry above oil. They had prized their public lives above their private lives. No one seemed to notice. Until now. But suddenly it was obvious to everyone. They had little to no oil. Little to no anointing. Little to no light.

Sobering.

And I probably don't need to tell you, when I finished reading Julie's chapter, there was only one phrase ringing in my spirit: *I…need…more…oil.*

BURNOUT

Now, I'm no lantern expert. But there's one thing I do understand. When a lantern's fuel is spent, out goes the flame. The oil is the fuel. The oil is what burns. The oil is what ultimately produces light. And if that oil—which can only be cultivated in the secret place—runs out, there is little left beyond a pleasant-looking hollow shell of a lantern. A form of ministry. Lacking substance. With no real light. No real warmth. No real evangelistic reach.

You've probably heard of this condition. *Burnout.*

Interestingly, many use this term in a way that speaks of something that has happened *to* them. A circumstance beyond their control. As a result of others laying too heavy a load upon them, causing them to be too busy. Exhausted. Overworked.

But wait. What if burnout is less a product of being busy, and more a product of missed assignment? What if burnout is not a product of being overworked, but of a misalignment of priorities? A result of prioritizing everything else—everyone else—except that which is of utmost importance?

Fellowship with God.

In the parallel parable, found in Matthew 25, Jesus' response to the five "empty" virgins is staggering. It's not something He simply shrugs off, saying, "Silly virgins. Please try not to live as ministry-oholics too much, okay?" No. He shuts and locks the door—undoubtedly the door to eternal life—leaving the five of them frantically pleading to be let in. His words ring out like swords clanging in slow motion.

> *"But while they were gone to buy oil, the bridegroom came. Then **those who were ready** went in with him to the marriage feast, and the door was locked. Later, when the other five bridesmaids returned, they stood outside, calling, 'Lord! Lord! Open the door for us!' But he called back, '**Believe me, I don't know you!**' So you, too, must keep watch! For you do not know the day or hour of my return"* (Matthew 25:10–13).

"I don't know you."

This phrase clearly speaks of relationship. Or the lack thereof. It speaks directly to those who have developed a closer relationship with religious activities then they have with the Father. Those who have proven through the choices they've made that they do not truly hunger for fellowship with God. That they do not truly thirst for close friendship with Him.

So the door is closed. Even to those with impressive ministries. Even to those with stunning lamps. Even to those who walk in the company of other believers.

Many of us—leaders, even—are running dangerously low on oil. We've grown close to the *activities* of heaven without growing close to the *King* of heaven. Still, we long to hear those famous words, "Well done, my good and faithful servant," and yet God *"is a rewarder of those who diligently seek Him"* (Hebrews 11:6 NKJV).

It's true. Daily intimacy with God is the only means by which oil can be multiplied within our souls. In the secret place. Where it's just you and God alone. You and the Word of God. You and your prayers. You and your songs. You and the King.

So we choose.

THREE-STRAND CORD

From where I stand, as leaders and as Christians, it only makes sense for us to spend time with God each and every day. Not as a religious duty, but as a source of relational fuel for our souls. The Bible is clear on the importance of the "one thing," and Jesus modeled this strikingly, as He often stole away with His Father in the early morning hours, even "wasting away" entire evenings deepening His communion with His heavenly Daddy (Luke 6:12).

It goes without saying. Our secret-place time with God should incorporate at least three things: reading the Word, praying, and worshiping in song. A three-strand cord of authentic relationship that cannot be easily broken.

Yet we need a plan, and we must be increasingly intentional.

So what does time alone with God look like for you? What does it look like for me? Let's peek in.

JUMPSTARTING YOUR PRAYER LIFE

Prayer is an interesting animal. If you ask someone to pray publicly to open a meeting, you might receive a variety of responses, anywhere from the "professional prayer" (the one who enjoys being seen reciting bold and provocative prayers), to the "apprehensive prayer" (the one who trembles at the thought of praying aloud in public). Many even seem to view prayer as a formality, where we don't really talk to God but we preach to others. This approach can greatly amplify our numbness toward prayer. And toward God.

Remember, the purpose of prayer is to foster a clear relational connect point with our God in order to increase our personal walk with Him. (Not surprisingly, this is one of the most practical things you can do to increase your authentic impact as a leader too.)

So let's hit the redo button as we look at a few strategies that have helped jumpstart my own prayer life.

1. Make a plan. I mentioned being intentional. This is number one. I find if I don't have a plan to pray, I'm very inconsistent. This is almost worse than scrapping prayer altogether. Plus, it's not the way I want to live my life. I want to talk to God consistently in the secret place *and* all throughout my day.

Spurred on by my parents when I was younger, I created a prayer calendar of sorts. (This is after talking to God as a friend and as a Father first.) Monday is immediate family day (I pray for my wife, Martha, and my kiddos, Roman, Evan, Channing, and Clara). Tuesday is extended family day, where I pray for my parents, sis, cousins, aunts, uncles, nieces, nephews, and more. Wednesday is church day, where I pray for my pastors and for our church culture. Thursday is Worship City Ministries day, where I pray over my personal ministry activities, including my touring, teaching, preaching, writing, podcasting, worship leading, etc. Friday is NCU day, where I pray for my fellow professors, students, and staff. Saturday is miscellaneous day, which can consist of praying for our nation and for other random things on my heart. Sunday is a day where I do most of my praying at church and in our family devotions.

We mostly mirror this prayer calendar at night with our kids too, as we gather together as a family before bed. Each of us prays for one family member on Mondays, one extended family member on Tuesdays, one pastor on Wednesdays, one teacher or politician on Thursdays, and so forth. These routines create powerful habits with just enough fluidity to keep things fresh. Of course, we don't always see it through every day, and sometimes we change it up. For example, if one of our pastors has an urgent need on Monday, we don't wait until Wednesday to pray. We adjust as necessary.

2. Don't chase emotion. Some days you're gonna feel it, and some days you're not. Quite honestly, anything we do over and over again has the potential of growing stale. While the routine is vital, we must beware of depending on emotion to drive our prayers. Pray when it feels good, and pray when it feels like you're as dry as the desert sand. Just pray. Your responsibility is not to *feel* like praying. It is simply to seek God. In prayer. By faith. Oftentimes, the refreshment of prayer doesn't occur until the faith of prayer takes action.

3. Don't simply talk about praying. I've found we often talk more about praying than we actually pray. Especially when we're in small groups. Make sure to redirect the focus to move yourself (and others) past talking or thinking about prayer needs and into the actual prayer itself. Also, don't confuse talking to yourself with praying to God. This can be a fine line as we process the needs we have in our personal lives. Make sure you direct your conversation to God, engaging Him directly concerning the issues of your life.

4. Don't start with requests. The Bible encourages us; *"Be anxious for nothing, but in everything by prayer and supplication, with thanksgiving, let your requests be made known to God"* (Philippians 4:6 NKJV). Even so, don't approach God with requests only. If we make this a habit, we won't have much to talk about with Him in the age to come. Imagine if my kids only came to me for money, the keys to the car, help with homework, food, etc. We wouldn't have much of a relationship. It's when they climb into my lap to snuggle or give me butterfly kisses (with no hidden agenda) that our real-time relationship is sparked. As a result, my heart is beautifully endeared to them, and I am moved even more so to provide for their needs.

5. Pray aloud. We need to speak our prayers aloud to God more times than not. Many folks don't feel comfortable praying aloud, but this should be normal behavior for mature believers. Your ears desperately need to hear your mouth talk to your Creator. And so do other people. It builds confidence, strengthens resolve, helps avoid stuffing our problems, and greatly strengthens our team dynamics. Of course, the only way to increase our comfort level for praying aloud is to do it. So jump in!

6. Get rid of the church lingo. This is huge. We've got to stop praying to God in King James English. The only reason we have the KJV is because it was the *modern* language of *that* time. But God understands our everyday language—just as He understands King James English. Yet He prefers for you to be you. So don't put on a face when you pray. Don't change the tone of your voice. Just talk to Him. Like Moses did, as a man talks with a friend.

7. Don't babble on and on. Often, we get in the habit of repeating ourselves in prayer, somehow believing that our repetition will help God know we're serious. This is a fine line. Matthew 6:7 tells us not to repeat our words over and over again, yet Matthew 7:7–8 tells us to ask, seek, and knock, and the door will be opened. My advice is to be specific and clear with God—in the same way you would when speaking to a friend. If you wouldn't repeat yourself over and over again to a friend, don't do so with God. Side note: I would also work hard to break the habit of repeating God's name over and over when you pray. Imagine if you talked to a friend this way: "Oh, Jeff, you're a great friend, Jeff. Jeff, you're such a nice guy, Jeff. And I really like your books, Jeff. Jeff, I'm going to buy your books and share them with everyone I know, Jeff. Oh, dude, Jeff, you're my favorite author, Jeff!" You get the picture.

8. Listen to God. Prayer is a two-way conversation, so I encourage you to make space to listen for God's voice when you pray. Set aside some time to be still and attend to His voice. Close your mouth and quiet your mind. God is often speaking to us in a still small voice, one that can easily be missed in our busy rushing. I also recommend being intentional to listen to yourself as you pray. I find when I'm praying aloud, I often say things that are inspired by God's Spirit—words directly from *His* heart that are flowing out of *my* mouth. This means I'm often learning and growing even while I'm praying.

9. Declare God's truth over yourself. Part of praying is speaking the Word of God over your life. Don't worry, I'm not a huge fan of the "name it, claim it" approach, but I do recognize the significance of proclaiming God's Word over myself, my family, and others. Something undeniable happens when we declare God's Word aloud. I often declare things like, "I am the son of the King," "I have Jesus' royal blood running through my veins," and "Sin no longer has any power over me, and there is a way out in every temptation." I also love to get specific when I quote Philippians 4:13. I'll pray things like, "I can (fill in the blank) through Christ who strengthens me." "I can *treat my wife with love and respect* through Christ who strengthens me." And so forth.

10. Pray the Lord's Prayer creatively. There's a reason Jesus showed the disciples a pattern for prayer. But, without a doubt, it wasn't so we would repeat it word for word every Sunday morning. I'm begging you. Please stop viewing this prayer as something we should regurgitate like a bunch of robots in order to be counted as spiritual. The Lord's Prayer is more of a guide. A template, of sorts. One we can expand upon as we pray through the different categories within. I absolutely support praying a *version* of the Lord's Prayer every day, using Jesus' different bullet points as launch points for specific prayers. (Note: For a detailed breakdown of the strategies I use when praying the Lord's Prayer, see the addendum.)

Prayer is an insanely powerful weapon to help us stand against the challenges and attacks of this world—as well as the internal attacks we face that can often be even more problematic. It is to declare *all-out war* on all that is coming against the Kingdom of heaven and its people. It is the ultimate revolutionary response to God, to our flesh, to demonic powers, and to a world that vehemently opposes God.

UN-NUMBING YOUR LOVE FOR GOD'S WORD

Have you or members of your teams struggled to connect with the Bible? I have, at times. Does it lull you to sleep with all of its hard-to-comprehend dos and don'ts? Is it more confusing than the payment directions on the back of a speeding ticket? Does it seem to parade around like an old-fashioned, outdated encyclopedia that boldly contradicts all of the greatest minds of our time?

This is how many feel these days.

Even so, let's take a fresh look and see if we can resuscitate our hearts—and the hearts of our team members—regarding the living, life-changing wonders of God's Word.

1. The Word of God is not a book. It is a person. *He* is alive. Don't forget. It is not a leather-bound manuscript with a river of words on an ocean of pages. It's unlike any other book that has ever been written. It is not a physical thing. It is a spiritual thing. It is a living, breathing being. *"For the word of God is alive and powerful. It is sharper than the sharpest two-edged* *sword, cutting between soul and spirit, between joint and marrow. It exposes our innermost thoughts and desires"* (Hebrews 4:12). *"In the beginning the Word already existed. The Word was with God, **and the Word was God**. He existed in the beginning with God. God created everything through him, and nothing was created except through him. **The Word gave life to everything** that was created and his life brought light to everyone"* (John 1:1–3).

Some people get hung up on the actual book itself, in its physical state. As if we should lock it away somewhere in a museum in a glorified glass case. As if the leather and the parchment themselves are holy. Honestly, the physical matter composing the Bible is entirely unimportant. It's just cowhide, wood, and ink (and possibly some other synthetic materials). It's not as if displaying a larger-than-life King James Bible on our trendy coffee table is going to give us a leg up on reaching heaven. The book itself is not divine.

Yet, it does *house* something divine. Something holy. Something beautiful. Something supernatural. Or better stated, *Someone* supernatural. It carries the very person of God. Jesus. God's Son. In the form of the written Word. Deep within the stories and parables and the dos and don'ts. Within the trials and the miracles. Within the persecution and the disappointments. Within the victories and the destruction. Within the mercy and the amazing grace exists the very person of God. His life. His being. His DNA. It carries the personality and nature of the one true God. The One who spoke galaxies into being and breathed His very existence into our lungs. The Bible is full of beauty. Full of hope. Full of life.

2. The Bible is a relational gateway. If the Word is a person, the Bible is not only meant to be read; it is also meant to be encountered. Yes, the Word of God is a gateway. A passageway. A doorway to something greater.

Some wrongly assume this "something" is truth. I mean, Jesus Himself is the Way, the Truth, and the Life, so if the Word of God is Jesus, and Jesus is the Truth, then the Truth must be the goal, right? No. It's like this: The reason we seek the truth of the Word is not so we can know the truth of the Word, but so we can know the Person of Truth found within the Word of truth. The Word gives us access to the God of Truth. Access. To His character. To His being. To His heart. That we might *know* Him.

Honestly, it's not important to *know* the truth. But it is important to know the Person of Truth. And this only happens as we gain access to the God of Truth via the truth of God. We can acquire all the knowledge in the world and still not know God (think the devil and the Pharisees). Better said, we can obtain knowledge and still not have revelation (spiritual understanding). Knowledge without revelation is dangerous. Knowledge without revelation is dead. Revelation is a springboard. Revelation is where God's knowledge meets God's Spirit, meets our spirit.

3. God's Word must be more than memorized. Junior Bible Quiz (JBQ) is a competitive Bible memorization program sponsored by the Assemblies of God. One website says, "JBQ offers a fun, exciting way to motivate children to understand the all-important truths in God's Word. Through cooperative learning, children work together on teams to learn and understand the questions and answers from the Bible Fact-Pak. Then, using cooperative competition, the children meet with other teams for a fun quizzing match. There are twenty questions in a match, with two teams of quizzers trying to beat each other to the buzzers to get the first shot at the answers."[4]

It's a ton of fun, and my own kids have been very involved. The problem is, any time we begin memorizing the Word of God, there is a danger of accumulating facts housed in the mind that are not translated into revelation for the heart. Isn't it still better to get the Word of God in these kids than not? Yes. I believe so. I mean, I hope so. We might even quote Isaiah 55:11 on the matter: *"It is the same with my word. I send it out, and it always produces fruit. It will accomplish all I want it to, and it will prosper everywhere I send it."* Even so, we must be engaged to guide our young competitors along in order to keep them from acquiring knowledge alone.

I recently heard a popular speaker on the topic of memorizing God's Word. She said, "It's not just so you can have it memorized; it's

---

4   "JBQ," *Christian Life Assembly,* https://clacamphill.com/jbq.

so that your mind will be changed and you'll start living out of a place that is congruent with your identity in Christ." This is good. On the surface. But God hasn't given us His Word primarily so we can cultivate a healthy identity. He's given us His Word so we can have access to Him. In relationship. When we have access to Him in relationship, we come to know Him. When we come to know Him, we begin to know His thoughts toward us, and we begin to see ourselves the way He sees us. We first seek relationship with God. And the result—or the fruit—of a healthy relationship with God is a healthy identity in God.

4. The Word of God is a love letter. My Aunt Judy (my mom's older sister) recently lost her best friend. Sorrowfully, my Uncle Bob passed away after battling dementia for several years. This was truly heartbreaking, and we hurt so much for my aunt and my cousins. In response, Martha and I encouraged our kids to join us in putting together a little care package with some drawings and a few goodies. I wrote her a personal letter from our family to let her know just how much we love her and to remind her that we are praying for her.

I thought about this when I was talking with our kids a couple of weeks later. We were discussing how the Word of God is like a love letter from our Creator. Just as we wrote a letter to my aunt, God has written a letter to us. The words we wrote to my aunt were more than just truth. More than mere words. They represented a relational connection from us to her. In fact, I imagine as she read our letter, it was as if she was actually imagining our voices, not simply reading words on a page. She was hearing our heart between the lines, lovingly communicating our care and concern for her.

It's the same with God's Word. As we thumb through its pages, we must be listening for something beyond the rules and regulations. Beyond the rights and wrongs. Beyond Kingdom "policy." Listen for His powerful and loving voice. In every story. In every adventure. In every rebuke. In every miracle. Think of it! God Himself is actually talking directly to you. To each of us—as a whole *and* as individuals. Personally. Powerfully. Poignantly.

5. The Word of God reveals God's heart. It is imperative we understand one of the great purposes of the Bible. To aid us in discerning God's voice. His heart. His tone. Many people complain about not being able to hear God's voice, yet they haven't spent enough time with Him to come to recognize it. If a complete stranger wrote the letter to my Aunt Judy, would she receive it in the same way? Probably not. It would be nice, but not nearly as meaningful. Why? The words might be the same, but there would be no relational connection to the people behind them. And since God has identified Himself as the overall Author of the Scriptures, His words now become a relational gateway, helping us distinguish His voice from all others.

Think of an NBA Championship game. Tied up with twelve seconds on the clock. Tens of thousands of fans in full throat. How does each team hear their coach's voice amidst the mayhem? Simple. They've spent hundreds of hours listening to his or her voice for just such a moment. They simply tune in precisely, like we might do with an old analog radio. In the heat of the moment, every other voice fades to the background, allowing the "frequency" of the most vital voice to break through. Clearly. Unmistakably. Just enough to hear and obey the call to win the game.

6. The Word of God is nourishment. Just as the body needs food for nourishment to sustain life, the soul needs nourishment to sustain spiritual vigor. We would never go a whole week without eating. Yet we often go days, weeks, or even months without cracking open the Bible. Ironically, some churchgoers roll their eyes when they hear preachers preach from familiar passages, as if the nourishment from each passage dissipates after a single serving. The truth is, the Word of God keeps giving and giving, no matter how many times it's consumed.

Imagine, you offer me a juicy cheeseburger with all my favorite toppings, but I turn you away, saying, "Thanks, buddy. I'm good. I've had one of those before." What? No way. Just because I've consumed a certain food one time in the past doesn't mean it can no longer provide me with much-needed enjoyment *and* nourishment in the present. It's the same with the Word of God. Every time you read it—whether it's a familiar passage or something new—it provides relevant sustenance for your soul. *"When I discovered your words, I devoured them. They are my joy and my heart's delight, for I bear your name, O LORD God of Heaven's Armies"* (Jeremiah 15:16).

7. The Word of God is a weapon. You may recall Ephesians 6 dubbing the Word of God the "sword of the Spirit." This reveals something profound about the Word: it is a weapon. And it is meant to help us gain the victory in the many battles in our lives.

We have been equipped by the Word of God—His foremost weapon of mass destruction—to be able to defeat our enemies by faith, via the Word of God and in the power of the Holy Spirit. This doesn't mean we won't face battles. And it doesn't mean we won't lose a few. But we will win the war in Jesus Christ if we continue to stand on the Word of God. *"No weapon turned against you will succeed. You will silence every voice raised up to accuse you. These benefits are enjoyed by the servants of the LORD; their vindication will come from me. I, the LORD, have spoken!"* (Isaiah 54:17).

Only through the Word of God did Jesus dispel the attack of Satan in the wilderness in Matthew 4. Satan attempted to use the Word as a weapon against Jesus by distorting it, as many still do today, but Jesus used the Word properly—as a weapon—in order to refute the devil. We also have this great power in the Word of God.

8. The Word of God shows us how to live. God's laws and directions are there for our good, not for our harm. They are not random primordial schemes thought up by the Big Man in the sky. His statutes are keenly motivated by one simple thing: love.

The good news is, by and large, we have few complaints with these "love lines." What? Yep. Whether we realize it or not. They are mostly straightforward—that is, until we decide to give ourselves a pass. Do not murder = love. Do not lie = love. Do not commit adultery = love. Do not steal = love. These are not hard to understand even if we don't always like them.

Ironically, the fact that the Bible tells us *who* we are is much more important than that it tells us *how* to live. Why? Because when we know *who* we are, it helps us know *how* we should live. The good news is, verse upon verse guides us into a greater understanding of who we are. And, of course, who we are is never a matter of our feelings, but a matter of fact. A fact established by the One who made us. No one can refute what the Maker says about the ones He created. We are 100 percent who God says we are. No matter what anyone else says.

As we come to grips with who we are according to God's Word, let me share a few things that help me as I strategize to consume it daily. Take what you like. Leave the rest.

1. When and how often should I read God's Word? This is simple. Plan to read something from God's Word every day. Could be ten verses or four chapters. But each one of us should consume a portion of God's Word every day, in the same way we eat every day. Our spiritual beings need the spiritual food of the Word just as much as our bodies need the nourishment from food. How much you consume each day is up to you and the Holy Spirit. I would create patterns and habits in your life that help you. Don't bite off more than you can chew, but also avoid eating only the crumbs that fall from the table.

2. What should I do before reading God's Word? One of the important habits I've established is to pray a short prayer before I read the Bible. This helps me approach God before diving into His Word, simply to say hello and to ask Him to help me understand and apply what I'm about to read. There's nothing worse than reading a bunch of verses, getting to the end, and having no idea what you've read or how it can impact your life. We simply need to ask for God's help when it comes to understanding of His Word. He will gladly step in.

3. Where should I begin reading in God's Word? I am surprised to discover how many people never actually start reading the Bible simply because they claim they don't know where to start. Honestly, I wouldn't be too concerned with *where* you start, but rather *that* you start. You could read one chapter in the Old Testament and one in the New Testament each day, moving forward through each chapter and each book in order.

You may also set aside a season of life to focus on Psalms and Proverbs. These are amazingly practical books to read over and over again.

My family recently finished reading through the Bible in a year, *chronologically*. I've never done that before, and I've found it interesting to know that the books of the Bible aren't necessarily compiled in order. No matter where you start, there should be a long-term goal of reading through the entire Bible, even if it takes you several years. Then, over your lifetime, you should continue to read it many times over.

REIGNITING YOUR HEART FOR MUSICAL WORSHIP

One beautiful Sunday morning in the summer of 2018, our pastor, Derrick Ross, invited me to preach on my upcoming book, *Awakening Pure Worship*. I preached my guts out, touching on several important topics, including a bold idea from chapter 7: "Worship is not for God."

A couple of Sundays later, a friend of mine came up to me and said something like, "Jeff, you've changed my life!" He went on to tell me that he had always thought of musical worship as the credits before the movie. He would stroll in late to the service, somewhat unengaged, waiting for the "main course": the sermon. His wife is a talented worship leader, so he had always thought of musical worship as something nice for her. Something nice for musicians and singers. A vehicle to aid creative types in offering their art to God. He would smile along but remain a spectator, applauding his wife for the brilliant job she did, all the while waiting for the real thing. The message.

All was good and fine until I said this: "Did you know that worship is *not* for God?" As you can imagine, he—along with many other folks—got a little wide-eyed. To many, this kind of talk may sound heretical, like we're attempting to steal God's glory. But we're not. Ask yourself these two simple questions: Who's changed more when I worship God, Him or me? Who needs me to declare and be reminded that God is holy, Him or me?

Worship is always *to* God and *about* God, but ultimately musical worship is a gift from Him that is *for* you. When we worship Him, He gets what He *wants*—deeper fellowship with us—but we get what we *need*—deeper fellowship with Him. He remains unchanged, and yet we are transformed in ways we can't begin to describe.

Suddenly, the light came on for my friend. "Wait a minute. If worship is for me, and I remain unengaged each time there's an opportunity to lift my voice to my Creator, it's not God who's missing out. It's me!" And from that day forward, he decided he would never approach the musical worship portion of the service the same.

HOW DO YOU WORSHIP GOD?

The good news? Musical worship need never be relegated to something we do in church. In the same way we wouldn't refuse to read our Bibles at home or pray at work, neither should we leave musical worship sitting on the church steps.

It's funny. That's how I used to think, yet now it nearly seems like a truth too obvious to state. Sadly, though, there are those flipping through these pages—leaders, even—who rarely if ever spend time outside a church service worshiping God with music. Outside of rehearsing the songs for Sunday. Ironically, many spend countless hours in front of people "worshiping" God with music, yet rarely lift their voices in song outside the public eye, in the secret place. As a result, many leaders attempt to minister to others through "worship" sung in the public place that has never truly taken root in the secret place.

It's time to turn that around so we can truly encounter God for ourselves and begin to lead from a place of authenticity. But how?

1. Draw close to God, and He will draw close to you. This may seem devastatingly obvious, but please don't pass over it. Many a well-meaning worship leader and lead pastor knows this truth cerebrally but not relationally. Intimately. As we seek to reawaken our hearts in musical worship, we need to be honest with ourselves. Have we actually cultivated a close and personal walk with God outside the work we do in ministry? This is monumental. Ask yourself: Am I truly satisfied with my fellowship with God? Or, better yet, is God satisfied with His fellowship with me? Do I hear His voice? Can I truly say I meet with Him face-to-face? Every day?

One of God's wonderful relational promises is found in James 4:8: *"Come close to God, and God will come close to you."* This is a beautiful assurance and one we desperately need to pull on. God started this whole thing by loving us. By drawing close. He opened the door for us to join Him in sweet fellowship. And now His invitation is simple: "If you will engage with me, I will engage with you."

At the same time, we can expect the opposite from God too. If we dodge opportunities to meet with Him one on one, He will not force Himself upon us. He will give us exactly what we seem to be asking for—space away from His presence. Thankfully, Scripture does *not* reveal a God who fails to seek us entirely when we ignore Him. Heaven forbid! Yet, He will give us our space if we will not have Him. It's a delicate balance. God continually woos us to Himself, rarely giving up on us, but He doesn't play the one-sided relationship game for very long. If, by our actions, we communicate a lack of desire to be with Him, He ultimately will let us have what we desire. Yet when we pursue Him—even just a smidge—He will respond with great love and affection.

2. Resist connecting solely with the music. If you're a worship leader, there's a pretty good chance you love music. Immensely. I know I do. I love everything about it. Especially writing it, arranging it, playing it, and singing it, as well as using it to express myself in worship. The problem comes when we make the mistake of trading a relational connection with God for a relational connection with music. Often without knowing it. But we must remember that music is only a tool. As wonderful as it is, it is not much more than a springboard for us. A springboard into authentic fellowship with our Maker, the One who created music to begin with.

I see music as one of God's greatest creations—an incredible gift that He's given us to enjoy! However, as always, the very things we love can also stand in the way of genuine connection with God. Ironic. How does this happen? Well, it's very easy to get caught up in the joy of songs and music or even in the great skill of singers and players. This is precarious, because it can move us off center enough to cause our worship to lose focus. If we're not paying attention, it can even cause us to remove God from the equation entirely. Unintentionally. To the point where we fall in love with His creation rather than with Him. To the point where we fail to worship God, all while worshiping worship.

3. Change it up. Engaging with God through singing in our time alone with Him can be tricky. It's not rocket science, but I find it's important to keep a healthy balance between routine and spontaneity. What I mean is, I try to keep both discipline and variety in mind concerning the music I choose and the time frame I set aside. Most often, my flesh gravitates toward the slow songs, where I simply soak quietly on the floor in my basement or office, and yet I've found I also need to challenge myself to put on a little Hillsong Y&F (or something with a danceable groove) to stir my heart to rejoice again. (How can I expect to worship authentically with up-tempo songs in public if I never cultivate a passion for jumping and dancing to up-tempo songs in private?) Truth is, if our worship in public looks very different from our worship in private, we may begin to wonder if our public worship is contrived, artificial, or manufactured—designed to please the crowd or simply to enjoy the gathering—rather than to actually enjoy the Father.

I love to vary the amount of time I worship with music as well as the order in which I read my Bible, worship in song, and pray. Sometimes I start with musical worship and other times I end with it, etc. I also experiment with songs I know and songs I don't. This can be challenging, but it's extremely important. It's no surprise that we lean toward songs we know, but we must continually fight to be open to new songs so we don't slip into the trap of loving songs more than we love God. We can also experiment by worshiping with different styles and genres. This may be difficult at first, but it will pull you into depths in Christ that you might never reach otherwise, plus it will allow you to grow in your ability to worship authentically in public when the music style is not to your liking.

4. Lift up a spontaneous song. I won't expound on this topic right now, since we cover the critical exercise of singing spontaneously in great detail in chapter 13. Even so, I want to whet your appetite concerning the significance of this beautiful—often misunderstood—highly biblical form of worship. If only for you.

Bold statement alert: Singing spontaneously in the secret place *and* in the public place regularly is something every believer must do. Think of it as comparable to our need to pray spontaneously, without a script. Truly. It's unbelievable the way this one exploit can open our hearts to God in ways other things can't. A seemingly insignificant thing, like lifting up your own song to God, can spark the moving of mountains in your life.

Don't get me wrong. I love singing "normal" corporate worship songs too. Publicly and privately. In fact, I typically start right there—with a song I know—just to get my blood pumping. But I often find it a struggle to stick to the previously written words. It's like I'm compelled to branch off a bit so I can be more specific and so I can keep my heart and mind engaged. Ironically, my mind tends to wander or disengage a little more when I'm singing a song I know. It's just way too easy to zone out, especially if I'm able to sing a song without thinking. Been there?

What to do? Well, I begin singing my own words. I slide off the main melody and begin experimenting with my own song to the Lord. Basically, it's like I'm setting my prayers to music. This helps me in so many ways, especially in avoiding singing words with my mouth while being completely distracted in my mind. As I sing my own song, I'm forced to think a little more about what I'm saying rather than simply regurgitating someone else's ideas.

5. Worship when you don't feel like it. I can't think of too many mornings when I get up, bound downstairs, and blissfully dive into musical worship. Rarely happens. At least not without a little faith. Even so, I want to encourage you to avoid waiting until you feel like worshiping God to do so. Especially regarding time alone with Him. We all know there are days we attend or plan a worship service with little to no emotion. The same can happen in the secret place. Yet as we step out in faith to open our mouths or lift a hand, something breaks inside. Like a dam. Why? Because, at the very moment we determine to worship God in faith—against our fleshly desires—it's as if He simultaneously pours transformation juice into our souls.

Sure, we don't always get goose bumps when we worship. I don't. But often, as we seek God by faith—even in the numb—deep and authentic emotions begin to rise up as we reach out and let go. Especially if we persevere and refuse to jump ship. Of course, we don't chase emotion. We chase God. Still, the point is, when we genuinely seek God, He often awakens—or reawakens—our spiritual senses to His heart in supernatural ways. When we truly seek Him, we will find Him, and when we truly find Him, we shouldn't be surprised when we are genuinely overcome by just how wonderful He is.

IF I FAIL AT EVERYTHING ELSE

As I've disciplined myself to spend daily time alone with God, I've also whispered a simple prayer over and over: "Lord, if I fail at everything else, let me not fail at knowing you. If I never have truckloads of money. If I never become a YouTube sensation. If I never make it on *The Voice* or pastor a world-renowned church. If this book's message never reaches the places around the world that desperately need it. If I fail at being a husband. If I fail at being a father. If I fail at being a professor at NCU or a pastor at Celebration Church. If I fail at being a songwriter, a podcaster, a worship leader, a speaker, or an author—please, Lord, let me not fail at abiding in close fellowship with you!"

This is my foremost prayer.

The irony? If I fail in my walk with God, I will ultimately fail in all of these other areas. *All* of them. But when I "succeed" in my walk with God, I will also succeed—in the truest Kingdom sense of the word—in all of these other areas. Additionally, if I seek God as a good Father, I'll be more capable of hearing His heart on effective parenting. If I spend time seeking God as the bride of Christ, I'll grow as a husband. If I succeed daily at communing with God relationally, I'll become a friendlier friend, a brotherlier brother, a neighborlier neighbor, a more employable employee. I'll also become a more inspiring teacher and a more anointed writer, speaker, author, and worship leader.

When I prioritize knowing Christ—in face-to-face real-time relationship—I am, in essence, buying oil for my soul. And this oil—this anointing, this Holy Spirit power—keeps my light burning, all while helping me accomplish all that God has called me to do. I become a better companion of Christ as well as a better worker in His fields, because I'm operating from a place of overflow rather than a place of lack.

Chapter Highlights

1. Part of growing as a leader is being willing to be transparent with your own personal walk with God, allowing others to sharpen you and keep you accountable. Seeing how it's so easy to wane in these areas, continued dialogue with your mentor(s) on the disciplines of spending time with God should remain a top priority.

2. According to Matthew 25:1–13, nothing is more important than "buying oil" for your relationship with God. This is the only way to continually spark the light in your life's lamp, keeping you from "burning out" in life and in ministry.

3. As believers, our daily time with God should consist of three things: studying the Bible, praying and listening to God, and engaging in musical worship. These three will keep your light burning brightly for Jesus.

4. The most important thing about spending time with God is to keep it all relational. It's so easy to read the Word, worship in song, and spout off prayers without genuinely engaging with the *person* of God. Resist the temptation to do the duty of daily devotions without employing these disciplines as a relational gateway to fellowship with God.

5. When we get to the end of our lives, few of us will wish we had done more *work* for Jesus. Rather we will wish we had spent more *time* with Jesus.

Chapter 4

PRIDE AND PURITY

Lie #4

*"The blood of Jesus excuses our
imperfections and impurities."*

What a conundrum we have. With creatives, that is. The very creativity meant by God to breathe life into a hurting world—our art, our songs, our handiwork—is the very thing that can monumentally corrupt. Both the hearts of the creative and the consumers of this creativity.

My heart is broken over the plethora of gifted artists and creatives around the globe who are either devastatingly insecure or who are unbelievably impressed with themselves. We've all watched with cringing hearts as leaders in the Church, in the music industry, in Hollywood, and in the corporate world have gone off the integrity deep end. And still—shockingly—we've seen many "believers" looking the other way, and even celebrating or defending highly gifted, immoral people.

But the focus of this chapter is not on them. It's on us.

With all the moral failures littering the popular skylines, what makes us think we'll be different? What makes us believe we can avoid the pitfalls so many others haven't? Especially when they believed this at one time too.

Shouldn't we be asking these questions? Shouldn't we be pondering these issues now—before it's too late? Shouldn't we be talking about purity, motives, and holiness before *we* become the next big moral catastrophe?

God is empowering you and me to become Spirit-led, gifted, passionate, humble servants who understand how to responsibly and resourcefully steward the gifts—His gifts—that He's entrusted us with. Without succumbing to pride and insecurity. You in?

CLEANSING OURSELVES

I used to wonder, *Who is responsible for the work—God or us?* I mean foundationally, as it relates to things as random as acquiring a new job, choosing a career, providing for the future, and even cleansing our souls.

It's a good question, really. How much of this depends on us, and how much depends on God?

In the Scriptures, with regard to pleasing God, we understand that He does the lion's share of the work within us. *"For God is working in you, giving you the desire and the power to do what pleases him"* (Philippians 2:13). Simple. Still, if God does *most* of the work, what's our role?

Back up one verse. *"Dear friends, you always followed my instructions when I was with you. And now that I am away, it is even more important.* ***Work hard*** *to show the results of your salvation, obeying God with deep reverence and fear* (Philippians 2:12).

So who does the work? Looks like we've stumbled upon another one of those *both*/and principles.

Take this precarious verse: *"Because we have these promises, dear friends, let us cleanse ourselves from everything that can defile our body or spirit. And let us work toward complete purity because we fear God"* (2 Corinthians 7:1).

Wow. Pause. Reread. That's a different level altogether.

We don't hear this one preached much. Maybe we're afraid that if we encourage people to work toward purity, we'll appear to be affirming a salvation-by-works theology, attempting to replace the work of Christ on the cross with human effort. To cleanse ourselves. By ourselves. We certainly don't want that.

Yet what is our role? According to this passage?

Paul touches on it again, this time with ferocity, in 1 Corinthians 15:10: *"But whatever I am now, it is all because God poured out his special favor on me—and not without results. **For I have worked harder than any of the other apostles; yet it was not I but God who was working through me by his grace.**"*

There it is. The unveiled irony. God is working in us to cleanse us, even as we work, in the power of His grace, to cleanse ourselves. This is important for many reasons, not the least of which is to allow the shimmer of God's transformational light to shine clearly and cleanly to others through the lens of our own lives.

C. S. Lewis writes captivatingly in *Mere Christianity*:

When you come to knowing God, the initiative lies on His side. If He does not show Himself, nothing you can do will enable you to find Him. And, in fact, He shows much more of Himself to some people than to others—not because He has favorites, but because it is impossible for Him to show Himself to a man whose whole mind and character are in the wrong condition. Just as sunlight, though it has no favorites, cannot be reflected in a dusty mirror as clearly as in a clean one.

You can put this another way by saying that while in other sciences the instruments you use are things external to yourself (things like microscopes and telescopes), the instrument through which you see God is your whole self. And if a man's self is not kept clean and bright, his glimpse of God will be blurred – like the Moon seen through a dirty telescope. That is why horrible nations have horrible religions: they have been looking at God through a dirty lens.[1]

Okay. That went well.

Don't worry. We won't attempt to unpack these impregnable words in their entirety.

The main point? Much of our ability to see clearly—spiritually—lies

1 C. S. Lewis, *Mere Christianity* (New York, NY: MacMillan Publishing, 1952), page 144.

in our ability, combined with the Spirit's ability, to keep our viewfinder unmuddied. Only a clear heart can see clearly. Only a clean heart can live cleanly. And though *our* work could never have been done had Jesus not done *His*, we must get *our* hands dirty in order to apply the cleansing properties of His blood to our lives. It's not Jesus by Himself. It's us along with a huge helping of Jesus. Together. He provides the blood, the wherewithal, and the power, and we apply our faith to work it all out. As His Spirit leads.

Many folks believe Jesus paid it all. That the entire cost of our reconciliation to God was paid by Jesus. Startlingly, this isn't entirely true. It's a nice song and everything, yet I suppose it all hangs on our definition of *all*.

If by *all* we are referring to Jesus' part as the *only* part that must be paid, then we're somewhat misguided. But, if by *all*, we're referring to the part that only Jesus Himself can pay, we're cooking with gas. Jesus paid His part, and now we can pay our part, by faith through the power of His Spirit. We couldn't do our part without Him first doing His part, but there's still a cost for us to pay as we lay down our lives for the Kingdom.

Make no mistake. We cannot do the work Jesus did. And we cannot obtain our desperately needed purification without the redemptive work of Christ on the cross. This is the lion's share (or the Lamb's share, if you will). We could never purify our own hearts—as the Scriptures command—without Jesus' great sacrifice. Still, if Jesus has done His part, and yet you and I have left our part undone—infinitesimal as it may be—the part we leave undone still nullifies the part Jesus has done on our behalf.

The Bible is clear. We are expected to work by faith to keep our hearts pure. As believers. As leaders. We must live in such a way that we do not invalidate Jesus' work on the cross or the work of the Spirit in our lives. To stand in purity. To walk in righteousness. To live in holiness. We must refuse to allow our character to wane even as our talents and giftings are often championed.

PURITY MATTERS TO GOD

You knew this. But it's still important to reiterate. Especially as we lead creatives.

Purity matters greatly to God. And it must matter greatly to us. As it

pertains to creatives and artists and innovators—to everyone, really—we must be clear. An untainted heart is the most important thing. Before talent. Before looks. Before money. Before success. Before accomplishments. Without a pure heart, all of these amount to nothing to God.

God is not looking as much for impres-
sive musicians as He is clean vessels. He is not searching the planet as much for extraordinarily talented performers as He is extraordinarily faithful followers. Don't be

> God is searching for genuine hearts who know how to powerfully and humbly wield the talents He has given them.

fooled. Though this world spends gross amounts of precious resources searching the highways and byways for the hottest talent, God is not awed by talents. Think about it. Why would He be impressed with our giftings, especially when He gave them to us in the first place? Rather, God is searching for genuine hearts who know how to powerfully and humbly wield the talents He has given them. This is the distinguishing factor for Him.

Not surprisingly, God is unamused when our lives are polluted—even a little bit. He hurts for us. When the fresh waters flowing from our mouths cease and the salt water pours forth. When the crystal-clear springs of our hearts and minds are fouled with even a small clod of pride or insecurity. When the entire batch of dough is tainted by just a touch of yeast. Yes, when our talk and our walk are diametrically opposed to one another, our talents and giftings become a greater detriment to the Kingdom than a help. In Matthew 15:8–9, God says, *These people honor me with their lips, but their hearts are far from me. Their worship is a farce, for they teach man-made ideas as commands from God.*

I imagine He would have us keep silent and remain out of the spot-light rather than ignore the duality of our lives. Not that He would have us reach for perfection, but that He would have us drop to our knees, admit our duplicity, do an about-face, and begin to depend again on Him to make us "worthy" carriers of His presence.

How can we be made worthy? Only Jesus is worthy, right? Yet, we are made worthy when we die to ourselves—completely by faith—and allow Jesus to become our righteousness. When we are crucified with

Christ, He lives our life on our behalf, and we are able to minister out of His righteousness, even as He is transforming our hearts and minds by His Spirit.

Incredibly, our pride-stained hearts can be turned pure white again via one beautiful drop of Jesus' blood. But we must avail ourselves to His blood so it can do its work. We must make way for a complete spiritual blood transfusion that we might begin to live and lead in complete purity.

MOTIVES MATTER TO GOD

This is a tricky one. Motives are harder to assess. Fact is, if you want to get somebody riled up, question their motives.

I suppose the reason we're a little touchy about our motives is because they seem to hint at what's hidden beneath the surface. And we don't want people delving so deep. Why? Because motives get right to the heart of the issue. The *reasons* we do what we do. Of course, it's one thing to do the right thing. It's quite another to do the right thing for the right reason.

While perceiving someone's motives can be very difficult, it's nearly impossible to distinguish our own. Even so, the Lord sees it all: *"People may be pure in their own eyes, but the LORD examines their motives"* (Proverbs 16:2). This is terrifying. But also refreshing. Why? Because it means we might as well stop pretending. God sees it all. But there's great freedom in living our lives humbly and completely openly before Him.

Without God's help, we can never understand the true depths of our own hearts, our motives. But God can, and He wants to bring them to light so that He can heal us completely: *"The human heart is most deceitful and desperately wicked. Who really knows how bad it is? But I know! I, the LORD, search all hearts and **examine secret motives**. I give all people their due rewards, according to what their actions deserve"* (Jeremiah 17:9–10). *"So don't make judgments about anyone ahead of time—before the Lord returns. For he will bring our darkest secrets to light and will **reveal our private motives**. Then God will give to each one whatever praise is due"* (1 Corinthians 4:5).

If these verses make us tremble a little, that is good.

But what to do?

Throw caution to the wind? Hope and pray for God's grace? Ignore it all, and hope it goes away?

Let's talk it through.

CREATE IN ME A CLEAN HEART

Our healing begins with a prophecy from Ezekiel, one of the most wonderful and hope-filled prophecies in all the Old Testament: *"Then I will sprinkle clean water on you, and you will be clean. Your filth will be washed away, and you will no longer worship idols. And I will give you a new heart, and I will put a new spirit in you.* **I will take out your stony, stubborn heart and give you a tender, responsive heart.** *And I will put my Spirit in you so that you will follow my decrees and be careful to obey my regulations"* (Ezekiel 36:25–27).

I'm deeply moved by these words. They're truly some of the most astonishing words found in the Old Testament, because they're so filled with eternal, supernatural love and healing for our souls—something a lot of people aren't used to encountering in the books of the Law and Prophets.

He doesn't slap on a little supernatural duct tape, leaving the old cracks and brokenness—as many well-meaning leaders teach. No. As the Scriptures say, He completely removes our old stony, stubborn heart and gives us a new one. Brand new. One born of His Spirit. One fashioned for obedience. One fully equipped for righteousness. His own spiritual heart surgically transplanted right into our spiritual chest.

This is wonderful news.

PERSEVERING IN PURITY

Walking in purity is not easy. But that's no reason to believe it can't be done. We simply must fully embrace Ezekiel 36 so we can stop trying to do it with *our* heart and, instead, do it with *God's* heart.

Here are a few practical areas we can grow in as we work toward nurturing our Ezekiel heart, the one God has given us by His Spirit.

1. Recognize that our gifts come straight from God.

It may be elementary, but I've found this to be one of the primary stumbling blocks we encounter as creatives. For some reason, there seems to be a proverbial disconnect between our talents and their source.

How do I know? The proof is in the pudding.

We need only look to the massive chasm between the ultra-gifted and their—and our—understanding of the source. Why else would folks parade themselves around with their sunglasses, their little foo-foo dogs, and their noses in the air? As if the world revolved around them. Somehow, they've missed something. And yet so have we, when we desperately seek to be them and/or to chase them around all googly-eyed while hoping to snag a photo.

We didn't create ourselves. We didn't create our gifts. Our beauty. Our prosperity. And we certainly didn't fashion this big blue ball called Earth, the planet that does *not* revolve around us. We didn't give ourselves sight. We didn't give ourselves intelligence. We didn't design our vocal cords or breathe air into our lungs.

Shoot, we didn't even give ourselves the drive to practice. Who's to say we truly grasp the miracle of "practice makes perfect"? We didn't even make our own two feet, let alone the path they walk on. And we certainly can't engineer our own success.

It's all a façade, according to the Scriptures.

> *"Don't raise your fists in defiance at the heavens*
> *or speak with such arrogance.'*
> *For no one on earth—from east or west,*
> *or even from the wilderness—*
> *should raise a defiant fist.*
> ***It is God alone who judges;***
> ***he decides who will rise and who will fall"*** (Psalm 75:5–7).

Wow.

The Classic Amplified version reads: *"Lift not up your [aggressive] horn on high, speak not with a stiff neck and insolent arrogance. For not from the east nor from the west nor from the south come promotion and lifting* *up. **But God is the Judge! He puts down one and lifts up another***" (Psalm 75:5–7 AMPC).

Love it or hate it, God raises one person up and puts another down. For His purposes. No matter how many prominent leaders tell us otherwise. No matter how many books on success we've read. God is working behinds the scenes for His purposes. He gives us assignments, and He controls our destiny. *"It is not that we think we are qualified to do anything on our own. Our qualification comes from God"* (2 Corinthians 3:5).

Can we speak into our destiny or learn principles that can help us move forward in life? Sure. Depending on our definition of the word *forward*. Still, He ultimately holds the powers of life and death in His hands. He places those in authority in their positions (see Romans 13:1), and He directs the hearts of Kings (see Proverbs 21:1) to accomplish His purposes. Yes. *His* purposes. His good and perfect purposes.

Remember, it's God who gave His great favor to people like Abraham and David. Esther and Mary. Peter and Paul. God gave it. And He wants to give you and me favor too. Not to do *our* work, mind you. But to do *His* work.

Joseph was successful because God gave Him success. *"**The LORD was with Joseph**, so he succeeded in everything he did as he served in the home of his Egyptian master. Potiphar noticed this and realized that **the LORD was with Joseph**, giving him success in everything he did"* (Genesis 39:2–3).

Samuel's words had power only because God gave them power: *"As Samuel grew up, **the LORD was with him**, and everything Samuel said proved to be reliable"* (1 Samuel 3:19).

David was loved by the people of Israel, ultimately, only because God made it happen: *"David continued to succeed in everything he did, for **the LORD was with him**"* (1 Samuel 18:14).

God even raised up unbelieving, godless leaders, giving them power to do His bidding—like King Nebuchadnezzar II, the King of Tyre, and Emperor Nero.

This is *real* power.

This is *real* authority.

Make no mistake. God chooses when and where and to whom He

will give His power. And for what purpose. Sometimes He gives it as a blessing. Other times as a test.

On top of all of this, whatever God gives to us—success, opportunity, blessing, breath, money, influence, and more—He certainly calls us to account for what we do with it. We must not allow ourselves to forget Jesus' sobering words in Luke 12:48: *"When someone has been given much, much will be required in return; and when someone has been entrusted with much, even more will be required."*

2. Understand that God's definition of success is different from ours.

Would it disappoint you to know that God's goal for us is not "success"—at least not as we define it? God's success, and the world's success. These are two vastly different objectives. As worship leaders, musicians, pastors, and creatives, we need to get our heads out of the clouds and reforge our understanding of *success*.

As always, it's all in a word. *Success*. What do we mean by it? What does God mean by it? Where do our definitions converge? If at all? God does want *success* for you and me. But are we really after the same thing?

Let's start with one of my least favorite words.

Refinement.

This is *success* according to God. And He's doing everything in His power—often against our stubborn wills—to aid us in this area. "Thank you very much, God. I'll have a little more refinement with that, if you please. Fill it right to the top. In fact, I want every last drop. You know, the part *some* ice cream vendors throw away once they've blended your milkshake? The part at the bottom of the metal blending cup that doesn't quite fit into the to-go cup? Yeah, I'll take *everything* you've got in the refinement category."

Ha!

Trust me, I don't like it any more than you do. And yet there is great reason for celebration:

> So be truly glad. There is wonderful joy ahead, even though you must endure many trials for a little while. These trials will show that your faith is genuine. It is being tested as fire tests and purifies gold—though

your faith is far more precious than mere gold. So when your faith remains strong through many trials, it will bring you much praise and glory and honor on the day when Jesus Christ is revealed to the whole world. (1 Peter 1:6–7)

The testing of our faith is part of the refinement process. It is necessary in order for us to truly know that our faith is real. To know that our faith is robust. How would we know—how could we—that our faith was fully operational unless it was tested?

You have tested us, *O God;*
  you have purified us like silver.
You captured us in your net
  and laid the burden of slavery on our backs.
Then you put a leader over us.
  We went through fire and flood,
  *but **you brought us** to a place of great abundance.*
(Psalm 66:10–12)

No doubt, you've already received teaching surrounding the silver-refining process. But let me briefly summarize.

In order for silver to be purified, it is subjected to overwhelming heat. Typically, several times over. Each time, the heat drives the impurities—or dross—to the surface, where they are scraped off by the silversmith and thrown out. The hotter the heat, the greater the chance the impurities will surface. The more times the silver is exposed to the process, the purer the results. This is what determines the worth of the silver. Of course, the silversmith always knows exactly when the silver is ready, because it sings when he rubs his fingers on it *and* he can see his own reflection in it.

Wow.

"Remove the impurities from silver, and the sterling will be ready for the silversmith" (Proverbs 25:4). This is God's idea of *success*.

And if that's not enough, other words come to mind. Words like *suffering, trials,* and *persecution*. Again, these are seemingly unwelcomed foes, but they're the core strategies of your and my *success* according to the Scriptures. Peter exhorts, *"For God **called you** to do good, even if it means suffering, just as Christ suffered for you. He is your example, and you must follow in his steps"* (1 Peter 2:21).

Ironically, when I think of my calling, I don't typically do so in terms of any perceived negatives. But here, things seem entirely flipped—as if there's a different formula by which God calculates success. And yet He speaks clearly through Peter—the one who fully embraced a life of hardship after first attempting to shrug off its very existence—to announce that suffering is a featured item on the menu of God's buffet for our lives.

Ironically, we can fail miserably in the eyes of the world and still succeed mightily in the eyes of God. Just as we can undoubtedly succeed in the eyes of the world and yet fail—fundamentally—in the eyes of God.

It's our choice.

3. Be willing to make important sacrifices to remain in God's purpose.

I've heard Lisa Bevere say that whatever you compromise to get, you must continue to compromise to keep. This is riveting and perfect for our discussion.

What does it mean to compromise? Obviously, this word has its goods and bads. When we comprise, or meet in the middle, regarding a disagreement with someone, it can be a very good thing. But what about when we compromise our character?

The verb *compromise* means to "accept standards that are lower than is desirable."[2] And in our case, lower than God desires.

I remember a story my friend Gabe Hagan shared. (He wouldn't want me to use his name, but his heart is commendable and needs to be heralded.)

Before I moved to Minneapolis to be a professor at NCU, Gabe was a student, pursuing his undergraduate degree in music performance as a drummer. A very good one at that. This would have been approximately 2008.

---

2 Oxford English Dictionary, s.v. "compromise," Lexico, https://www.lexico.com/en /definition/compromise.

I was looking for a new touring drummer, and word spread to some friends at NCU that I was in need. Gabe heard about it and was suddenly faced with a dilemma. He had just made a commitment to a local artist to play for several regional dates over the course of the next couple of months. Right during the time I was in need of a drummer.

As he tells it, the local opportunity was great but paled in comparison to the national touring opportunity I was offering. Not only that, but the local tour was much shorter while mine was further reaching and longer term.

What to do?

We all have to decide. And ironically, the decision must often be made *before* the second opportunity presents itself. It has to be made in the darkness of anonymity. In the void of opportunity. Because if we wait until opportunity knocks, we can always find a way to justify compromise.

The psalmist chimes in and answers his own question, *"Who may worship in your sanctuary, LORD. Those who despise flagrant sinners, and honor the faithful followers of the LORD, and **keep their promises even when it hurts**"* (Psalm 15:1–4). Proverbs 11:3 echoes, *"The integrity of the upright guides them, but the unfaithful are destroyed by their duplicity"* (NIV).

Easier said than lived.

Please highlight my next sentence.

Don't compromise. *Ever.*

So, what did Gabe do?

Of course, he sought the Lord, even while wrestling with logic. He faced up to the demon of compromise right there on the mat of his big break. And he went for the take down. He could have called his buddy and asked to be released from his commitment. (This is a reasonable option. See Proverbs 6:1–5.) But Gabe had a conviction. And he stuck to it. For the pin. And the win.

We have to be careful, because, in the end, we simply want God's best for our lives. And He will often test us by allowing us to commit to one thing while presenting a "better" second option immediately following. (Get used to this. It's often His way.)

It's personal for me too. Every time I book a tour date for my ministry—even now—it seems I get an inquiry in the next week or so, asking me to book something for twice the pay and twice the reach on exactly the same day. Bummer. But I smile. Because I realize there's more at stake than the opportunity. What's important is not the opportunity, but the test of my character. Which ultimately leads to three things: peace with God (because I obey Him), favor with man (because I'm not burning bridges), and a good night's sleep (because I know my Provider).

Warning: The beauty of Gabe's story is one I want to caution you about. See, unlike many stories, his *did* come full circle. In real time. In good time. In his lifetime. But many times, it doesn't.

Gabe ultimately passed on the opportunity to be my drummer. All without knowing I would join the faculty at NCU two years later. All without knowing I would continue to tour professionally. All without realizing he would quickly become my touring drummer as well as my good friend. All without having to break his word or hurt his relationship with his other friend.

Amazingly, I wasn't even aware of this story until much, much later.

Good on him. And good on those who are committed to making decisions based on the big picture. Those who refuse to jump haphazardly from one "big-break" opportunity to another. Attempting to justify burning bridges and burning people, all without regard to the long-term consequences.

Here's David's word on this subject to his son:

"And Solomon, my son, learn to know the God of your ancestors intimately. Worship and serve him with your whole heart and a willing mind. For the LORD sees every heart and knows every plan and thought. If you seek him, you will find him. But if you forsake him, he will reject you forever. So take this seriously. The LORD has chosen you to build a Temple as his sanctuary. Be strong, and do the work" (1 Chronicles 28:9–10).

THE NEBUCHADNEZZAR FACTOR

As creatives, we are not strangers to pride—or its second cousin, insecurity. Truthfully, they go hand in hand. One minute we're flying high on the praises of the people—as if we've hung the moon—and the next we're sinking deep into a dark depression, thwarted by the glorious mob of critics outside our door.

History records King Nebuchadnezzar II as one of the most fascinating pagan leaders of all time. The Bible does not disagree. And yet, as the poster child of egotism, he serves us greatly by demystifying God's feelings on pride while providing powerful inspiration to help us avoid the unsightly casualties his arrogance achieved for him.

His duplicity is fascinating. One minute he's found tossing Shadrach, Meshach, and Abednego into a blazing furnace for refusing to worship the detestable image he had set up, and the next, he's making this celebrated statement concerning the Most High God:

> "His rule is everlasting,
>   and his kingdom is eternal.
> All the people of the earth
>   are nothing compared to him.
> He does as he pleases
>   among the angels of heaven
>   and among the people of the earth.
> No one can stop him or say to him,
>   'What do you mean by doing these things?'
>   Now I, Nebuchadnezzar, praise and glorify and honor the King of heaven. All his acts are just and true, and he is able to humble the proud" (Daniel 4:34–35, 37).

Bravo, Nebuchadnezzar. Bravo. I'm telling you, you just can't make this stuff up.

But the real question is, what caused him to shift his perspective so dramatically?

Glad you asked.

GOD IS ABLE TO HUMBLE THE PROUD

King Nebuchadnezzar II reigned for forty-three years, from 605–562 BC, and was one of the greatest kings of the ancient Babylonian Empire.

Babylon (whose ruins now lie in modern-day Iraq), was one of the enemy nations assigned by God—unbeknownst to Israel—to oversee and administer Israel's discipline for their outright rebellion against Him.

Between 587–586 BC, Nebuchadnezzar II conquered Jerusalem for the second time and took much of Israel's people into exile. Daniel was one of his prize subjects. As you may remember, Daniel 4 describes a dream the king had, recounted to Daniel (or Belteshazzar, as the Babylonians called him) as such:

"While I was lying in my bed, this is what I dreamed. I saw a large tree in the middle of the earth. The tree grew very tall and strong, reaching high into the heavens for all the world to see. It had fresh green leaves, and it was loaded with fruit for all to eat. Wild animals lived in its shade, and birds nested in its branches. All the world was fed from this tree.

"Then as I lay there dreaming, I saw a messenger, a holy one, coming down from heaven. The messenger shouted,

'Cut down the tree and lop off its branches!
*   Shake off its leaves and scatter its fruit!*
Chase the wild animals from its shade
*   and the birds from its branches.*
But leave the stump and the roots in the ground,
*   bound with a band of iron and bronze*
*   and surrounded by tender grass.*
Now let him be drenched with the dew of heaven,
*   and let him live with the wild animals among the plants of the field.*
For seven periods of time,
*   let him have the mind of a wild animal*
*   instead of the mind of a human.*
For this has been decreed by the messengers;
*   it is commanded by the holy ones,*
so that everyone may know
*   that the Most High rules over the kingdoms of the world.*
He gives them to anyone he chooses—
*   even to the lowliest of people.'*

"Belteshazzar, that was the dream that I, King Nebuchadnezzar, had. Now tell me what it means, for none of the wise men of my kingdom can do so. But you can tell me because the spirit of the holy gods is in you" (Daniel 4:10–18).

Daniel proceeds to interpret the mysterious dream starting in verse 24:

"This is what the dream means, Your Majesty, and what the Most High has declared will happen to my lord the king. You will be driven from human society, and you will live in the fields with the wild animals. You will eat grass like a cow, and you will be drenched with the dew of heaven. Seven periods of time will pass while you live this way, until you learn that the Most High rules over the kingdoms of the world and gives them to anyone he chooses. But the stump and roots of the tree were left in the ground. This means that you will receive your kingdom back again when you have learned that heaven rules" (Daniel 4:24–26).

Daniel adds this heart-felt warning: *"King Nebuchadnezzar, please accept my advice. Stop sinning and do what is right. Break from your wicked past and be merciful to the poor. Perhaps then you will continue to prosper"* (Daniel 4:27).

But the self-righteous king couldn't resist. Daniel 4:28–33 records how one year later Nebuchadnezzar was strolling on his palace roof bragging aloud about his accomplishments when he suddenly professed, *"Look at this great city of Babylon! By my own mighty power, I have built this beautiful city as my royal residence to display my majestic splendor"* (Daniel 4:30).

While the words were still in his mouth, a voice from heaven called down to him, saying he would immediately be disavowed from his position as king over Babylon for seven years, and the events in the dream would come to pass until he indeed learned that *"The Most High rules over the kingdoms of the world and gives them to anyone he chooses"* (Daniel 4:32).

Pride is devastating. Pride kills. Pride destroys. And God is able to humble those who are prideful. Quickly. And easily.

And though King Nebuchadnezzar did finally give up pride for humility after being made to eat grass like a cow for seven years, there's no reason we need to embrace such a path to get there ourselves. Why not take the necessary measures now to avoid this disparaging trap—a trap that has plagued so many leaders? Leaders like Pharaoh, who claimed, "The Nile River is mine" in Ezekiel 29 (and was thereby punished as God promised to reduce Egypt to one of the lowliest nations on the face of the earth), and Herod Agrippa, who was eaten by worms in Acts 12:20–23 (as a punishment for accepting the worship of the people instead of giving the glory to God).

Note these important action points that will help us keep pride at bay:

- **We are only tools in God's hands.** Nothing more. Can a hammer drive a nail by itself or build a table and chairs alone? Neither can we do anything apart from God (see John 15:5).
- **God does not need us to accomplish His purposes.** Though this can be disheartening, we cannot let the enemy's distortion of the truth win the day. Never have we wanted to serve a God who needed us. But thank goodness, we serve a God who wants us, in spite of the fact that He does not need us.
- **We did not create our giftings or make ourselves great.** People who experience "worldly" success typically start from much humbler beginnings. Remembering these facts will serve us well in maintaining a grateful heart toward any success we might experience now or in the future.
- **Every good and perfect gift comes from God (James 1:17).** We covered this earlier, but it deserves a second mention as we consider the unnatural attributes of humble Kingdom leaders.
- **Always redirect any praise you receive.** This is what Herod Agrippa did not manage as he was greeted with the ostentatious praises of the people in Acts 12. Don't misunderstand. The best response when someone compliments you is still, "Thank you." Just make sure you don't receive the praise without realizing where the ultimate praise belongs. Thus, our attitude should

always be that of Psalm 115:1: *"Not to us, O LORD . . . but to your name goes all the glory."*

- **Believe only the Lord's report.** The devil is always working both sides. If he can't lead us into pride, he'll drag us into false humility. Whether we're successful in man's eyes or not, all that God requires is that we hold to His perfect thoughts of us. We are sons and daughters of the King, and this knowledge is what will keep us from swerving off course.
- **Beware of the fear of man.** This was a big part of King Saul's downfall, as displayed by his remarks to Samuel in defense of his disobedience from 1 Samuel 15:24: *"I was afraid of the people and did what they demanded."*

Pride is one of the greatest enemies of the Church. As creatives and leaders, we do well to guard against Satan's tactics, remembering that we still overcome the Accuser by the blood of the Lamb, by the word of our testimony, and by being unafraid to die (see Revelation 12:11).

Chapter Highlights

1. The Bible is clear that purity matters to God. This is a common area of struggle for many creatives and leaders. Though the ultimate cleansing of our souls starts and ends with Jesus' blood, part of our role as believers is to "cleanse ourselves" in the power of the Spirit (see 2 Corinthians 7:1). We must engage in the process as God works deep within us to sanctify and purify our souls.

2. Paul presents a peculiar balance when it comes to the work we do in our lives. While some believe Jesus did and does all the work necessary for us to walk in purity with God, Paul reveals that Christianity demands we join God in the work, similar to the way the Israelites were commanded to join God's shout with their shout in order to bring down the walls of Jericho.

3. God has ordained that we engage in the great heart exchange. He has not planned to simply duct tape our hearts back together, but to *remove* our stony hearts of sin altogether and replace them with brand-new ones, directly from His Spirit.

4. God's definition of success is often different from ours. We must keep from comparing ourselves to others while resisting the temptation to make our core decisions based on our deep longing for earthly success. Kingdom success may not bring the applause of men, but it will provide a great reward in the end.

Chapter 5

THE ULTIMATE EXPRESSION OF WORSHIP

Lie #5

*"My life is mine to do with as I please. Jesus
carried the cross, so I wouldn't have to."*

Dick Brogden is a friend. He's also an inspiration. I love *and* hate when I have a chance to hear him preach. His words are an onslaught to my flesh. I am stirred. I am challenged. I am grateful.

During the fall of 2016, he made a statement that rocked me during an NCU chapel: "If you want to be a life-giving Christian, it starts by dying."

Okay. So let's start with this one little sentence before moving on. How does this impact our worship?

As a leader. As a worship leader. As a musician. As a believer in Christ. Do we really aspire to be a life-giving Christian? Do we know what this means? Are we really prepared to die? To lay down our lives? To forego our earthly desires? Or does this idea simply scare the bejeebers out of us?

He continued inspirationally, "In the physical world, first we live and then we die. In the spiritual world, first we die and then we live. The lost of this world do not need our putrid, uncrucified selves. The unreached do not need your tyrannical nature leading the way. The lost of the world need the fragrance of a crushed will, a broken heart, and a contrite spirit.

The Lord is very near to the crucified. He hung amongst them. And he is very far away from those who dwell on self-made thrones."[1]

Stop. Ponder. Reflect. Cry.

Reminds me, in some ways, of Proverbs 14:12: *"There is a path before each person that seems right, but it ends in death."* Do you see it there? The end? *Our* end? When we go our own way? Make our own path? It doesn't end well. Yet, paradoxically, what seems to start excruciatingly in the Kingdom—through crushing, brokenness, and suffering—ends well. Very well indeed.

The path I choose now inevitably encapsulates my life here on earth. A few short years. A few forgettable moments. When I choose *my* path, I may be afforded the opportunity to live my life my way in the immediate, after which I, like everyone, must die. Here on earth, "living" comes first. Death comes second. Death everlasting. But if I choose to flip it and embrace *God's* path, my experience will be exactly the opposite. I may spend a significant portion of this short life dying to my own desires—seemingly unable to attain all this world offers me—and yet, as a result, I will spend eternity with God, truly attaining all the splendors He has to offer. Truly living. Fully. Forever.

It's as if we've been given the most unbelievable choice. We can embrace all the "pleasures" of this world—for a very short time—ending with eternal death, or we can die to the pleasures of this world—for a very short time—and enjoy all the wonders the Father has to offer for all of eternity. The irony? By choosing to die to earthly pleasures in the *here and now*, we are additionally granted access to the most abundant life this planet has to offer. Even *before* arriving on eternity's shores. The best of both worlds.

LIFE IS SHORT

The other day, I saw an interesting anonymous post about life. As a leader who works diligently to help others discern right from wrong, good from evil, it saddened me deeply.

---

1   Dick Brogden, North Central University chapel, Minneapolis, MN, 2016

Time passes so quickly, you literally do not even notice it until it begins to show. So, don't wait to use the good china, go on the trip, eat the cake, watch the late movie, read your favorite book, and take a chance in life… the time is now. Tomorrow is promised to no one.

Hmm. Do you see it? Look again.

It seems almost perfect. Inspirational. But ask yourself, at its core, what is it really saying? "Your life is yours. Go ahead. Live your dreams. Life is short."

Sure, there are some nice things listed, but if you look closely, most of them are already things we're doing and, quite honestly, should probably be doing less of.

Eat that cake. Seriously? You're gonna give this advice to the most obese generation to ever walk the face of the earth? Trust me. I think we've had our cake and eaten it too. *Watch that late movie?* Really? This is supposed to help empower the generation that coined the term *Netflix binge?*

The intention of the post is admirable. It's probably aimed at the workaholic who's consumed with work, work, work. Or the person who's holding back because of fear. I get it. It's attempting to motivate us to do the stuff we've always wanted to do but never took the time to do so we can get the most out of life.

Thing is, I have a feeling we could write a much better post if we were to filter our thoughts through Matthew 7:13: *"You can enter God's Kingdom only through the narrow gate. The highway to hell is broad, and its gate is wide for the many who choose that way. But the gateway to life is very narrow and the road is difficult, and only a few ever find it."*

Maybe it would read much better—and be more Kingdom minded—if it said something like this:

Time passes so quickly, you literally don't even notice it until it begins to show. So don't wait to tell your loved ones about Jesus, go on that mission trip, spend more time fasting and praying, attend your daughter's play and your son's baseball game, take your wife dancing, sign up for that theology class, and reach out to the Muslim family across the street. Take a chance in life…the time is now. Tomorrow is promised to no one.

Don't you dare roll your eyes. Ha! You know it's true.

While the author of the other post may have meant well, we simply cannot afford to spread half-truths, especially while so many are barely aware of God's existence. The last thing we need to peddle is more of that good ol' fashioned "do what makes you happy" ideology.

I'm going to be bold here. If you didn't see anything wrong with this post the first time you read it, you might need to reexamine your world view. You may need to ask yourself if it's possible you've grown numb—unintentionally or not—to the *authentic* ways of God. If you've grown ever so gradually deafer to His voice. If you've somehow managed to get God's truth flipped around in your heart. *Even* if you're a leader in the church. *Especially* if you're a leader in the church. We need to be much sharper than this.

What are we living for? Are we just playing games? Singing the songs and doing the dance? Just doing the church thing? Faking the funk? Or are we laying it all down? With every breath, in every minute of every day, desiring to offer up the ultimate expression of worship. The beautiful aroma of lives laid down before the King.

THREE SIMPLE WORDS

Speaking of laying it all down, what exactly *is* the ultimate expression of worship? What key is it in? (Kidding.)

Is it excellence? Authenticity? Proper theology? Scriptural doctrine? Singing? Dancing? Giving to the poor? Feeding the hungry? Social justice? Prophecy? Good works? Is it living in Spirit and truth? Is it the Tabernacle of David? Prayer? Miracles? Banners? Speaking up for the marginalized?

What?

For starters, we need to clarify our meaning. If we're talking about the ultimate *act* of worship, it is clear from the Scriptures that our highest pursuit in worship is relationship. Simply, fellowship with our heavenly Father. Connection. Intimacy. Friendship. This is the greatest *act* of worship, from which, of course, should flow an outpouring of good works and good deeds to minister to believers as well as those we might call "pre-Christians."

Even so, when we speak of the ultimate *expression* of worship, this is something different altogether. The ultimate *expression* of a life devoted to worship—devoted to fellowship with the Father—is one lived via three simple words: Death. To. Self. *"My old self has been crucified with Christ. It is no longer I who live, but Christ lives in me. So I live in this earthly body by trusting in the Son of God, who loved me and gave himself for me"* (Galatians 2:20).

> Laying down our lives for the Kingdom is the most fragrant expression of worship we can ever offer. This is the highest form of praise. The sweetest song there is.

Call it what you want. A living sacrifice. Denial of self. Carrying your cross. But know this: Whatever we call it, laying down our lives for the Kingdom is the most fragrant expression of worship we can ever offer. This is the highest form of praise. The sweetest song there is.

EMBRACING THE CROSS

You knew I would get here eventually: *"Then Jesus said to his disciples, 'If any of you wants to be my follower, you must give up your own way, **take up your cross, and follow me. If you try to hang on to your life, you will lose it. But if you give up your life for my sake, you will save it.** And what do you benefit if you gain the whole world but lose your own soul? Is anything worth more than your soul?'"* (Matthew 16:24–26).

Saving our soul is God's ultimate goal. His foremost desire. Why? Well, if we're not saved, we can't give Him what He wants *and* we can't have what we need: Relationship. With. God.

I've wrestled with this. What does it mean to take up your cross? How can we actually do this as individuals? As followers of Christ? As the body of Christ? As leaders? Musicians? Creatives?

Jesus leads the way brilliantly on this topic, all while inviting us to join Him. Yet, it still seems He routinely models leadership very differently than we do. For starters, He's always talking to people He shouldn't talk to (the woman at the well), going to the homes of people He shouldn't associate with (Zacchaeus), and refusing to condemn those everyone else has already condemned (the adulterous woman). He's always doing things He shouldn't be doing (washing the disciples' feet), taking actions at the worst of times (healing on the Sabbath), and "rabble rousing" when everyone else is being political (turning over the tables in the temple).

Then—if these examples aren't enough—He continues by saying things that deeply offend people (let the dead bury their own dead), traveling by means others would never dream of (riding the colt into Jerusalem), and healing those shunned by everyone else (the lepers and countless others).

There's got to be a lesson in here somewhere. Even for worship leaders and musicians. How exactly does embracing the cross affect your life? My life? Specifically? Are we talking only about a superficial "religious" posture—or is it something more?

I think it's safe to assume Jesus isn't speaking literally about embracing the cross. So what exactly is He saying, figuratively? Here are a few ideas:

- What if it means going across the street to mow your elderly neighbor's yard or simply taking a few minutes to sit down with her for a chat?
- What if it means giving up a cup of coffee each day to increase the amount you send to the child you sponsor in Haiti?
- What if it means deleting your Facebook app so you can spend more time in the Word? With the Word—the Person? (Lord knows your scrolling thumb would thank you!)
- What if it means turning off that flick to watch a thought-provoking sermon with your kids? And then discussing it?
- What if it means reducing the number of gifts (toys and stuff) purchased at Christmas in order to give some gifts to kids in foster care whose parents abused or abandoned them?
- What if it means humbling yourself before your parents and finally telling them you're sorry? Even if they're in the wrong, too?

- What if it means holding the hand of your hardhearted uncle as he lies in bed dying of cancer?
- What if it means putting off the basement makeover to use the time you'd save to start a neighborhood Bible study?
- What if it means refusing to lead a dancing/shouting song from the stage until you've actually cultivated a heart for dancing and shouting in the secret place?
- What if it means refusing to step on another platform until you've developed a love for your congregation by praying for them each by name?
- What if it means confessing the sin of comparison and jealousy that we embrace regarding other worship leaders with greater notoriety? (Believe it or not, I'm right there with you.)

This—and many other things—hint at exactly what it means to take up our cross to follow Christ. This is the life song God wants to hear emanating from our hearts. From our stages. From our teams. From our church folk. From our pastors, board members, elders, and volunteers.

This is what it means to be dead—and yet *so* alive. This is what it means to be sparked by the Spirit.

Please hear me. It's not about doing *more* stuff. It's about doing the *right* stuff.

But how do we turn things around?

It ain't easy.

THE LIVING DEAD AND THE DEAD LIVING

As committed leaders and followers of Christ, how do we transform our minds to become the people God has called us to be? How do we rid ourselves of the all-too-common natural desires to build our own kingdom? To love our lives too much? Especially when those tendencies disguise themselves as passion for ministry.

Romans 12:1 is so popular, we've almost grown numb to it. Even so, let's take another look. *"And so dear brothers and sisters, I plead with you to give your bodies to God. ... **Let them be a living and holy sacrifice—the kind he will find acceptable.**"*

As you know, the Israelites were required to bring animal sacrifice after animal sacrifice to the Lord in order to cleanse themselves from sin. But Jesus ended all of this by standing in as the final sacrifice. One man for all. One Lamb for all. One sacrifice for all time.

Jesus died a physical death so that we might have a chance to live a spiritual life. Yet, in order to receive the life Jesus offers we are invited to die to the life our flesh desires. To walk this earth as those who are fully dead to earthly things and fully alive to Kingdom things. For our overwhelming gain!

When we live dead...

- We don't have an identity crisis. Because *He* is our identity.
- We don't have a lust problem. Because lust has *lost* its power.
- We don't have a "sharing the glory" struggle. Because dead people can't attain glory.

When we live dead...

- Life stops revolving around us. Because our decisions revolve around the Son.
- Joy stops depending on circumstances. Because real joy transcends the good and the bad times.
- Fear stops holding us back. Because we are dead to fear, and fear is dead to us.

When we live dead...

- We are not defined by an ugly past any longer. Because the past is *dead* and gone.
- We don't have a disappointing present any longer. Because we know God has us right where He wants us.
- We don't have a hopeless future any longer. Because we *know* who holds the future.

When we live dead...

- Christ is alive *in* us.
- Christ lives our life *for* us.
- We view everything *through* His eyes.
- We see everything *with* His eyes.

When we live dead…

- We have the *heart* of Christ.
- We have the *mind* of Christ.
- We have the *nature* of Christ.
- We are fully, completely, 100 percent *dead*, and are now fully *alive*!

MY NAME IN "LIKES"

Of course, all this goes completely against our natural desires.

Peter struggled right alongside us. He's like, "Why can't I have an influential, longstanding ministry like John's? Why does *he* get it so good?" (see John 21:18–23). I've struggled with it too. Why can't I have the same level of influence I had when I was in Sonicflood? Why can't I be connected to Bethel or Jesus Culture like Brian and Jen Johnson or Brian and Katie Torwalt? Why can't I write a song that is sung in every church around the world? Why can't I have flowing locks of thick hair like other men? (Oh shoot, did I just write that?)

My kingdom and God's Kingdom cannot *coexist*. But…

I desire success and influence so much.

I long to be noticed and recognized by everyone.

I want my name in lights.

I want my name in "likes."

Oh, you want to be an effective Kingdom leader? Don't listen to the imposters who would say, "Live your life. Dream your dream. Work extra hard, so you can silence the haters. You only get one life. Get after it!"

Want to empower people to walk with God in real victory and humility? In real fervency and faithfulness? In real surrender and holiness? Give your life away. It's not popular, but this is the culture God is calling us to instill into our teams and our congregations.

Ironically, many preach that Jesus had a popular earthly ministry, saying things like, "That's why everybody liked Jesus and wanted to hang around Him all the time. The rich and the poor. The Jew and the Gentile. Everyone. And we should be like Him!"

Really?

Not so fast.

They're only looking at a small sample size of Jesus' ministry, early on, when the Bible says: *"Jesus grew in wisdom and in stature and in favor with God and all the people"* (Luke 2:52). They're only considering the part where He had crowds of people following Him everywhere, hanging on every word, wanting to touch Him and glean from Him and, honestly, to just be in the same room with Him. But that was the part of His ministry *before* people really caught on. Before He went "Kingdom" on them, saying things like, *"I tell you the truth, before Abraham was even born, I Am!"* (John 8:54). Or, *"I tell you the truth, unless you eat the flesh of the Son of Man and drink his blood, you cannot have eternal life within you"* (John 6:53). Or, *"The Father and I are one"* (John 10:30) (which profoundly enraged the Jewish leaders by asserting that Jesus was equal with God).

No wonder we are tempted to imitate the first half of Jesus' ministry. Because, well, it's much easier to swallow. Think of it. When we choose to preach the inspirational first half of Jesus' ministry over the not-so-prestigious second half, we can still say we are preaching Scripture. Yet we mislead people by failing to truly represent what really happened over the entirety of Jesus' public ministry.

It's fun to share about Jesus' glory days. When the throngs of people were following Him and everyone was being healed. When the disciples where all pals and everything was peachy keen. But what about when everyone abandoned Jesus? The Israelites? The Jewish leaders? His own disciples? Even His own brothers? Of course, many people eventually flipped the "psycho switch," demanding His brutal execution shortly after watching Him heal and deliver their own family members. It was crazy town.

Hmm. Still want to be a worship leader? Still want to be like Jesus?

THE DARK SIDE OF THE MOON

For better or worse, Jesus wasn't about building earthly kingdoms. At all. He was about building His Father's Kingdom. A spiritual Kingdom. And He knew exactly what that meant. It meant completely dying to His—or anyone else's—agenda. It meant doing the opposite of what most people are doing.

For us, it means realizing that most folks who jump on the Jesus train early often make a quick exit once things get bumpy. It means understanding that the seed planted in the shallow soil will almost always fail as a result of its inability to flourish in difficult times (see Matthew 13:21–22). It means discovering that many people who seek after Jesus because of His healing miracles will ultimately turn away from the faith, refusing to turn from their sins (see Matthew 11:20).

The writer of Hebrews 11 gives our evanescent lives another dose of Kingdom perspective. He leads, of course, with the exciting stuff.

> *How much more do I need to say? It would take too long to recount the stories of the faith of Gideon, Barak, Samson, Jephthah, David, Samuel, and all the prophets. By faith these people overthrew kingdoms, ruled with justice, and received what God had promised them. They shut the mouths of lions, quenched the flames of fire, and escaped death by the edge of the sword. Their weakness was turned to strength. They became strong in battle and put whole armies to flight. Women received their loved ones back again from death"* (Hebrews 11:32–35).

Hallelujah!

But this is only half of the story.

What about my friend Jeff Grenell, who lost his beautiful, caring wife, Jane, to cancer on December 18, 2016? What about my amazing, godly, and once healthy friend, Justin Burns, who suddenly dropped dead in a friend's home on January 24, 2016, at the age of thirty? What about our friends Josiah and Elizabeth Urlaub whose toddler son, Toby, was diagnosed with leukemia? What about my friend Joel Stockstill, whose wife died of cancer a few years back, after students from all over the world prayed desperately for her healing? What about my friend and mentor James Goll, who lost his wife and ministry partner, Michal Ann Goll, to cancer after fighting and beating cancer himself? What about the pastor of our friends in Mozambique who lost his life in March 2019 during Cyclone Idai when his house suddenly collapsed on him while he slept?

What about the countless stories of believers who have endured pain and suffering and persecution in their lives? Those who have been killed—even in our day—for their faith? Do we simply ignore them? Do we do what some do and assume they must have done something wrong to bring these troubles upon themselves? Maybe it was the devil? Or the curse on this world?

We wonder. What do we do with these things as God's children? As leaders of God's children. How do we answer the unbeliever who laughs at this seemingly unjust suffering? Who mocks the very God who can't seem to take care of His flock? Is there anything in the Bible to give me supernatural peace and strength when things in life go horribly wrong?

Yes, there is.

The writer of Hebrews continues:

But others were tortured, refusing to turn from God in order to be set free. They placed their hope in a better life after the resurrection. Some were jeered at, and their backs were cut open with whips. Others were chained in prisons. Some died by stoning, some were sawed in half, and others were killed with the sword. Some went about wearing skins of sheep and goats, destitute and oppressed and mistreated. They were too good for this world, wandering over deserts and mountains, hiding in caves and holes in the ground. (Hebrews 11:35–38)

Sometimes I wonder; *If the disciples were alive today, would they also be outcasts in the Church? Would those of us in modern-day "Churchianity" also look down upon these culturally incorrect castoffs?*

How did many of the Old Testament prophets' ministries end? Persecution. Murder. Exile. How did John the Baptist's ministry end? Beheaded in prison. How did most of the apostles' ministries end? Prison. Beatings. Martyrdom. How did Jesus' ministry end? Alone on a cross. Rejection. Desertion. Betrayal. Total humiliation.

There are *always* two sides of the story. Here's the B side:

*All these people [those who died and those who overcame] earned a good reputation because of their faith, yet **none of them received all that***

God had promised. For God had something better in mind for us, so that they would not reach perfection without us. (Hebrew 11:39–40)

The point? If things are going well for you as a leader, stay humble and remember that your success comes only from God (see 2 Corinthians 3:5). If you are one of the many leaders experiencing rejection, betrayal, and hardship in your ministry, yes, self-evaluate and ask God how you can adjust, but do not despair.

You may be one of those mentioned in the second half of Hebrews 11. One who feels like you're living on the dark side of the moon. Or maybe you're one who is right in the middle of a painful season, but your breakthrough is on the way. Hold on. Don't give up! Continue to pursue God with all your heart, soul, mind, and strength. Your Kingdom reward is coming. Even if it isn't in this life. Even if it doesn't come with grandiose applause and wonderful accolades from men. Even if you spend the entirety of your earthly life hidden in a corner, seemingly unnoticed.

God sees. He is working in mysterious ways. And the eternal joys that are coming in the next age will make the great sorrows and disappointments we face today seem like the tiniest blip on the radar screen of this life.

BEAUTIFUL SLAVERY

Enter Paul. And more ancient ideas. (Those believed to be obsolete.) He announces daringly, *"Or don't you know that your body is the temple of the Holy Spirit, who lives in you and was given to you by God?* **You do not belong to yourself, for God bought you with a high price"** (1 Corinthians 6:19–20).

Elsewhere, He continues, *"And remember, if you were a slave when the Lord called you, the Lord has now set you free from the awful power of sin. And if you were free when the Lord called you,* **you are now a slave of Christ. God purchased you at a high price"** (1 Corinthians 7:22–23).

A slave of Christ? Purchased by God?

Beautiful slavery.

Enter the Creator. Intriguingly, He alone is able to claim actual ownership. Of anything. Of all things. To say to us indisputably, "You are *mine.*"

The psalmist writes, *"The earth is the LORD'S, and everything in it. The world and all its people **belong** to him"* (Psalm 24:1). (Paul echoes this verse in 1 Corinthians 10:26.)

Ironically, some of us are so blindly committed to fighting for self-ownership that we miss the enigmatic freedom that is born when we submit to the One who made us. Yes, submit. Against our very nature.

Not only is it illogical to refuse to submit to God and to recognize His complete and utter dominion—considering He formed us from the dirt with his very own hands—it is decidedly arrogant. (Especially when we so often lead our congregations in singing songs of surrender.)

Many perceive God's "demands" of submission and obedience as equal to primitive slavery. But God's "slavery" is not the slavery many have known in this world's checkered past. It is something completely different. Something completely paradoxical. Slavery to God is the ultimate freedom. It means escaping bondage and the powers that bind us to depression, anxiety, and fear. To death, hell, and the grave.

Paradoxically, we're now talking about inescapability to *goodness.* Inescapability to kindness. Inescapability to righteousness. Inescapability to freedom. Who doesn't want that? To be found "powerless" to escape all that is good in life?

And so it is. There are only two possibilities. Slavery to God or slavery to everything *not* God.

Don't you realize that you become the slave of whatever you choose to obey? You can be a slave to sin, which leads to death, or you can choose to obey God, which leads to righteous living. Thank God! Once you were slaves of sin, but now you wholeheartedly obey this teaching we have given you. Now you are free from your slavery to sin, and you have become slaves to righteous living. (Romans 6:16–17)

Slaves to righteous living? Sign me up.

We can choose to resist God's undeniable, loving authority—and remain slaves to slavery—or we can gladly, *willingly*, embrace God's ways and enjoy slavery to abundant life. There is no middle ground. (As if we needed any.)

What a beautiful bondage!

But wait. I thought freedom was all about doing what *we* wanted to do? Having our own way? Running our own lives? Not so fast. Anyone can live that way. True freedom at its core is having the ability to completely surrender to God and to recognize that His ways are entirely good, right, and lovely. The ability to obey God. The ability to live as He pleases. The ability to say no to our sinful nature and yes to our new, upgraded, elevated, new and improved spiritual nature.

Strange as it may seem, this is precisely how we know we are truly free. When we die to our old selves and become alive to the new creation God has fashioned within us.

This is the irony we have been invited to embrace. For ourselves. For our families. For our congregations. The only question is, will we? Will we boldly go where only the God-fashioned minority has gone? And proudly profess, "I am not my own. I am dead to my will. I fully and wholly belong to God"? This is the catalyst to sparking true Kingdom culture while activating our teams in ways that cause the Father's face to shine upon us.

This is the undeniable launch point for instilling Kingdom DNA into the hearts of everyone in our churches. It's not that we are free in and of ourselves, but that we are gloriously bound to freedom as a result of our beautiful slavery to Christ.

It's not that we are free in and of ourselves, but that we are gloriously bound to freedom as a result of our beautiful slavery to Christ.

Chapter Highlights

1. Carrying our cross and dying to self are foundational characteristics of core believers in Christ. As Dick Brogden said, "In the physical world, first we live and then we die. In the spiritual world, first we die and then we live." In a ministry where things seem to start and end in the public eye, we must remember to lead from a place of being "crucified with Christ."

2. It seems that Jesus was always leading with a countercultural posture. In ways that seem to erode His ability to be celebrated by powerful people. We must constantly reassess whether we're leading in the ways He would lead or simply imitating the leadership patterns of this world.

3. When we live dead, we allow Christ to live our life on our behalf. In doing so, we die to insecurity, comparison, and fear, and come alive to communion with God, empowering others, and building the Kingdom.

4. If you are one of God's beloved who has faced great pain, disappointment, and trials in your life, don't give up. God has great purpose in all of your struggles. Not unlike the disciples, you can praise Him all the more—and lead others to do the same—because of His great strength spawned from your weakness.

ACTIVATING TEAMS FOR PURE WORSHIP LEADERSHIP

Chapter 6

TOGETHER OR NOT AT ALL (FOSTERING UNITY)

Lie #6

*"I could never grow into
a truly unifying leader."*

CHAPTER NOTE: *Many well-meaning leaders may skip ahead to this chapter in order to get right to the practical ministry strategies. But I beg you. Don't do it. Go back, and start from the start. In the same way the best parents are the ones who prioritize their marriage first, before their kids, the best leaders are the ones who truly learn to love their First Love first.*

I don't know who originally coined this phrase, but I love it: *Together or not at all.*

I don't think I've always done a good job of leading my teams from this mindset. Honestly, in my past—and sometimes in my present—I tend to forget that leadership is less about my agenda and more about loving the people right in front of me. I can get so focused on the task at hand, especially a task given to me by God, that I inadvertently begin to view my team as cogs in a machine (existing only to accomplish my work) rather than as friends and partners with whom I am linking arms to live, breathe, and build together.

With great fervency, I rush to battle. In error, I work toward checking a box on my spiritual to-do list, instead of embracing the progression of doing life, solving problems, and wrestling with issues. United. With my team. With all of the beautiful people God has put into my life.

If you're like me in the slightest, your teammates may have felt used and abused at times rather than empowered and encouraged. Like they've been run over rather than run alongside. This is not healthy, and it can be fairly difficult to detect in oneself. Worse yet, it is quite common among gifted ministers of the Gospel.

Regrettably, many leaders continue to bulldoze people no matter how often they change churches. It simply becomes part of their leadership modality, typically out of ignorance or insecurity. Or both. Thankfully, this is where circling back to section one of this book serves us extraordinarily. Why? Well, it seems the only way to discern our deficiencies in this area is to hear it straight from the Holy Spirit. And, of course, this is much more likely when we are walking in close fellowship with God.

Recently, our student ministry (Celebration Youth) in my home church (Celebration Church) has been lifting high this mantra in a way that has been refreshingly unifying. After serving as a volunteer youth leader for over twenty-seven years, it blesses me to serve in a ministry where we seek to love and serve both God and people. All people. (Of course, embracing *together or not at all* does not mean we affirm everyone's way of life or count everyone's individual choices as "equal," but we begin by recognizing that every human being is equal in their inherent value, as determined by God.)

TOGETHER

It seems to me, most of us face a serious dilemma concerning our desire for independence. Call it selfishness. Or insecurity. Or fear. Or narcissism. People in general—including me—have an innate desire to make things happen on their own. To be self-sufficient. To avoid asking for help. It can be as simple as believing—and therefore living in such a way—that we embrace this popular idiom: *If you want it done right, you have to do it yourself.*

While this could be "true," we still have to ask if it is best.

I suppose it depends on whether we're talking about the short term or the long term. Initially, difficulty seems to increase when we branch out to finally add that second employee. Similarly, it is much more of a challenge to motivate fifty-three guys on a football team toward a common goal than it is to motivate one person in singles tennis.

Why?

Well, from the onset, involving more people can actually intensify the workload, because we are forced to navigate the often-so-awkward period of transference that must take place before we can experience the increase. Since this is highly problematic, many of us are tempted to sidestep the team approach all together.

In the short term, doing the work alone seems best and easiest, but I would argue that in the long term, working together with a team multiplies our effectiveness and our outcomes. Despite the immediate struggles presented.

Of course, I'm convinced that God does this on purpose. Coaxing us to work together. Not to make things harder, but to keep us from siloing ourselves and to help us become more fruitful than we could ever be on our own. To prove it, He designed the world in such a way that we need to work together. Almost as if a self-destruct sequence is initiated if/when we attempt to work entirely alone.

Of course, as worship leaders, we operate day in and day out with one of the premier examples of teamwork: our worship bands. Each individual is dependent upon each of the others to create a symphony of sound that could never be fully imitated by an individual in real time. Think of the ways we limp along when one of our teammates is missing. Think of the overwhelming sense of accomplishment we have as we create. Together. Sharpening and inspiring and loving each other. Lifting and empowering one another.

Though it is possible to be effective alone—with a piano/guitar and a vocal—few would discount the multiplied impact that arises as musicians with great expertise complement one another within a band setting. Each leaning on the other. Each gleaning from another.

It doesn't take a genius to grasp the importance of team. From the angels, to the disciples, to the Church, to the family, it's clear that God enjoys giving each individual a role and a purpose in order to entice us into working together. Right? I find this to be true: Just when I've come up with the next big idea, I hit a major roadblock in the finalization process. I'm convinced God interrupts me purposefully—often keeping me from bringing my work to completion—in order to compel me to reach out to another for help.

> From the angels, to the disciples, to the Church, to the family, it's clear that God enjoys giving each individual a role and a purpose in order to entice us into working together.

Think of it. If God granted each of us the ability to accomplish His purposes alone, we would never venture out to discover what we can accomplish together. We might even attempt to cruise through life on an island—and, in many ways, miss the beauty of bonding, fellowship, and collaboration. There would be no need to reach out. To seek additional perspective. To embrace others' strengths in the face of our weaknesses. To step past our fear of working together as well as our desire to go solo.

NOT AT ALL

Adopting the phrase *together or not at all* could be viewed as embracing hyperbole, especially considering the *not at all* bit. In fact, I admit it's possibly too ambitious to contend that we should *never* do anything alone. Yet, knowingly overstating this point serves to counteract our negative inclination to wander alone and also helps us better grasp the inherent value of team.

It may feel like paddling a canoe up a waterfall, but intentionally collaborating with others—rather than "going it alone"—goes a long way toward fostering greater love and creativity to the profit of all.

It's true. Going together is ultimately better. Yet, we can be honest about the challenges. In fact, most would agree that our work with people is the most difficult aspect of leadership. Don't fool yourself. If your first inclination is to point to the music as your greatest challenge in worship ministry, you'll quickly discover this is not the case. In fact, music is the easy part. And that's okay. It's not that our fellow musicians or congregants are the source of the problem, but God has placed before us a unique and electrifying challenge. If we want to build something beautiful, we'll need to understand the potential of each individual to be a part of the problem *and* the solution.

Even as I pour into up-and-coming leaders in the classrooms of NCU, it's all too obvious that regurgitating the nuts and bolts of leading worship is easy—things like creating and reading charts, running sound checks, organizing Planning Center Online (PCO), and even engaging a congregation. But the "real-time" wrestling match we face with people in ministry is difficult to simulate in a controlled classroom environment. There's nothing quite like the bono fide person-to-person struggles, complications, and consequences of actual Church ministry.

EFFECTIVE WORSHIP TEAM PHILOSOPHY

In *The Language of Influence and Personal Power*, author Scott Hagan states, "There are two types of leaders. Those who love power and those who love people."[1]

Not surprisingly, it's easy to shift the focus of caring for people to the bottom of the ministry to-do list—unintentionally. Our tendency is to continually aim to love the people "out there" in the congregation, all while missing the obvious need to love those on our teams. The good news? When we begin by loving our teams—the ones we're closest to—there is an authentic trickledown that reaches our congregations.

Here are six important strategies for keeping these priorities straight:

1. Prioritize spiritual growth. All too often, we fail to prioritize the most important thing when we meet: gathering together to grow spiritually. To change this, we must discipline ourselves to make time to circle up—without our instruments—for a short but intentional devotional, preferably right at the top of our rehearsal. This could take place immediately after a quick line check or immediately upon arrival (we'll discuss this in the next chapter).

---

1   Scott Hagan, *The Language of Influence and Personal Power* (Minneapolis, MN: KPT Publishing, 2019), page 34.

If you know me, you know I believe that *musical excellence* is one of several highly important biblical focal points that serves the ultimate vision of "loving God and loving people." However, if we're honest, we'll recognize that many of our church systems have begun to overemphasize the perfection of craft over the development of spirituality. It's rare that any leader is forced to correct their team, saying, "Hey, guys. We're simply spending way too much time in God's presence, and as a result, the quality of our music is beginning to suffer." All we need to do is tally our team's total rehearsal time against our team's total devotional time, and it's clear.

Am I saying these two things need to be uniform? Well, no. I wouldn't go that far. But I would ask that we consider "tithing" to God with the time we set aside to rehearse. What if—at a bare minimum—we spent 10 percent of our time together seeking God? Twelve minutes out of a 120-minute rehearsal, and so forth? What if we also agreed to stop worshiping God together on a stage until we've made it a practice to worship God together off the stage? (Remember chapter 1—Digging the Well? If digging the well is important for cultivating individual authenticity, perhaps it's also essential for cultivating team authenticity.)

> What if by setting aside time up-front for our teams to seek the Lord together, we could revitalize the efficiency of our entire rehearsal?

"But, Jeff, we have a very limited time for rehearsal. We barely get through all the songs. We can't afford to take time for a Bible study in every rehearsal!" Okay. I get it. It's tough. I've been in countless rehearsals in my time, many of which have run long. Still, I wonder if part of the problem is that we misuse the time we have? What if by setting aside time up-front for our teams to seek the Lord together (ten to fifteen minutes off the top), we could revitalize the efficiency of our entire rehearsal?

What if by asking different team members to lead a short devotional or worshiping together with a couple of tunes in the sanctuary or sharing prayer requests and praying for one another *before* rehearsing, we were increasing team unity and thereby more likely to maximize our rehearsals? What if by building our team spiritually, we were actually developing them in every area—spiritually, relationally, and musically? I'm telling you, if you get this right, most of your other issues—attitudes, competition, sarcasm, insecurity, rebellion, superiority—will fade away into the sea of forgetfulness. Could it be?

2. Communicate the vision and the plan. A second reason to gather as a team, before playing any music at all, is to quickly and concisely communicate the plan for the rehearsal as well as to reiterate the vision of the "house." This assures greater "buy-in" in the overall Kingdom culture God is asking you to build. It's a known fact that people learn through repetition as well as through clear communication, so it's vital that we repeatedly share our lead pastor's vision so our teams and leaders are able to clearly reiterate it. Take sixty seconds after your devotional, and be creative in the way you cast this vision once again.

Once complete, move from macro to micro, and share the vision for *this* rehearsal (assuming you've already established your specific rehearsal culture—things like making sure everyone honors each other by not "jamming" at the wrong times, etc.). By communicating your goals for this week's rehearsals up-front, you greatly increase the likelihood of accomplishing all you set out to do. Plus, you'll add greatly to the joy of your team, since there's nothing much worse than a leader showing up to a rehearsal without a plan. Been there? You find yourself forever stuck on one song. You can't remember if it's 12 or 17 bridges. Or you mistakenly discover midstream that the chords on the YouTube video are different from the ones on the PCO chart. Now you're wasting everyone's time.

Easy fix. By scheduling a time at the beginning of rehearsal to communicate the plan, we force ourselves to be more prepared and better organized. Why? Because the only way we can effectively communicate the plan is if we actually know the plan. This fosters good accountability and streamlines our rehearsals.

3. Emphasize relationships. Remember, few things are worth losing a friendship over. Arguments. Musical differences. Power struggles. Who sings the solo. Seriously. We're not at war with each other, yet this is oh-so-easy to forget. Especially when we're family. As I lead my worship teams at NCU and Celebration Church, I continually remind myself that we no longer wrestle against flesh and blood (see Ephesians 6:12). Check it. People are not the enemy. Even the mean ones. No. The devil is forever tempting me to spar with my brothers and sisters, hoping I will remain oblivious to the fact that he is the true foe. He baits me in order to distract me, hoping I'll believe he is on the other person's side. Truth is, he's on his own side and is attempting to kill, steal from, and destroy both of us.

The devil and his spiritual forces in the heavenly realms are the *real* enemy. They hate the teammate who keeps disrespecting us in front of our team just as much as they hate us. Then, when we decide to turn our guns on our teammates, not only does it erode team unity, but it gives power to the enemy. It's when we turn our love toward that person and our guns against the devil that we make great strides toward winning over our ornery teammate.

This reminds me of the time a worship-leader friend was dealing with a condescending team member who was aggravated by the time they were taking for spiritual growth in rehearsal. "It's like you're trying to get us to have revival!" he quipped. Hmmm. Wow. These are the moments where Holy Spirit guidance is crucial as we attempt to spark the culture of unity within our teams. When we show love and patience—even to our most troubled team members—it transforms the way the rest of the team interacts with one another. And of course, if we presume to ask our team members to love each other, we must also learn to love our team members.

4. Celebrate character. As discussed in chapters 4 and 5, a musician's character is something every leader must champion over and over. The importance of this is nearly impossible to overstate. With all of the well-intentioned applause given to gifted musicians—coupled with a great void in character reinforcement—we must double down on balancing the scales. Admittedly, it's a bit of an uphill battle, but we must emphasize a culture that is as equally committed to advocating for high character as it is to discouraging low character. Unfortunately, musicians and singers are often fooled into believing that their personal worth is derived from talent rather than from who they are in Christ. Many churches unknowingly—but selfishly and irresponsibly—reinforce this sentiment by turning the other cheek when questions of integrity arise. As a result, they end up prostituting musicians for what they can *do* while undervaluing the development of who they *are*. This just cannot be.

I saw it over and over again during my seventeen years in Nashville. I was naïve, to say the least. I assumed everyone on stage at Christian events—singers and musicians alike—was boldly living in harmony with the lyrics of their songs. Yet, so many times, the opposite was evident as we gathered backstage. There are no Dove Awards or Grammy nominations for high character, of course, which makes capturing the hearts of talented musicians on your team much more complicated. The same happens in our churches. There are no grand trophies for guitarists who quietly spend their early mornings alone in God's presence. And yet vigorous applause awaits them as they play with pristine tone and vibe.

> Our team members must never—consciously or unconsciously—walk away from our rehearsals or services believing the primary reason they are loved is because of their skill.

As leaders, we must remain diligent in searching for ways to celebrate character first. Our team members must never—consciously or unconsciously—walk away from our rehearsals or services believing the primary reason they are loved is because of their skill. This affirms a culture where our team members are encouraged to walk in holiness as well as to sharpen each other in other areas. The good news? When people participate in a culture that proactively encourages a commitment to godliness, it is often a place where the commitment to increased musicianship resides as well. Win-win.

5. Pick your battles. Confronting conflict is something few relish. But what do you do when you've asked your sound engineer to sprinkle a little reverb on your voice and he agrees, but then removes it secretly during the service? You're going to need an extra allotment of Holy Spirit fortitude here. It's true. No one enjoys sending—or receiving—that dreaded text: *Hey, can we talk for a minute after rehearsal tonight?* Yet, as leaders, we must not shy away from these situations but step into them with boldness and sincere loving-kindness.

Here are a few recommendations I'll share concerning conflict resolution.

- Resist the temptation to correct obstinate team members in front of the whole team. Very few folks function well when corrected publicly. Unless harsh rebellion is coming your way, pull the person aside to talk later.
- Never approach a team member from a position of top-down "I'm your boss" authority. Leadership is much more than a title. It's a mantle of service and facilitation that has been imparted to us from the Lord. Lead humbly out of who He is within you rather than out of who you are. *"Care for the flock that God has entrusted to you. Watch over it willingly, not grudgingly—not for what you will get out of it, but because you are eager to serve God. Don't lord it over the people assigned to your care, but lead them by your own good example. And when the Great Shepherd appears, you will receive a crown of never-ending glory and honor* (1 Peter 5:2–4).
- Pray. Often. Continually ask God to help you in every area as you lead your team. To have the right words. To remain gracious. To remain calm. To help you throw off insecurity. To know when to speak up and when to remain silent. To remember James' words, *"Understand this, my dear brothers and sisters: You must all be quick to listen, slow to speak, and slow to get angry"* (James 1:19).
- Be careful with the way you speak. When it comes to tone and language, I highly recommend heeding the words of Proverbs 15:1: *"A gentle answer deflects anger, but harsh words make tempers flare."* Speaking softly not only keeps you from going off the anger cliff, but also shows great maturity and restraint. This approach will often win your teammate over as well as gain you much respect from the rest of the team.
- Don't forget to lead with confidence too. It's been said by many; "An indecisive leader is a poor leader." You'll be faced with making

many difficult decisions. Seek the Lord. Weigh the options. And make a godly decision. Of course, when faced with the "right" decision versus the one you prefer, always—*always*—go with the right one. God continuously places these types of choices before us to test us, and He will honor integrity every time. Remember, being decisive also means not waiting too long to deal with the Negative Nancys on your team. Sensitivity regarding good timing on these matters ensures you don't leave your most faithful team members frustrated.

- Big one: Don't think you need to have all the ideas. In fact, that type of approach will derail your leadership almost instantly. Simply realize you're a *facilitator* of ideas. You have the joy of unearthing a treasure of creativity from within your teammates with the hope of identifying the best overall path for everyone.

- Fear not. You won't need to address each and every issue within your team. Listen to the voice of the Spirit, and pick your battles. Some problems take care of themselves, while others require varied amounts of attention. By all means, refuse to make big things out of little things, and *never* make little things out of big things. Search for and champion greatness in others, and hold loosely to your own personal preferences. Always operate with Kingdom urgency while remembering to avoid taking yourself too seriously.

6. Be an empowerer and an encourager. This one came at a price for me. It's like I had some serious blinders on when it came to the power of encouragement in leadership. I seemed to regularly focus on the negative rather than the positive. It's like I was afraid to compliment people for fear that I would give them a big head or, worse, distract them from other important areas that needed work.

Sadly, there was a time when I was known for "the look"—a glance I would shoot scornfully at my band behind my back during musical worship, all with the misguided hope that they would be "encouraged" to fix that one little musical mistake. I was ignorant, and it took some loss and pain to finally look in the mirror and make some necessary changes.

Who knew? Encouragement is a real thing! John Maxwell's book *Developing the Leader Within You* changed my life and my perspective.

> I became steadfast in adopting a leadership style that motivates people through love rather than through fear.

Even though it took some time for these "encouraging words" to emanate from an authentic space in my heart, I became steadfast in adopting a leadership style that motivates people through love rather than through fear. Thankfully, like you, I had a strong desire to be a mentor and a father figure for those under my care. But I didn't know exactly what that looked like. Truthfully, I was adverse to the term "father" at first, because I didn't feel "worthy" of it and because I thought it meant I would be cast to the sidelines as a "non-player." I believed moving from player to coach was a demotion rather than a promotion, because I didn't understand that empowering others didn't equate to "depowering" me.

This valiant quote from Scott Hagan has helped me greatly: "Nobody's success is robbing your potential. There's plenty of wind in the harbor to sail more than one ship."[2] That means I'm free. Free to lay down my worry. Free to lay down my competitive, ladder-climbing spirit. It also means I can boldly speak up for the highly gifted *and* the underdog. You never know who might surprise you when you begin to champion things in someone that they can't even see in themselves. God often purposes to use the least likely, knowing they are the most likely to give Him all the glory.

LOVE RULES

There are many strategies we can highlight in leading a team—probably too many to count—but the one thing we must never forget is that love trumps everything. Love must become and must remain the foundation for every policy, idea, and strategy we implement. Love must be the motivator for every plan, speech, and project. It must be the filter through which everything flows.

---

2 Scott Hagan, *The Language of Influence and Personal Power* (Minneapolis, MN: KPT Publishing, 2019), page 3.

Love is what compels us to work together. Despite the difficulties. Love is what keeps our priorities straight. Despite dangerous temptations to compromise. Love is what ultimately births creativity and unity in the face of our carnality and pride.

Love rules.

Of course, there is much misunderstanding of love in leadership. Especially in an increasingly entitled generation. As always, the enemy turns God's truths upside down in an attempt to deceive, and he is increasingly effective today in the area of "love."

Misled, many have come to believe that love is celebrating people as they are rather than celebrating them as God intends them to be. Many believe love never confronts or corrects. Many believe love overlooks sin rather than opposes it. Many believe love is first and foremost sexual rather than first and foremost relational.

What is love? *"This is my commandment: Love each other in the same way I have loved you. There is no greater love than to lay down one's life for one's friends"* (John 15:12–13).

Real love lays down its agenda. Real love lays down its rights. Real love lays down its need for superiority. Real love, even at times, deprioritizes the work of the ministry "out there" for the sake of the team's long-term health "in here." This keeps us grounded and helps us avoid the tendency we have to step over people to achieve theoretical ministry goals while embracing this often-forgotten truth: people are the goal. All people. In the end, our ministry "out there" multiplies greatly in effectiveness when we begin first with our ministry "in here."

Kingdom love must spark every decision we make as leaders. It must be infused into our vision and mission statements. It must be infused into our rehearsals and sound checks. It must be considered as we construct our service orders and set lists. It must be woven into our schedules and gatherings. Love must rule the agenda. Love must rule the house. Love must rule the day. And love always begins with relationships—with God *and* with people.

Chapter Highlights

1. We must discipline ourselves as leaders to prioritize the spiritual growth of our teams. This is vital for us and for them as believers, and it will also produce the greatest team unity and creativity we can imagine.

2. Great leaders communicate well with their teams. They repeatedly reiterate the vision of the house, the heart of the worship ministry, and the desired culture of the team rehearsal.

3. People are the number one focus of ministry. After spiritual growth, there is nothing more important than loving, equipping, correcting, and walking with our team members. Each and every one.

4. Though there is a real biblical precedent for cultivating talent and skill in our worship ministries, losing sight of character development will always serve to derail our best musical efforts. When we champion increased godliness in musicians, increased musicality typically follows close behind.

5. There will be endless challenges to overcome as you aspire toward team unity. Always lean in to Holy Spirit discernment concerning which battles to step into and which ones to let go of.

6. Be intentional and lavish with encouragement, all with the goal of empowering your teams and congregation. This will go a long way toward lifting up even the most discouraged or disillusioned team member. Encouragement is one of your greatest resources.

Chapter 7

WHEN TEAMS MEET (REHEARSALS AND TEAM NIGHTS)

Lie #7

*"As creatives, we'll never flourish
in the areas of organization that can keep
our worship teams healthy and stress free."*

We've already established that "team" starts with love and relationships. And, if this is true, there's no better place to grow together than in the many spaces we gather together: sound checks, rehearsals, services, team nights, potlucks, BBQs, game nights, etc. These meetings provide incredible opportunities—often missed opportunities—to bond with everyone on the team, including singers, musicians, sound techs, lighting directors, camera ops, slide presenters, choir members, producers, etc. The question is, are we taking full advantage of the gathering opportunities we've been given?

THE SOUND CHECK

Ian Allison is a friend and very gifted bassist. A few years back, he suggested I consider teaching our class on rehearsals and sound checks at the Pure Worship Institute. Now, if you know me, it wouldn't surprise you to learn that my love for worship leadership has been mostly spiritual in nature, so I was largely uninterested.

But he pressed the issue. He told me that I had significantly impacted the way he thinks about sound checks and rehearsals. I don't know. Maybe I just took it for granted. I was only trying to get the job done. But he believed I had developed an efficient way of doing things that was different from other bands he'd worked with and that it needed to be shared.

A Little History

Sound check has changed a lot over the years. My experience on the road with Sonicflood was mostly with professional engineers, forty-eight-channel analog FOH consoles, side-stage twenty-four- to thirty-two channel monitor boards, and wireless in-ear monitoring systems. In those days, most churches didn't own this type of gear. Many were fortunate to have a sixteen- to twenty-four-channel analog console with four monitor mixes and two or three wedges on the floor.

As prices dropped and technology improved, digital boards became more accessible to churches. Next came digital monitoring systems, the first and most well-known of which was Aviom. These systems revolutionized our sound checks. Gone were the days of standing around waiting for the sound tech to give us more of this and less of that. We could simply make our own adjustments to our own mix. This season paved the way for in-ear monitors for all, allowing us to greatly reduce our overall stage volume, protect our ears, improve the house mix, and clean up the stage by ditching those cumbersome floor monitors (more on this in chapter 8).

Of course, I realize some of you reading this book are still using floor monitors with a small analog board. No problem. But I do want you to be aware of some of the ways churches are modernizing their approach to their stage setup. Thankfully, technology is less foreboding and less expensive than ever.

Meanwhile, here are some valuable sound-check principles for you, no matter where you land on the technological spectrum.

1. **Sound check is not rehearsal.** I know this seems obvious, but unfortunately, many enthusiastic musicians and singers seem to forget this the moment they plug in to the big church sound system. My good friend Doug Gould continually asks me to remind our bands of this fact in order to foster good vibes between the band and the sound techs. He would tell me, "The rehearsal is for the band, but the sound check is for the engineer." This is a rudimentary but important distinction that will help everyone on your team remember that sound check can be as long or short as we want it to be.

2. **Before sound check comes line check.** Line check is that thing we do right before we begin building our mixes. It's very important to make sure we have a clean signal flow traveling through each line—from each instrument and mic, back to the console, and all the way out through the speakers. Multiple lines must be connected properly if we're going to provide good, clear sound for the congregation, as well as for each band member. Much of this can be done prior to the band's arrival to keep from wasting too much time troubleshooting, but a proper line check must be completed prior to sound check. Typically, the sound tech asks each singer and instrumentalist to briefly play or sing in order to confirm that all cables are connected and functioning properly as well as to set the input gain levels.

3. **Come prepared with everything you need.** Sometimes there's confusion over who brings what to the band setting. Make sure you communicate with your team members concerning who's responsible to provide things like instrument cables, direct boxes, tuners, picks, sticks, batteries, ear buds, etc. Also, encourage your teammates to have extras on hand for emergencies. Note: Typically, keyboardists and guitarists are expected to provide their own quarter-inch cables, while the church or venue is expected to provide everything from the direct boxes to the console. Everyone normally provides their own ear buds, while the church or venue provides wireless in-ear packs or wired digital monitoring system stations to plug into. Some churches provide one-size-fits-all in-ear monitors for team members who need them. Communication is the key.

4. **Appoint a music director (MD).** The term *MD* has changed in recent years. It has most often characterized the person assigned to oversee the instrumentalists—whether in extra rehearsals or in achieving the sound(s) and tone(s) the worship leader is looking for. This person can also serve as the main go-between for the sound tech and the band. This is a great way for a worship leader to delegate some of his or her responsibilities all while raising up another leader. Most recently, the term *MD* has evolved to include the person (typically an instrumentalist) designated to communicate additional directions or reminders to the team through a microphone that sends only to the band's in-ears. For example, the MD can remind the band about the upcoming big musical "stop" without the congregation hearing him. He can also aid the band with flow during spontaneous worship moments, providing chord changes and unexpected dynamic shifts. Caution: Do not overuse the MD by asking them to communicate every little detail. This becomes distracting for your team and to a congregation who has no idea why someone is speaking into a microphone that can't be heard. It can also diminish the overall musicianship of your team, as they rely too heavily on the guidance of the MD rather than on their own musicianship. Incorporate sparingly and judiciously.

5. **Utilize a sound check song.** This approach may surprise you, but it will save boatloads of time. After many a lengthy sound check, I noticed at least one thing we need to avoid at all costs: playing an entire song all the way through while everyone attempts to adjust their mixes. The reason this doesn't work is because there are sections in each song where the guitarist plays softly or the keyboardist doesn't play at all. Why attempt to adjust your mix while the guitarist is playing softly or the keyboardist isn't playing at all, only to have them burst onto the scene in another part of the song, blowing your ears out? The solution is simple. Together as a band, with tracks and loops, play the loudest section of one of your songs (often the last chorus) over and over again while everyone adjusts their in-ear mixes. Understandably, this approach won't wow casual listeners, but it will guarantee a better mix for obvious reasons.

6. **Sing or play at your loudest planned volume.** Ever heard your band complain vigorously about the sound tech changing their mixes during the service? The tech swears he didn't do it, only to be met with frustrated snarls from the team. Honestly, most of the time the tech is telling the truth (and if he's not, he's in *big* trouble). Most often, the changes are a result of the band playing at lower levels during their sound check than they play during the service. Adrenaline is often the culprit. More often than not, singers sing louder and instrumentalists play with greater intensity during the actual service, and, as you can imagine, these subtle/not-so-subtle differences can drastically change our mixes. The solution is two-fold:

   • First, each person needs to discipline themselves to stop over-singing and overplaying during the service. This harms our voices long term and results in tuning issues and bad tone from guitarists, bassists, and drummers.

   • Second, during sound check, everyone needs to make sure they play or sing at the loudest level they plan to play or sing at during the set. This can be annoying, especially for singers, but it is much less annoying than the alternative: bad mixes.

7. **Play in the style/genre of the songs on the set list.** When asked to sing or play for the engineer, many well-meaning (but insecure) musicians are known for bursting into some random song not on the set list. While this may be inspirational (or not), it wastes time and does very little to help the engineer or other band members. What good is it for the keyboardist to sound check with a soft, jazzy Rhodes sound when he's planning to play loud synth stabs during the set? The engineer is left to gain, balance, and EQ sounds that aren't even going to be used, giving him less time to work on the overall mix. Note: I suppose this is as good a time as any to remind instrumentalists to resist the temptation to play when they should not be playing. This is extremely frustrating and steals valuable time from the team by making the rehearsal last longer and be less productive.

8. **Learn how to build a good in-ear mix.** Building a good in-ear mix can be downright maddening, especially if you or your team are new

to in-ears. I understand. One of the first things I recommend is to ask yourself, "What can I turn down?" Obviously, the norm is to turn things up louder and louder, but this can make matters worse, cluttering the mix and hurting your ears. Often, finding one or two instruments to turn down goes a long way toward bringing greater overall clarity.

Here are some additional tips:

- **Overall pack volume** – Don't forget to keep your pack volume around 7 or 8, leaving enough headroom to adjust your overall volume to taste during the service.
- **Your hearing** – Remember, one of the beauties of having your own separate in-ear mix is that you control your overall volume. Trust me. Long term, this is going to preserve your hearing in ways you cannot imagine. I must admit that I didn't do this when I was younger, and I am now paying the price with subtle hearing loss. Condition yourself now to monitor your mix at lower levels. It'll take some discipline, but you'll establish a healthy habit that will keep you enjoying music for years to come.
- **Panning** – When your in-ear mix is in stereo, it simply means you can position the instruments and vocals (pan them) from left to right anywhere between your two ears. (If your mix is generally mono, skip ahead.) This greatly helps with the clarity of the mix. Drums and keyboards should be the first things you adjust. Toms and cymbals can be panned similarly to the way they would sound if you were playing the drums yourself, and keyboards should typically be panned hard left and right with each stereo patch. If there are two mono electric guitar sends, these can be panned left and right (possibly at ten and two o'clock), and singers can be panned as well, possibly in accordance with how they're positioned on stage for perspective. Experiment with panning and discover the best fit for you.
- **A little of everything** – Normally, we place our own instrument or vocal at a louder level than everything else in our mix to make sure we can hear ourselves properly. Some people like

to have everything in their ears mixed like a recording, while others like to emphasize certain instruments or even turn some off completely. Note: Make sure the chordal instrumentalists always mix in a little of everything to their ears to avoid inevitable train wrecks caused by missed chord changes. Also, make sure to keep the lead singer's, MD's, and speaker's mics at reasonable levels for communication purposes.

- **Ambience and reverb** – Singers in particular often struggle with feeling uninspired by a dry or "dead" mix, causing them to feel detached from the congregation. The temptation to pop one ear monitor out can be overwhelming. (I personally wrestle with this regularly.) But we need to take seriously what our sound tech has probably told us a thousand times already: that taking one ear out can severely damage our hearing over time. To compensate, consider these options:

  - If your in-ears have adjustable ports for ambience, try opening them further so you can hear more of the congregation.
  - If your tech can add some ambient congregational mics, this will allow your team to mix in more of the congregation. You can also try mixing in slightly more of the overhead drum or vocal mics to pick up more of the congregation or to add ambience.
  - If your personal in-ear systems have built-in effects, you can add reverb or delay to taste. Use discretion though, because I've found adding effects can give me a false confidence, causing me to believe I sound better (and more in tune) than I actually do. I personally prefer no effects. I figure, if I sound in tune with a dry mix, it's going to sound even better in an ambient room.

- **The click** – Always keep the click at a significant volume so it can be heard at all times, even when the band is playing its loudest. This can be tricky, because it means the click may end up sounding louder than you'd like during the soft parts. CAUTION: Be careful not to leave one ear out during soft moments, or the congregation may hear the click bleeding into your mic through your open in-ear monitor. (For more on the philosophy and purpose of using a click, refer to chapter 8.)

9. **Work out hand signals to aid communication.** There are two distinct reasons to develop hand signals, and both have to do with enhanced communication.

    •   The first is for those who are *not* using personal monitor units (like Aviom, MyMix, etc.). When relying on the engineer to make your mix changes, you should develop basic hand signals for each instrument in order to better communicate mix changes to the sound tech during the service. For instance, clicking your pointer finger and thumb together and then pointing upward with the other hand can tell the engineer to turn up the click. Likewise, making a slight pounding motion and then pointing downward can mean you want less kick drum. (IMPORT-ANT: Always avoid the thumbs-up signal for turning up an instrument. This is confusing since thumbs-up can also mean "everything sounds good." Simply use your pointer finger (or drum stick) to point up or down as needed while using an "okay" sign to convey that everything sounds good.)

    •   The more important reason to develop hand signals is to com-municate directional changes/reminders to your team during the set—especially in spontaneous moments. I've really simpli-fied my signals to avoid stressing out my team. I also make my hand signals low and down by my side to avoid distracting the congregation. (Of course, if you lead with an instrument, you'll need to devise signals you can make with your feet, body, and/ or instrument, but please know this is still vital.) IMPORT-ANT: Don't forget to utilize body language and changes in vocal intensity to augment your signals. For example, when you want the band to grow in volume, use your standard "increase vol-ume" hand signal together with a rising intensity of vocal tone and body movement. This enhances your ability to communi-cate the song flow to your team, your lyric presenter, and your congregation. Feel free to judiciously utilize vocal cues as well (such as, "Let's sing that chorus again"). Here are a few of the signals I use to keep things simple:

- THE FIST – This is the classic sign for "we're about to end this song."

- PALM UP, WAVING UPWARD – This tells the band to bring the volume or intensity up. I wave more rapidly when I want them to do a larger/quicker build.

- ARM STRAIGHT OUT, MOVING SLOWLY DOWNWARD – This tells the band to bring down the volume or intensity. IMPORTANT: Ask the band to utilize at least three distinct volume levels to keep from dropping so drastically from 10 to 2. They should be able to go from 10 to 6 (and then from 6 to 2) if you make a second signal. Playing at a 6 means everyone is still in but they're playing more sparsely at a medium volume.

- HAND/FOREARM MOVING IN A CIRCULAR MOTION – This tells the band to continue "looping" (repeating) the current section. When the band is unsure about repeating or moving on, this helps them know for sure to stick with the current section. This signal is supposed to be subtle and natural, so it draws little attention from the congregation.

- POINTER FINGER POINTED DOWN – This signal means "next," and it is my *most important signal*. I use it in two different ways, and it combines three signals into one, eliminating the need for the classic "C" sign for chorus and whatever you currently use for "verse" and "bridge."

  - First, this signal means "next song." It tells whoever is running the tracks/click to start the next song at the next possible, logical moment. It only means "next song" when we're clearly near or at the end of a song, most often *after* the fist sign has been given.

  - Second, this signal also means "next section." When the click is currently running and we are *not* at the end of a particular song, it tells the band to move on to the next section (like a chorus or bridge). This is incredibly helpful, because it means we no longer need three different signals for the verse, chorus, and bridge. Most often, we only move freely between the chorus and the bridge—rarely do we go back to the verses after playing them as normal. So, if we're currently in the chorus and want to go to the bridge, we simply give the "next section" signal. Similarly, if we're flowing on the bridge and want to go to the chorus, we use the same signal. This works perfectly in conjunction with the previous signal—"hand/forearm moving in a circular motion"—because you can now easily communicate that you are either going to repeat the chorus or you are about to go to the bridge. This allows you to spend as much time on these two sections as you want, building up and down and singing spontaneously without allowing the music to grow stale. (It can also help less-experienced musicians remember when to change sections in a set song arrangement.)

▸ POINTING TO THE DRUMMER – This one is obvious. It simply tells the tonal instrumentalists to prepare to drop out while the drummer and singers take over. Utilizing a "drums-only" moment can be very inspirational, because it allows the congregation to feel the energy of the drums while hearing the strength of their own voices. Then, when the band comes back in, there is a "lift" similar to that of a key change. NOTE: Always ask the band to play all the way through to beat 1 of the measure in which you want the "drums-only" moment to begin. Confidently hitting the downbeat and then dropping out together increases the potency of this moment. I also encourage incorporating longer-than-normal "drums-only" moments, since the response from the congregation is normally over the top.

Then, use the "palm up, waving upward" signal to bring the band back in at the appropriate moment.

10. Avoid staring at charts and lyric monitors.

- **To read or not to read** – This may be a tough pill to swallow, but reading music (from charts, lead sheets, or hymn books) decreases your ability to lead worship effectively. I know. People have done it for eons. But think of the anointed worship bands we see out there. Have you ever seen them with a music stand? Only with big bands and orchestras do we see this. Imagine your favorite indie band reading charts—the guitarist squinting, with his nose in the music, playing his solo note for note. But it loses its flair. Why? Because he's *thinking* the music rather than *feeling* the music, and because, at the same time, he's erecting a huge wall between the stage and the seats. Of course, we're not interested in being "watched" in a worship service, so that's not the issue. The issue is relationship. The music stand (with an iPad or chart notebook) becomes a barrier, making it more difficult for us to be connected with our church family as we worship. Even worse, when we use music, there's a 100 percent chance we'll look at it more than we need to. In actuality, we may only need the first line or first couple of chords to jog our memory, yet, because it's there, we gaze blankly at the music throughout most of the song. Unfortunately, every moment we spend looking at a stand is a moment our congregation feels disconnected from us, which increases the chances of them feeling disconnected with our community and with the One we're inviting them to worship. What to do? Practice. This will help us grow as musicians while keeping us from constructing a giant barricade between the band and the people. If you absolutely cannot memorize your music, or you're leading a more lengthy time of worship, it's better to place a set list on the floor with a few key lyrics and chords. Glance down when you need to while keeping your focus on loving God and serving the congregation.

- **The confidence monitor** – Friends, we've only really been
dealing with these monsters—I mean monitors—for the last
few years. I love the fact that we've developed a system to
help with lyrics, but we've got to reel this baby in. First of all,
who named this thing? Confidence monitor? Really? The last
thing we need is to encourage a lack of confidence by tightly
clutching our lyric security blanket. Ha! I'm just so weary of
watching worship leaders attempt to lead us while staring at
the back wall. I know. You think we can't see your eyes. But we
can. (Remember, you have a bright light shining on you.) Plus,
staring at the back wall is the same as putting your nose in a
music stand. Some of you would never be caught dead doing
that, but staring at the confidence monitor has the same effect.
Disconnect. It also makes you appear unprepared, which hin-
ders your ability to lead. I have simply trained myself to scan
the congregation front to back and side to side. If I need to
reference a lyric, I slide my eyes from one side to the other, taking a quick glance at the back wall, while staying completely
engaged with my church family.

THE WEEKLY REHEARSAL

I realize you've probably run thousands of rehearsals, but I encourage
you to—at the very least—skim through my ideas as I lay out a rehearsal
structure for your team to consider. Remember,
bad rehearsal culture will always spark negative
worship team culture.

> Remember, bad
> rehearsal culture
> will always spark
> negative worship
> team culture.

Here are a few key questions to help you
break down your current rehearsal culture.
Take a few minutes to answer and/or discuss
these in detail:

- When and where do you meet? How often?
- Do you start and end on time?

- How much total time is taken for your rehearsals? For your set up, line check, discussion, spiritual growth, tear down, etc.?
- Who is required to attend? What exceptions do you allow?
- What is your typical strategy for rehearsing the songs? What order, etc.?
- What specific areas do you normally emphasize in your rehearsal?
- Who stands out as a leader on your team (in good ways or bad)? Who sits on the sidelines and could bring more to the table?
- What is the relational culture of your team at your weekly rehearsals? Sarcastic or genuine?
- Where does the musical culture of your weekly rehearsals land? Between sloppy and perfectionistic?
- Do you typically accomplish all you had hoped to accomplish?

BEFORE YOU REHEARSE

What did we do before Planning Center? How did we communicate the plan? "Wait," you say, "What is Planning Center?" Uh-oh. We're in real trouble if you haven't heard of Planning Center. (Incidentally, if you discover you need more detailed info about Planning Center Online, you can find it in chapter 8.)

For now, rest assured that PCO is there to help us prepare in detail for every aspect of our services. It is effectively our one-stop shop for all-things-communication between us and our team. Every ounce of organization we once did on our own can now be accomplished through this powerhouse online hub. It's the place we gather, formulate, edit, organize, and communicate our detailed service plan(s), all significantly in advance of our scheduled rehearsals. This is the point. And since we all understand the importance of getting next week's plan to the team in a timely manner, PCO is even more desirable since it helps us dodge most of our miscues, no-shows, and lost-in-translations.

I remember a few years back, I took a poll, asking my NCU Worship Leading class how many of them used PCO, and only 15 percent or so raised their hands. Now, it's easily 95-100 percent. Clearly, there was a great need within the worship community for this handy tool. (FYI, there are a few similar sites that pop up online, like worshipteam.com, but none as widely used as PCO.)

Here are a few essential steps you need to take *before* you rehearse, whether you use PCO or not:

1. **Solidify your band.** This is something you should work on way in advance, possibly up to ten weeks ahead of schedule. PCO is a whiz at helping with this, but either way, it's vital to manage the schedules of all your team members. Whether you're barely scraping together a band of five each week or managing one hundred plus musicians, you'll need to devise an organized system to help you designate who's playing when. Part of choosing your band each week is also deciding who's doing what. Who's playing lead and who's playing rhythm. Who's singing soprano or who's singing alto, etc. Whatever you do, make sure to communicate way ahead of time (no less than three weeks), so team members can commit to you before their calendars are overrun with the busyness of life.

2. **Communicate the rehearsal schedule.** Hopefully you already have this established, but there are always new team members who don't know your rehearsal culture yet. Make sure you let everyone know *when* and *how long* you rehearse, as well as *exactly* what time they should be ready to play. Should everyone arrive at the designated start time on PCO, or do team members with more gear need to come earlier? These are important distinctions. (For specific ideas on when and how long to rehearse, keep reading.)

3. **Select the songs.** Song choice is highly important. So many things go into compiling the songs for a Sunday or Wednesday set list. You'll need to be aware of all the factors, including sermon topics, the church's calendar, as well as important holidays. You should allow these items to inform your song choice as much as you and your pastor deem appropriate. Of course, you'll want to consider things like new

songs, older hymns and choruses, songs with the best fit for your congregation, songs with the best fit for your singers and team, songs that flow nicely together, as well as songs that rise high on the singability meter. Even so, don't pull your hair out over song choice. Attempting to match each and every sermon topic perfectly is less important than choosing songs that help people worship God extravagantly. And, while leading well-written, theologically correct songs is important, leading with heart and anointing is even higher on the list.

4. **Choose the best keys.** If you are the only "lead singer" for your church, make sure the keys you choose sit nicely within your particular range, so you don't hurt your voice. You should know what your top note is, and then you should determine the highest note for each particular song. I don't like to sing much higher than an E above middle C, so if the highest note in a given song lands on the 5th note of the scale, I would put the song in the key of A (The 5th note of the A scale is E.) If it lands on the 1st note of the scale, I would put the song in the key of E, and so forth. Then, also consider your congregation, since you want to make your songs as accessible for them as possible. (In the process, don't forget that our voices typically fly at lower altitudes in the morning.) If you typically spread your songs between several singers, make sure you reach out to them at least two to three weeks in advance to determine the best key(s) for them. Make sure you also take into account—as a lower-priority item—the way in which the keys of your songs might flow together.

5. **Communicate the song list.** I suggest working three to four weeks ahead with choosing your songs (sometimes even further, considering special events/holidays, etc.). Of course, communicating the set list includes things like the order of the songs, the keys of the songs, and who is singing which song. Make sure the band has the song list absolutely no later than the Monday before the Sunday they are leading (typically much sooner).

6. **Provide the charts.** These days, most worship teams utilize chord charts, either created by the worship leader or found online (often

through CCLI.com). Providing chord charts for each song in the correct key (with the correct chords) is paramount. Make sure you double-check your sources, because there are often multiple versions available. Some churches still provide sheet music for musicians and singers who only read notes, while others have taught their teams to use number charts (the Nashville number system) rather than traditional letter charts. Do what works best for your team, while gradually pushing them to grow musically.

7. **Specify the song versions.** Since there are many different recordings of the different popular worship tunes out there, make sure you indicate on your charts which version you want your team to learn. This includes designating the song map (the order of the sections; how many verses, choruses, and bridges). Of course, it's best practice to point your team to a particular YouTube video or MP3 for reference.

WHEN TO REHEARSE

After serving in many churches around the world, I've noted multiple variations on the timing for rehearsals. Days vary. Times vary. Durations vary. But we can learn a ton from what others are doing.

The length of your rehearsal is going to depend on several variables: the desired quality level of the music, the number of songs in the set, the number of days per week set aside for rehearsal, and, certainly, the overall experience and expertise of your team. Some churches find 60 minutes does the job, while others are a bit more ambitious—delving deep into arenas of excellence and creativity—and aren't content with less than 120 minutes or more. (Please remember that preparation is hugely beneficial for several important reasons, including increased freedom in worship, heightened focus on hearing the Holy Spirit, and strengthened ability to create a sense of community with your congregation—all while not burying your head in your iPad.)

In general, there are three main options when choosing which days to rehearse:

1. **Sunday only** – Some churches plan a lengthy rehearsal for early Sunday morning and call it a day. Anywhere from 90 to 150 minutes. This is a great way to go depending on how many morning services you have and how early you'll need to start. (Hint: If your church has five Sunday morning services, I highly recommend avoiding this plan to keep from starting rehearsal at three a.m.!) The good news is, this approach keeps you from asking your team to come out on a separate night. The bad news is, it's going to require a little more faith in your team. Along with some very intentional prep work on your part. When you decide to rehearse on Sundays only, you are telling your team a couple things:

   • They can expect you to communicate the details of the service (songs, song versions, song keys, flow, musical changes, who's singing/playing what, etc.) significantly in advance of Sunday.

   • You can expect them to work ambitiously on the songs at home during the week, showing up 100 percent prepared and ready to go.

   • You can expect them to reach out to you *before* Sunday morning with any questions they might have.

2. **Sunday + one** – Many worship pastors ignore the whole issue of asking their teams for another night in order to divide up the rehearsals with hopes of taking their teams to the next level. I suppose it depends on the culture you want to build. In the end, it's hard to ask for more than two hours for a Sunday morning rehearsal, but you may be able to get a little more from your teams overall by splitting up the rehearsal over two days. The most common way this happens is Thursdays and Sundays (though I also know of churches with a Saturday night service who simply rehearse on Saturday afternoon and Sunday morning). You can shoot for two rehearsals of 90 minutes each, or hit it hard for 120 minutes on Thursday with a 60 minute refresher on Sunday. Of course, Tuesdays or Fridays can work too, but Thursdays work best, because it's late enough in the week to give the team time to prepare, but not so late that there's no time for the band to improve before Sunday.

3. **Sunday + Wednesday** – Another less common idea is one we've implemented at Celebration Church. We rehearse on Sunday mornings in addition to Wednesdays (during our midweek adult, youth, and kid services). The idea is, we avoid asking people who normally attend Wednesday nights to come out on yet another night. It's great, because they can come with their kids and spouse and find something for everyone, but it can get a bit complicated. First, we had to move our adult midweek service out of our sanctuary to facilitate our rehearsal. (For us, rehearsing in a different room from where we lead on Sunday morning would hinder us more than help us. Plus, we have another room that nicely facilitates our adult service.) From there, it's pretty much a piece of cake, aside from these important realizations:

- By doing this, we keep our worship teams from participating in the midweek services.
- By doing this, we place extra demands on our media teams (lighting, sound, presenters, etc.). For this reason, we do our best to keep a decent rotation so we have enough people on hand to cover our midweek media requirements while still managing our rehearsal effectively.
- By doing this, some of our worship team members often double as worship leaders for our other midweek services. For this reason, we start our rehearsal fifteen to twenty minutes later than our midweek services. Our main adult service goes from 6:45 to 8:00 p.m., so we run our worship team rehearsal from 7:00 to 8:30 p.m. This allows our worship leaders to lead for ten to fifteen minutes in our other services without being too "late" for our rehearsal. Of course, we ask them to come early to set up their gear in the sanctuary if needed, so they're ready to go right when they arrive. The thirty-minute delayed end time is not an issue since many families stay and talk after service anyway. (Honestly, the jury is still out on this idea for me. It works well in some ways, but also has its drawbacks.)

GROUND RULES FOR REHEARSAL

Once you've established the plan for *when* you will rehearse, you can begin to implement the plan for *how* you will rehearse. As mentioned in chapter 6, I highly recommend beginning each rehearsal by gathering the team for some type of spiritual-growth activity. Following this, you'll want to keep everyone circled up briefly to communicate—or reiterate—the plan for the rehearsal itself. Make sure to provide an opportunity for the team to ask questions, and then release them to their stations to rehearse. Above all, make sure you're clear and concise. People typically respond with greater confidence when they know what to expect.

Of course, we aim to start right on time, and I typically ask my team to finish set-up and line check *before* rehearsal begins. For example, if our rehearsal spans 7:00 to 8:30 p.m., those who need to arrive and set up early should plan accordingly. As always, make sure you strike a healthy balance between work and fun. It is detrimental to the team when we operate from either extreme.

WHAT TO REHEARSE

Before we dive into the process of running the actual rehearsal, let's quickly highlight the most important rehearsal elements. Identifying these things up-front keeps us from wasting precious time and goes a long way toward boosting team morale.

1. **Smooth out the trouble spots** – You know 'em. These precarious musical moments typically present a higher level of difficulty than others. A tempo change or a key change. A borrowed chord or a big drum stop. Whatever they are, the temptation will be to practice your trouble spots until you play them perfectly one time. Please don't make this mistake. Make sure you hit these babies correctly three or four times so your team will be able to play them accurately and confidentially during the service. Doing this should take only three or four minutes each since you can begin and end no more than four bars on either side of a particular trouble spot.

2. **Utilize dynamics** – This is one of the most vital and often glossed over elements in music. Think of it like a movie. If the plot holds stagnant for a long time, people go to sleep. Same with music. Dynamics play a critical role in inspiring and engaging people. Rehearsing the dynamics together as a team will greatly multiply your team's impact and—believe it or not—increase your congregation's desire to participate. A couple notes:

   • Subtle changes in dynamics make a big difference. Practicing these nuances increases your effectiveness and brings joy to the music-making process for the team.

   • Avoid operating as many bands do, with only two dynamic levels, soft and loud. Make sure you incorporate at least one nice medium level as well (mezzo forte), and then navigate between all of these with a variety of sudden and gradual rises and falls.

   • Attention keyboardists (and other instrumentalists who carry softer moments by themselves): When the band is playing loudly and suddenly goes soft (or drops out), the common approach is to suddenly go soft with them. Unfortunately, this creates an extreme vacuum in volume, causing the musical momentum to dissipate inopportunely. Think multiplication and division rather than addition and subtraction. Consider this: If each instrumentalist is playing loudly (at a volume of 9 out of 10) and suddenly drops to volume 2, there is much too great a loss in overall volume, causing the congregation to shrink back. In this case, the lone musician standing (often the keyboardist) need only drop to level 5 or 6 for there to be a substantial (and wonderful) dynamic shift. Please resist the temptation to play too softly, especially after the rest of the band drops out. Keeping some of the energy going in the soft moments will allow for the desired shift in dynamics without pulling the rug out from under the congregation.

3. **Know when *not* to play** – Teaching your band to leave musical space for others perpetuates a glorious "less is more" mentality. For some, *not* playing is a foreign concept and desperately needs to be rehearsed.

Ironically, some bands assume (naively) that more notes = better music, when in actuality, playing fewer, more intentional notes typically yields a more palpable soundscape. For drummers, make sure they understand, for example, that overuse of cymbals and fills actually causes these precious elements to lose their value. Playing too many fills or cymbals causes the mind to begin to tune them out. Incorporating them calculatedly (*after* avoiding them for a stretch) helps to create a heightened interest for the listener.

4. **Play in different registers** – You will need to guide your team in understanding the concept of playing in different registers. For example, when the keyboardist is occupying the lower/middle of the sound spectrum (around middle C or lower), it makes good sense for the guitarist to play higher inversions up on the neck. Likewise, asking your keyboardist to play only single bass notes in the left hand (just below middle C), instead of full octaves, creates greater space and clarity in the low register for the bass guitar. (Of course, there are times we do want that low-octave key's power to hit in conjunction with the bass guitar just as there are times we would ask the keyboardist to play with the right hand only, mostly above middle C.)

5. **Refresh your song arrangements** – We will discuss the purpose of creativity in detail in chapter 8, but our rehearsals should always allow time for developing unique and intentional variations on the common songs we cover—partly to keep the congregation from slipping into a coma, but also to keep our team from becoming a "karaoke band." First, ask your team to prepare a "default" version of each song, and then work together (either in advance and/or during your rehearsal) to brainstorm a few new twists. This provides some additional excitement and ownership for the band and keeps the congregation from developing a "been there, done that" mindset, subconsciously believing they already know how all songs are going to go. Trust me, the worship police won't show up if we alter a song from its originally recorded version.

6. **Excel in spontaneous worship** – For now, I'll simply say your team's ability to flow skillfully in spontaneous worship will always correlate directly with your commitment to rehearsing spontaneous worship. We must rehearse spontaneity if we hope to be effective (skilled and anointed) in this area. Seems like an oxymoron, right? Do we really need to practice being spontaneous? Moreover, *how* do we practice being spontaneous? Glad you asked. Chapter 13 is dedicated to answering all of these questions and more.

7. **Prepare for the altar response** – There's no question. Altar-response moments can serve as one of the most impactful moments in our services (I cover the heart behind them in chapter 11). The problem comes when the altar music is not rehearsed and becomes an afterthought. This happened to our team once. Near the end of our rehearsal, we quickly discussed *which* section of *which* song we would play and even *how* we would get into it. But, regrettably, we forgot to discuss exactly *where* we would end. No big deal, right? Well, unfortunately, this particular song didn't contain an easy off-ramp like most songs, and we found ourselves looping eternally before awkwardly careening through a guardrail and over a cliff to an abrupt stop. Discussing and rehearsing your post-sermon song moments is vital. For longer altar moments, consider choosing progressions, sections, and songs that flow together in the same key/tempo to help you achieve the maximum impact, all without starting and stopping eight different songs or, worse yet, beating one to death.

8. **Win with transitions** – These little beauties are so often forgotten that we're going to dedicate some serious time to them right now. (Note: Do not skip!)

NAVIGATING THE NARROWS BETWEEN THE SONGS

The number one most overlooked rehearsal component for every worship team is transitions. You know, those often-so-awkward spaces between the songs, loaded with key changes, tempo changes, patch changes, pedal changes, and wardrobe changes—wait, no. Scratch that last one.

Let me set the stage. We're cruising along brilliantly through one of our most beloved Elevation tunes when out of nowhere the end approaches. Oh no. The song itself has flowed flawlessly—we even hit that dramatic stop before the last chorus. But in the rush of rehearsing each song in the set, we suddenly realize—with three bars left in the outro—that we forgot to work out the particulars of *how* we would move from this song into the newly arranged—and quite spectacular, I might add—version of that new Jesus Culture tune.

Gulp. Hope the band knows sign language.

Sometimes a transition is like two opposite sides of the Grand Canyon trying to join together seamlessly. We take a running leap off the edge of one song and desperately try to hang glide, parachute, high-wire walk, or even cannonball to the next one. Unfortunately, many times, if we're honest, we forget to rig the high wire or pack the chute properly. We get so caught up with the intricacies of each individual song that we figure we can just wing the transitions.

Then the end draws near. Eyes dart between band members. The pad fades out too early. The drummer nervously scrolls to the next song and accidentally starts—and then stops—the wrong tempo. The worship leader says something canned to fill the space. The crowd looks down and pretends not to be there. Everyone on stage closes their eyes hoping to time-travel 120 seconds into the future. Crickets start chirping. Pins begin dropping. Microphones start moaning.

Then, after what seems like thirty-seven minutes, the next song begins, and praises arise—mostly out of relief that the moment has passed. All is fine. All is good. All is forgiven. All is forgotten. Disaster is avoided. Sort of. Right then and there we make a mental note to *never* let this happen again. Until three bars from the end of the next song. Oops. Next week.

And so, in honor of these treacherous transitions, let's look at a few helpful hints that will turn them from tragic to terrific:

1. **Practice your transitions.** This may seem obvious, but the idea here is to make transitions seamless. Seamless to the point where no one

in the congregation notices them. Not so we can be "awesome," but to maintain the flow. Flow helps everyone stay focused on God. Flow is a good thing. Flow helps each song blend neatly into the next like one stream merging with another. This takes practice.

2. **Be confident with your transitions.** If we're uneasy about our transitions, the congregation will be too. This of course happens when we're not properly prepared and may create unnecessary turbulence when flying at high worship altitudes. Our feelings of apprehension are typically transferred to our passengers through small hesitations or indecision that can be as untimely as those seatbelt announcements right in the middle of a 37,000-foot nap. They pull people out of a deepening connection with God by creating a preventable disturbance. Of course, nobody has sinned here, but we all agree: less turbulence is better for maintaining favorable worship cruising altitudes.

3. **Don't underestimate your transitions.** Songs in the same key with minor tempo shifts can fit together nicely. Yet, these simple transitions are often the ones that sneak up on us. We overlook them because they seem rudimentary, yet without proper communication, we can easily drop the ball here too. Succinctly discussing the smallest nuances of the simplest transitions goes a long way toward cultivating team unity, even while preserving true communion in God's presence.

4. **Use words or singing to smooth your transitions.** Often, instrumental music alone can make for a perfect transition. But sometimes, interjecting a prayer, a Scripture passage, or an exhortation can help massage problematic tempo and key changes. Be careful, though. Many leaders misstep in this area, using churchified clichés and empty hallelujahs (discussed in the next point) in an attempt to distract or "hype" the congregation. Our main desire is to keep the congregation's focus on God and away from tricky musical transitions. The mistake many worship leaders make is waiting until the next song *starts*—essentially *after* the transition—to sing or say something, when, clearly, the best approach is for them to talk, sing, or read Scripture just *before* one

song ends (during a crash-out or final chord). The leader should continue over top the musical transition all the way past the intro of the next song in order to help meld the two songs together. Again, I ask, if we're going to talk between songs, why wait until *after* an awkward musical transition instead of doing so *over* the entire transition? Aim to layer your exhortations over your transitions, and this will keep your congregation focused on the Creator rather than on the distraction of the musical transition.

5. **Be authentic in your transitions.** We don't need to speak between every song. Please avoid this at all costs. In fact, I would encourage you to prepare a greater number of instrumental transitions, especially between up tempo tunes. Then, when we do speak, it should not be manufactured, but concise, anointed, and heartfelt. We've all heard robotic-like exhortations between songs that inevitably do the opposite of their intention. Pray ahead of time about what the Spirit would have you say and let it flow out sincerely. (I know some worship leaders who find it helpful to write out exactly what they want to say and memorize it so they don't ramble on incoherently.) Sometimes I pause for a split second upon approach, letting the music at the end of a song carry the first part of the transition. Then, relying on the Spirit, I step boldly and humbly into the moment, speaking to the people (or to the Lord) with all my heart. Of course, steer clear of "Christianese"— common Christian verbiage. Refer back to chapter 1 for "Digging the Well" strategies that will help you increase your authenticity.

6. **Teach the congregation to worship through the transitions.** This is big. Part of the challenge we face as worship leaders is establishing a culture where people realize they don't have to stop worshiping when the band changes songs. Few churchgoers understand the concept of gliding right on through the yellow caution light—continuing to engage with their Creator—regardless of what the band is doing between songs. Even if the transition is a complete disaster. We must teach these concepts to our spiritual family if we expect them to understand. Why make things more difficult for ourselves when

we can easily caution our congregants against slipping into spectator mode between songs and, instead, encourage them to sing or pray spontaneously with their own words and melodies during the musical transitions and instrumental sections? As a result, they'll be able to stop lurching in and out of God's presence with each song change.

7. **Be creative with your transitions.** This one is huge. God made us in His image. He is highly creative, which means we should be highly creative too. Let the Holy Spirit amplify your transition's creativity, incorporating fresh melodies, rhythms, and swells to help you navigate the tempo, key, and feel changes. Check out these super-practical ideas designed to help you with even the trickiest of transitions.

   • **When you have an odd key change**—like C to B—you can sing the chorus of the first song a cappella a couple times. This is powerful and encourages the congregation to sing out. From here, as the last word of the a cappella chorus ends, pause sensitively and fade in the pad/keys in the new key. Voila! Removing the chordal instruments distracts the congregation from the key change and allows the band to move astutely to the next song. Another creative technique to help smooth odd key changes is starting your next song with a drum groove. For example, if you end a song on the 1 chord in the key of A (and your next song is in Bb), try swelling on the A, and then, *before* fading out, click off the tempo of the next song and have the drummer play a creative four-bar groove that leads directly into the intro of the next song. The band should wait to fade out the key of A until somewhere around the third or fourth bar of the drum groove in order to leave a little empty tonal space between the two songs. Again, the drum groove serves as an inspirational distraction for the listener, allowing them to stay in the flow.

   • **When moving between songs of different keys that share a chord or two,** try ending on the chord both songs share—often the 4 or 5 chord. This helps establish a new 1 chord—a new tonal center—for the new key. For example, when going from C to F, try ending on the 4 chord in the key of C (which is F) and swelling on it just long enough to establish it as the new 1 chord for the key of F. Even if you're moving from C to G, you can sometimes end on the 5 chord (G), thus establishing it as the new 1 chord for the new key of G. Intentionality is important.

• **When moving from a mid-tempo song to a slower song** (even from one slow song to the next) it really helps to create a definitive "ending." Use subtle instrumental swells to communicate to the congregation that the song is coming to a close. Realize the congregation is constantly searching for cues. They wonder (subconsciously) whether we're singing the chorus again or going back to the bridge. By swelling softly and even retarding slightly, we tell them things are changing. This means, even if everyone but the keyboardist has stopped playing, others should swell in delicately on the final chord together—cymbals, guitar, bass, etc.

• **When going from one fast song to another in a different key**, it works best to leave no dead space between songs (unless the space is very intentional). Why not just crash out boldly at the end of song one and then do a hard key change right into the next song? Follow the drummer's lead as he starts the click for song two and counts it off *before* the crash-out from song one ends. In other words, don't fade out the crash ending completely until right as the next song begins (*after* the count-off). Playing the downbeat of song two definitively exudes confidence and assures continuity. In this way, we can get away with just about any key or tempo change.

> Always look to discern what creative musical modifications need to be made between songs in order to keep the flow.

• **When moving from a fun, up-tempo song to a slower song**, always avoid switching songs too abruptly. One effective technique is to sing the chorus of the up-tempo song at a slower tempo, one or two more times, with keys and guitar swells only. This helps lower the intensity of the up-tempo song while foreshadowing the mood change that is about to take place. In this way, we utilize something from the song we just sang (lyrics) in order to blend it with something from the song we are about to sing (musical mood). This makes for a *mucho grandioso* transition-o.

Fun story: I remember suggesting this type of transition to my NCU Worship Live team back in September 2019. They were attempting to flow between "Alive" and "It Is Well," but since one song ends super big and the other begins super soft, it created an awkward moment. I encouraged them to change the intro of "It Is Well" and start with a full-band, anthemic instrumental (the 7/4 part). After the intro, they could simply drop into the first verse as usual. They tried it and loved it! I challenged them to stop thinking of each song individually and to start seeing the entire set as a whole. Always look to discern what creative musical modifications need to be made between songs in order to keep the flow. This approach keeps us from jerking people around in God's presence and also helps us revive older songs (or overly used songs) by making them less predictable.

- **When ending an up-tempo song,** I highly recommend utilizing longer crash-out endings. I'm convinced people are longing to respond passionately to exciting declarative songs, yet often they aren't given much of an opportunity to do so when we crash out for three seconds and abruptly move to another song. Playing a longer crash-out ending helps us practically as well, by giving the band more time to adjust pedals or add a capo, etc. Even more importantly, it provides the congregation the chance to celebrate more freely without worrying about getting caught singing or shouting loudly just as the band dies down. *Awkward!* If we allow these endings to extend just a few seconds longer—maybe even fifteen to twenty seconds total—people will learn that it's "safe" to let go and praise God a little longer and a little louder.

Some may read my extensive exposé on the importance of transitions and become concerned that by emphasizing these areas, we'll miss the organic and raw presence of God. Honestly, it's just the opposite.

True. People will survive if things aren't "just so" in the transition department. Making musical mistakes or botching things between songs won't prove to be the end of the Church as we know it. Unquestionably, we don't want to crash and burn on anointing and authenticity while flying high on form and function. Yet, is there any reason we can't have both? Is there any reason we can't strive for both? Why else would God design us with such amazing creative musical abilities if not to serve His people lovingly *and* exceptionally, genuinely *and* extraordinarily? Much like a believer who builds a home, pilots a plane, or performs surgery with a passion to do his or her work with tender loving care *and* great attention to detail, smoothing the transitions between the songs increases the likelihood that our congregants will engage in the process without finding themselves overly concerned by potential mechanical failures. This, too, is spiritual! What a beautiful thing when servant artists concern themselves with skillfully and carefully operating the craft so others can sit back and enjoy the ride, unhindered, in the presence of the Lord.

RUNNING THE REHEARSAL

Okay, now that we've considered *when* to rehearse and *what* to rehearse, let's get into the nitty-gritty of *how* to maximize an actual rehearsal.

1. **Start with the least-known song.** Of course, you'll regularly incorporate new or lesser-known songs into the set (though I wouldn't introduce more than one every three to four weeks). Rehearsing your newest song at the beginning of the rehearsal—rather than simply starting with the first song in the set—guarantees you'll give it the attention it needs and you won't risk running out of time by overemphasizing songs the team already knows.

2. **Rehearse the extras.** Go through the list of "what to rehearse" from earlier in this chapter. Clarify the plan for the transitions and then run through each of them. Consider the possible spontaneous moments, the known trouble spots, the dynamics, the potential off-script arrangements, and the altar-response song(s) right away. This will keep you from forgetting to rehearse important elements.

3. **Run the whole set from top to bottom.** Now that you've touched on all the extras—answered the team's questions and worked creatively together—it's time to hit the entire set (assuming everyone has worked through the songs on their own *before* coming to rehearsal). Don't forget to simulate the service countdown (if your church uses one) as well as the speaking moments; a welcome, a Scripture passage, a prayer, or a teaching moment. (Hopefully you've thought through these items before your final rehearsal so you can simply say something like, "Talking, talking, talking," or "Praying, praying, praying" in order to keep the rehearsal moving. Of course, if your church asks that everything be perfectly timed, you'll need to speak each word as planned.) Then, as you work through the set, hit important "fix it" spots as needed, but do your best to keep things moving.

4. **Revisit any additional trouble spots.** If there's still time, make sure you touch on any lingering issues. If not, you can talk through these things (especially your transitions) in your second rehearsal or backstage (if this is your only rehearsal). If you have extra time, I recommend playing through the transitions again. This can be done quickly by playing the first eight to sixteen bars of the first song, then stopping to jump to the last eight to sixteen bars of that song. Play the specified transition together the first eight to sixteen bars of the next song and so forth. You should be able to play all three to five transitions in a matter of three to four minutes, boosting everyone's confidence.

5. **End on time.** It's highly important for you to establish a culture of honor where you begin and end on time. Take it from me. This can be difficult, especially if this is your midweek rehearsal. (Oh, how I struggle

with ending on time!) Even so, you have to remember that you still have another rehearsal to touch on missed elements, so trust the process and leave some things for later. (If this is your Sunday rehearsal, you won't have much choice, because the countdown won't wait.)

6. **Circle up again.** If this is your first of two rehearsals, make sure you gather everyone together one more time at the end of your rehearsal to direct them on what to work on before Sunday. You should end with a word of sincere encouragement and thanks and then close in prayer. (If this is your Sunday morning rehearsal, make sure to gather everyone backstage for your pre-service walk-through.)

7. **Talk through the entire service.** Our church does a six- to seven-minute "all-volunteer huddle" forty minutes prior to service. This marks the drop-dead ending time for our rehearsal and provides the perfect space for energizing everyone. Following this, our entire creative team meets together to quickly talk through the full order of service with our service producer. This keeps us all on the same page with the details and allows for any last-minute questions or clarifications.

8. **Pray together.** With the five to ten remaining minutes, we gather to refocus our hearts on the Lord one final time before the service begins. This helps to settle our nerves, cultivate unity, and help us keep from forgetting why we're doing what we're doing. I often take this opportunity to invite several individual members of the team to lead us in seeking the Lord. This can also be a good moment for a short devotional teaching, depending on the time.

Remember: Always encourage the culture of excellence in your rehearsals, not perfection. (I am a recovering perfectionist myself.) Be sure to remind everyone to be ready to go with all their gear and music. Encourage team members with similar musical roles to communicate with each other outside rehearsal so they know who's playing or singing what. Above all, foster unity and spiritual growth at every turn. Encourage each person to remember that their individual role is vital to the Kingdom but also to the team.

For perspective (and to help steer your team clear of pride and insecurity), I would remind them that our gifts and songs are much like the little boy's lunch (see John 6:9). They are insignificant yet still precious and useful in the Master's hands. Compared to the great hunger of the people, our loaves and fishes will never be enough to meet the need. But when placed in the Master's hands, our little offering of songs and chords is multiplied to become more than enough to nourish hungry souls.

AUDITIONING NEW TEAM MEMBERS

One of the beautiful things about teams is they tend to grow. That is, when teams are healthy. And there's nothing more exciting than bringing new people into the fold. Even so, adding members to your worship team can present some challenges as well as make for some significant administrative work.

Here are a few ideas meant to spark efficiency when it comes to adding new members to the team:

1. **Spread the word.** Most churches are not turning away loads of musicians. In fact, most are borderline desperate for more participants. For this reason, you're going to need to learn to do a little marketing on behalf of your worship team. There are many ways to do this, but I would encourage the following: concise quarterly announcements in the main services (either via video or on the microphone, with the blessing of your pastor), engaging social media posts, a connect portal or email widget on the church website, and regular worship team gatherings specifically designed for inviting potential team members to attend.

2. **Create online auditions.** Let's be honest. Not everyone who wants to join the worship ministry is capable of doing so. One way to discover some unknown gems—as well as to "weed out" those who are not ready—is to create an online audition system. This can be as complex or simple as you want it to be. It could be as simple as having would-be team members email you a video (preferred) or audio file

of them singing or playing. Or it could be as complex as designing an online submission system for your website.

3. **Schedule an annual or biannual audition.** Our church has been known to schedule all-team auditions to attract new team members as well as to check in on the growth of current team members. There are many ways to do this, but I suggest providing lunch after a Sunday service and then holding auditions for a couple hours afterward. Give everyone one or two songs to learn in advance and have them rotate in and out with different band members to see how they work together. You can decide whether to involve everyone on the current team in the audition or to simply allow the newbies to jump in with the current team members. Either way, this is a fun way to find new talent and to strengthen community.

4. **Mentor young and upcoming musicians.** This is *huge*! Many churches make the mistake of ignoring the youth worship band until they come back from college. But I've found the best ministries are continually pouring into the younger generation in order to prepare and equip them for the future. By investing in students now, you foster relationships and improve their skills, which will pay off greatly over time. A strategy some worship leaders use is inviting students to join the team for a Sunday morning (or midweek service) *before* they're ready. This may seem odd, but doing so can help you speed up the process of equipping young future team members. Plus, you can always give them this valuable experience while keeping their volume slightly lower in the mix, if necessary. You could also invite them to your team nights as well as to any formal team audition days.

5. **Schedule coffee hangs.** If you have potential team members who are nervous about jumping in or who you're not sure about, schedule lunch or coffee with them. These types of get-togethers can help provide some much-needed insight for you and some much-needed encouragement for them.

6. **Invite proven musicians to your rehearsal.** If you know a musician you want to fast-track onto your team, one way you can do so without adding them to a Sunday morning too quickly is to invite them to participate in a regular rehearsal. They can come early, meet the team, participate in the pre-rehearsal meetings, and then watch from the front row. This will help them get a taste of your culture while allowing you to see how they handle themselves. If you want to take it up a notch, you can ask them to learn one of the songs ahead of time and have them play it once or twice with the team in place of your scheduled team member.

7. **Consider paying your musicians.** Ahhh, the age-old question. To pay or not to pay? Here's the thing. We have a *serious* cultural problem. How so? Well, most churches approach the money issue as if there are only two options: 1) enlist committed volunteers who may or may not have talent, or 2) pay talented "hired guns" who have little commitment beyond the Sundays they're scheduled. This might surprise you, but there is another option (which also happens to be more biblical).

   As you know, the singers and musicians in the Old Testament were part of the tribe of Levi (the Levites), and the Levites didn't have jobs like everyone else. Ministering to the Lord in the Temple on behalf of the people *was* their full-time job. They and their families lived off the sacrifices and offerings brought by the other twelve tribes (see Numbers 18:21). Think of it. What if we could turn the current system on its head and, at the same time, avoid losing our best musicians to the world? Of course, we can't stop this altogether. But what if we could begin paying (investing in) our musicians (not just our singers) to a level where they could provide for themselves and/or their families? And, instead of expecting *less* from them (as we do with "hired guns"), we would expect *more* from them? We'd add them to our church staff (possibly part time at first) with the same level of accountability and responsibility as other pastors. Hmmm. I know. It would require a serious financial paradigm shift, but why not start with one or two musicians and then work our way up? When we invest, we can expect a return, right? So, as our musical worship increases in quality and anointing, there's good reason to believe attendance will go up too. This would provide more resources, allowing us to continue to invest in similar ways. Of course, our staff musicians would not be treated as rock stars. They would be expected to do other things around the church as well. They would take part in staff meetings, possibly do the graphic-design work, or help with church maintenance. Could it be that there's a better option behind door number three? A guy can dream, right?

Above all, determine to be deeply prayerful as you add team members. While getting the right people on the team can help you tremendously, bringing people on too soon or keeping them on the perimeter too long can create problems that are difficult to overcome. As always, we must never stop emphasizing character development as we champion spiritual maturity and musical growth. Commitment to the local church body is a must, while a teachable, servant heart should always separate the haves from the have-nots.

THE TEAM NIGHT

Many pastors and worship leaders have discovered that weekly rehearsals alone don't allow enough opportunities to build the culture necessary for anointed worship teams to flourish. In an effort to counter this, some have instituted an additional bimonthly or quarterly gathering called a "team night."

A team night provides another occasion to build on what's already happening in our weekly rehearsals, with the specific purpose of fostering deeper connections with God, richer fellowship with teammates, and practical growth in areas of music. The team night provides many benefits for our worship ministry without the simultaneous pressure of preparing for a Sunday morning service—an important distinction. It also gives us the chance to reinforce the overall vision of the church and the worship ministry.

> The team night provides many benefits for our worship ministry without the simultaneous pressure of preparing for a Sunday morning service.

I would consider a quarterly Friday night gathering of between 90 to 120 minutes long. Of course, food should *always* be a part of these meetings, and I would recommend establishing four different emphases for each month. Here's a possible scenario for your quarterly gatherings:

1. **February (spiritual growth)** – A great way to start off the year is to come together for food and fellowship while spending some significant time growing together spiritually. February can be a good month to dive back in after the holidays (and after a season of prayer and fasting hosted by many churches in January). This gathering should include a lengthy time of musical worship as well as a time of teaching from you or another pastor (possibly in reverse order, preaching followed by musical worship, to emphasize the concept of *revelation and response* discussed in chapter 11). You may also consider inviting a worship-leader friend from another local church to lead a time of acoustic worship in order to give your team a much-needed opportunity to *receive*. (Consider reciprocating this as a favor in return.) Another approach would be to utilize a YouTube playlist for the musical worship part. I know this might seem less than inspiring, but it will be better received than you think. Trust me. The simple act of getting your team together to worship through song *without an "audience"* will transform them as few things can.

2. **May (musical training)** – After a time of food and fellowship (possibly a classic potluck dinner or the always beloved Chick-fil-a feast), settle in together for a practical musical teaching (maybe songwriting secrets, tips on engaging your congregation, or strategies for playing together as a band). This is a great way to give back to your team while helping them grow as musicians. Learning builds confidence, and confidence + work = the fruit of excellence. You can change it up by inviting four to five different workshop hosts to meet with each area/instrument on your team for an hour or so. This could come in the form of voice, drums, bass, guitar, and keys clinics, taught by local or national experts, as well as possible teaching in the areas of mixing, lighting, slide creation, set design, Ableton, or camera work—as

needed. This keeps everyone motivated and growing in their area of interest. (Incidentally, you could also start a separate weekly songwriting collaboration for interested team members. This is a great way to begin building a catalog of songs birthed right from your community, all in preparation for recording your church's first EP.)

3. **August (fellowship and encouragement)** – Meet at a park or a beach somewhere for a picnic or BBQ. Play some volleyball or kickball and then sing together around a campfire or down by the water. Take some time to encourage your team members concerning all the positive things you see God doing in and through them. (Remember, as a leader, you're gloriously tasked with helping your team understand who they *are* as well as who they can *become*. It's your job to speak these things into existence even if you can't always see them with your natural eyes. Your team members will always become who you say they are.) Also, consider opening things up for a few team members to share encouraging thoughts about each other and/or to share some prayer needs. You can end the night by praying together for individuals, for your other pastors, and for God to increase the spiritual fervor within your church.

4. **November (leadership)** – This is the month to provide a killer build-your-own-sundae bar. Also, invite your lead pastor or another local worship pastor to pour into your team on the subject of leadership. (For more of a personal feel, you could host this gathering in your home, if the team isn't too big. Being vulnerable in this way can go a long way toward building rapport with members who are on the fringe.) Helping your team understand biblical leadership is one of the most important things you can do. Sometimes your team can slip into the erroneous (and convenient) belief that what they do (on and off the stage) doesn't really matter since they aren't "in charge." Help them understand the truth: that we are all always leading. People are always watching, and more importantly, God has gifted and called us to serve His people, regardless of rank or file. We are all leaders, all the time, whether we like it (or admit to it) or not. It's time to invite

our teams to rise to the occasion as servant leaders in the power of the Spirit of God.

Don't forget, you can always do these gatherings more often or add a weekly forty-five minute Zoom call to spice things up. Also, going through a book like this one together over several months can be an incredible way to foster team growth.

Gathering together in various ways is paramount to the overall well-being of your team. In doing so, you provide opportunities for team members to get to know each other better as well as to walk the journey of life with one another. In many ways, your team will function similarly to a close-knit small group—one where you don't simply make music together, but where you also laugh and cry together too.

Is it easy? Nope. In fact, I would say it would be much easier to focus on perfecting the music rather than building relationships (at least in the short term). I promise, it will get messy. It may even get downright ugly at times. It will demand many hours and a few tears. But if you stay the course—with the help of the Holy Spirit—you'll be a part of building something beautiful that will transform your church family, impacting the lives of people across every culture and generation.

Chapter Highlights

1. Remember, sound check is not a jam session. It's a time for the engineer to serve the team in getting everything "audio" working for the rehearsal. Everyone should do their part to speed the process along in order to increase the productivity of the limited time you have together.

2. Communicating the plan for the rehearsal *at the beginning of the rehearsal* will go a long way toward keeping everyone engaged and getting everyone out on time. This is monumental for building healthy team dynamics.

3. Don't forget to rehearse all the needed items for your service, especially the transitions. No matter how well things go in the songs themselves, the greatest chance of pulling people out of the flow of God's presence comes in those precarious moments between the songs.

4. There are a lot of worship ministries that take a random approach to team auditions. I highly recommend spending serious time developing an intentional strategy that continually sparks an inflow of new people, including young and old, experienced and novice.

5. Getting together for a monthly or quarterly team night—apart from weekly rehearsals—will do more for building unity than just about anything else you do.

Chapter 8

WALKING THE TIGHTROPE OF MODERN WORSHIP (CREATIVITY, EXCELLENCE, AND TECHNOLOGY)

Lie #8

*"Technology is here to stay, and we just can't
build an effective ministry without it."*

Ever heard of a funambulist? It's the Latin word for *tightrope walker* (from *funis*, or "rope," and *ambulare*, or "walk"). When it comes to some of our more modern worship approaches, it seems we walk a fine line with keeping things in balance.

So which is it? When it comes to musical worship, is technology a blessing or a curse? Is excellence important, or does it stand in the way of authenticity? Should we sprinkle in a little extra creativity into our musical arrangements, or do we risk distracting people as they connect with God? Are these elements a hindrance, or are they a springboard for true worship?

Super glad you asked.

Imagine. A Jesus-follower attends a service where the worship band is very gifted, the sound is loud, and there is substantial use of automated lighting and haze. And yet, there's an arrogant, performance-driven air about them. The result? Obvious. This Jesus-follower learns. She begins to equate the use of technology and skill with pride and showmanship.

Another believer attends a different life-changing service where technology and musical excellence are tip top, but, this time, the band appears to be uniquely humble and powerfully anointed. The possible assumption? The transformative presence of God simply cannot be experienced in a worship service *without* the use of technology and highly skilled singers and musicians.

Ironic. Extremes.

Yuck.

We tend to go to extremes easily, mostly as a result of our personal experiences. We allow these one-time (often skewed) experiences to color our entire perspective moving forward, right or wrong. Most of us view the musical worship aspect of the service as either best *with* creativity, excellence, and technology or best *without* them. As either our greatest aids or our worst enemies.

Let's pump the brakes.

Truth is, creativity, excellence, and technology are all amoral. Just like any other tool. Inherently, they aren't good or bad. They're benign. They certainly can be used for good, but they can also be used for great harm. It's true. Technology, creativity, and excellence are *not* our worship fix-alls. But neither are they our greatest adversaries. It all depends on our approach.

CREATIVITY

As mentioned briefly in chapter 7, there are many compelling reasons to utilize creativity in our worship services. The most obvious—and least surprising—is that we've been fashioned in the image of God. Certainly, creativity is one of God's foundational attributes, as displayed by the way He formed the universe, the way He guides His people, and the way He strategizes against His enemies. No doubt. He is always doing a "new thing."

Have you ever been complacent in your relationship with God? Have you ever found yourself slipping into robotic worship mode on a

Sunday morning? As a leader, have you ever struggled with losing heart when singing the same old songs over and over again?

Of course you have. So have I.

These are real battles, and we all face them. Even more so at times, in leadership. But thankfully, there are a few things we can do to reverse our natural inclination toward apathy. For ourselves and our congregations.

Creativity is one of the most helpful, practical resources we've been given.

How so?

Well, from where I sit, there's a threefold purpose tied to creativity:

- To bring glory to God
- To bring joy to life
- To serve others in their pursuit of God

Glory to God

When we act creatively, we reveal God's likeness in us. Just as He desires. This brings Him glory by helping us maximize our effectiveness for His Kingdom.

Some imagine that God's creative side completely evaporated the moment the sixth day came to an end, almost as if He intended to set the world in motion and then sit uninvolved for all of eternity. This could not be further from the truth. The very idea that God took a Sabbath *rest* implies that there was still work to be done. Otherwise, He would've rested on the eighth, ninth, and tenth days as well. And every day following.

But no.

Beginning no later than the eighth day, God rested from resting and got back to work (see John 5:17). To this day, He is continually creating, renewing, reworking, and reviving. He is constantly building, nurturing, making, and molding. And He calls us to the same. Six days a week.

Don't just take it from me. The Bible supports the idea of God's continual creative involvement in our world, long after it was formed. Here, Isaiah reveals God's incessant passion to remain in the business of creating: *"For I am about to do something new. See, I have already begun!*

Do you not see it? I will make a pathway through the wilderness. I will create rivers in the dry wasteland" (Isaiah 43:19).

Dead Set Against Boredom

Another reason God invites us to utilize creativity in our services is to keep things fresh for ourselves, our teams, and our congregants—to bring joy to life! This may seem unspiritual, but I assure you it is not. It is the servant's service. It is love.

As tough as it may be to admit, we've all rolled our eyes—at least internally—when leaders overuse certain phrases, songs, structures, and prayers, all birthed out of ritualistic religious habits. We've all grown tired of hearing the same ol' songs played the same ol' ways, over and over, to the point where we can predict every build, every dynamic change, and every end-of-song clap offering. In our sleep.

This is not God's heart. This is not God's approach.

Haven't you noticed the way He fashioned a world where everything is constantly moving and changing? Haven't you noticed the way He created His children to experience new and wonderful things every day? Haven't you noticed the way the Scriptures are written in such a way that there's level upon level of intrigue, line upon line of hidden meanings, story after story pertaining even to the most mundane parts of our lives?

One thing is for sure. God is passionate about inviting us to live in a world beyond our capacity to discover it all. For the express purpose of affording us the joy of newness. Day after day. For all of our lives. And ultimately, for all of eternity. With love as His primary motive.

Thankfully, God is also dead set against boredom. Even if our churches often are not.

"You have heard my predictions and seen them fulfilled, but you refuse to admit it. Now I will tell you new things, secrets you have not yet heard. They are brand new, not things from the past. So you cannot say, 'We knew that all the time!'" (Isaiah 48:6–7).

Wow. Does God have us pegged or what? It's funny. Still we're surprised to discover how well He knows us. What a blessing to know He has infused His own supernatural creativity into our beings to keep us from falling into that oh-so-dangerous "been there, done that" mentality. We certainly owe it to our teams and congregations to do the same.

Serving Our Congregations

I'm not a huge fan of nicknames. But recently, one of my former students gave me one I really like. You see, I'm always reminding our worship leaders that our job is often more about bringing *confirmation* than providing *revelation*. What I mean is, most times, we're not attempting to present ideas and perspectives that our congregation has never heard before—*revelation*. But we're absolutely attempting to serve our congregations by presenting ideas and perspectives about God that re-establish compellingly what they've already known—*confirmation*. The best leaders find creative ways to remind us of the God-things we've grown numb toward in order to awaken our hearts to them once again.

> The best leaders find creative ways to remind us of the God-things we've grown numb toward in order to awaken our hearts to them once again.

One of the most common frustrations concerning the Israelites is this: "They forgot" (Judges 3:7). They forgot God's ways. His love. His kindness. His provision. His healing. They also forgot their God-given purpose, their God-given identity, and their God-given joy. They even forgot, regularly, God's very existence. As we do.

That's why they decided to call me Chef Deyo. Because I repeatedly reminded them of a leadership strategy I learned from a pot of soup. I'm not a good cook by any means, but my mama taught me enough to know that if I don't stir the soup when the burner is cool, the top will crust over. Likewise, if I don't stir the soup when the burner is hot, the bottom will burn.

Think about it.

Not surprisingly, a large portion of worship leadership is simply about stirring things—the foundational things—from day to day, from week to week. Reminding people of all the incredible wonders of God and the reasons we worship Him. Reminding people of the ways He's taken care of us in the past, and how we can trust Him to take care of us in the future. Incredibly, our efforts are often helped or hindered in direct correlation with whether or not we are inventive in the way we present the truths of God. In the way we order our songs. In the way we arrange our sections. In the way we use our dynamics. In the way we handle our transitions.

Continuing to copy and paste our songs, arrangements, and service orders often accomplishes the very opposite of what we desire. Spiritual apathy. And yet God has graciously given us creativity—by His Spirit—as a weapon to push back.

Karaoke Bands

During the Denver Broncos' 2015 Super Bowl run, player Antonio Smith was asked how the team kept from growing complacent over the course of a sixteen-game season. Look at what he said: "It seems like a simple thing to say, but complacency is real. When you're feeling good and everybody is patting you on the back. You get to feeling, 'Aw, this feels comfortable. This feels nice. Let me enjoy it.' But the one thing we don't do is let that happen."[1]

Sadly, this happens to us in our churches every week. Much more than we would like to admit.

I remember something a friend told me during his time in a popular Christian band. After dreaming for years of hitting the road full-time, he now found himself bored and counting people with red shirts in the massive crowds. Just to pass the time. Why? Because after one hundred cities of doing the same set list the same way, night after night, it all started to lose its appeal. It all started to lose its meaning. And he began to lose heart, along with the joy of playing.

As leaders, this is the paradox we face. People are largely jaded toward the same old same old even while being hostile toward change. Even our team members will begin to disengage when things are always done the same way. Played the same way. Sung the same way. Said the same way. It's like we all slip into a coma. Spiritually. Emotionally. Relationally.

---

1   Antonio Smith, DenverBroncos.com video, 2015.

This is a leader's reality. And one of his greatest challenges.

I've heard some leaders wisely call for the end of the karaoke-band approach. Where local worship teams mindlessly cover popular worship songs in exactly the same manner as the popular worship bands recorded them. Down to the exact vocal licks and guitar solos.

Taking this approach may *seem* like a smart way to reproduce the same results of other influential worship bands, but it never does. Those bands didn't do that. They didn't copy other bands. They did something fresh. For *their* congregation. For *their* spiritual family. With the help and direction of the Spirit.

Copying always backfires. Why? Because God is protecting us from attempting to prefer recreating above creating. Imitation above formation. Copying over crafting. Knowing full well that blind replication serves only to quickly erode the abundant life God designed us to walk in.

The question is not, "How can we package and redistribute the things other successful worship bands have already created?" The question is, "Lord, what are You doing in our church? What are You speaking to our people. What is needed in this moment, this time, this hour?" Of course, this is not to say we shouldn't learn from other bands, but it is to say that God has put His Spirit of creativity in each and every person. When we ignore this and simply regurgitate what others have done, it is counterproductive to the advancement of the Kingdom of heaven.

Protection from Predictability

Have you noticed our passion to formulize everything? All while noticing Jesus' express passion to keep us from doing so? Why? Because if we're allowed to formulize spiritual things, ultimately, we will arrive at a place where we stop listening to the voice of God's Spirit. A place where we believe, blindly, that we're self-sufficient. A place where we believe we can switch on autopilot and simply cruise toward "success."

This is something that God, in His kindness, will not allow. For our own protection. In fact, let me be as blunt as possible. When our sermons, prayers, sets, and service orders become predictable, we can know unquestionably that we are not following the Spirit of God. Believe it or not, the moment we believe we have "figured it out" is the moment we subconsciously begin attempting to manufacture church. Embracing self-reliance causes us to gravitate toward manipulating people's emotions rather than to rely on the voice of God's Spirit.

Just look at the way Jesus purposefully avoided formulizing healing the sick. One minute He was rubbing dirt and spit together to put on some blind dude's eyelids. The next He was letting healing power flow from the hem of His garment. In one instance, He spoke healing to a lame man standing before Him. The next, He healed the centurion's servant from miles away. He commanded the dead to rise, and brought healing to others by casting out demons. Some lepers didn't even receive their healing from Jesus until they began to walk away.

Can we see that He is attempting to protect us—lovingly—by keeping us from formulizing supernatural healing? He intentionally brought healing to people in different ways. Each time. Why? First, because each situation was unique and required a creative, supernatural approach. And second, because He wanted to keep us from attempting to cut Him out of the process.

Sadly, when it comes to Kingdom things, our natural inclination is threefold: discover it, reproduce it, and then distribute it to the masses. Mindlessly. We simply attempt to learn it and then regurgitate it with no thought of the importance of walking together with God in the process. Thankfully, God is inviting us to be engaged creatively—together with Him—in each and every encounter. Each and every service. Wrestling. Questioning. Listening. Responding. In harmony with His Spirit. This is good for the Kingdom, and it is wonderful for us.

The Hillsong Police

Keeping things fresh helps everyone. Ourselves, the band, and the congregation. Implementing simple strategies like playing slow songs fast, or playing fast songs slow can usher in a new perspective (and even awaken zombie-like worshipers). Something as simple as starting the occasional service with a slow song instead of with the typical fast one can help break people out of the numb.

Heaven forbid! Start with a slow song? What will people think? That could be very uncomfortable. Sure. Maybe. But ultimately, it will help break up the norm while sparking exactly what we are looking for: vibrant, awake, and alive Christ-followers.

Trust me, the Hillsong police aren't going to show up if we decide to play their songs a little differently than they do. In fact, Hillsong may send you a special thank-you note to applaud your efforts. (If not, I guarantee your band and congregation will.) Sure, Hillsong chose one way to record their songs on the album, but that doesn't mean they lead them exactly the same way in their church.

"But, Jeff, what if we're using Ableton or MultiTracks? Doesn't that mean we're stuck to the static form?" No. The good news is, you can edit the tracks in Ableton, which means you can have the best of both worlds. Crazy, right? You can cut and paste sections creatively—in any order you like—which allows you to do something wildly radical like start with the bridge instead of the chorus. Or repeat the instrumental before the bridge as many times as you like. You can even add an additional chorus near the end or create a medley of songs by linking them together.

Have you ever wished there was an extra bar or a "drums-only" moment in your favorite worship song? Make it happen. That's what the Spirit of God is urging you to do by giving you creative ideas. He is very aware of the ways in which creativity helps our congregations awake from the deep sleep we've often put them in by serving up yet another cookie-cutter service or song arrangement.

Because people's natural tendency is to aim for the path of least resistance, one of our most important jobs is to lead creatively in the way we seek God together. This encourages a vibrant, authentic worship culture. The kind of culture that shakes people free from mindless, robotic worship. The kind of culture that launches people toward connecting with God rather than with a religious system.

"But what if we start focusing on how great we sound or on being creative for creativity's sake?" Then I'd simply say, "Stop doing that."

Really. I love this quote from Stephen Miller, taken from his book *Worship Leaders, We Are Not Rock Stars*: "While creativity is a wonderful servant to worship, it is a terrible master."[2]

So be careful. Continually remind yourself and your teams that creativity is a tool. A tool to help people love God. It is fun, and it should be. (And this is certainly one of the valid reasons to champion creativity within your worship teams.) Yet, there's an even greater purpose for creativity—to aid us in the awakening of the Church—as we follow the creative nudges of God's Spirit.

> Because people's natural tendency is to aim for the path of least resistance, one of our most important jobs is to lead creatively in the way we seek God together.

EXCELLENCE

A few years back, I ran into a well-known worship leader who told me emphatically, "We shouldn't be concerned about skill in worship. There's nowhere in the Bible that emphasizes this."

Hmm. I couldn't help but wonder if we were reading the same Bible.

Fear not. We will focus in on the biblical precedence for excellence in worship in the pages ahead, but first, let's grapple with a different question; what exactly is it that could cause someone to buy in to the lie that excellence, talent, or skill are the enemy of authentic worship?

As always, the answer is found in a seemingly connected—actually disconnected—circumstance. One whereby a highly gifted musician flaunts his skill in order to draw attention to himself. It's clear. His entire guitar solo was me-focused, offered in an attempt to turn the spotlight in his direction. Those ultrafast riffs were a royal distraction from the one true purpose of musical worship—to bring honor and glory to the one true God. (Incidentally, you simply must look up the YouTube video "Over the Top Piano Player 'Amazing Grace'" for a hysterical example of this!)

---

2   Stephen Miller, *Worship Leaders, We Are Not Rock Stars* (Chicago, IL: Moody Publishers, 2013), page 110.

That said, aren't we still missing the point?

The question is not, "Did the guitarist act pridefully in the way he played his guitar solo?" but "Is the guitarist's skill the real culprit in his crime?" We have to ask—just as we did with creativity—is skill inherently bad? Or is it simply a scapegoat?

When someone shows off in worship, is excellence the root of the problem? If so, we should forever banish excellence in music *and* in everything else we do. (Sorry to overdramatize.) Think about it. If excellence is the root cause of pride, we should be able to rid ourselves of pride on the church stage by expelling excellence from the church stage.

But, alas, this makes little sense. We've all known people who were full of pride and yet who were *not* full of talent—possibly unbeknownst to them. And certainly, we have all encountered a few blessed souls who walk in complete humility despite their extraordinary gifts. Surely, deleting excellence from our church platform is not the answer. If anything, we've heard many a critic's cry for *more* skill in the church, not less.

What gives?

Heart and Skill

Here's a crazy question: What if we stopped believing that heart is more spiritual than skill? What if we embraced the biblical truth that *both* are spiritual? Like David. *"He [David] cared for them with a true heart **and** led them with skillful hands"* (Psalm 78:72). Yes! This is the most concise verse on the subject. And it seems to emphasize skill *and* heart not skill *or* heart? What if both are fully spiritual? Together? And what if leading skillfully in worship is actually a key component of leading authentically?

What if the real problem is not being too skillful, but refusing to give God glory for the skill we've been given?

I was on a panel a few years back where we were discussing the issue of skill in worship. Unfortunately, it was getting pretty heated. Some folks were up in arms about the emphasis some musicians place on skill, even pointing out a "competitive spirit" that seems to be encouraged in worship auditions as we choose one musician over another.

I totally get it. These are real concerns.

Then someone spoke up and said, "I grew up with a few people in a house church singing passionate songs—all out of tune, with little skill. It was some of the *best* worship I've ever been a part of. We seem to be too worried about playing everything just so. Besides, raw just feels more authentic."

Sounds convincing, right?

But is "raw" really more authentic? Isn't this the same thing we've been saying? Isn't "raw" more of a style preference for some instead of a mandated preference of God? Haven't we watched people whose music is considered "raw" bubble over with pride, and yet, also watched people whose music is slick and produced embody the role of a servant? Is there not also a godly purpose for excellence in music just as there is in other disciplines?

Remember chapter 2, where we identified the type of music that's noise to God's ears? What was it, according to Amos 5? Did God say He rejects fancy or ornamented music? Of course not. Did God say He despises complex music? Nope. What He said was this: He rejects songs and lyrics that are incompatible with the way we're living.

Think about it. If raw is authentic and elaborate is sinful, we'd better stop training musicians. Seriously. But I don't think I'd last very long as a professor at NCU if I strolled into the classroom and said, "Whatever you do—if you want to be authentic—make sure you avoid excellence. Certainly, don't practice, because you don't want your skill to become a stumbling block to other worshipers."

The problem has never been that we've had too much skill, but how we've handled the skill we've been given. The problem is not talent; it's the human heart. We can't throw out skill and expect to become authentic any more than we can embrace "raw" and expect to become godly. We can sing out of tune all day long and still be just as lost and arrogant as the guy with the unimaginable gift.

But don't take my word for it.

Skillful Is Scriptural

You've read Psalm 78:72, but let's take a quick look at a few other passages.

- **We must be good stewards of God's gifts.** Nothing we have is ours—including our gifts and talents. Honestly, most of our issues would be solved immediately if we would simply walk in this truth. We didn't give ourselves life, and we didn't give ourselves talent. We didn't give ourselves breath, and we didn't give ourselves skill. We didn't even create within ourselves the desire to practice, let alone create a world wherein doing something repeatedly (practicing) produces growth in our skills. As you might imagine, we will be held accountable for how we use God's stuff. Our talent is His stuff, and we are responsible to use it for His glory. Otherwise, He could find reason to take it away. *"To those who use well what they are given, even more will be given, and they will have an abundance, but from those who are unfaithful, even what little they have will be taken away"* (Matthew 25:29).

- **We must become trained and accomplished musicians.** One of my favorite passages on skill in worship is found in 1 Chronicles 25:6–7. Let's look at the surrounding verses too: *"All these men were under the direction of their fathers as they made music at the house of the LORD. Their responsibilities included the playing of cymbals, harps, and lyres at the house of God. Asaph, Jeduthun, and Heman reported directly to the king. **They and their families were all trained in making music before the LORD, and each of them— 288 in all—was an accomplished musician.** The musicians were appointed to their term of service by means of sacred lots, without regard to whether they were young or old, teacher or student."* This is undoubtedly the way God set things up. He didn't assign just any old type of musician to minister in His "house." He wanted *trained* and *accomplished* musicians. Specific people called and gifted by Him to do His work with anointing and excellence. Don't miss this, because it hasn't changed. This is still God's plan—to release authentic *and* skilled people to serve His Church.

- **We must serve the Lord with skill.** *"So the people of Israel who were present in Jerusalem joyously celebrated the Festival of Unleavened*

Bread for seven days. Each day the Levites and priests sang to the LORD, *accompanied by* **loud instruments. Hezekiah encouraged all the Levites regarding the skill they displayed as they served the** LORD. *The celebration continued for seven days. Peace offerings were sacrificed, and the people gave thanks to the* LORD, *the God of their ancestors"* (2 Chronicles 30:21–22). This isn't hard to grasp. Hezekiah didn't *discourage* the Levites from utilizing skill as they sang to the Lord, accompanied by *loud* instruments. He *encouraged* them to continue in this manner—not behind closed doors, but in public—as they served the Lord. The next verse adds, *"Kenaniah, the head Levite, was chosen as the choir leader because of his skill"* (v. 23). Of course, just because something is recorded in the Bible does not mean it is automatically endorsed by God and is something we should emulate. But since there are multiple Scriptures affirming the importance of skill in music, we can assume David's decision to select Kenaniah as the head Levite was sanctioned by God. Psalm 33:1–3 adds, *"Let the godly sing for joy to the* LORD; *it is fitting for the* **pure** *to praise him. Praise the* LORD *with melodies on the lyre; make music for him on the ten-stringed harp. Sing a new song of praise to him;* **play skillfully on the harp, and sing with joy.**"

Dirty Jobs

How would you feel if I told you we don't get to choose our roles in life, but we do get to discover them? This seems to be a hot button these days. Sadly, people are being taught—even by pastors and Christian leaders—that

> The problem has never been that we've had too much skill, but how we've handled the skill we've been given.

they can do anything they can dream in life. And yet, Scripture doesn't affirm this. In fact, God is pretty clear: *"Just as our bodies have many parts and each part has a special function, so it is with Christ's body. We are many parts of one body, and we all belong to each other. In his grace,* **God has given us different gifts for doing certain things well**" (Romans 12:4–6).

What if this is really true? What if God decided long before you or I were born what talents and skills He planned to divvy out, and He simply affords us the opportunity—and the joy—of discovering, developing, and deploying them?

Maybe this is exactly why we've seen so many want-to-be singers failing and flailing publicly on *American Idol* and *The Voice*. Maybe because so many are attempting to do exactly what they were *not* designed to do. Maybe.

Are we offended by a God who would make these choices on our behalf? A God who might restrict our abilities to do some things while opening wide the floodgates for us to do other things—the things He created us to do?

To me, it makes perfect sense. He makes us each unique, with different skills, persuasions, and bents so we might steward—with excellence—all the wild and crazy tasks He wants us to accomplish around the earth. He deposits within us seeds of talent connected to a particular skill set and then invites us to have at it as we cultivate the skills to accomplish His assignments. In a sense, He's giving us each something special to do, while avoiding the problem of everyone wanting to do the same thing, and thereby, leaving scores of tasks undone.

Take the show *Dirty Jobs*—the one from Animal Planet with host Mike Rowe. Why would anyone choose to do the jobs no one seems to want if we didn't all have innate, God-given skills and preferences? Who would want to be the worm dung farmer or the roadkill cleaner-upper? Surely nobody would sign up to remove chewing gum from the subways or pigeon droppings from public parks (yes, these are real jobs). Who would want to be a chimney sweep, an oyster harvester, a hot tar roofer, a garbage pit technician, a fuel tank cleaner, or a painter?

A painter? Yes, a painter.

The reason I bring this up is because I recently discovered that my wife, Martha, loves to paint. Not pictures or art, but walls. People have recently begun hiring her to paint their kitchens and bathrooms and even entire interiors. She'll paint your walls, your ceilings, and even your trim, giving it all a fresh new look. She'll even patch your holes.

And the best part? She's good at it.

Incredibly though, I have absolutely no desire to paint walls. None. Zero. *Nada.* It gets really old really fast. After eight minutes I'm ready to go "Tom Sawyer" on that thing. But not her. She loves it, and she—unlike me—has the innate ability to paint without leaving those dreaded streak marks.

Could it be that God actually placed within her a natural—or supernatural—bent to enjoy—and to be good at—painting? And, at the same time, could it also be that He did *not* give her other skills? Could it be that she was designed to play a role and play it well, actually doing something she is gifted to do *and* that gives her a sense of accomplishment?

What if it's the same with musicians? What if they, too, are endowed with certain gifts and are charged with serving God's people with authenticity *and* excellence with their gifts? And what if—just like in other professions (pilots, hairstylists, surgeons, pastors, etc.)—those who are *not* gifted or accomplished workers are not permitted to work in these areas?

Honestly, I don't believe we can reach any other logical conclusion. In fact, I dare say—as controversial as it may sound—that those who lack training and giftedness in music are simply not called by God to regularly lead others in music.

Sure, it's a hard call, and some may continue to see the inclusion of skill in creative disciplines as unspiritual. But God doesn't see it this way. He created each person to play a specific role in the Kingdom and to play it well—with skill and excellence.

The Upside

Let's take a quick look at some of the incredible advantages of cultivating a culture of skilled worship leaders, singers, and musicians in your church.

- **Being skillful glorifies God.** Everything God does is done with excellence. When we refuse to operate within the giftings and callings assigned by God, we do the opposite of bringing Him glory. Imagine a stick figure painting on the ceiling of the Sistine Chapel rather than Michelangelo's masterpiece. How would this bring glory to God? Would we simply say, "Well, his heart was in it. He meant well." No, because the work we do ultimately reflects our Creator. We are certainly all in process, but it could be said that if we aren't excellent at what we do, it's because we are either lazy or we aren't operating within the realm of our calling.

- **Being skillful serves God's people.** When we're skilled, we become inspiring rather than distracting. Imagine a speaker who keeps fumbling over his words, using incorrect exegesis, or making points that don't make sense. How many people would sign up to attend his church? Over the long haul? Likewise, a preacher who continually talks above his congregation—using words only scholars understand—is also missing the point. In the end, when balanced rightly, skillful worship gives way to serving and inspiring God's people.

- **Being skillful helps us flow in the Spirit.** To grow and flow in skill requires practice. I've heard Lindell Cooley say that we should practice, practice, practice off the stage, so we don't have to think so hard when we get on the stage. When speaking at our Pure Worship Institute gathering in 2015, Bob Sorge said, "It is preparation (developing your talent) that gives you courage to get out of the boat (and into the river)." In his book *Following the River*, he adds, "Preparation empowers you to deviate from your preparation. Preparation is not confining but releasing."[3] It's true. Playing, singing, and leading skillfully in worship—as with anything—demands considerable practice. But much practice makes a more confident, less distracted musician. And a more confident, less distracted musician equates to one who knows the music so well that she can keep her focus *off* the notes and lyrics and *on* the flow of the Holy Spirit!

- **Being skillful strengthens and displays team unity.** What would we think of a professional big band that kept playing the wrong notes and fumbling through their music? No doubt, we would assume they hadn't been practicing or hadn't been playing very long together. Or both. The same is true when we observe a group of skillful worship musicians. We're inspired

---

3   Bob Sorge, *Following the River* (Kansas City, MO: Oasis House, 2008) Page 29.

by them and their commitment to the task at hand as well as to their ability to function together as a unit. It's also like in sports, when a team brings in a highly gifted athlete. It raises the bar for everyone, setting a new standard and creating a sense of positive peer pressure to move things forward. As they say, a rising tide lifts all boats. In this way, we can expect the skill of each individual team member to increase, while also expecting the community and the impact of that community to increase.

Are there risks involved with encouraging your teams to operate with skill in musical worship? Of course. We could become prideful, or we might begin to focus too much on the program rather than God's presence. Beware! Don't let this happen. But again, let's not throw out skill for fear that we might get it wrong. Skill is not the problem. Human desire, pride, insecurity, and selfishness are the problem. Eliminating skill will not eliminate these problems. Increasing our time in God's presence and availing ourselves to accountability, mentoring, and correction will help us remain humble, even as we increase in skill and giftedness.

God Equips the Called

You've heard it said, "God doesn't call the equipped; He equips the called." This is a great quote. However, don't miss it. Remember, those He calls, He *does* equip. Right? Of course. So, it would stand to reason that if you're not equipped, you're not likely called.

Don't hear me saying if someone is fourteen years old and not skilled that they're not called. It's a process. But if God assigns us to do something and we fail, He doesn't simply pat us on the back, and say, "Well, you tried. I know your heart was in it." No. He expects us to dust ourselves off, get back to work, and go at it again. All with the end goal of accomplishing our assigned tasks with excellence. For His glory.

The fact remains: Our goal is to do everything we do for God with great skill. Maybe that's why Jesus waited until He was thirty to begin

His public ministry. I don't imagine He needed to wait, but maybe He was giving us a pattern to follow. A pattern to suggest that we should spend more time in preparation than we might think.

It's true. Authenticity is *vital*. (That's why we spent the first five chapters poring over this concept.) But because our work reflects our God, authenticity is never enough by itself. God requires *both* heart and skill. This is the scriptural model He's given us to follow, so that His Kingdom will be effective, and so that He'll receive all the glory for the work He's doing in and through us.

TECHNOLOGY

One stormy night in Phoenixville, Pennsylvania, at the University of Valley Forge, my band and I had just finished sound check for a special night of worship. Everything was going just so as we gathered to pray before taking the stage.

We launched into the first song—and just as we began singing the second chorus—the lights went out. Every single one of them. The power was gone. No amps. No keyboards. No microphones. No sound system. Nothing but several hundred stunned people.

I motioned for one of the leaders, and they informed us the storm had knocked out the power to the entire building. There was no reason to believe it would come back on any time soon. So I sent him hunting for an acoustic guitar (we only had electric instruments), and he came back momentarily with a single musical apparatus.

With no amplification or lighting, we began to lift our voices together. Musically, it wasn't as fulfilling as we'd hoped. Honestly. But spiritually, it was overwhelming. Hands and harmonies soared throughout the room as the Spirit of God touched everyone present.

Admittedly, the night didn't go the way I'd envisioned, and I can't tell you I resolved to scratch all sound systems and electric guitars henceforth, but I did gain some perspective as well as receive a poignant reminder that technology should never become my main focus. Technology, too, is amoral, of course. It's not the enemy, but neither is it the solution. We should be capable of leading a Spirit-drenched worship service whether we're in a megachurch with a massive sound, lighting, and video system, or in a small group with a miniature keyboard.

The Revolution

Things have changed immensely in our worship bands in the last twenty years. Some for good and some for bad. In fact, if you're reading this book after the first year it came out, there's a good chance you'll be using technology that didn't exist when I wrote it. Nevertheless, technology is playing a major role in the local church in ways it hasn't before, and we need to embrace the fact that it is not going away.

Few churches—besides the largest ones—were using click or in-ear monitors back in 2000, and almost no one was using tracks and loops. There were no such sites as Planning Center Online or MultiTracks.com, and programs like Logic and Ableton were mostly inaccessible to local church worship leaders.

Even so, we were already incorporating these precious tools back when I was in Sonicflood in 1999–2000. We were using a click and in-ear monitors, and we readily incorporated loops and programming into many of our songs, as did a few other touring worship bands, like Delirious and Hillsong. Back then, because we were discontented with playing the songs the same every time, we were editing our tracks and loops in Logic so we could change things on the fly, as led by the Spirit. The difference now is that this technology is accessible to almost everyone because of its rapid development and much lower price point.

I'm guessing you can easily carry forward the principles I've mentioned a few pages back, concerning creativity and excellence. We dare not blame technology for our lukewarm services or our performance-driven worship models. Undoubtedly, problems with me-first worship teams existed way before technology moved in and took over. It's true. Musicians have always struggled with the temptation to make it about our gear rather than about our God. Like any tool, we must simply learn how to wield technology for Kingdom good, all while standing against the temptation to let it own the room.

Exploring the Possibilities

That said, let's take a fresh look at a few practical ways technology can be harnessed to cultivate the Kingdom in the context of a modern worship setting.

1. **Planning Center Online (PCO)** – Back in 2006, a group of leaders in a local church recognized their great need for a system that could help organize their services. Like you, they had mountains of material to manage, including dozens of volunteers, thousands of songs, and an ever-evolving Sunday morning service schedule. So they decided to design the software we now know as PCO to make things easier. Soon after, they realized other churches around the world had similar needs, so they began offering their new technological services to anyone and everyone. Today, as of 2021, PCO is one of the most prominent tools churches use—not only to organize the musical portion of their services, but every part of their services. Here are a few of the things PCO can do for you:

   - It comes as a downloadable app, making it easy for your teams to engage with any of your church's upcoming services on the go, right from their phone or tablet.
   - It organizes and tracks everything and everyone. All your volunteer contacts, your service schedules, your communication, your charts, and your songs.
   - It provides each user with a personal profile in order to keep track of each team member's details.
   - It will email all your volunteers—musicians and singers, plus volunteers in every category—in order to help manage the schedule of everyone involved in serving. You can set it up to send email updates or to invite specific volunteers to participate each week—days or months in advance.
   - It allows your volunteers to accept or reject your invites with one click, as well as to create blackout dates stored in the main calendar. Everyone involved in each service can clearly see who is "on" and who has or has not responded to their invitation. This makes assembling your worship team super quick and easy.

- It is your one-stop shop for attaching and linking MP3s, YouTube videos, and charts for all of your songs. No longer do your teams have to guess which song or version you're playing. You simply add charts (through CCLI) and YouTube links within the song order, and they can access each one from the app. PCO will even change the key of your charts as well as the key of the pre-recorded versions of your songs. For example, if Bethel does the song in the key of A, but you need it in the key of C#, it's as easy as 1-2-3.
- It even details the section arrangement or "map" of each song so team members can know exactly how many verses, choruses, and bridges each song has. This gives you a great starting point while making it much easier to go off-script in order to make the song your own.
- It lets you, your pastor, or your service producer organize every part of your service in outline form, from the pre-service music to the baby dedication to the sermon notes to the altar songs. You can insert the times for each section, list who is leading each song or section, and add as many notes as are needed. Then you simply copy and paste your template to edit for the next week.

2. **In-ear monitors** – If you're still not sure about in-ear monitors, don't worry. I'm going to give you some helpful tips to consider. Basically, in-ear monitors are glorified miniature headphones that fit inside your ears, giving you the ability to discontinue the use of floor monitors and, more importantly, giving you the ability to precisely mix the volume of each individual instrument and vocal into your ears according to *your* preference. Some folks purchase inexpensive one-size-fits-all in-ear monitors (ranging from $50–$250) while others opt to invest a little more by purchasing custom-molded in-ears from companies like AlClair (alclair.com) for anywhere between $250–$1,500. Shockingly, my very first personal set of custom-molded in-ear monitors, purchased back in 1999, cost upwards of $3,500. Thankfully, the prices have dropped incredibly without seriously impacting the quality of the product.

- Again, custom molds are higher-end in-ear monitors that are specifically molded to fit only your ears. They block out the outside noise as well as increase the quality of your monitoring experience. Companies like AlClair even allow you to customize the look of your molds (with sparkles, logos, and vibrant colors, etc.), all while choosing from vastly different types of drivers (miniature speakers) that greatly enhance the clarity and quality of your experience.

- For detailed information on how to create a good in-ear mix, turn back to chapter 7 under "Sound Check."

- Though moving from floor monitor to in-ear monitors can be daunting, there are incredible benefits of making the switch.

  ▸ **Your ears will love you.** Why? Because you now have complete control over the balance of every individual instrument as well as the overall volume. You are no longer fighting with the musicians next you just to hear yourself. This makes for a much more satisfying monitoring experience as well as a longer life for your hearing.

  ▸ **Your engineer will love you.** Why? Because he can ditch those heavy floor monitors that take up so much space and create so much stage volume. When the stage volume is loud, the engineer has a very difficult time overcoming the loud muffled instruments coming from the stage to get a good mix in the house.

  ▸ **Your team will love you.** Why? Because using in-ear monitors will help everyone hear better, which means everyone is going to play better. Frustration levels will be lower, and team members will be able to focus more on worshiping God. Isn't that the point? (It also means you'll be able to use a click [discussed in the upcoming pages] and potentially an MD [discussed in the upcoming pages] to increase the effectiveness of your band.)

  ▸ **Your congregation will love you.** Why? Because you'll play better as a band, and because the congregation will have a much cleaner and clearer mix (less muddy sounding) after getting rid of those pesky floor monitors. Win-win-win.

- Important cautions:
  - ▸ When you first use in-ear monitors, it will likely feel like you're underwater. It may also feel like you're disconnected from your band and your congregation—locked inside a bubble. This isn't actually true, and these feelings won't last. It just takes practice. And persistence. Whatever you do, don't give up after the first try. Think of all the benefits we mentioned above, and press on, my friend!
  - ▸ Whenever we use technology, there's always a chance it could fail. If your in-ear pack goes out (because of the battery or some other issue) you'll be unable to hear temporarily. You'll have to pull your monitors out and carry on the best you can, listening to the front-of-house sound as it bounces off the back wall. The good news is this rarely happens.
  - ▸ While using in-ear monitors certainly decreases your chances of hearing loss by 1,000 percent, if you're undisciplined, you can end up doing more damage to your ears by turning up your volume too loud. This is easy to monitor since you have a master volume on the pack at your hip (or on the master unit near your station).

3. **The click** – There are many debates over whether to use a click or not. (Using a click basically consists of putting a computer-generated metronome in everyone's ears to help keep the band "clicking" along at the correct tempo.) Recently, I was in a church in Devil's Lake, North Dakota, where I spent the weekend pouring into the worship team through sessions and workshops on a Saturday in preparation for leading together on Sunday. They were using in-ear monitors but had never used a click before. Quite honestly, they were very nervous about making the switch (some members were even a bit perturbed by the idea). Nevertheless, after assessing the situation, I determined they were ready

to make the leap. It wasn't easy, and we definitely had some near train wrecks over the course of the weekend, but I dare say, after stepping into the unknown, the overwhelming majority of the team was positive about the experience and had determined to make this their new reality.

The click and its purpose:

- The common thought is that by using a click we are cheating somehow, even becoming less of a musician. This is absolutely not the case. While some professional bands don't utilize a click, nearly every pro pop/rock band—both Christian and secular—does. Think about it. Cultivating the musical skills to stay locked as a band to a computer-based click is a talent all its own. Plus, once you start using a click, you will discover just how much your tempo tends to waver without it, speeding up as things grow in dynamics and slowing down when the dynamics drop. By regularly using a click, you'll actually grow in your ability to stop rushing so you can play better together.

- Many fear their minds will go numb from the constant beating of the click in their ears. But amazingly, the brain has the insane ability to tune out the click, as long as you keep it at a reasonable volume, just above the volume of the band when everyone is playing their loudest. My friends at the church in Devil's Lake experienced this phenomenon, commenting that they only really noticed the click in the moments they got off of it.

- Using a click in conjunction with a program like Ableton can offer many practical extras for your team, including:
  - Count-offs that will allow you to start together confidentially
  - Vocal cues that remind you of upcoming musical changes
  - Programmed tempo changes
  - The ability to play along with programmed synth or percussion tracks
  - The ability to play along with pre-recorded instruments (such as the bass guitar) when your bassist gets the stomach flu early on Sunday morning.

4. **Sound and volume** – Let's touch briefly on sound; not so much pertaining to the latest in technological amplification standards, but regarding the issues of "volume wars." It's true. Believe it or not, there are a few churches out there who have had a tiff here and there concerning the overall volume of the music in their church. Been there? Question is, should we cater to those who like to feel the music or to those who prefer the softer side? Either way, we must come to grips with the fact that we can never please everyone. That said, here are a few things to consider:

   • **Understanding decibels (dB)** – Most folks know about dB meters: devices that measure the overall volume of the sound in a room via decibels (dB). Using the A-weighted scale (rather than the C-weighted scale) is preferred with music, since it measures the frequencies the human ear is most sensitive to (2–5 kHz). OSHA standards are best and run along a sliding scale, projecting hearing loss to begin when sound exposure is constant at 90 dB for eight hours. The scale continues with times cut in half for every gain in 5 dB (95 dB for four hours, 100 dB for two hours, 105 dB for one hour, and so forth).

   • **The sliding scale** – It should be clarified that, because of the nature of the sliding A-weighted scale, cutting the volume from 100 dB to 50 dB does *not* cut it in half but, in essence, turns it off. There are different descriptions, but the most pervasive is that the human ear can detect changes in volume about every 2–3 dB. In that light, we perceive a move from 100 dB to around 90 dB as nearly cutting the volume in half, decreasing it significantly.

   • **Orchestras are loud** – It should be noted that a thirty-member choir can easily hit 95–100 dB while singing at a good volume, even without microphones or amplification. Interestingly, many folks perceive incorrectly that their frustration is with volume when it is simply a matter of style preference. This comes to light when we understand that a symphony orchestra, musical, or opera can easily top 105 dB several times throughout the evening. Thus, it is often not so much the volume of the instruments that frustrate, but the difference presented by various tones and style.

- **Safe levels** – Determining the best dB levels for your church can be complicated, but the good news is, it's relatively easy to keep the volume at a safe level. Most church services include anywhere from fifteen to forty-five minutes of music and, of course, do not produce a static rate of volume over that time. Typically, volumes fluctuate continually between 85–100 dB, making it very safe to average 95 dB over this time, since it takes approximately four hours of *constant* exposure at 95 dB to damage a person's ears. This helps us understand that at these levels we are not damaging people's ears. That said, there's certainly nothing wrong with keeping the average below this if the church leadership agrees to do so.

- **Love and ear plugs** – We must continue to be sensitive to the needs of the whole body. We never want to cater to one group without considering another. Case in point, I—like many—truly enjoy the feeling of the low frequencies hitting me in the chest, while some others literally feel physically assaulted under these conditions. I appreciate my friend and former president of NCU's "missionary-type" perspective. Though he personally never preferred louder sound levels, he recognized the need to cater to our students' preferences first, within reason. I encourage you to do your best, together with your pastoral staff, to find a "reasonable middle point," even while attempting to educate everyone about truly safe volume levels. Thankfully, there are other things we can do besides yanking the volume around like a yo-yo (based on who's putting the most in the offering plate). Providing ear plugs for people who want them can be a fitting and welcome gesture.

5. **Ableton Live, Logic, and Mainstage**
   - Ableton Live is a digital audio workstation (DAW) and a software sequencer that came on the scene in 2001. Many artists and worship teams have been using it for twenty plus years to create

and run tracks during their live concerts and church services. Ableton Live is designed primarily for live performances as well as the remixing of songs, but it can also be used to record music, automate lighting and visual effects, run lyrics, and much more.

- Many worship teams have come to love Ableton Live as a result of their passion for creating modern soundscapes with soft synths and sampled percussion sounds that are nearly impossible to recreate live. Instead of hiring two or three keyboardists to do this work on stage, they simply record the music in Ableton, sync it to a click track, and play along with their analogue-style band instruments (drums, bass, piano, and guitar). We did this with Sonicflood back in 1999. After creating many unique drum and keys sounds for our recording—and with only a five-member touring band—we decided to add these "tracks" or "stems" to our live sound by playing along with them through another similar program, Logic. While some bands play along with full tracks (even adding guitars, lead and background vocals, or even bass guitar—when the bassist is absent), we chose to only use Logic to play back the recorded instruments we couldn't reproduce live, all while actually playing the instruments we could play live. This gave us a very unique combination of live and programmed music to augment our overall vibe.

- Mainstage, released alongside Logic in 2013, is a software-based live workspace interface that allows the user to place sounds into regions in order to group them and their parameters (like volume, filters, panning, effects, etc.) together for live playback. It comes packaged with bundles of sounds and effects and is designed to be linked to a controller keyboard or drum pad for live performances. Many bands have jumped on the live DAW bandwagon, taking things even further, thanks to these programs being much more readily accessible.

- Probably the biggest misconception with regard to using DAWs for your team's live worship sets is that we lose the ability to flow in the Spirit. This is simply not true and was something I was unwilling to budge on as far back as my days in Sonicflood.

Thankfully, long before Ableton perfected this approach, our gifted keyboardist rigged Logic to repeat and/or jump to different section markers (A=verse, B=chorus, and C=bridge), giving us the freedom to follow the leading of the Spirit (potentially differently each night). Now, worship leaders easily import either original programmed tracks or tracks from their favorite worship artists and add markers and/or chop them up in order to play new and fresh arrangements of their favorite songs on the fly.

6. **iOS Apps/Tracks (MultiTracks.com and Loop Community)** – Speaking of tracks, many local worship bands have added vitality to their sound by purchasing a subscription with companies like MultiTracks.com or Loop Community. These companies have created collections of full-band stems and tracks from all of your favorite worship songs with two purposes in mind: 1) to help your team better recreate "that sound" from "that song," and 2) to help smaller churches fill band-member roles when team members are ill or unavailable. Known artists and bands used to randomly make their tracks available on their own websites until these companies organized their sites into one-stop shops for all known artists. Now we can subscribe or simply purchase individual tracks and then import them into DAWs like Ableton and Logic. Additionally, Multitracks.com offers their own easy-to-use DAW called Playback, while Loop Community provides a similar product called Prime. Both are designed specifically for use with purchased tracks. Once imported, these tracks can be used in part or in whole by muting the undesirable instruments and playing along with the desirable ones. As mentioned, this allows for bands who might be missing a rhythm guitarist on a certain Sunday to add the pre-recorded rhythm guitar part into the mix via the tracks. Multitracks.com even "rents" rehearsal tracks so team members can "solo" certain instruments in order to hear more clearly exactly what is being played. Note: Don't forget, you still have the best of both worlds when playing with tracks. Section arrangements (maps) can still be altered endlessly to taste within Playback, Prime, Logic, or Ableton so as to maintain a spontaneous, creative flow.

7. **Worship Pad Apps** – While many worship bands are exploring the seemingly unending possibilities delivered by programs like Ableton, Logic, and Mainstage, others may prefer a simpler route, especially when it comes to adding a static keyboard pad into the mix. Whether it's for full-band usage or to beef up a solo acoustic worship set, apps like Ambient Pad are free and can help augment your sound. The idea here is to give anyone the ability to easily generate a keyboard-like droning sound that fills in the spaces, creating "atmosphere," especially for your "down" and in-between moments. Simply choose the key and hit the start button. A lush keyboard sound is automatically generated as if a keyboardist was playing live. Typically, the sound is built around the root and the fifth of the chord, making it a perfect aesthetic addition to whatever song you are playing. When you're ready to change keys for the next song, simply touch the key you want, and the app fades smoothly to that key, avoiding the often-so-awkward pitfalls that tend to occur between songs. Of course, you can take things to the next level by downloading apps like Pads Live or SoftPads or Prime and purchasing beautiful sonic bundles, including sounds like Guitar Sky, Organ Drone, Orchestral Strings, Bright Wave, etc. These apps can be run straight from your phone or be paired with your DAW.

8. **Other Helpful Apps** – From guitar-tuner apps to metronomes, there is never-ending accessibility to worship-help apps in your device's store. If you don't like PCO, you can always try worshipteam.com. Smart Chord is an app that can help your team with the how, why, and what of playing in a band, while Shazam becomes a personal assistant to help you find and name songs. Anytune Pro can help you learn to transcribe and play songs by slowing them down with tempo and pitch changes, and Capo Touch can help you increase your ability to learn by ear. Onsong will help you manage and access a huge library of charts, while Frozen Ape has created apps to help manage your tempos and pitch. Yousician becomes your personal music tutor, while Worship Leader Worldwide gives you access to songs and charts in many languages. It's a brave new world. And the beauty is, if you can't find an app for your particular need, you can develop one yourself.

9. **Lighting and hazers** – Just a couple quick notes on lighting. First, I would never ask my lighting director to attempt to *create* an environment during the musical worship. His job should be to enhance what the Spirit of God is doing by reflecting colors and movement appropriate for the moment. This means there could be times of flashing and swooping that are in line with celebratory musical expressions as well as sweeter and more majestic visuals that coincide with softer, more placid moments. Again, lighting is a tool, and it can be used to help or hinder. Even so, there's no reason the lighting director shouldn't be able to worship the Lord with her skills, just like any other member of the team. Using hazers (machines that fill the room with a thin, fog-like mist) to subtly augment the beams of light on the stage can add yet another layer of creativity that points to the beauty of our Creator. Just be careful not to overdo it to the point where the lighting becomes the main focus.

10. **Lyrics and projection** – Long have we utilized tools to help our church attendees sing the words of the worship songs. From hymn books to overhead projectors and now to massive, high-definition projector screens, things continue to evolve. There are many takes on how to utilize these screens. Some keep it simple with white lyrics on a black screen. Others employ exquisite videos and motion graphics that are beautifully designed and timed to go with the music. No matter your style, I would suggest a similar approach to the one I mentioned with lighting, in the sense that we never want our creative tools to become the sole focus. Overall, our screens should continually point us to the Creator rather than point us to His creation. This should also hold true as we encourage our lyric operators to stay one step ahead of the game by displaying no more than two or three lines on a slide at a time and by advancing to the next slide just as the final word from the previous slide is being sung.

Whatever you do, don't allow yourself to feel pressured into using technology or into making too many major changes all at once. Just take things a step at a time, as budget and know-how allow. Remember, creativity, excellence, and technology are simply meant to be helpmates on the way to launching people into greater connection with God. Anointing and love, paired with these tools, can help take us to greater heights in God's presence, as we keep our main focus on the One who created it all.

Chapter Highlights

1. Cultivating a higher level of creativity within your team can be a great source of joy for your musicians. Doing this will help keep them engaged and also develop them musically over time. It will also help to pull your congregation out of dangerous ruts that promote a "been there, done that" mentality. Just be careful to continually posture music as a servant to worship and not the primary focus.

2. Increasing in musical excellence and preparation has strong biblical backing and will go a long way toward serving your congregation, allowing more space for the Spirit of God to move, and establishing team unity.

3. We can worship passionately and authentically with or without technology, so as we travel further and further into the modern age of worship, let's be sure to utilize the latest and greatest in technological toys to enhance rather than create the atmosphere in our services.

Chapter 9

GOD WANTS YOUR BODY (ROMANS 12:1-2)

Lie #9

"I wasn't raised in a church where people
expressed themselves physically in worship,
so there's no reason to change that now."

I f you're like me, you grew up believing people who lifted their hands or danced in worship were a little "out there." You know what I'm talking about. There was always that one lady "distracting" everyone with her "overly expressive" worship. Even so, in the second half of my life, I've discovered that much of the Bible—as well as so many of our songs—speak to the incredible blessings of engaging our physical bodies in worship. Ultimately, it got me thinking, *Who is the "weirdo"? The one who worships extravagantly, or the one who points a finger at the one who worships extravagantly?*

I was talking with a close worship-leader friend recently, and he told me about a decision his church leadership had made recently to provide a "distraction-free" worship environment for their congregation. Sounds nice. (They were referring to a desire to increase their musical excellence, but also to a desire to limit physical expression in worship, on stage and in the congregation.)

Now, I do believe this is a conversation worth having, especially since we do want to discourage people from worshiping in ways that are carnal or that seek primarily to draw attention to oneself. That said, this is

a difficult thing to discern, especially in a day and age when the majority of worshipers in Western churches have adopted an extremely docile (dare I say lukewarm) approach to worship. Who's to say if the worshiper needs to be tamed or if the rest of the body needs to be wakened from the dead?

> Many church leaders seem more committed to protecting passive worshipers from "distractions" than to protecting them from apathy.

As my friend and I talked, our frustration grew over the idea that many church leaders seem more committed to protecting passive worshipers from "distractions" than to protecting them from apathy. Truth be told, many who are "distracted" by exuberant worshipers simply use this as an excuse to justify their own inaction.

Real distractions in worship services are truly rare. Subsequently, we needn't pour too much energy into safeguarding our sheep from exuberant worshipers but simply into educating unbelievers and believers alike concerning the importance of passionate worship as exemplified in Scripture.

If there's any doubt, we can look to the way Jesus continually encouraged and affirmed the "distracting" actions of people in the Bible. Then, if, by chance, we find ourselves desperately "distracted" by other passionate worshipers, for heaven's sake, let's not tone them down. Let's refocus our gaze on the Savior of the world and seek to join in with them. Otherwise, we may find ourselves in good company with the men who disparaged the woman who poured expensive perfume on Jesus' feet.

GIVE YOUR BODY TO GOD

Don't get offended. Just open your heart.

If we're going to lead our teams and our congregations in biblical worship, it's time we took a long look in the mirror to determine once and for all if we're going to worship God with our whole being or not. Bodies included.

Romans 12:1 exhorts, *"And so, dear brothers and sisters, I plead with you to give your bodies to God."* As a follower of Christ—a worshiper—I want to honor God with every part of myself and every part of my life. Heart, soul, mind, and body. I don't want to compartmentalize worship as something I do at church but not at work—something I do in my "quiet time" but not when I'm out with friends. Nor do I want to worship God with my mind and not with my heart or with my soul and not with my body. I want to give Him every area of every part of my being.

And so do you.

And still, it seems that many of us resist this notion blindly when it comes to worshiping God with our bodies.

So, what about it?

Need we concern ourselves with worshiping God with dancing and shouting? Is singing really *that* important, especially seeing how the New Testament only mentions it a few times? What about kneeling or lying prostrate? Are these actions at all relevant for the twenty-first-century Church? And what's with all the hand raising? Is there any *real* purpose in it?

Honestly, if you would've asked me these questions twenty years ago, I would have been fairly disagreeable. I grew up in a good conservative church. No one ever stood up, spoke up, or lifted a hand up. We sang a couple of songs quietly from the heart and didn't dare make a peep otherwise.

Like some of you, I was conveniently unaware—or unmoved—by Scriptures like Psalm 95:6 (bowing before the Lord) and Psalm 63:4 (lifting up our hands to God). I guess I assumed many of these passages didn't apply to me, like Psalm 150:4 (praising the Lord with dancing) and Psalm 98:4 (shouting our praise to God). Worshiping God with outward expression was culturally unnatural to me and was therefore easy to explain away. Honestly, the idea itself made me...well, uncomfortable.

Even so, I was vaguely aware that God is sometimes known for asking people to do uncomfortable things. So, with reticence, I began to look a little deeper, beyond the obvious Scriptures in Psalms. And that's when the Lord began highlighting some powerful principles I had overlooked.

1. Our bodies are not our own.

1 Corinthians 6:19–20 reminds, *"Don't you know that your body is the temple of the Holy Spirit who lives in you and was given to you by God?* **You do not belong to yourself**, *for God bought you with a high price. So you must honor God with your bodies."* I reason that if my body isn't my own, then ultimately, I don't get to make the decisions about what to do with it. I'm completely subject to the Scriptures.

Paul also said, *"But you can't say that our bodies were made for sexual immorality.* **They were made for the Lord, and the Lord cares about our bodies.***"* (v. 13). He wrote in 1 Corinthians 6:14–15, *"And God will raise our bodies from the dead by his marvelous power, just as he raised our Lord from the dead. Don't you realize that* **your bodies are actually parts of Christ?***"*

Whoa, that was something I'd never thought of before. Our bodies were made for the Lord, and they are *actually* parts of Christ!

2. We will be judged for what we do or don't do with our bodies.

Second Corinthians 5:10 takes things up a notch: *"For we must all stand before Christ to be judged.* **We will each receive whatever we deserve for the good or evil we have done in this earthly body.***"* It's simple. If I borrow someone's car and wreck it, I'm responsible for the damages. If I wreck God's property—including the body He's lending me—I'll be held responsible. If I use my body in ways it wasn't intended to be used, I'll be held responsible. My body was created by Him and for Him, not for me. It was created to do His work, not mine. I'm simply called to be a steward of His property. He's the owner, and He knows what's best for "my" body.

3. Worshiping God with my whole heart is not enough.

I made another discovery. God created us for whole-self worship. Not solely for heart worship or mind worship or body worship, but for all of the above. *"And you must love the Lord your God with all your heart, all your soul, all your mind, and all your strength"* (Mark 12:30).

Worshiping God with our *whole heart* is certainly way up on the list, but surprising to some, it's not enough by itself. God is asking us to worship Him with our *whole being*. When we worship with our heart and mind but *not* our body, it's as if our body is functioning in disagreement with (or in rebellion against) the rest of our person—disunified—thereby creating conflict within our soul. The ultimate goal is for our entire being to come into agreement regarding our worship expression, whether we worship God with humility or joy, sadness or adoration.

4. Learning to worship God with my entire being requires training and discipline.

As I mentioned, I didn't grow up expressing myself to God with my body in worship. Yet, in my commitment to become a biblical, whole-being follower of Christ, I discovered I would need to be open to significant change, even if it meant unlearning many of the traditions from my younger years. As a result, I've endeavored—with the help of the Holy Spirit—to imitate Paul as he imitates Christ. In every way. In fact, I see no way around it. Despite my conservative upbringing. Despite my initial awkward attempts at physical worship. I now *"run with purpose in every step. I am not just shadowboxing.* **I discipline my body like an athlete, training it to do what it should** *[in worship and in lifestyle]. Otherwise, I fear that after preaching to others, I myself might be disqualified"* (1 Corinthians 9:26–27).

5. My natural personality must not dictate the level of my expression in worship.

What can I point to in all of God's Kingdom that meshes nicely with my personality? How about carrying my cross? Dying to self? What about loving my enemies? Maybe tithing? Fasting?

Why would we expect worship to be any different? Kingdom activities always invite us outside of our comfort zones—beyond our natural personalities—yet not for our loss but for our gain.

Remember Romans 12:1? "

And so, dear brothers and sisters, I plead with you to give your bodies to God because of all he has done for you. Let them be a living and holy sacrifice—the kind he will find acceptable. This is truly the way to worship him."

Last time I checked, crawling up on an altar to become a living sacrifice is not comfortable. Gratefully, God is not requiring us to lay down our bodies through crucifixion—as Jesus did—but He *is* requiring us to lay down our entire being (heart, soul, mind, and body) in order to die to everything we consider "natural" in life *and* in worship.

Am I suggesting Romans 12:1 refers solely to worshiping God with our bodies? No. Am I saying God requires each of us to praise Him in exactly the same manner, erasing the diversity in our worship expression? No. But God *is* requiring us to step beyond ourselves into deeper dimensions of action that aid us in shifting from natural expressions in life and worship to supernatural expressions in life and worship. Why? Because this is part of what it means to live an abundant life.

6. Jesus used His body to communicate His great love for us.

Thankfully, Jesus never asks us to do anything He isn't willing to do Himself. Think about it. What was the number one most powerful expression of Jesus' love for us? His Word? His miracles? His glory? No, those are all fundamentally important, but it was His bodily action—action He took on Calvary—that provided the most impactful assertion of His love. Why? Simply because actions speak louder than words.

This was a huge revelation for me personally, especially as a leader. Jesus knew full well that using His body to communicate His extravagant love was hands down the best way to express it. There's no getting around it. It wouldn't have meant quite as much to us if He'd only said it (in His Word) while sitting piously on His heavenly throne.

Of course, God has designed us to communicate our love for Him in many ways, but when we leave out bodily expression, we do so in direct contrast to the way Jesus loved us. With His whole being. With words *and* with actions. Just as He gives every part of Himself to us, He asks us to give every part of ourselves to Him in return.

NO MORE EXCUSES

As we endeavor to worship God with our whole being, let's debunk a few common excuses.

1. Won't people think I'm weird if I worship with my body—if I become *that* **guy?** Maybe. But 1 Corinthians 1:18–29 reminds us that God often purposely confronts us with "foolish" instructions in order to mystify those who think they are wise. What could be more "foolish" than using our bodies to worship a God we can't see? And yet, ultimately, which is more foolish, worshiping God with our bodies (and our entire being) or using our bodies to exalt the god of this world? Of course, simply acting foolish in worship doesn't guarantee godliness, but in this case, I'll quote David on the subject of physical expression in worship: *"Yes, and I am willing to look even more foolish than this, even to be humiliated in my own eyes!"* (2 Samuel 6:21).

2. What if I wasn't raised that way? Yes, what if my family brought me up to worship God in a more reserved, reverent fashion? Cool. But we're all in a new family now. A spiritual Kingdom family. With a new, heavenly Father. Plus, if there is ever a conflict, the truth in God's Word for His family always trumps our natural upbringing. Welcome to the family.

3. What if I'm not inherently a good dancer? Good question. I would simply ask, "Were you ever good at anything before you practiced?"

4. What if I'm physically unable? What if my knees hurt when I bow down or dance? I totally get this, and each person needs to be wise with their own choices here. But honestly, some of the most beautiful worship offerings originate from those who make astounding physical sacrifices to bring them.

5. But I've heard God is not a God of disorder. Some ask, "Don't we risk affirming chaos and selfish ambition in our services if the physical worship gets out of hand?" Sure, we do, but we must never, never, never... *never* make decisions about the way we follow God based on the *fear* of what *might* happen. We simply stand upon and act upon God's Word no matter what—despite any logical objections. Despite our fears. Despite those who might take it "too far." Despite our upbringing. Despite our comfort. Despite our boxes. Period.

Note: 1 Corinthians 14:29–33 is certainly one of the most manipulated passages in the Bible. When it reminds us that *"God is not a God of disorder but of peace,"* it is simply reminding us to keep the number of prophecies we share in a service to two or three, making sure each prophet speaks in turn. This is hardly a frantic warning to avoid wild Holy Spirit dance parties. In fact, if anything, this passage encourages complete submission to the movement of God's Spirit in our churches. (Incidentally, this type of complaint sounds a lot like one Michal [David's wife] might have raised in order to cover up her pride and insecurity. See more in 2 Samuel 6:16, 20. Steer clear.)

7. Fine. So bodily worship is for believers, but what will unbelievers think? "Surely, we don't want to scare away the many tenuous seekers with all of our worshiping mayhem, do we?" Absolutely not. And at the same time, maybe. Yeah. Maybe this is exactly what we need to do. Ultimately, it's not the crazy worship dancers and the banner wavers who will frighten away the unbelievers. If anything, it's the cross. It's the splinters and the blood. It's the whole "dying to self" thing. And the "crazy talk" surrounding hell and demons and the antichrist. It's the idea of sin and holiness and the whole "loving your enemies" thing.

Come on, are we planning to strip away everything in the Bible that makes people uncomfortable? Like it or not, the true gospel isn't slick or flawlessly packaged in the way many of our modern church services are. Why? Because when we try to sugarcoat the gospel to avoid frightening unbelievers, we actually do them more harm than good. You may disagree, but I'm convinced pre-Christians are desperately searching for something godly to do with their bodies. Sure enough, many have participated in scores of activities that have accomplished just the opposite. Most would be thrilled to discover that there is a truly godly purpose for our bodies. Honestly, most probably don't know their bodies were made for the Lord, made to worship and exalt Him. Maybe because we never told them.

WORSHIP WITH KINGDOM BENEFITS

Fortunately, God doesn't mandate physical expression in worship "because he says so." Remember, worship is *about* God and *to* God, but it is *for* you. When we worship Him His way, He is exalted and we are transformed. Therefore, we should know that there are astonishing, practical God-ordained benefits to be enjoyed by those who worship Him His way. (Consequently, these same benefits are forfeited when we determine not to worship Him His way.)

Here are four of the beautiful blessings connected with fully releasing our bodies in worship to God:

1. Worshiping with our bodies helps keep our hearts tender toward obedience. When we worship with our whole being, it helps remind us—and others—that we're more interested in obeying God and His commands than catering to what others think. This keeps our hearts from growing numb toward our Creator while keeping us alive toward His desires.

2. Worshiping with our bodies helps to keep our heart, soul, and mind focused on God. When our body is truly unified with the rest of our being in worship, it's much less likely to distract or tempt us with other "pleasures." Whether it's a desire to sleep or eat or even a craving for sexual pleasure, all it takes is a disengaged body to increase the chances that we might be distracted. It's simple. Involving our body in worship—together with our heart, mind, and soul—keeps it engaged in the activity of musical worship and helps us remain focused on God.

3. Worshiping with our bodies helps to keep our flesh crucified. Humble worshipers continue to gravitate toward whatever it takes to die to the demands of their flesh. Physical worship can serve as the ultimate pride killer as it continually beckons us beyond our comfort zone. Additionally, when we submit to God's instructions for physical worship, our flesh is no longer in the driver's seat, making it much easier for us to approach Him with childlike abandonment (see Matthew 18:3).

4. Worshiping with our bodies helps us avoid physical sin. Simply put, while we are worshiping God with our bodies, we are much less likely to be sinning with our bodies. "But doesn't this make worship more about going through the motions and less about the heart?" No. Remember, we aren't elevating physical worship above heart, soul, and mind worship. We're simply placing them all where they belong, on a level playing field.

UNCOVERING THE HIDDEN HEBREW WORDS FOR *PRAISE*

As we prepare to embark on the incredible journey to discover the seven Hebrew words for *praise*, I can't help but revisit the words of Chris DuPré from when he spoke at the Pure Worship Institute in 2016: "Worshiping is not about performing or striving to get God's attention. It's a *response*. We don't dance in worship to get God's approval. We do so because we already have it! We don't sing or shout to gain His attention. We do so because we already have it! We don't bow or kneel so He will notice us. We do so because He already has!"[1]

Words are important. They help us renew our perspective. When put together uniquely, they're like a puzzle. Arranging them in different ways allows us to paint colorful pictures and communicate distinctive messages that can free people's hearts.

As you might imagine, translating words from one language to another—like Hebrew to English—provides a great challenge. Part of the reason for this is that there are often subtle meanings that don't transfer entirely.

Take the Greek words for love: *Agape, philea, storge,* and *eros.* Unfortunately, there's only one primary word for *love* in English, which means communicating the heart of *philea*—brotherly love—requires a few more adjectives to get the point across. Likewise, the exact meaning of *agape*—love for God—can easily be misconstrued when we simply utilize the word *love.* One could easily misunderstand, assuming we mean *eros*—sexual love.

The dilemma is similar with the English word *praise.*

In the Hebrew language, there are multiple words for the word *praise,* yet we regularly end up on the wrong end of the translation deal in a futile attempt to pack each Hebrew word into our one little English word.

If you decided to ask a congregation to "praise the Lord," how should

---

1 Chris DuPré, Pure Worship Institute 2016.

they respond? Maybe they would sing or shout out or simply pray in their hearts. Maybe they would clap or lift their hands or simply lend a hand to the poor. Point being, each person would do whatever they wanted, since everyone has different ideas of what it means to praise the Lord.

But what if there's more to the word *praise* than meets the eye? What if we're actually failing to comprehend the message from the original text? And what if our partial misunderstanding is holding us back, aiding us in our failure to respond with biblical praise?

Thankfully, there's a hidden treasure of understanding many are unaware of. One that can change our lives. A hidden answer that provides great clarity surrounding the numerous biblical meanings for the word *praise*.

Let's dig in.

1. *Zâmar* (zaw-MAR) (Strong's H2167) – *"Instrumental worship. To praise with instruments. To touch the strings. (Includes the act of prophesying on the instruments.) (Release the prophetic instrumental song.)"*

I hope you've gathered from this book that when I speak of worship leaders, we're talking about everyone who's involved in facilitating the musical worship portion of our services. Clearly, this goes way beyond the singer with the microphone in her hand. It extends to the bassist, the drummer, the keyboardist, and the guitarist (even the tympanist). It extends to the lyric operator, the lighting folks, the camera people, the sound engineer, and more. All of these people—our teammates—play a monumental role in helping people engage well with God in musical worship.

It's ironic. Many times, we singers can be caught believing we're the most important people in the room. At the same time, I've watched as many instrumentalists have—just as assertively—determined to be the least important. These issues combined can cause instrumentalists to casually disengage behind the singers, often evading their true calling as a Levite. As a worship leader.

That's what I love about the Hebrew word, *Zâmar*. It doesn't let anyone off the hook. It marks us all as worship leaders, reminding us that we all play an important role in serving people through worship leadership.

Moreover, *Zâmar* serves our instrumentalists in refocusing their efforts.

No longer should they—or we—view themselves as "back-up" to the singers. In fact, because of *Zâmar*, we all begin to recognize that they, too, are singing. Singing with their instruments! We begin to see that when they play, they are actually releasing their own "language" of worship, which speaks just as loudly—for good or for bad—as a singer's voice.

When I was in Sonicflood, I used to ask the instrumentalists to sing at all times, but that was before I understood *Zâmar*. Encouraging the instrumentalists to sing is wonderful, but what we must grasp is that our instrumentalists are *already* singing. Prophesying. Pushing back the darkness. Breaking strongholds. With their instrumental praise.

Just as singers can give all the glory to God—or choose to keep it for themselves—instrumentalists can do the same.

Thankfully, this is going to revolutionize the way we cover those amazing Lincoln Brewster worship tunes. Seriously. How awkward are these moments? Our hometown guitarist gives it his best but often can't pull off the solo quite like Lincoln. Who can? We smile awkwardly as a few bobbled notes grace our ears, *or* we cringe uncomfortably because of the arrogance of our "somebody-stop-me" super guitarist.

Psalm 108:1 reads, *"O God, my heart is fixed; I will sing and give* **praise** *[Zâmar], even with my glory"* (KJV). Notice that singing (vocally) and giving *Zâmar* are two different things. We certainly can't forget the way God used David's anointed and skillful harp playing to drive away the evil spirit tormenting King Saul (see 1 Samuel 16:23).

That's it! *Zâmar.*

Can you imagine what would happen if our instrumentalists grabbed ahold of this concept? If *we* did? What if we actually believed and encouraged the biblical truth that our instrumentalists can join us in setting the captives free and healing the blind with anointed instrumental playing? What if the congregation knew this too? Wow. Our congregants might even put two and two together and realize they can begin *Tehillâh*-ing (see the next Hebrew word) every time an instrumentalist begins *Zâmar*-ing. Now that's a beautiful combination.

2. *Tehillâh* (teh-hil-LAH) (Strong's H8416) – *"To sing with songs or hymns; laudations of the spirit. The song of the Lord; spontaneous song to the Lord."*

In our platform-driven church worship culture, we are certainly used to singing corporate songs written by talented writers, either out of our hymn books or via our video screens. Brilliant. But what if we discovered that we're missing something significant here? Would we remain indifferent?

It's clearly wonderful to adopt the songs of Chris Tomlin, Jeremy Riddle, Steven Furtick, Jenn Johnson, and Chandler Moore. But from a biblical standpoint, there's reason to believe we should also learn to express ourselves with our own personal God-songs.

This is *Tehillâh*.

Many non-singer types may see this as daunting, but God invites each one of us to praise Him with spontaneous singing. And, as we'll discover in greater detail in chapter 13, this type of spontaneous *Tehillâh* can unlock deeper levels of connection and freedom in God that otherwise cannot be experienced.

Astoundingly, the meaning of the popular Psalm 22:3 is completely flipped on its head as we read, *"But thou art holy, O thou that inhabitest the* **praises** *[Tehillâh] of Israel"* (KJV). Suddenly—with eyes wide open—it dawns on us that God doesn't inhabit just any old praise. He "lives in" or "abides in" or "is enthroned upon" the *Tehillâh* (the spontaneous praise) of His people. Wow. How did we miss this?

As you might imagine, there's remarkable purpose surrounding God's invitation for us to lift our *Tehillâh* to Him. Not only does it help us learn to express ourselves more personally to God, but it also empowers each individual to bring forth worship to God on their own. With their own words. This is incredibly rewarding for worship leaders as we watch our congregants mature in their ability to express themselves to God right before our eyes. Thankfully, it's not too late to begin lifting our *Tehillâh* praises to God in the secret place and in our corporate gatherings.

3. Bârak (baw-RAHK) (Strong's H1288) – *"To kneel, to bow in worship; prostrate, to fall down. (Often translated 'bless'.) Can also mean to salute."*

This is one type of praise we're generally familiar with—bowing before the Lord. At least in principle. Even so, when we read a verse like

Psalm 72:15, which instructs, *"And let [the people] pray for him continually; let them bless and **praise** [Bârak] him all day long"* (AMP), we would never guess in a million years that the word *praise* here actually means to do so by bowing down. How could we?

The end of the verse reads slightly differently in the King James: "And daily shall He be *praised*." This is supremely meaningful as we discover that *Bârak* is not simply referring to a generic form of praise—where we sit comfortably sipping our coffee—but instead to a profound falling-to-our-knees praise that screams "surrender" to the King of kings. Two very different things.

Unfortunately, it's quite rare these days to find people bowing down before the Lord. Why do you think this is? Maybe because it's physically uncomfortable? Maybe because no one on the stage is doing it? Or maybe because we've simply lost our awe of God so much that we find it unnecessary to bow before the Author of the universe.

Bârak could change all of this, serving to restore a true sense of the fear of the Lord by boldly beckoning us to increase in reverential praise. (Note: Make sure you don't miss my intriguing story about a young woman who came face-to-face with the word *Bârak*. It's just ahead after the seventh Hebrew word for praise.)

4. *Yâdâh* (yaw-DAH) (Strong's H3034) – *"To revere or worship with the hands. (Wringing, extending, waving.)"*

This word is one we've likely become a little more comfortable with. At least in the last twenty to twenty-five years. These days, you might even walk into a small conservative country church and see quiet worshipers lifting up a hand during the musical worship. (You never know. Maybe they, too, came across the seven Hebrew words for *praise* and began to see these beautiful expressions as biblically relevant—not simply for the emotionally charged, but for the everyday Christ follower.)

Psalm 67:5 reads, *"May the nations **praise** [Yâdâh] you, O God."* I love this because, once again, if we didn't have access to the behind-the-scenes story here, we wouldn't think much of this verse. We'd just "praise the Lord" and be done with it. But here, the psalmist is being oh-so-specific. He's inviting us to praise God with a particular type of praise. Praise with the hands. And he isn't simply inviting the charismatic folks to do it. He's expecting the *nations* to join in. Everyone.

Psalm 9:1—and many others—echo this same sentiment: *"I will* **praise** *[Yâdâh] you, LORD, with all my heart; I will tell of all the marvelous things you have done."*

Fascinatingly, the first time *Yâdâh* was uttered in the Bible was when Leah gave birth to Judah, her fourth son. Genesis 29:35 reports, *"Once again Leah became pregnant and gave birth to another son. She named him Judah, for she said, 'Now I will* **praise** *[Yâdâh] the LORD!'" And then she stopped having children."* After being barren for many, many years, and then miraculously birthing four sons, Leah praised the Lord—not simply with her words—but also with uplifted hands.

Could it be that God is longing to birth new praise in you after years of barrenness in praise? Could it be that *Yâdâh* is part of the answer? I believe so. For us all.

5. *Tôwdâh* (toe-DAH) (Strong's H8426) – *"A confession of thanks and praise for what God is going to do; extending hands in praise for things to come. Also, a sacrifice of praise; a procession of worshipers (a choir)."*

This is an astounding word. Interestingly, it's found, among other places, in the title of Psalm 100, which is commonly translated, *"A Psalm of* **praise** *(or thanksgiving) [Tôwdâh]."* Yet, it is more than that.

Of course, we might not be surprised to discover a Hebrew word—like *Yâdâh*—which specifically points to praise with the hands. But *Tôwdâh* takes things to new heights by inviting us to lift up our hands in total thanks to God with the same intensity we might if God had suddenly fulfilled a long-awaited, miraculous answer to prayer. But *before* it happens. As *if* it had already happened. By faith.

Picture this. Your sister needs a kidney transplant, but there are no kidneys to match. Yet, in faith one night, you begin to lift up your hands in praise to God anyway—in advance—just as exuberantly as if you had received word that the matching kidney was already on its way. This is the kind of praise that tells God you are trusting Him fully, believing your answer *is* on the way. Even if you can't see it yet.

In his book *Holy Roar*, co-written with Chris Tomlin, Darren Whitehead asks these illuminating questions about *Tôwdâh*: "Have you raised your hands for your wounded marriage, your troubled career, your wayward son or daughter? Have you raised your hands believing God will give you the guidance and the direction you so desperately need? Have you raised Tôwdâh to God for healing?"[2]

These are real questions. Maybe some folks in your congregation have given up. Or lost hope. Maybe it's time to begin introducing them to *Tôwdâh* so they can begin praising God in faith—with uplifted hands—as the Bible instructs. When they do, they'll be joining David who did so immediately after being captured by the Philistines. Imagine the horror! Psalm 56:11–12 tells us he sang these words in faith: *"I trust in God, so why should I be afraid? What can mere mortals do to me? I will fulfill my vows to you, O God, and will offer a sacrifice of thanks [Tôwdâh] for your help."*

Yep, even *before* David was delivered—before he knew the end of the story—he offered faith-filled praise, with uplifted hands, to his Deliverer. This is *Tôwdâh*.

6. *Shâbach* (shaw-BAHK) (Strong's H7623) – *"To command, triumph; to shout before God in praise."*

Remember the walls of Jericho story? I love it. Why? Because it typifies our often-outlandish role in God's miracles. Remember Gideon and the clay pots? Jehoshaphat and the singing soldiers? Elijah and the sopping-wet altar? This is one of those stories too.

Here, God has the brilliant idea to ask the people of Israel to march around an enemy city one time each day for six days, and then seven times on the seventh day. Then, as the ram's horn is blown, He instructs them to shout with a mighty shout and watch as the massive walls of the city come tumbling down.

Huh?

My mind goes back to VeggieTales (sorry), where the people of Jericho (the French Peas) snickered and threw slushies down at the Israelites. My favorite line comes as they holler—accompanied by a gloriously animated accordion—these words: "The awesome powers of this

---

2   Darren Whitehead, *Holy Roar* (Nashville, TN: Thomas Nelson, 2017), page 62.

wall, we've clearly demonstrated. But out here in the hot, hot sun, perhaps you're dehydrated?"[3]

Of course, the French Peas' actions are largely inaccurate—since the Scriptures record the people of Jericho being terrified by the Israelites—yet you have to wonder, even in their fear, did they never question the Israelite's peculiar battle tactics? Or their sanity?

What an odd way to fight a battle!

Yet we often fail to recognize the supernatural power in a shout. A power that is much greater than anyone can imagine, apparently. In fact, the Bible tells us the Israelites shouted "*with a great shout*," which can be translated, "*with **The** great shout*," which gives us this glorious equation; the people's shouts + God's shout = walls tumbling down. Gargantuan city walls, that is. Look, I could be wrong, but I have a sneaking suspicion that this is also a metaphor for the way spiritual walls are meant to come tumbling down. As we shout in our praise to God.

In Psalm 63:3, David bellows, "*Your unfailing love is better to me than life itself; how I **praise** [Shâbach] you!*"

"But, Jeff, what about those of us who are quiet worshipers?" Okay. Ask yourself, "What would I have done that day? When God told Joshua to have *all* the people shout? Would I have nervously raised my hand to ask if I could sit this one out? Or would I have reached courageously into the depths of my spirit—beyond my natural personality to my supernatural personality—to stir up the loudest, deepest, most robust shout I could?"

If so, you would have joined the likes of Daniel as he declared, "*I thank and **praise** [Shâbach] you, God of my ancestors, for you have given me wisdom and strength. You have told me what we asked of you and revealed to us what the king demanded*" (Daniel 2:23). I have no doubt. You and I *should* be found responding just as enthusiastically, knowing all that God has done for us. Yet, we often remain relatively unmoved, offering, at best, a golf clap to God.

Daniel offered a robust, nearly involuntary *Shâbach*, I guarantee

---

3 "Josh and the Big Wall!" *VeggieTales Wikia*, www.veggietales.fandom.com/wiki/Josh _and_the_Big_Wall!.

you. For King Nebuchadnezzar had just threatened him and his friends with execution if they didn't interpret his dream by morning light. And yet, God came through, providing Daniel with the interpretation he so desperately needed. Ever been there? When God comes through in an unbelievable way for you or your family? How might you respond? This is the essence of *Shâbach*.

7. *Hâlal* (haw-LAL) (Strong's H1984) – *"To shine, boast, celebrate; to sing, act clamorously foolish."*

According to Bob Sorge, "When asked why the people dance when they worship, a brother in Spain replied, 'I suppose we dance because we cannot fly.'"[4]

Perspective.

Isn't it illuminating, the way we wrestle so fiercely to keep dance out of our Western worship? Other cultures have no problem making the leap, yet predictably, we do what so many believers do. We throw the baby out with the bathwater. Why? Maybe because we've seen too many carnal examples of dance. Sure. Even so, God created dance to bring honor and glory to Himself, and still we find ourselves discarding it in its entirety for fear that it might be abused (or that it might scare away unbelievers). And the devil wins.

What if we uncovered a little word like *Hâlal*, hidden neatly behind some of our English words for praise? Would it change things? Would it spark curiosity?

What if we discovered that *Hâlal* is the root word for the word *hallelujah*?

What if we put fresh eyes to the very last verse in the book of Psalms, specifically the popular Psalm 150:6? It reads, *"Let everything that breathes sing **praises** [Hâlal] to the LORD! Praise the LORD!"* Everything that has breath. Everything that breathes. Every single created being.

Are you breathing?

What if we took a closer look at Psalm 22:23 and realized it reads,

---

4   Bob Sorge, *Exploring Worship third edition* (Kansas City, MO: Oasis House, 2018), page 27.

*"You who fear the LORD, **praise** [Hâlal] Him"* (NIV). Okay. Sounds like an important distinguisher of Jesus followers.

We all know the story of King David, supposedly dancing naked before the Lord, in 2 Samuel 6. (By the way, I don't recommend this. Dancing naked, that is.) Alas, David was not dancing naked. He was doing something even crazier. After recapturing the Ark of the Covenant from the Philistines, he placed himself at the front of the celebratory march, intending to lead all Israel in a massive worship block party back to the temple in Jerusalem, the rightful home of the "presence of God."

On the way, he did something strikingly beautiful, inspired by the customs of the day. You see, in those days, when a nation won a battle, the victors would often place the captured enemy king at the front of their victory parade, strip him naked, and force him to dance foolishly as they marched loudly and proudly all the way home.

Apparently, this sparked an idea.

Maybe it was because it was hot. Maybe it was because he was sick and tired of wearing those cumbersome kingly robes. Or maybe it was because he simply longed to let loose in exuberant praise before the Lord. So he did. The Bible records it this way: *"And David danced before the Lord with **all his might**, wearing a priestly garment [linen ephod]. So David and **all the people** of Israel brought up the Ark of the LORD with shouts of joy and the blowing of rams' horns"* (2 Samuel 6:14–15). (Note: For a thorough layout of biblical passages detailing the importance of all people worshiping God expressively, see the addendum entitled "All the People.")

Incidentally, the linen ephod David wore was typically worn over a priestly linen robe (see also 1 Chronicles 15:27). The problem with David's attire—as sarcastically highlighted by David's wife, Michal, in 2 Samuel 6:20—was that it wasn't the kind of attire a king would normally wear. Metaphorically, by "stripping off" his kingly garments, David had stripped himself of his power. In this way, he exacerbated Michal by temporarily divorcing himself from his kingly authority in order to identify more closely with those under his rule.

The author of the article "No, King David Never Danced Naked Before the Lord" clarifies, "He chose to wear a Levitical robe and then he likely girded it [pulled it up, exposing parts of his legs] so he could dance. Certainly, this act would have been undignified in multiple ways. First, he wasn't dressed as the king. Second, he was dancing like a fool. Third, he probably girded the linen and ephod which was not a priestly thing to do. On every level he was undignified."[5]

Here's the kicker.

As King David danced in such a way few had ever seen, he was communicating something beyond our imagination. Just as the Israelites might have placed an enemy king at the front of their procession to dance foolishly as a captured king, David now placed himself at the front of his Creator's victory parade—dancing wildly, divested of his symbolic royal garments—declaring that he, too, was a captured king. A captured king to the King of kings.

Wow.

Does it freak you out to imagine yourself dancing freely in worship—like David did—in public? Does it make you even the tiniest bit nauseated? Even so, maybe now you could begin to picture yourself and your congregation experimenting in these things as a result of learning about the word *Hâlal*?

Clearly, exuberant praise is biblical. Again and again, we see it in Scripture, even as Psalm 35:18 boldly states, *"I will **praise** [Hâlal] you before all the people."* Yes. Together. Joyfully. In public. Untamed. Unafraid. Unashamed.

Could you? Would you?

Look, I know where you're coming from. It seemed weird to me too. Imagining myself "flailing around" before the Lord in *Hâlal* in church. But then suddenly—thankfully—God flipped my perspective, and I realized it was even weirder to continue to offer Him my stoic response. After all He'd done for me? It was largely hypocritical of me to use religious justification for my refusal to celebrate God's wonderful works exuberantly even while continuing, in many ways, to exuberantly celebrate man's works.

---

5   "No, King David Never Danced Naked Before The Lord," *Dusting Off the Bible*, November 23, 2015, www.dustoffthebible.com/Blog-archive/2015/11/23/no-king -david-never-danced-naked-before-the-lord/.

As a result, I did what every truly hungry follower of Christ must do. I humbled myself and determined to change. To become a doer of God's Word and to lead the people under my care to do the same. In every area. Including this one.

I would begin first by training myself in *Hâlal* in my time alone with God—with the doors closed and the music blasting—even if it killed me. And I did. And it did. And I haven't looked back.

TO SALUTE OR NOT TO SALUTE

Here's a crazy story you have to hear.

It was Wednesday, and we were in the middle of our 2015 week-long worship conference, Pure Worship Institute. This means it was Seven Hebrew Words for *Praise* Experience day, a favorite among our PWI attendees. (*Huge* shout out to Ray Hughes and Brian & Ramey Whalen for introducing me to the seven Hebrew words for *praise* back in the day.)

After the session, I made a beeline for my next breakout. Before starting, I asked a couple of attendees to share a testimony from their Seven Hebrew Word for *Praise* Experience. One young lady in the back shot her hand up. She shared how she'd been in the military, and how difficult it had been for her to participate in the last session.

Now, before I continue, notice again the definition for *Bârak*. It reads *"to kneel, to bow in worship; prostrate, to fall down. (Often translated 'bless'.) **Can also mean to salute**."* One of the things we ask attendees to do, before bowing down, is to *Bârak* the Lord by saluting Him. I love this part, because no matter how naturally expressive a person may be, few have ever saluted God in a worship service before.

Picture it. With a flat hand raised to our brow, we stand there at attention for two to three minutes (which feels like ten). Stiff as a board. Head straight. Shoulders cocked. Eyes fixed. On Jesus. Incredible! Honestly, it's nearly impossible for the hardhearted to remain hard while participating in this simple but transformative act.

The woman went on to explain that it is highly inappropriate for military personnel to salute anyone other than an officer. Ever. And there was no way she was going to act dishonorably and salute Jesus in our little worship service. This was her initial thought.

My mind was racing. I had never heard this before. Makes sense. Sort of. Wait, you mean to tell me, we can salute man, but we can't salute Jesus? King of kings? General of generals? Officer of officers? Hard core.

She went on.

About sixty seconds into the experience, she couldn't take it any longer. Should she? Could she? Would she? Yes. And so with trembling fingers, she slowly began to lift her hand toward her forehead.

No one else seemed to notice.

Then, just as her hand touched her eyebrow, something broke. Wide open. Tears gushed down her face, and her body began to buckle slightly. She stood. Trembling quietly. God was touching her. Profoundly. Beautifully.

FULL CIRCLE

You cannot believe the Holy Spirit revelation that flooded my soul as she recounted her story. You see, I'm typically exasperated by well-meaning pastors who approach me after a service to say, "Jeff, thanks so much for leading an anointed time of worship. You plowed the hard ground with worship in order to make a way for the seed of the Word to be planted!"

> It has always been abundantly clear that our worship does not make a way for the Word as much as the Word makes a way for our worship.

While I genuinely appreciate this sentiment, I do take issue with it, because it encourages the notion that the end goal for every person is simply that they hear the Word of God. But God's end goal for every person is not simply that they hear the Word of God but that they fully engage in loving fellowship with Him, the God of the Word. It has always been abundantly clear that our worship does not make a way for the Word as much as the Word makes a way for our worship.

Which of these two is going to cease upon our arrival in heaven? The preaching of God's Word or musical worship? Certainly, the singular reason we preach the Word of God is so that the hearer might begin to grasp the reason for his existence. Which is, of course, to become a true worshiper of God (in song and in life).

Worship is our *response* to the revelation of the person of God, while the Word is the *revelation* of the person of God that compels us to respond to Him in worship. Simply stated, we cannot worship a God we have no knowledge of.

Okay. What does this have to do with our story of the woman who didn't want to salute? You see, as the woman came face to face with the biblical revelation surrounding *Bârak* (as a result of my preaching), she had a choice to make. Would she respond or not? Would she obey or not? Would she worship or not?

At first, she refused to respond to the revelation (the preaching), but then she changed her mind. (I had understood this much previously: the *revelation* came first—giving her knowledge of the Bible's clear instruction to salute God. Her *response* came second—as a result of her decision to obey the revelation she had just received. Cause, then effect. Revelation, then response. Preaching, then worship.)

That's when the Holy Spirit opened my eyes to the second half of the truth. I began to see that neither I nor the well-meaning pastors were wrong. In fact, we each understood one half of a *both*/and truth. A truth that is cyclical.

Amazingly, by obeying the Word of God—even when she didn't fully understand—the woman opened the door for something extraordinary to happen. Suddenly, the gift of greater understanding (that which goes beyond knowledge) was dropped into her heart—by the Spirit—as a "reward" for her faith-filled obedience. She was now being permitted to understand the *why* behind the importance of her salute to God. Wow.

Take it from Jesus: *"To those who listen to my teaching, more understanding will be given. But for those who are not listening, even what little understanding they have will be taken away from them"* (Mark 4:25).

Fascinating!

Think of it. Had the woman clung to her initial response to keep her hands in her pockets, she would not have received the deeper revelation—and the personal breakthrough—she needed. It was only *after* she acted upon the revelation (in faith) that she was provided with the *why* behind the command to *Bârak*.

Round and round in circles it goes. Like so. God sends His revelation. We respond in obedience. Our response opens our heart to receive even greater revelation from God. (Which opens us to even greater response.) And so on.

Or the other way around. God sends His revelation through His messengers—apostles, pastors, prophets, teachers, and evangelists—but this time, we refuse to respond. Now everything goes quiet. No more revelation from heaven. No more understanding from the Spirit. Even less response from us. (Not because God is mean, but because *we* closed the portal between heaven's truth and our heart.)

Ouch.

Are you beginning to understand the power behind our faith-filled response?

BRINGING IT ALL TO BALANCE

Sorrowfully, responding with "faith-filled" praise is something we've largely lost in our day. We stand by, logically responding—or not responding—in whatever manner our personality or circumstances deem appropriate.

Please note; I have no desire to overemphasize outward expression in musical worship. Rather, I beg us to consider the ways we've underemphasized it to our great detriment. To the point that it has hurt the Church profoundly.

Though God invites us to worship Him with our whole being, some worship with intellect only but not with their hearts. Others enjoy the physical aspects of worship but never engage with their minds. Ironically, this is something I began to understand more completely on my trip to Mozambique during the summer of 2019. Our black African friends at A Palavra informed me plainly that when it comes to worshiping God with heart, soul, mind, and strength, worshiping Him with their minds—intellectually—is the most difficult. The most unnatural. The least culturally fitting. This shocked me, yet it really came as no surprise that heart and strength worship were naturally at the core of who they are.

Question is, should we conclude—since intellectual worship is apparently somewhat incongruent with the Mozambican culture—that they needn't worry about worshiping God with their minds? Of course not. The command to worship God with heart, soul, mind, and strength surely applies to Christ-worshipers from Mozambique, just as it does to people from every other country around the world. They simply need to be encouraged to grow—as do we—in all four expressions of worship, *especially* the ones that aren't culturally naturally.

We understand. Worshiping God with our bodies won't magically transform us into authentic worshipers. Yet, every authentic worshiper does endeavor to worship God with his *whole* being—heart, soul, mind, *and* body.

Incidentally, the Bible tells us in 2 Samuel 6:23 that Michal remained barren over her entire life, while David was treasured by God in spite of his imperfections. Here in lies the choice we have. We can become like David—someone who was passionately sparked to seek after God's own heart—or we can follow in Michal's footsteps and express our utter contempt toward those who sing, dance, and bow freely in worship. Gratefully, worshiping God with our whole being helps to transform a life that was destined for spiritual barrenness into one ordained for eternal fruitfulness.

Chapter Highlights

1. According to Scripture, our bodies do not belong to ourselves, and we will be judged for what we do and don't do with them. Physical worship is a small but important part of disciplining our physical self to submit to the Spirit of God.

2. Worshiping God with our body (and with heart, soul, and mind) is vital to our ever-increasing connection with God and our growth as a full-on follower of Christ. We must cultivate these things in our personal life, in our teams, and in our congregations if we want to be fully spiritually healthy.

3. Just because we weren't raised to worship God with our bodies doesn't mean we're excused from doing so. Likewise, having a more passive personality doesn't give us permission to sit on the sidelines when it comes to lifting our hands, dancing, or kneeling. We only hurt ourselves when we don't do the things God deems "good" for us.

4. Worshiping God with our bodies launches us in ways nothing else can. It's entirely reasonable to say that if God asks us to worship Him with our bodies, He is not trying to hurt us but to help us. When we refuse, we are refusing His kindness and revelation that comes as a result of our obedience.

5. The seven Hebrew words for *praise* provide an invaluable roadmap for equipping ourselves, our teams, and our congregations in the biblical forms of physical worship. Please learn them and teach them often.

Chapter 10

LEADING BY EXAMPLE: THE HINGE PIN OF LEADERSHIP

Lie #10

*"My worship team members are too jaded to become
the authentic leaders God wants them to be."*

This is where we dive deep to uncover the practical things we can implement to help our team members grow into more effective leaders—all with the purpose of letting their authenticity reignite our congregations for sweeter fellowship with God.

In all the years I've been leading worship and teaching at worship conferences, one question from worship team members stands out above the rest. Repeatedly, after presenting a session or two on worship leadership—as we turn to the Q&A portion of our time together—someone raises a hand and says something like this: "I often show up at our church on Sunday morning excited and ready to go. I rehearse with the band. We work out all the kinks. I encourage and unify the team. We pray and seek the Lord. Then we step up on stage to worship God with everything we've got, only to look out at a sea of zombies. Is there anything we can do?"

Been there? Can you picture it?

Hands in pockets. Scattered yawns. Mouths barely moving. Arms folded, or cups of coffee in hand. A few scowls. Some glancing at their watches. Counting down the minutes. To lunch. To freedom.

Of course, some of us are oblivious. We're more concerned about the sound of our voices, the hipness of our clothes, or how we look in the stage lighting than we are about loving people and helping them break through into authentic worship. Still, many of us really do have a genuine heart to be a vehicle for the transforming work of God in people's lives. Desperately. We really long to see the supernatural activation of our church family as they lift up their hearts to God in musical worship. Truly. We really hunger to help people encounter the love of their heavenly Father. Deeply.

We just don't always know how to do it.

We wonder, *Is it arbitrary? Is there a formula?*

Is the key found in some hidden chapter in the Bible?

Is it about talent? Looks? Charisma?

When it comes down to it, what responsibility do we and our teams really have to help people connect with God? Is there anything else we can do to accelerate a genuine connection with God, beyond singing and playing well?

BREAKING DOWN THE WALLS

As you can imagine, I wouldn't have written a book like this if I didn't believe I could give you some extraordinary techniques that will revolutionize your ability to serve people. Techniques that will help you strengthen your teams spiritually and musically. Techniques that will help break down the towering wall between the stage and the seats, revitalizing community. And techniques that will set the stage for increased fellowship between God and His people. Your people. The ones right there in your church. Your spiritual family.

This is our heart's desire, right? To help people grow in God? To be conduits of His presence? To be more than a church attendee?

Great. But first, let's do something about that wall.

What wall?

You know. Sometimes it seems like there's a twenty-mile-high, twenty-foot-thick concrete monstrosity between the stage and seats. A chasm that is even greater than the one described in Luke 16 between the rich man and his servant, Lazarus—between hell and Abraham's bosom. Uncrossable.

We've probably all experienced it from the performer's perspective *and* from the listener's. Everyone feels it. Without saying a word, each person is slowly sinking farther and farther into the folds of their seat. The band is busy doing what they do—rocking out, completely oblivious to the fact that they've lifted off into outer space, leaving myriads of spectators on the earth below. They're off on their own journey, almost as if the very purpose of the "performance" is lost on them altogether—which, clearly, is to take us all on the journey *with* them. Not to leave us sitting alone on the launch pad, staring up in utter astonishment at the power and beauty of their rocket ship.

Ironically, this approach accomplishes exactly the opposite of what most bands were aiming for by building the wall of separation higher and higher, thicker and thicker. All while the rest of us sit in our seats fighting the urge to hold up large homemade signs that say *DON'T FORGET ABOUT US.*

My heart is to help each of us avoid this common occurrence. The one that causes many frustrated churchgoers to wrongly diagnose the problem. They know something is wrong, but they don't know what it is. They know there's a disconnect between themselves and the stage, but they can't quite put their finger on it. Unfortunately, they often decide it's a *performance* issue when, in reality, it's a *community* issue.

ENGAGING YOUR CONGREGATION

Engaging your congregation is one of the main strategies worship leaders can utilize to make sure we're not perpetuating the problem—no longer building high the wall—as we lead. Yet, few of us have a full picture of what this means. On top of that, there are even a few folks out there who become highly agitated when we discuss things the worship leader can do to bring down the wall. As if we have no part to play. And as if leaders have no right to do anything besides worship God from the stage.

I was blown away. Why? Because there's an older video on my YouTube channel (YouTube.com/JeffDeyoPodcast) with 126,000+ views that discusses these "Engaging Your Congregation" strategies. It's called "What to Do When the Congregation Isn't Responding?" and unbeknownst to me, negative statements and brutal brawls have been piling up in the comments below like cow patties in an unkept barnyard. It's true! Some folks went full-on pit-bull attack mode to prove their point, arguing that the type of loving leadership strategies I present in this chapter (and in that video) are unbefitting a godly worship leader.

Check out some of the *actual* negativity:

- *I have a better idea. How about trashing this no good, sorry, pop culture garbage you're trying to pass off as worship, and get something with some depth and meaning, not just what's trendy. Modern worship music NAUSEATES me. It is pure hype. It is worthless. Disgusting!!! UGH!!!*
- *The congregation isn't an "audience". I just worship my heart out when doing worship, if they don't respond, that's their choice. It's not a gig, you don't need to make them respond at all.*
- *You, my friend, are an idiot.*
- *More than likely it is the volume of the music (too loud) .... If we don't know the song and we can't hear the singers singing (to know where you are up to in the lyrics) ... this is the most irritating. I find that when the music is soft it seems to be more inviting for the Holy Spirit to move you ... loud music is distracting. I am sure that the Lord God loves to hear the voices of his saints ... but they are drowned out be music ...*
- *First, I believe that we're commanded to worship. But having a hissy fit about not "responding" to your music or "performance" in a way you deem appropriate is kind of childish. I mean, who are you really looking for a response from, them or God? I think if you'll examine what you're saying, it looks as if you're measuring the success or failure of your worship service on the emotional response you get from the audience.*

Wild stuff, right?

I agree 100 percent that it's not my job as a worship leader to "perform a show" or mandate a response from the congregation so I can feel better about myself. (I'm really hoping that much is obvious.) I considered responding to each of these complaints individually, but decided not to. The bottom line—the thing these fine folks don't grasp—is that leading is about serving. And serving is a good thing. Since when is it childish or idiotic to try to help God's people love God more? The response I'm looking for is not for *me*, so I can feel good about my leadership. It's for *them* so they can be blessed with the beautiful opportunity to engage with God in rich fellowship.

Here's the question: what if we discovered we could greatly increase the possibility of an authentic connection between God and those in our church family by altering some of the ways we lead them? Would we be excited? Would we be willing? Additionally, what if we suddenly realized we were leading in ways—habitually, but unintentionally—that were hindering our congregation in their attempts to connect with God? Would we consider adjusting?

As worship leaders, our first goal should always be to cultivate an atmosphere where God receives all the glory. Absolutely. But second—and nearly as important—we must serve our congregants in the power of the Spirit in order to help them respond rightly to God's love. This also brings *great* glory to our Father!

We can't *make* people worship God, nor should we try. I just wonder, *if we can help people worship God more completely—with authentic, biblically based passion—and stop hindering them in certain ways, shouldn't we?* Isn't this what worship leadership is all about? Loving? Helping? Serving? God *and* God's people?

Of course.

Tell me, if you could address these worship leaders—the ones who are convinced we shouldn't help our church family from the stage—what would *you* tell them? What's *your* advice? Think about it. Take a few minutes and brainstorm. Right now. Jot down a few things in the space below. I bet you have some incredibly relevant thoughts concerning ways you've already fought to help your church family encounter God in order to break through the spiritual numbness that can birth fear and choke out joy.

_____

_____

_____

_____

_____

This is what I long to do. For you. As leaders. To empower you. Encourage you. Educate you. Equip you. To help others. To serve others. Effectively. Passionately. Not by throwing a few trivial, untested ideas your way. No. What I've gathered in this chapter is an arsenal of proven biblical strategies—bathed in love—that will aid you in tearing down that stubborn wall between the stage and the seats *and* between the floor and the heavens. Once and for all!

Ready?

COMPONENT ONE: LEAD BY MODELING

Establishing Kingdom worship culture in your church begins with implementing three main components of leadership: modeling, teaching, and doing. In this chapter, we'll start with the most foundational component, modeling (leading by example). Be careful. You may be tempted to gloss over this one because of its simplicity. But I've found that many, many worship leaders struggle mightily in this area.

Don't get me wrong. They don't mean to. But it often takes a video camera to convince us of our struggles. What? Yes, a video camera. You see, few of us are fully prepared to concede our lack of engagement in worship leadership until we see it for ourselves. On the big screen.

Mirror, Mirror

We've found that videoing our worship teams at NCU is extremely helpful. Also enlightening. Afterward, we settle in with some popcorn (not really) to critique the videos as a team, encouraging serious self-evaluation as well as offering valuable feedback to help each team member grow. This would be a great idea for one of your team nights. But don't forget, the whole purpose and process of giving feedback must be built on a foundation of love.

Paul gives us this foundational leadership advice in 1 Corinthians 11:1. *"Follow my example, as I follow the example of Christ"* (NIV). This is the very least we can expect. Those under our leadership should be able to pattern their overall worship activity after ours and know with certainty that they're moving in the right direction—toward authentic, biblical worship.

This goes for lead pastors as well. In the end, they truly set the tone for the entire congregation—even more so than worship leaders do—since few congregants ever burst through the ceiling their pastor creates with his worship. It probably shouldn't be this way, but only about 10 percent will break through the barriers set up by their leaders. The rest are looking for someone to show them the way. To go before them. To go *with* them.

In the New Living Translation, 1 Corinthians 11:1 uses the word *imitate* instead: *"And you should imitate me, just as I imitate Christ."* Interesting. The thought-provoking question is, "Are we imitatable?"

I know. *Imitatable* is not a word. But the question still looms. Can the people in our congregations—on our teams—imitate our actions, and be confident that they're on the right path toward becoming a true worshiper?

As you might imagine, many of us overlook this idea, because we hold to a skewed perception of ourselves. We see ourselves as we'd like to be seen rather than as we're actually seen. When we finally see ourselves on video, we say things like, "Oh, shoot, I thought I was moving more than that," or "Wow, I guess I did close my eyes the whole time," or "I really did stare down that confidence monitor!"

It's true. We must be willing to first take a look in the mirror if we're going to be more effective in helping others grow as authentic worshipers.

The Lead Worshiper

Interestingly, things began shifting for me when I embraced a slight tweak in the title we traditionally give to those leading the singing in our churches, *worship leader*.

I remember Matt Redman using this "new" term, *lead worshiper*. I loved it. He argued that we could fine-tune our understanding of worship leading by simply flipping the words around. Using the term *lead worshiper* seemed to bring a renewed perspective while encouraging us to remember that we are not simply worshipers, but leaders too.

> Worship leadership is 100 percent worship *and* 100 percent leadership. We cannot separate the two.

Most leaders recognize the weight the word *worship* has as a part of the term *worship leadership*, but many well-meaning worship leaders gloss over the importance of the second word, mainly *leadership*. It's as if we're afraid to discuss the term *leadership* in *worship leadership* for fear that we'll be mistaken for those who are rather unconcerned about the *worship* element. Some fool themselves into believing it's more spiritual to lean on the *worship* element of worship leadership rather than to embrace *both* aspects as spiritual: *worship* and *leadership*.

I like to say it this way: Worship leadership is 100 percent worship *and* 100 percent leadership. We cannot separate the two.

The Grand Canyon

Remember the tour guide analogy? Digging the well? The Grand Canyon? I discussed these things in chapter 1 with the *worshiper* in mind. As noted, fellowship with God in the secret place is absolutely the most important pursuit of our lives, worship leadership aside. From there, though, we can bring things full circle and focus more on the concept of the tour guide as it relates to the *worship leader*. In this sense, *tour guide* is the perfect substitutionary term for *worship leader*.

Again, if being a worship leader means becoming a *tour guide*, what does this imply? Primarily, that we must know the tour. Backwards and forwards. Simply put, if we're going to show people the way to genuine love for God, we must know the way for ourselves. And the only way to know the way is to have walked the path. We simply cannot guide people to a place we've never been. We cannot help people find God in the secret place if we've rarely found Him there ourselves.

With this in mind, we must ask—whether we're a lead singer, an instrumentalist, a sound engineer, or anyone else involved in ministry, "How long has it been since I've been on the tour? By myself? Just me and God?" And then, "Can I honestly say I'm "imitatable"—capable of showing others the way—if I haven't been on the tour myself? Regularly? Recently?"

Remember, I'm not trying to discourage you in any way. I'm simply stating the facts. *We just can't take people where we haven't been.* And if we want to be a part of the solution as leaders—to be a part of tearing down the walls between the stage and the seats and between the people and their God—we must understand how leadership works. We hurt our church family (and become less effective as leaders) when we prioritize the public tour over the private tour. Conversely, we greatly empower our church family (and become more effective as leaders) when we prioritize our First Love.

Oh, Happy Day

One of my great frustrations is a leader who expects more of their congregation than they do of themselves. Ever seen this? The worship leader steps up to the microphone at the end of the song and shouts, "Let's give the Lord a huge shout of praise." Then as the people pour their hearts out with loud cries, he quietly bows his head and tunes his guitar. Oh, baby, this is maddening. Why? Because it's a situation that is abusive in two important ways: 1) The purpose of the shout has been undermined, because—truth be told—the command to shout was never about the Lord, but about a few seconds the worship leader needed to transition to the next song, and 2) The worship leader has just asked the congregation to do something he's unwilling to do himself, and this grossly violates a foundational principle of leadership; leading by example.

Remember the Jesus Culture song "Happy Day" from the 2008 album *Your Love Never Fails*? The one Kim Walker sang? I loved it! Especially since so many worship bands have largely stopped writing and recording celebratory worship songs.

Thing is, there's nothing worse for a congregation than trying to sing "Happy Day" while staring at a worship leader who has that angst-like, prune-faced worship-leader look. Right? Can you see it? Eyes scrunched. Cheeks clenched. Eyebrows furrowed. Borderline angry. All while singing about the wonderful joy of our sins being washed away and our lives being forever changed!

I'm convinced we're not bothered by this, because we still don't fully grasp the wonder of our *own* sins being forgiven. I mean, if we really knew what it meant for our sins to be forgiven—for our souls to be cleansed by the blood of Jesus, for our shame to be thrown into the sea of forgetfulness—wouldn't we sing and lead these lyrics from a totally different place?

Instead, we focus more on the music delivery than the heart. Often completely unaware that our face is communicating something opposite from the lyrics.

I'm telling you, it would be next to impossible to pry that genuine, childlike grin off our sweaty little faces if we really understood. All that Jesus stands for. All that Jesus has done. All that's before us when He finally returns. Smiles would abound. Not because we've finally mastered our leadership skills and by plastering a gloriously religious smirk on our faces. No. Because we are truly, insanely grateful for the unfathomable mercy and grace of our God. We finally get it. It's not lost on us. And, as a result, that oh-so-happy smile is pinned neatly between our ears, even as we sing these profound words.

What about the song "I Am Free," from the 2010 Desperation Band album, *From the Rooftops*? How many worship leaders have you seen sing this one standing still—often safely behind a mic stand—all while blasting lyrics that boldly declare our passionate desire to run and dance in worship. Huh? This song was sung over and over in congregations, but peculiarly, very few people were running and dancing. Few in the congregation and few on the stage.

Seem odd?

Maybe. Maybe not.

"But Jeff, we're running and dancing in our hearts."

Okay. It's a metaphor, then? I think it's more than that. I'd play along, except these expressions have long been a part of the biblical norm in worship for true believers. As we've discussed, we find dancing—among other places in the Bible—in Psalm 149 and 150, and we find running as a beautiful example of the way the prodigal son's father—a type of heavenly Father—broke social norms to express his deep love for his son.

Jesus Culture's 2018 single, "Freedom" sung by Kim Walker, is another profound example. There is a line hidden in the pre-chorus that is a deeply profound, declaratory call to action—but I wonder, do we even know what it means? What it means to dance like the weight has been lifted? Are we really free? Or are we still carrying the weight? Is it real? Or is it only words? Can we sincerely ask our congregations to sing songs with lyrics that invite them to dance, run, and shout if we refuse to lead the way from the stage? (Not only the singers, but the musicians as well?)

> Can we sincerely ask our congregations to sing songs with lyrics that invite them to dance, run, and shout if we refuse to lead the way from the stage?

As leaders, I beg us to be transparent. Rarely should we be found leading these types of songs—singing about the freedom we have to worship with dance—when we are truly *not* free to dance. When running, shouting, and dancing are the furthest things from our minds as we lead these songs. And when running, shouting, and dancing are not actually a part of how we seek the Lord behind closed doors.

Let's be real. It's not that we *really* believe these activities are metaphorical. It's that we believe the enemy's lie that these expressions are only for a few overly extravagant people. All the while, the issue is one (or all) of three possibilities: 1) We are spiritually immature (insecure) in our walk with God, 2) We haven't taken the time to cultivate this type of worship in our alone time with God, or 3) We truly haven't grasped the incredible wonder of the miracle of Jesus' saving blood.

You pick.

We grow more frustrated with our congregations, wondering why they won't respond. Wondering why they simply stare back at us with coffee cups in hand and little to no passion in musical worship. All the while, we refuse to ask ourselves why we expect our church family to respond in ways we refuse to respond ourselves. This is poor Christ-followership and poor worship leadership, and it will have to change if we're going to see the kind of transformation in our churches we desire.

Operating with Kingdom Authority

The devil has done a number on us musicians.

Truth is, if we're going to become the leaders God has called us to be…if we're going to serve our congregations and help them encounter God through musical worship…if we're going to love them as we lead them—we must throw off our own insecurities and embrace who we are in Christ. This is a desperately needed paradigm shift in the Church today. Too many of us are attempting to lead out of who *we* are—our talent, our looks, our own leadership prowess—rather than leading out of who *Christ* is within us. My friend and mentor Chuck Porta talks about this in the way leaders often lead out of their souls (who they are) rather than out of their spirit (Christ in them).

Why do I bring this up? Because I meet many worship leaders who are naturally timid. They often defend their timid leadership, pointing to their natural personality. The world has told them, "Embrace who you are. Be you. And don't be ashamed to be you. Whatever your limitations, embrace them. It's who you are."

Of course, this is a mixed message. In some ways, it's good advice. But at the same time, if we fully embrace this ideology, we miss the whole point of Christ living in us. Christ didn't come to affirm who we are. He came to instill within us the person of Himself, who He is. His personality.

This is a game-changer.

And yet, we must buy into this biblical thinking—by faith—if it is to produce results.

What do I mean? Well, if you believe your leadership will always be timid because you're a naturally timid person, there's nothing we can do to change that fact. But if you embrace what God says about you—that you are a son/daughter of the King and an overcomer who is strong in weakness—then you'll live out of a revitalized Kingdom personality that will guide you powerfully as a leader. Congratulations. You're now tapped into a newfound ability to lead, from Christ's strength rather than from your weakness.

Curiously, I find that people assume I'm an expressive worship leader as a result of my personality—inferring that those of us who are exuberant in worship on stage are driven mostly by emotion and natural temperament—thus excusing themselves to remain docile. But this isn't the case. Worship expression is not driven by *personality* as much as it is by *revelation*. The greater the revelation we have of Christ, the greater our response will be. Inward and outward. This is how God made us.

Question: Is the Spirit of Christ alive in you? Yes. Of course. Do you believe it? If so, you can lead from the same position of spiritual authority as Jesus. Jesus knew who He was. Do you?

> *Then Jesus went to Capernaum, a town in Galilee, and taught there in the synagogue every Sabbath day. There, too, the people were amazed at his teaching, for he spoke with **authority**. Once when he was in the synagogue, a man possessed by a demon—an evil spirit—cried out, shouting, "Go away! Why are you interfering with us, Jesus of Nazareth? Have you come to destroy us? I know who you are—the Holy One of God!" But Jesus reprimanded him. "Be quiet! Come out of the man," he ordered. At that, the demon threw the man to the floor as the crowd watched; then it came out of him without hurting him further. Amazed, the people exclaimed, "What **authority** and power this man's words possess! Even evil spirits obey him, and they flee at his command!" The news about Jesus spread through every village in the entire region.* (Luke 4:31–37)

I find it interesting that the Jewish people were so impressed with Jesus' leadership acumen when there were plenty of other religious-leader types around who were scratching and clawing for attention. Why all the marveling at Jesus?

"Because he was *Jesus*," you say.

Yes. But what was it about Jesus that made Him so different? Besides the fact that He was God? What was it about this God-man, Jesus, that made Him different from the everyday leader?

The Scripture above provides the obvious answer: *authority*.

Jesus carried Himself oh-so-very-differently from your average Pharisee or Sadducee. Why? Because He really knew who He was. He was operating out of Sonship rather than out of performance. He was leading from a place of God-security rather than self-insecurity. The people were amazed at the way He walked. At the way He talked. To the demons. To the sinners. To the governors. And to the governed. He was different. He was bold. But He was not arrogant. He was humble. But He was strong. He was a respectful listener and a profound communicator.

Jesus is calling us to lead from this same place. Out of *His* authority. Not because we're great, but because He is great within us. Not because of self-confidence, but because of God-confidence.

This type of shift in our thinking transforms our worship leadership. We all know there are days when we don't feel "worthy" to lead. We all know there are days when we feel intimidated or insecure or weak. Or just plain old exhausted. We all know there are days when we don't feel like leading at all.

But it doesn't matter how we feel. It doesn't matter if we're having a good day or a lousy one. We must stop leading out of who *we* are. Yes, Jesus is special, but He boldly invites us to lead out of who *He* is within us. From *His* strength. Because we're part of *His* family. *His* sons and daughters. Grafted in. Carrying *His* DNA. Loved and forgiven. Cherished and empowered.

Jesus says, "Look, I have given you **authority** over all the power of the enemy" (Luke 10:19). And because we now embody *His* authority, we can become the lead worshipers we were meant to be. Standing tall when we feel two feet high. Bringing light to the darkness when we feel the darkness surrounding us. Producing an atmosphere where chains are broken, prison doors are opened, dry bones are awakened, and spiritual captives embrace true freedom. All because of His supernatural power and authority living within us.

Body Language Rules

As we attempt to model what it looks like to worship God—to lead by example—we can't afford to underestimate the power of body language. Studies tell us that body language—non-verbal communication—is hands down the most powerful form of communication there is. Actions always speak louder than words. Truth is, our body language

LEADING BY EXAMPLE ◆ 221

screams ten times louder than our words ever could. Even in worship. Definitely in worship.

Consider this old adage, often attributed to Ralph Waldo Emerson: "What you do speaks so loud that I cannot hear what you say." Maybe we could alter it a bit for our purposes: "How you live [and lead] speaks so loudly that I can barely make out the lyrics of your song."

Gulp.

If this is truly the case, why do we so often miss this in worship leadership?

Can you see it? The overworked worship leader steps guardedly to the platform for the opening of the six a.m. Easter Sunday sunrise service. He searches for the mic. It's not on the stand. There's an awkward silence. He appears irritated. Someone runs up with a mic. He pauses. He speaks. But we hear only the faint echo of a voice unamplified. He tries again, his fist grasping the trunk of the microphone more tightly than usual. The mic bursts onto the scene with a loud ear-piercing squeal. Everyone reels. He attempts to regain his composure. His face tells the story. How many times does he have to endure this incompetence? How is he supposed to lead worship with these types of technical faux pas? He continues in a garbled monotone with a defeated countenance, "Welcome to God's house on this wonderful Resurrection Sunday, saints. This is the day the Lord hath made. Let us rejoice and be glad in it. Amen."

And the music begins.

Been there? I understand.

But his body language said so much that it virtually nullified the words he spoke. Powerful words, indeed! And the congregation couldn't receive most of what he said for the dead pan expression on his face.

Hear me out on the importance of body language.

What if one day an Olympic-gold-medalist swimmer shared with you the most important aspect of effective swimming—proper arm movement. You had honestly been looking for ways to improve, and yet you decided to ignore her advice, instead focusing, as usual, on proper foot movement alone. You rolled your eyes sarcastically, citing the ridiculous advice given to you by this "quasi-professional swimmer"—the one who clearly doesn't understand *today's* swimmer. Still, you remained greatly frustrated with your inability to succeed as a competitive swimmer.

It sounds ridiculous, I know, but this is exactly what many worship leaders do. They've heard about the power of body language. In high school speech class, no less. They've experienced the challenges of leading a congregation without utilizing passionate body language (and even watched themselves lead this way on video).

> Yes, it's all about the heart, but the heart communicates through the mouth and the body.

They've even seen others lead with good body language who continue to see results. Yet they still refuse to change.

Yes, it's all about the heart, but the heart communicates through the mouth and the body. We must grasp this. Everything we do while we lead communicates. Everything. Especially our bodies. (Remember chapter 9? Remember the way Jesus communicated with His body?) You see, I began to discover that physical expression in worship involves more than randomly waving my arms and legs toward God. It is more connected to our hearts than I thought.

Are there exceptions we can cite? Artists who still seem to be successful with heads bowed and bodies frozen behind a microphone stand? Sure. But they're one in a million. And they're typically so insanely gifted that no amount of poor stage presence could derail them. This is not me. This is not you. This is the extreme exception, and we mustn't base our hopes for connection with our congregation on those types of odds. Especially if we love them. Especially if we love God.

Eyes Wide Open

Before I was in Sonicflood, I was in the band Zilch. Believe it or not, we opened for the band Third Day one night. Ironically, though, they weren't the headliners. Nope. Can you guess who was? None other than MC Hammer.

Crazy, right? Can't touch this.

That night, I remember having a riveting conversation with Third Day's production manager, Denny Keitzman, who was also our manager. He was describing a technique that lead singer Mac Powell often used to keep a very large crowd engaged from front to back. Mac would lift his eyes and head above the crowd, glancing to the back of the venue—as we might expect—but then he would do just the opposite as well, engaging with individual people up near the front. He would do so briefly but intentionally. His eyes would float around, smiling at different attendees throughout the evening, communicating the love of Christ to one person at a time.

Somehow, almost supernaturally, the continual ebb and flow between engaging the crowd as a whole—the macro—and engaging them as individuals—the micro—seemed to keep everyone joined in community, all focused on worshiping God with songs like "Agnus Dei," "Your Love Oh Lord," and "God of Wonders."

I never forgot this, and I began to incorporate it into my own worship leading, rooted in a love for God's people and a passion to encourage everyone to join together in exalting God.

Even so, many find it odd that we would consider opening our eyes to engage with congregants during *worship*. At first glance (no pun intended), it seems this technique might be counterintuitive—especially if our goal is authentic worship. But remember my heartfelt recommendation from a few pages back—that we must continue to build our worship leadership on the foundation of "loving God *and* loving people"? Well, this is one area where we must pay close attention.

Have you ever noticed the way many instrumentalists hang their heads while on the stage, looking highly uncomfortable? Vocalists do this too. Especially while waiting for that verse two lyric to come back around during an instrumental break.

Have you also noticed the way this uncomfortableness is extremely catching in the congregation? You know what I mean. Often, when the band on stage looks uncomfortable, it makes everyone else feel uncomfortable too. Much of this is an easy fix. Maybe the band simply needs to learn the songs better so they can look up from their instruments more often, displaying a more inviting appearance.

Still, it's reasonable to believe it goes a little deeper than that. Often, eyes downcast signifies something else. Insecurity. Or paralyzing stage fright. And while these things can seem relatively harmless, they can become a real hinderance in encouraging others to seek the Lord. That's right. Our eyes are one of our greatest assets we have for communicating our genuine love for God. And for others. Especially while mouths and hands are busy doing the practical work of music making.

Our eyes communicate powerfully—for good and for bad. Consequently, we must become more aware of exactly what they're communicating so we can use this power for good. Believe it or not, keeping our eyes closed during most of the worship set makes us appear detached. Disengaged. Uncaring. Even untouchable. Or possibly just too busy with God to bother with the "common folk."

This is important, especially as we desire to break down the towering wall between us and the congregation. In contrast, opening our eyes to spread the love of Jesus helps keep the "family" unified—that is, unified on giving all the glory to God! Plus, a genuine glance of authentic love toward your congregation can be exactly what is needed to encourage them in expressing their authentic love toward their God.

I regularly assign my worship leaders at NCU the task of leading in our classes by themselves. Often, as a particular student finishes, I'll ask them to sing the chorus or bridge one more time. But this time around I'll direct them to put on an infectious smile while keeping their eyes open—maybe even in an exaggerated way. The results are incredible! After doing something this simple, the transformation is palpable. I've watched as a student's engaging eyes and pleasant smiles transformed their worship leadership so drastically in sixty seconds that their peers burst into a loving ovation.

Side note: If you're suddenly becoming agreeable to this idea—which I trust you are—you must promise to never take things to the opposite extreme. Whatever you do, please resist the temptation to smile nonstop or to stare down your now extremely uncomfortable congregants. There's a balance needed for using your eyes and smiles in worship leadership. I call it "ebb and flow." Simply close your eyes at times, and make sure you're indeed connecting with God relationally, and then come back up for air so you can lovingly invite the congregation to go with you as everyone pursues the Father together. Back and forth. In and out. Fully alive to God and fully engaged with His people.

Good Performance Is Good

When I arrived at NCU in the winter of 2010, our chapels were already vibrant. Yet the worship leadership had a very distinct posture—a culture. It was as if someone had said without saying, "Everyone who steps onto this platform had better be very, very careful. Careful not to do anything to draw attention to themselves. For fear of infuriating God and ruining everything."

I get it. We've all seen too many attention-seeking singers, instrumentalists, and worship leaders, and our natural response is to draw back violently. As a result, we focus erroneously on doing the extreme opposite of our iniquitous spotlight-lovers. And so we do—again—what the body of Christ has been so good at. For centuries. Throw the baby out with the bathwater. Seriously. We're beyond experts.

Instead of recognizing that "performance" isn't inherently bad, we allow the devil to deceive us into disavowing *all* performance. But we must come to terms with the real truth: bad performance is bad, and good performance is good.

We attend musical and sports performances religiously. We applaud and relish them sincerely. We have performance degrees and performance halls. And performance plays an important role in nearly every career, from business management, to sports, to sales, to medicine, to the arts.

Performance. It can be good. It can be bad.

But what makes it bad? Pride? Insecurity? Yep. Both.

And yet, coupled with humility, good performance is genuinely heart-warming. Anointed. Moving. Life transforming. Kingdom purposed. Good.

We've seen both good performances and bad performances. And we can tell the difference. Easily. Yet, at some point in our past, someone somewhere pointed a finger in our face and told us we had better stop drawing attention to ourselves in worship in an attempt to steal the glory of God. From that day forward, our general assumption has been that "performance" in worship leads to God's fiery judgment raining down upon us.

But what if the correct response to "bad performances" isn't simply attempting to expel *all* performances, but is to focus on redeeming each and every performance for the glory of God?

Spiritual Posture Communicates

As with all things, from facial expressions to clothing, our posture on stage communicates. Did you know you have a spiritual posture? The question is, what is yours—what is mine—communicating?

Wild story alert.

There was a time, back in the day, when some of my band members came to me to report something terribly disturbing. They needed me to be aware that there were a growing number of times when young women would proposition them immediately following our nights of worship.

What?

Here we were, travelling to a town somewhere far from home. We'd all been practicing and praying. We were all focused on the transformation we hoped would result from our time of community worship, and then, with complete disregard to the supernatural work at hand, a few young ladies attempted to seduce my band members.

How could this be?

What should we do?

What *would* we do?

And then this ridiculous thought came into my mind: *How come I never get propositioned?*

Oh my. Hold on. I didn't mean to think that. I didn't mean to think that at all.

Yes, yes, I know. I'm far too "spiritual" to have thoughts like that. Yikes.

But I was just processing the *whys*. Why was this happening? Why are these girls chasing after my band mates? And not me? I thought about it. After all the years of touring, I had never personally been approached in this manner. Never. So…were my band guys doing something wrong? Was I doing something right?

I pondered. Was I ugly? Old? Unattractive? Did I smell? Eeeeek! Then it hit me.

I've always carried myself in a certain way. I've always worn my wedding ring loudly and proudly. I've always talked about my wife and my children with clear and passionate affection. I've often showed pictures of my family from stage. And I've never put myself in a position to bring into question my love or commitment to them. I give only side hugs—carefully. I never communicate extra "intentions" with my eyes. And I never allow myself to be alone with anyone of the opposite sex.

I have determined to posture myself on and off the stage in a way that subtly but clearly communicates that I am completely off limits when it comes to potential sexual or emotional relational encounters.

There's a posture we can hold on stage that says, "I'm taken." There's also a posture we can hold on stage that says, "I'm available." Let's be real. You know what I'm talking about. There's that little glance we can throw across a room to someone that says a million things. Maybe, "Hey, girl. I love Jesus, and so do you. You are fearfully and wonderfully made, and it would be fun to discover whether or not you'd be interested in me, even though I'm mostly unavailable. But still, it'd be nice to know that I could have you if I wanted you."

Yikes.

Point is, posture communicates. Our physical posture *and* our spiritual posture. People are constantly reading us. Our intentions. Our purposes. Our goals. Our authenticity.

Wow. That seems pretty daunting for us as leaders. So what's the answer? Run and hide for fear of failure? Poke our heads in the sand, completely overwhelmed? Look the other way and pretend the issues don't exist?

No.

Simple. Look Jesus straight in the eyes and intentionally cultivate a deeper, more genuine relationship with Him, so we can serve others out of purity and holiness. Embrace the Spirit of self-control during those tempting moments, and determine to be faithful and above board in everything you do. In this way, we will grow increasingly in our ability to engage those under our leadership. To carry ourselves with humility. To minister with spiritual heads held high. To sing with genuine joy on our faces. And to lead with godly love and affection in our hearts.

Chapter Highlights

1. Some leaders will be tempted to skip this chapter, believing they've got it all down. But this is one of the most overlooked and under-accomplished forms of leadership there is, especially as it concerns worship in our churches. Without realizing it, we often expect a level of response from our congregation that we're not giving ourselves. This must change.

2. Worship leadership is so much more than worshiping God on a stage. This is not your time with God. This is not your secret place. This is your moment to serve the body by leading them to encounter God for themselves.

3. We tend to lead out of who we are rather than out of who Christ is in us. Shifting our perspective in this area will help us step into the boldness and authority we have in Jesus, amping up the effectiveness of our leadership, even if our natural personality is more reserved.

4. Body language in leadership is *huge.* If you sing the words but employ a bland tone or posture, no one is going to hear what you're saying or singing. Actions always speak louder than words.

5. Your eyes communicate more than we can possibly imagine. Worshiping God on a stage with our eyes closed 90 percent of the time significantly undermines our ability to build community and inspire others to worship God passionately.

Section Three

INSTILLING THE HEART OF PURE WORSHIP INTO YOUR CONGREGATION

Chapter 11

EMPOWERING YOUR CONGREGATION, ONE WEEK AT A TIME

Lie #11

"That could never become a part of our normal church culture."

One ordinary Wednesday night, in the middle of leading worship for the youth of Bethel's Rock Church, Lauren Freitag was led by the Spirit to ask the students to kneel. (Lauren is one of many passionate worship-leading students who studied at NCU.) She was leading the song "Nothing Else" by Cody Carnes and had just landed on a spontaneous moment when she suddenly felt the Spirit's nudge. But there was a problem. She was conflicted by the instructions He had whispered. What if it doesn't go well? What if people complain? What if no one responds?

These days, few adults—let alone students—find themselves kneeling in a typical worship service. It's just too awkward, I suppose. Plus, high school students are often seemingly more responsive to up-tempo tunes where they can jump around and have fun. We've been instructed many times to avoid spending too much time "soaking" in God's presence with students for fear that their short attention spans wouldn't survive.

Lauren was nervous.

Even so, the direction from God's Spirit was too strong. In fact, she explained to me after class one day that it was one of the most powerful unctions she'd ever sensed while leading worship. Thankfully, in that moment, she remembered our Worship Leading class and how we often pressed the issue of listening to the Spirit in the middle of a worship set. She also remembered our discussions about the importance of "teaching-and-doing moments" and how they empower people to go deeper.

The possibilities ran through her mind. She knew it wasn't a question of whether she wanted to serve these students well or whether she wanted to obey the Lord's instructions. But how? Maybe her main responsibility was only to model worship. Nothing more. But her heart told her otherwise.

In spite of her almost-crippling fear, she decided to step out in faith. She took a breath and began quietly teaching the students about *why* we kneel before the Lord. Straight from Psalm 95:6–7. Just like we learned in class. A hush came over the room. *"Come, let us worship and bow down. Let us kneel before the Lord our maker, for he is our God. We are the people he watches over, the flock under his care."* She also shared about the Hebrew word for *praise*, *Bârak*, which means "to kneel, to bow in worship; prostrate, to fall down." Finally, she invited every student and leader in that room to kneel. Together. Before the Lord their God.

To her astonishment, they did.

After a few minutes, they returned softly to singing the chorus of "Nothing Else." Yet, this time, it was from a posture of deep humility, accentuated by their reverent physical posture.

Then something broke. In her and in them. Many students were weeping on the floor. So was Lauren. Tears rolled down her face as she observed students being touched lovingly by the Lord, all as a result of a simple teaching-and-doing moment led by the Spirit. She couldn't help but sense God's undeniable confirmation on her calling to lead others in musical worship.

But wait.

What happened?

Could it be this simple? Could a tiny posture shift really make way for a colossal perspective shift? The song wasn't different. The band wasn't different. The room itself didn't change. The leadership didn't change. The only variation came in two parts, as this humble, faith-filled leader beckoned her fellow worshipers to 1) *hear* the Word and 2) respond by *doing* the Word. Just that simple.

Think of it.

Kneeling isn't a terribly demanding action, as physical acts go (except for those with serious knee troubles, of course). It's rather a routine posture. We kneel for many reasons. To pick things up. To reach under the bed. To tie our shoes. Yet, somehow, in worship, it's like we think we're asking people to scale Mount Everest when we ask them to kneel. And still, it's not us who's asking. It's God. Why? Because He knows He created us to respond physically to Him in worship (in addition to spiritually, mentally, relationally, etc.). He literally coded these essential actions into our DNA. And He—above all others—knows the difference a simple change in physical posture can make to help accentuate a spiritual posture.

This was the first time Lauren had stepped out to lead a teaching-and-doing moment outside of class. Afterward, she spoke to a few mentors and expressed her newfound passion to leave the old way of leading worship behind—the way of running up on stage, singing a couple verses, a chorus, and a bridge as usual, and then making a quick transition to the message. Kind of going through the motions. Mechanical.

I mean, seriously. If teaching congregants all that the Word says about worship *and* then inviting them to do what it says can inspire these types of cataclysmic paradigm shifts in people, she was determined to make incorporating teaching-and-doing moments her forever approach. Her new norm in leadership.

Sing. Teach the Word. Do the Word. Sing some more. Then sit back and watch God do what only He can do.

Then do it again.

THERE'S MORE TO LEADERSHIP

Many worship leaders mistakenly believe the only role they play in leading worship on a stage is worshiping God from their heart. Remember the big YouTube controversy I shared from chapter 9 concerning my popular/not-so-popular video "What to Do When the Congregation Isn't Responding?" Many are strangely offended by the idea that we could ever play a significant role in worship leadership beyond simply worshiping God.

Even so, while I believe becoming a true worshiper is the most important foundational element in worship leadership, this is just the beginning. Truthfully, becoming an authentic worshiper represents only what it takes to pour the concrete to secure the footers as a Kingdom worship leader. Yes, this is the rock-solid foundation upon which we must build, but there's considerably more to effective worship leadership than simply pouring a foundation—for singers and instrumentalists alike. We must begin to build upon it.

> Every worship leader must enjoy worshiping God, but not every person who enjoys worshiping God qualifies as a worship leader.

If becoming an authentic worshiper was the only qualifier of an effective worship leader, anyone could lead worship, for we would simply employ worshipers. But this is like saying the only qualifier to piloting a plane is loving to fly. Clearly there's much more to flying than enjoying the view. And there's much more to worship leadership than enjoying God alone. Hear me: Every worship leader must enjoy worshiping God, but not every person who enjoys worshiping God qualifies as a worship leader.

For instance, take this classic lead pastor/worship leader struggle.

SERVING IS WORSHIP, TOO

My good friend, who is a lead pastor, once hit me up for some advice on this very topic. He spoke of his continuous wrestlings with his worship pastor of three years. Week after week, he would sit down with him, attempting to find different ways to communicate the importance of leading the congregation into a balanced worshipful expression toward God. Sunday after Sunday, the young, well-meaning worship pastor would stand against his pastor's wishes by opening the service with a slow song.

Now, whether you agree on opening the service with an up-tempo song each week or not, most people agree that a worship leader should do his or her best to uphold the vision of their lead pastor. Not blindly or without consideration of biblical congruency, but prayerfully and with a sincere trust that God is able to lead the lead pastor.

My friend explained again and again that he wanted to give their congregation the opportunity to praise God with enthusiasm and joy *before* asking them to move into a deeper, more intimate type of expression (similar to the way people in King David's time would come through the outer courts before stepping into the inner courts.)

Finally, it all came to a head one day as they were meeting for the umpteenth time. His worship pastor blurted out these curious words: "My ministry is to God, not to people."

Okay, now we're getting somewhere. The truth of his frustrations finally came tumbling out in a way that could be understood. Honestly, I find his heart on the topic to be somewhat inspirational. Yet fundamentally flawed. Why? Because he is wrong. Or better stated, because he's only half right.

It's certainly true that our *first* ministry is to God. Period. We have established this unbending truth again and again in this book, and nothing we add from this point should be seen as an attack on this idea. However, our ministry to God doesn't begin on a stage. It begins in the secret place where intimacy is cultivated between us and God. Then its effects flow out in the public place, helping us serve our congregations by propelling them into intimacy with God just the same.

You know the problem, don't you? My friend's worship pastor has likely stood by in frustration while other worship leaders shined in the light of their own glory—building their own ministries—while appearing to build God's Kingdom. This is bad. Very bad. But he's also likely concerned that, by starting with an up-tempo song, we're playing to the desires of man and wasting precious time that could be used to bring our people into deeper depths of true worship.

The first mistake my friend's worship pastor made is assuming the fix for "showmanship" is to get our focus off leading people while leading worship. But this idea isn't found in Scripture. God never tells us to stop leading. He simply tells us—very pointedly—to stop leading from a place of hypocrisy. The focus, therefore, is not to stop leading others boldly, but to make sure we are leading ourselves off the stage, even as we attempt to lead others on the stage.

The second—and more egregious—mistake my friend's worship leader made is holding to the idea that up-tempo music is less spiritual than slow "soaking" songs. Of course, it doesn't matter when we do them in our set, but removing up-tempo praise songs entirely from our church services is one of the biggest mistakes we're making in musical worship today. Up-tempo songs are much more difficult to "fake" our way through than slow songs, and they tend to expose our complacency toward God as we struggle for motivation to respond enthusiastically. When we remove these songs from our services, we effectively remove the joy of the Lord from our services.

No doubt, we desperately need our worship leaders to be God-lovers, but we also need our worship leaders to be people-lovers. Helpers, servants, guides, harvesters, etc. We must remember that worship leadership is 100 percent worship and 100 percent leadership. And of course, great leadership starts with great servitude. Servants serve God by serving and loving people—and this blesses and honors God and fulfills a significant part of His calling for our lives.

Ironically, the Bible establishes this fact in Matthew 25:40: *"When you did it to one of the least of these my brothers and sisters, you were doing it to me."* So, yes, even our attempt to serve those in our congregations by giving them a cup of cold water for their thirsty souls equates to ministry to God.

Let me say, if your ministry is only to God, you should seriously consider leaving the planet as quickly as possible, because there's no longer any real reason for you to be here. While on earth, we know all of our earthly ministry is for God, divided into two parts: love for God and love for people. As always, our service to people in the public place is proof of our love for God in the secret place.

This brings us to the second component of leadership.

COMPONENT TWO: LEAD BY TEACHING

As you might guess, I'm going to suggest that our role as worship leaders is much more important than some think. Should it be this way? Maybe. Maybe not. But it is. People need us to lead them, show them the ropes, exhort them, correct them, inspire them, and remind them over and over again *who* it is we worship and *why* it is we worship.

If our first step is to lead by modeling (discussed in chapter 10), step two is to lead by teaching. This is results-producing leadership at its very best. We simply cannot lead people effectively if we refuse to teach them effectively. Proverbs 9:9 instructs, *"Instruct the wise, and they will be wiser. Teach the righteous, and they will learn even more."*

Some might tell us to simply shut up and sing, discouraging worship leaders from opening their mouths to teach, but we must continue to do what we can to help people understand the beauty of *why* we worship.

At the same time, we must understand there's a critical balance. Our role is *not* to take over the pulpit, but to lovingly build a bridge between the truth of God's Word and the worship of God's people in order to repeatedly highlight the real reasons for our worship.

> It stands to reason that we as leaders must do everything we can to foster an environment primed for God-given revelation.

Sadly, many churchgoers are ignorant of what God desires and requires from them in worship, because they're not studying their Bibles. Should this be the case? No. But it is. As a result, a vital part of our role as worship leaders is to present the Word of God to help reawaken God's people toward passionate friendship with Him.

I spoke of this in my first book, *Awakening Pure Worship*, but it bears repeating: Worship is always a response to a revelation. In essence, our worship toward God always shows up in the form of a response, in life or in song, to God's revelation of Himself through His Word or through His people. If this is true—that the worshiper is aided greatly in his ability to respond to God as a result of supernatural revelation given by God—it stands to reason that we as leaders must do everything we can to foster an environment primed for God-given revelation.

This is where some are tempted to jump ship.

What they hear me saying is *we should attempt to manipulate the revelation of God in order to manipulate the response of the worshiper.* But that's not what I'm saying at all. I'm simply suggesting that we have a profound responsibility to use all of our God-given resources—primarily the Word of God—to bring forth the truth of God in order to inspire the people of God to worship God. We are His hands and feet. I don't fully understand why, but God has chosen to use us—all believers, that is—as His conduits to bring forth His revelation in order to help each of us see Him more clearly.

The question is, are we prepared to be His conduits?

Fifty-Two Sundays to a Different Congregation

Matt Redman writes in his book *The Heart of Worship Files,* "Too often, when I lead worship, I'm driven to get a response out of the people. I want to see results. But, I should be far more interested in what lies behind these responses (or lack of them). Before we become consumed with how people are responding, it's good to be mindful of what they're responding to. Let's bring songs so full of our glorious Jesus that they ignite a fresh fire and a heart-filled response from those who sing them."[1]

This is perfect. But it's only part of our responsibility.

Yes, we must analyze our songs vigorously to ensure they're chock-full of God's supernatural truth, yet we must also bear in mind the opportunity we have to increase our impact ten times over. Can you comprehend the difference in your church between fifty-two Sundays that include a short scriptural teaching on musical worship and fifty-two Sundays without one? Would it make a difference?

You'd better believe it!

This is exactly what I'm asking you to do as a leader. Teach your people what the Word of God says about worship and about God's character with the purpose of increasing their ability to respond authentically and compellingly toward Him. Each and every week. Fifty-two Sundays a year. With one little 60- to 120-second biblical teaching or analogy that has the supernatural power to ignite a fire of response from

---

1 Matt Redman, *The Heart of Worship Files* (Ventura, CA: Regal Books, 2003), page 14.

your congregation. Why? Because there's a massive disconnect between God and most of His people, and there's nothing more effective to help bridge this gap than the truth from His Word.

Don't misunderstand. I'm not asking you to attempt to manufacture a response from your congregation. I'm simply telling you that if you will intentionally present the Word of God regarding the worship of God to the people of God, you will increase the chances that they'll genuinely worship Him a million times over.

Hallelujah! We become like an old-time operator—connecting two parties—as we share God's Word with the purpose of establishing a clearer connection between God and His people in worship.

Here's an example.

God's Presence Isn't Found in the Music

One night, I was leading at a worship conference, and the Holy Spirit began teaching me. As usual, when this happens, His purpose is two-fold. First, He's helping me understand a truth I may have misunderstood, and second, He's bringing an important revelation to my attention with the purpose of having me share it with His people.

In that moment, He dropped a simple but poignant truth in my heart: "I want you to remind my people that my presence is not found in the music." Now, of course, I had to process exactly what He meant by this. I thought, *What do you mean, Lord? If your presence isn't found in the music, why do we connect your presence so directly to our times of musical worship? Are we missing it?*

He replied, in essence, "It's not that my presence cannot be experienced within your times of musical worship; it's just that my presence is not bound to music alone. I want you to teach my people that it's just as important for them to learn to encounter my relational presence outside musical worship as it is for them to learn to encounter my relational presence within their musical worship."

He continued, "Many have mistaken my presence for the pleasant emotions that arise as a result of listening to powerful music. They're connecting with music, believing they have connected with me relationally. Then they leave the event or gathering having never truly enjoyed me, but having simply enjoyed my creation. This is a subtle deception that must be set right."

Imagine people attending conferences and church services and believing they've encountered God, when all the while they've only encountered emotions, skilled musicians, and super-charged atmospheres. I can see why God asked me to teach the congregation this truth—otherwise, they might continue in this fallacy.

This is an example of the type of teaching the Holy Spirit wants to bring through you to your congregation as you lead worship. There are endless perspective-shifting truths that must be taught to God's people if we're to aid them in becoming the authentic worshipers He designed them to be. (Incidentally, don't leave your team members behind as you teach Biblical truth about worship to your congregation. They will need the same teaching behind closed doors, preferably 4-6 months beforehand.)

Enough Truth to Go Around

You might be thinking, *This all sounds wonderful, but is there really enough worship content in the Bible to give us fifty-two Sundays' worth of relevant teaching nuggets?*

Why, yes, there is. Absolutely. In fact, there are mountains of teaching from God's Word that need to be brought before God's people—repeatedly—so we can all know Him and worship Him rightly for all of eternity. There's simply no end to it, and yet we must treat it like a treasure hunt, leaning in to uncover these beautiful biblical truths in our own lives before inevitably imparting them to those under our care.

Here are a few examples of what we should be teaching:

- **Why do we sing?** Have you ever been brave enough to ask yourself why we sing in church to begin with? Yes, yes, *because the Bible says so.* But I believe this is a question that many might be asking without asking. And we must be all about helping our church family understand the reasons we do what we do in church. I mean, is singing simply a tradition started by man hundreds or thousands of years ago, or is it something more? As a worship leader, I believe we have the high honor and responsibility of helping people understand even the simple things about worship, such as why we sing and why we gather in the first place. Of course, as you know, if you're going to teach on this subject, this means you must understand it for yourself. So study up.

- **Who is God?** I love this one. It seems so simple, but we barely comprehend it. The way in which helping people awaken to God's true character serves to greatly increase their response to Him. When I finally grasped the revelation from Psalm 103:8 that *God is slow to anger and full of unfailing love*, it revolutionized my passion to worship Him. Unbelievably. Think of it. This God of ours is so wild in His love for us that He holds back His otherwise justified anger and showers us with love instead—and not just any kind of love, but with unfailing, abounding love. This tiny little truth will serve to move your congregation to respond with greater potency to their God. But remember, we're not the ones invoking the response. We do our part—presenting biblical truth—and then God does His part, turning the truth we presented into genuine revelation. And since the truths about God's character are limitless, there's no end to your ability—with the help of the Holy Spirit—to release your congregation into a greater, more worshipful response to God.

- **Why do we raise our hands in worship?** If you didn't grow up in a church that encouraged people to lift their hands to God in worship, you might be surprised to know that this is not a Pentecostal or charismatic expression. It's simply a biblical expression. Period. It's not something typical of those who have more expressive personalities, but simply something typical of those who truly love the Lord. (You may still be surprised to know that there are at least as many examples in the Bible of people lifting up their hands in prayer or to bless people than there are of people lifting up their hands in singing.) Regardless, we must help our teams and our congregants understand two important things: 1) the Bible invites *all* people to lift up their hands to God in worship (and in prayer), and 2) *why* it does so. These are simple truths that many casual churchgoers still don't truly comprehend. To their chagrin. Yet, when provided with the *why* from the

Word, they now have the provocation they need—through the teaching of God's Word—to step out in faith.

- **What does the Bible say about dancing?** We've already discussed the importance of each person learning to worship in freedom through worshipful "dance." And this, of course, is a truth that must be taught. Repeatedly. As we might expect, people regularly assume dancing in worship is only for those whose personalities and giftings lend themselves to this. And while this may be partially true, God is inviting us all to respond to Him in ways that are outside our comfort zone. I ask again; which is more foolish? Dancing for men? Or dancing for God? Exalting God's creation? Or exalting the Creator of all things? Abandonment in sexual perversion? Or abandonment in worship? Some make excuses. "Yeah, but I'm not really the expressive, shouting, or dancing kind of worshiper." Sure, I get it. I'm not the giving kind of person either. Yet I'm still asked to give. I'm not the humble kind of person either. Yet I'm still required to cast off my pride. Clearly, God calls us all beyond our natural personalities to express ourselves to Him through supernatural means, and we have the responsibility to invite our congregations to dare to trust Him in this. Why? Because when God asks us to dance before Him, He's not attempting to hurt us; He's attempting to free us.

- **Why is worshiping God not just for church?** If you truly want to see your congregants be transformed into the true and passionate worshipers God desires, you'll need to teach them to worship at home too. (We'll dive into this in some detail in the upcoming chapters.) Certainly, we would never tell our church family to refrain from reading their Bibles at home simply because they read them at church. Moreover, we would never teach them to stop praying at home simply because they already pray at church. Yet, it's almost as if we've done this with worship—taught them that the only place to worship God with singing is at church. We must flip this narrative. You simply won't believe the transformation that will happen when families realize that worshiping God at home is one of the fast tracks toward squashing our ever-annoying numbness toward God. Louie Giglio says it this way: "Trust me, church is a lot better when our gatherings are filled with people who have been pursuing God for six days before they get there."[2]

- **Are those song lyrics really biblical?** Not only must we carefully select songs that are biblically accurate, but we must also embrace the responsibility we have to help people understand exactly how the lyrics apply to their lives. You'd be surprised by how many people make very little connection between the lyrics of our worship songs and the lives they lead every day—concerning both old hymns and new choruses. Incredibly, I'm convinced that many folks believe Chris Tomlin originated the idea *if God is for us, no one can stop us, and if God is with us, no one can stand against us.* Unbeknownst to many, this is straight out of Romans 8:31, and it is our job to help people identify the scriptural concepts that are strewn throughout our old and new songs. We must help them comprehend these concepts as originating not simply in the minds of songwriters, but deep in the heart of God. We must regularly take time before singing some of our songs—like "Our God"—to share the biblical truth associated with that song:

"What shall we say about such wonderful things as these? If God is for us, who can ever be against us? Since he did not spare even his own Son but gave him up for us all, won't he also give us everything else? Who dares accuse us whom God has chosen for his own? No one—for God himself has given us right standing with himself. Who then will condemn us? No one—for Christ Jesus died for us and was raised to life for us, and he is sitting in the place of honor at God's right hand, pleading for us" (Romans 8:31–34 NIV).

We might take a moment to explain the line "I'm not backing down from any giant" from Elevation's song "See a Victory," so we can empower people to respond to the giants in their lives—attacks,

---

2   Louie Giglio, *The Air I Breathe* (Colorado Springs, CO: Multnomah Books, 2003), page 115.

difficulties, suffering, sickness, depression, etc.—in the same way David responded to Goliath:

David said to the Philistine, "You come against me with sword and spear and javelin, but I come against you in the name of the LORD Almighty, the God of the armies of Israel, whom you have defied. This day the LORD will deliver you into my hands, and I'll strike you down and cut off your head. This very day I will give the carcasses of the Philistine army to the birds and the wild animals, and the whole world will know that there is a God in Israel. All those gathered here will know that it is not by sword or spear that the LORD saves; for the battle is the LORD'S, and he will give all of you into our hands" (1 Samuel 17:45–47 NIV).

You might think to yourself, *Jeff, people already know this stuff. Why do I need to teach it?* Well, first of all, I disagree. Most people do not process the way in which these random biblical truths apply directly to them. They are entertained by biblical stories and by the bravery of men like David, but they don't always recognize these instances as examples of how they can stand in the strength of God in their own lives. And even if they do recognize them, it often takes a leader in their life who is brave enough to say it aloud. Then and only then, does it rise from the recesses of a person's subconsciousness so they can truly begin living out the truths of God's Word.

This is one of the greatest joys of a worship leader. We are invited to repeatedly pull back the veil on many of the lesser-known truths of the Bible so people can boldly rise up as the worshiping warriors they were meant to be.

This, however, is just the beginning, because teaching the Word without doing the Word is almost as bad as not teaching the Word.

This brings us to leadership component number three.

COMPONENT THREE: LEAD BY DOING

So far, I've asked you to consider increasing your intentionality in two major areas of leadership: leading by modeling and leading by teaching. I've done so with one purpose in mind: that you'll be able to better serve your teams and your congregation by cultivating in them the culture of the Kingdom. A great blessing to everyone under our care.

Even so, if we stop here, we might as well not begin at all. Modeling (leading by example) is an incredibly powerful form of leadership. Without it, we'll muster something much less than we desire: little to no authentic response from our church worshipers. Why? Because people rarely go beyond the level of their leader. In any arena.

At the same time, modeling by itself is also ineffective. Why? Because modeling is often excused by those who view the modeled activity as something fit for only a few people and their unique personalities. They say to themselves, *Isn't it just so nice how Fred leads us in worship so passionately? I wish I could muster half his energy.* All the while, what they're really saying is, *Fred is different from me, and I could never worship God with the passion he has. God made him special that way. I mean, he's the worship leader, for crying out loud. He's supposed to be passionate.*

This is extremely dangerous thinking, because it excuses us from cultivating the passionate worship expression God requires of all His people. Remember, spiritual passion is not found in personalities; it's found in revelation. Listen to what Jesus said to the Pharisee about the woman who poured perfume on His feet: *"I tell you, her sins—and they are many—have been forgiven, so she has shown me much love. But a person who is forgiven little shows only little love"* (Luke 7:47). This Pharisee had little understanding (revelation) of how much God had forgiven him, so he in return had little love to give to God. The woman was just the opposite. She had great understanding (revelation) of all that God had done for her, and she responded with extravagant love. Again, our ability to love well is not connected to our personality. It is connected to the revelation we have (or the lack thereof) of all that God has done for us.

As we've discovered, teaching in worship takes our leadership to another level. Think of the increased response that will begin to flow from our congregations as we equip them with knowledge and wisdom from the Bible. The absence of teaching restrains the revelation of God and keeps His people in a state of lifeless indifference, while the increase of teaching invites the increase of God's revelation which fosters new life in His people.

Of course, we can't force people to receive revelation. If only! Yet, neither should we withhold the teaching of God's Word in order to simply model worship. We must bring forth the Word of God as we lead, knowing the Word will not return void but will produce fruit (see Isaiah 55:11). This is the wonderful work of God's Spirit that results from the obedience of His leaders as they commit to the preaching and teaching of the Word of God.

Leading by modeling and leading by teaching will do wonders in terms of empowering our teams and our congregations to worship with greater authenticity and passion. Even so, modeling and teaching are still limited when it comes to our full capacity to lead biblically. How so? Simple. *"But don't just listen to God's word. You must do what it says. Otherwise, you are only fooling yourselves"* (James 1:22).

It's not rocket science. When we lead people to hear the Word, we've done a good thing, but when we lead them to *hear* the Word and then to *do* the Word, we've done a great thing.

Doing Takes Hearing to Another Level

Imagine I invite you to my home for a gourmet meal. Because you arrive early, you're present for the entire preparation process. Now envision me talking you through exactly what I'm going to cook—with mouth-watering detail—followed by me preparing the meal before your very eyes. You watch with anticipation as it all comes together. You take in the wonderful aromas of each dish as the tantalizing tastes begin to fuse together.

Then, just as things are sliding out of the oven, I ask you to leave. I thank you for coming but am suddenly determined to exclude you from partaking in the scrumptious meal you've been expecting to enjoy. What?

This, my friends, is exactly what we do to people when we model and teach on worship and yet fail to invite them to step into it with action. Boldly and intentionally. The *doing* part of our worship leadership is the part that lends power and purpose to the *modeling* and *teaching* parts. This is the end goal! To lead people to the point of decision. To lead them to the point where they're compelled to take action to worship God in the wake of His glorious truth. To respond with action based on both what they've seen modeled *and* what they've been taught concerning the Word of God and worship. To quote a friend of mine, "To stop talking about it and to start being about it."

This is an amazing experience as a leader. This is where people start to move from being lukewarm church attendees to becoming on-fire followers of Jesus Christ. From being "religious" to being relational. From being spectators to being participants. From being song-lovers to being God-lovers.

Passing the Baton

This is the moment of truth. It's the moment in our leadership where we finally grab hold of what we've come to understand (our personal revelation) and begin to hand it off to our spiritual family with the purpose of encouraging them to join the race—to stop watching us run—and to begin running for themselves. It's a beautiful thing.

You see, up until now, many congregants have been sitting on the sidelines watching us run purposely and passionately around the track. Many churchgoers have been resting comfortably in the bleachers blessed and encouraged by our love for running, all while entertaining no plans to jump into the race themselves. Truth be told, they may not even realize they're supposed to leave the bleachers and join the race. Often, as a result of our poor leadership, they assume we're just fine doing all the running. We must change this and boldly invite them to join us.

But it won't be easy.

Think of it. Suddenly you show up one Sunday morning, and you move from demonstrating the act of running with a baton to reaching out with it to pass it on to them. In that moment, they may look back at you wide-eyed, thinking, *What! Me? Certainly not me. No way. I can't run. You're doing just fine running this "worship race" on everyone's behalf. You're the talented one. And truthfully, I'm just fine sitting here cheering you on.*

This is our challenge. To do everything in our power—in the power of the Spirit of God—to help people engage with God on their own. To join the race of the pursuit of God in relationship and in life. (Ironically, this is also the point where many worship leaders stop short of engaging their congregation, because they're just fine keeping their adoring fans in the stands.)

Modeling, teaching, *and* doing helps us get over the hump. Sure, we must show them how to worship, and we must teach them about biblical worship, but at some point, we have to boldly invite them to put on their running shoes. With compelling, biblical reasoning, we must beckon them to change out of their fan garb and join us on the track. We must ask them to stop being spectators and start being true worshipers, as we step into worlds unknown. But this can only happen as we move from modeling and teaching worship to doing it. Together.

Incredibly, when we invite people—even those who are the most resistant—to worship God in response to biblical revelation, their hearts are often softened, and they begin to respond in ways you and they would have never imagined possible. Some will sing boldly or fall to their knees for the very first time. Others will open their hearts or their minds to a new level of relational worship.

Just as beautiful is what we all build together when we worship according to the God's Word. Community. Yes. Kingdom community. And there is little that is more encouraging to a pastor and his worship leader than seeing God's people love Him in the ways they were made to love Him. All together as one.

What Can We Do Together?

It's not difficult to introduce your congregation to these powerful teaching-and-doing moments in musical worship. We can simply revisit the list of biblical items we should be teaching our congregations (from a few pages back) and ask them to respond—little by little—by taking the obvious/not-so-obvious parallel action.

For example, if I just finished sharing a teaching moment from 1 Timothy 2:8 on the biblical precedent for lifting up our hands to God, this is the perfect time to present a clear invitation for the entire congregation to do this—to lift up their hands to the Lord—together. Of course, there's a little positive peer pressure at work here as well, and, as a result, there will be folks who lift up their hands for the very first time (or for the first time in a long time).

Again, if lifting up your hands to God is already normal in your church, you might think, *What's the big deal?* Remember, there will always be new people coming into your church along with many others who just need a little extra push. *Doing*, in response to biblical *teaching* (even without complete understanding) will always produce greater spiritual revelation, leading to greater willingness to take action, leading to greater heart transformation. Do you want this for your congregation? I believe you do.

Now, let's identify a few examples of revelatory *doing* moments that you can introduce to your congregation during musical worship:

- **Sing in the Spirit.** Paul reminds us in 1 Corinthians 14:15, *"Well then, what shall I do? I will pray in the spirit, and I will also pray in words I understand. I will sing in the spirit, and I will also sing in words I understand."* As you train your congregation in *Tehillâh* (the Hebrew word for *praise* tied to singing a spontaneous song to the Lord), why not invite them to sing to the Lord in their Holy Spirit prayer language, just as Paul instructs.

- **Spread out around the room.** I can't find a Scripture verse instructing us to give ourselves more room during musical worship by spreading out around the room, but neither can I find one that insists we sit in rows facing the stage as we gather. Go figure. Nevertheless, take it from me, inviting people in your congregation to step into the aisles, to the front, or even to the back of the room to worship can help them break free from the numb. Being willing to move to a different physical place during musical worship can serve as a symbol that our hearts are ready to move to a different spiritual place in life.

- **Be still and know.** Psalms 46:10 appeals to us to be still and know that God is God. The context is one that encourages fear and trembling as we come into a full knowledge of how terrifyingly awesome God truly is. This awareness can stir a much greater sense of reverence as we worship. Even though "being still" is somewhat of an inaction, it still serves as a compelling biblical *doing* moment that can transform our musical worship moments. Few of us spend significant amounts of time being still or without some sort of stimuli, and, similarly, few of us are intentionally seeking a greater sense of the fear of the Lord for our lives. Thus, educating our congregants on the wonder and majestic power of the Lord—and then inviting them to be still and humble in His presence—is an incredible fruit-bearing strategy in worship leadership.

- **Enter with thanksgiving.** Psalm 100 reminds us to *"enter his gates with thanksgiving; go into his courts with praise. Give thanks to him and praise his name."* Expounding on this verse and the many reasons we have to be thankful will no doubt stir up a heart of gratefulness in your congregation (the kind of gratefulness that opens gates to relationship and welcomes us into God's presence). Once you've exhorted the people concerning a passage like Psalm 100, ask them to begin singing out the reasons for their thankfulness as part of their worship to God. This brings transformation that cannot be achieved in any other way.

Warning: One thing many worship leaders attempt to do is decrease the awkwardness of the *doing* process by asking people to simply *think* about doing something instead of actually doing it. For example, they might teach on humility and then ask people to *think* about this concept as they sing. Technically, thinking is a type of action, but this lets people off the hook too easily. Thinking by itself is too passive to lead to real transformation. It's like asking someone to think about giving money to the poor, believing it will have the same impact as actually asking them to give to the poor. Our *teaching* gets them thinking, but our invitation to "action" gets them *doing*.

Remember, all of these *doing* actions function best when they are tied to scripture and to songs that address similar topics. For example, why not lead your congregation into a time of repentance in worship by reading a Scripture verse like Proverbs 28:13: *"People who conceal their sins will not prosper, but if they confess and turn from them, they will receive mercy."* Invite them into action by singing or praying their confessions quietly to God as everyone humbles themselves before the Lord. Then, after a few moments, lead them in a song like "O Come to the Altar" by Elevation or

"Nothing Else" from Cody Carnes. In this way, you multiply the impact of your teaching-and-doing moments in every conceivable way.

THE POTENCY OF AN ALTAR RESPONSE

Whether or not your church currently incorporates a traditional "altar call" or "musical response time" near the end of your service, I want to make the case that setting aside a few intentional moments for praise and worship after the sermon is vital to empowering your congregation to go to the next level.

Again, our ultimate goal is to empower God's people by any means necessary (within biblical guidelines) to grow closer to God. It's that simple. And one of the most powerful ways we can do this is to provide a time for our church family to process "aloud" (response) all that they are receiving from the Word of God through the pastor's message (revelation).

The last thing we want is to fire loads of spiritual ammunition at them—in the form of a potent sermon—and then send them directly off to lunch, staggering and gasping for breath. This does our congregation a huge disservice by keeping them from participating in a vital part of the spiritual growth process: the *response* part.

As discussed earlier, worship is a response to a revelation, so this begs the question: Why set our church family up to receive great supernatural *revelation* from God and then steal the opportunity they have to *respond* to all they've just heard?

Here's a bit more on revelation and response as I wrote it in chapter 10 of my book *Awakening Pure Worship*:

> One of the more prevailing themes connected to corporate worship has been best branded *revelation and response*. This idea is best characterized by authentic, impactful, transformational worship (our response to God) flowing out of Holy Spirit-inspired, supernatural, eye-openers (God's revelation to us). Or you could say it this way: **A worshipful response *to* God is always born out of an insightful revelation *from* God.**[3]

---

3   Jeff Deyo, *Awakening Pure Worship* (Shippensburg, PA: Destiny Image, 2018), page 116.

To me, this concept is extremely rudimentary, but still so profound.

In an interview with Danielle DuRant on rzim.org, discussing his book *Facedown*, Matt Redman explains, "I think all true meaningful and pure worship is a response to a revelation. One way I like to define worship is 'the all-consuming response to the all-deserving worth and revelation of God.' When we see him, it commands a response to his holiness. Worship starts with us seeing him."[4]

Yes! And this only stands to strengthen the notion that we love because He first loved us.

It also begs some questions: How can you—how can I—love a God we do not know? A God we have not *seen*? A God of whom we have no understanding—no revelation? It's like saying "I do" to someone after shaking their hand for the first time. There's no basis for commitment. What could you possibly commit to?

Still, many leaders mistakenly characterize corporate worship as something that paves the way for greater revelation—for the preaching of the Word—nothing more and nothing less. But let's take another look. Yes, worship should pave the way for the preaching of the Word. But not exclusively. The truth is connected—oddly enough—to the seemingly arbitrary question of the chicken and the egg. You know. Which comes first—response or revelation?

Stay with me.

Because we know God created adult humans first and not babies, and because we know he created animals in their adult state, we can assume he created the chicken first. Not the egg. Likewise, it's illogical to assume that response comes first. Response to what? Response to God? In the form of worship? How can we respond to nothing? How can we love or worship a God who is entirely unknown to us? Impossible.

---

4 Matt Redman, Interview about *Facedown* book with Danielle Du Rant, www.scribd.com/document/7308949/Danielle-DuRant-with-Matt-Redman

God must first awaken something in us toward His existence. Toward His glory. Toward His power. Toward our need for Him. Toward our need for a Savior. *"For no one can come to me unless the Father who sent me draws them to me, and at the last day I will raise them up. As it is written in the Scriptures, 'They will all be taught by God.' Everyone who listens to the Father and learns from him comes to me"* (John 6:44–45).

Think back to the day you realized your own great need for a Savior. You didn't truly worship Him before that day, did you? But now—in response to an incredible revelation received through the Word of God and/or the Spirit of God—you fall to your knees, repent, and cry "holy," all in a flurry of response. In worship. In adoration. As a result of a supernatural revelation.

It doesn't start with a response. It starts with a revelation. The revelation that *He first* loved us. That *He first* gave of Himself. That *He first* bridged the gap. That *He first* broke through time and space, shoved Himself into a tiny human-skin suit, if only to reveal something we could never conceive. Something that should startle even the most jaded among us. Something that inspires billions of people around the globe—throughout all of history—to join together in one song with one voice. Not because they have to, but because there is no other fitting response.

It's hard to imagine reading all of this and then charging blindly onward with our often-so-typical Sunday service order. You know, the one where we ask our congregation for an immediate response (through song) right at the top of our services—just as people are getting in their mid-morning stretches. And with no real context for *why* or *whom* we should be worshiping. Then, following the musical worship, we offer a stirring but lengthy revelation from God's Word (the preaching), and then fail to offer our congregants the chance to do what God made them to do. Respond to His Word. Respond to His love. Respond to God's transformational revelation for our lives. To shout. To kneel. To cry. To be thankful. To love. To be grateful. To really worship.

We tie up the message with a perfect little bow, say a nice prayer, and send the people on their merry way—wishing them a wonderful week—full to the brim with pleasant truths but with little opportunity to process the application before stuffing their faces and forgetting it all.

At what rate do you suppose we forget the things we hear in a sermon? I'll refrain from making up a stat, but let's just say it's high. After a couple of weeks, very little of what we hear on a given Sunday sticks. Yet, we let the greatest chance we have to help things sink in slip away.

Of course, some churches do set aside two to three minutes of response time at the end of the service—maybe one song or part of a song. But after feasting on forty to fifty minutes of incredible God-breathed truth (revelation), can this really serve to satisfy the need we have to express our gratitude (response) for all God has given to us?

"But Jeff," you say. "Our people would never put up with the idea of lingering after the message to respond in worship. They're ready to go. Seriously. We've done well just to keep them from leaving a few minutes early."

Again, this is where we have to stop with the crazy pills. As I explained in the introduction, whatever people are feeling... however they are responding... whatever their natural tendencies are in our services... it is simply a result of the culture we—the leaders—have established. Another way to say it is, the culture we have is the culture we've built.

It's simple. If you have any hope that your congregation will grow in their desire to take part in a longer altar-response moment, only one thing is stopping you. You. It's true. If you long for a particular aspect of culture that doesn't currently exist in your church, you can—you must—become a part of building that culture. Please don't say something silly like, "Our church would *never* do *that*!" Why? Because the only reason they would never do *that* is that they don't currently do *that*. But if you will take the time to model, teach, and do *that*, they will grow significantly in their openness to *that*.

Yes, it's going to take time, and it's possible some folks might walk away during the transition. Fine. But don't forget: There are others in your congregation who are contemplating leaving if you refuse to take them deeper. Plus, you'll undoubtedly add new members to your church family who have been searching for a church just like the Kingdom-driven one you're building. Point is, it can be done. It can be built. Some will leave. Some will stay. And some will flood in.

FACILITATING AN EFFECTIVE ALTAR RESPONSE

Hopefully, at this point, you're at least considering inserting a significant amount of musical response time into (or back into) your service. If so, there are a few essentials you'll want to consider regarding the mechanics of leading an effective altar-response time:

- **Communicate with your pastor beforehand.** The first step in facilitating an effective altar-response time is getting the details from your pastor. You'll want to know:
  - How much time is going to be set aside for musical worship?
  - What is the cue for the band to come back up?
  - Is there a preferred altar song or two?
  - Should the band simply play instrumental music or sing as well?
  - How will the service come to a close following the time of response?

- **Communicate with your team.** After discussing things with your pastor, make sure to clearly communicate the information to your team. In addition, you'll need to work out the following:
  - The section/chord progression you plan to start with.
  - Whether you'll start with click right away or not.
  - Who is playing what, when.
  - Whether you plan to play a full song or only parts of songs.
  - How the band will know to switch between song sections as well as how they will know where to go dynamically. (What cues will they watch for?)
  - What the band should do musically and dynamically if the pastor suddenly decides to jump in to talk.
  - How you plan to end the altar time musically.

- **Be prepared to flow.** Many altar-response times are less structured than the sets prior to the message (of course, by now you're beginning to grow in your excitement to flow during every worship set). I would choose a song from the beginning of the service to reprise (keeping another easy-to-flow song or two in my back pocket). This can work really well, because it keeps things familiar, which helps people get out of "head mode" and stay in "heart mode" during these pivotal Holy Spirit moments. I recommend staying away from doing the songs exactly as they are on the recording. Start with the chorus or bridge—something repetitive—and also consider adding in a little spontaneous worship to glue everything together. Everything should ebb and flow over the course of the response time to keep things from feeling stagnant—dynamics, song sections, instrumental parts, spontaneous worship, etc. There's a fine line we walk between engaging-repetition and disengaging-monotony.

- **Learn to adjust in the moment.** This goes along with learning how to flow as a team, but goes a little deeper. For instance, make sure you're able to adjust musically to provide the correct atmosphere for each moment. For example, I remember a situation where the worship leader planned to use "Lion and the Lamb" during the response time, but decided to do it exactly like the recording, with tracks and everything. He quickly discovered this approach rarely works, especially since the band was unable to tag-team with the pastor between song sections. Starting with the traditional intro was extremely abrupt and therefore awkward coming out of a prayerful moment. A good way to utilize "Lion and the Lamb" for an altar response would be to start with the bridge.

- **Be decisive when directing your team.** One of the most important things about leading your team during an altar-response moment is being clear about where you're headed musically. Indecision can lead to confusion as well as to serious train wrecks. (This is why communicating the plan ahead of time is absolutely vital.) Devising simple hand signals and utilizing an MD to communicate your intentions to the team through a microphone will help you all stay locked into the flow. (See chapter 7 for help with simplified signals.)

Inviting our people to take specific actions to carry out the many worship-oriented instructions found in the Bible is one of the most impactful things we can do as worship leaders, that is, if we truly desire to empower our congregants. It's when we regularly *model* biblical worship, *teach* biblical worship, and invite our congregations to *do* biblical worship that we multiply our impact even while demonstrating an authentic desire to bring them into greater and greater alignment with God's Kingdom culture. This practical, three-strand-cord approach will continually stir the hearts of baby Christians and rekindle the fire of long-time believers by helping them step out of the bleachers and onto the track.

Chapter Highlights

1. Some worship leaders believe their only job is to worship God on a stage, but while this is a must, one of our primary goals is to help people remember *why* they are worshiping God in the first place. Even leaders and longstanding believers need to be reminded and inspired—through short teachings from the Word—concerning the incredible worth of our great King.

2. Teaching a little of what God asks from us in worship each week will slowly but surely establish Kingdom culture and transform your congregation into the biblical worshipers God desires them to be.

3. You'd be surprised by the number of people in our congregations who don't understand the purpose of singing, the purpose of physical expression in worship, God's expectations from us in worship, or that learning to love and worship our heavenly Father is the one thing we will continue to do throughout all eternity. These, and many other biblical truths, must be taught repeatedly so that they will be caught eventually.

4. Teaching our congregations to *understand* what the Bible says about worship is an incredible step toward revitalizing Kingdom culture in our churches, but failing to invite them to *do* what the Word says—right in the service—is tantamount to reversing everything we've ever taught.

5. In a spectator church culture, our ultimate goal in worship leadership is to get people out of the bleachers and onto the track. Inviting our congregants to do things like sing to God spontaneously, celebrate and lift up their hands, or shout with the voice of triumph aids us significantly in handing them the worship baton. This, in turn, moves them more and more toward worshiping God on their own, without our poking and prodding.

Chapter 12

LOVING AND LEADING:
A SYNTHESIS

Lie #12

"Influence is the primary focus of leadership."

Here's a question: Do you love the people on your teams? And another: Do you love the people in your congregation? One more: Have you considered the stunning possibility that loving people is as important—in worship leadership—as loving God?

Take a minute and ponder these questions. Please know, in no way am I suggesting that you don't love the people on your teams or in your congregation. Nor am I suggesting that loving people is a significant part of worshiping God. Yet, I do want to remind you that, *in worship leadership,* loving people is paramount to helping people love and worship God.

I don't remember where I first heard it. It was probably part of some random church's stunning catch phrase. But if you know me, you know it's one of my favs: *Love God. Love people.* We discussed it briefly in chapter 9, but let's dive in a little deeper here.

Like you, I'm not a big fan of Christian clichés, but I am a big fan of boiling it all down to the lowest common denominator. In the end, I just want to get to the bottom-line issues. You know, before we wind up getting lost in the weeds.

I've realized my own natural tendencies to get caught up in the peripherals—potentially the wrong ones—often to the point where I inadvertently neglect the most important aspects of my life. "Forest for the trees" stuff. Heaven forbid I get to the end of my life and realize I've spent my live-long days doing the lesser things, all while believing I was doing the greater things.

And so, when I heard the "love God, love people" slogan, I was like, "That's it! Now there's something I can use to help us grasp our life's purposeful purpose. Something I can impart to my kids, all of my students at NCU, and everyone in my home church congregation to help us make sense of this crazy thing we call *life*. Simple. Yet powerful."

AN OXYMORON

All the same, I couldn't help but wonder if this little mantra was really at home among our foundational worship-leadership strategies. It does seem a bit like an oxymoron. Loving people in worship? Really? I mean, we get the loving God part. That's unmistakable. But loving people in worship seems… well, odd. Even a bit counterintuitive.

Fascinatingly, some consider this idea to be worse than counterintuitive. Even despicable. Offensive. Detestable. To God. Something that slyly aims to displace the real heart of worship—altogether. Something that doesn't bring glory to God at all, but violently tears down the structure of biblical worship as a whole.

Hmm.

> Could it be that loving people—when coupled with loving God—is actually the mortar that holds all things in worship leadership together?

Or could it be that loving people—when coupled with loving God—is actually the mortar that holds all things in worship leadership together? Could it be that loving people in worship leadership actually brings fullness to the expression of loving God? That loving God is a significant part of loving people, and that loving people is a significant part of loving God?

Let me ask this question: *How can we lead people when we don't love people?* We may be able to disconnect ourselves for a time from all their quirks and issues, but eventually they will catch up to us. In fact, often—if we're honest—we recognize that the people in our congregations often account for the lion's share of all that is disheartening in leadership. (You know this isn't a stretch if you've been in ministry for more than five minutes.)

This is not to say that choosing the songs, arranging the tracks, and organizing the rehearsals isn't challenging. But so often, the difficulties we face with people are considerably more arduous. More personal. Difficult situations with people can sometimes even become the straw that breaks the camel's back. Welcome to ministry.

SERVING PEOPLE IS OUR DELIGHT

That said, please don't hear me saying that people *are* the problem. It's just that people are often used by God to stretch us as leaders, and vice versa, in ways we'd never expect—even if only to help identify the many flaws and character issues that exist within us. The very ones God desires to heal and transform so we can grow as servants to His people.

We might joke at times, saying, "If we didn't have to deal with people, ministry would be a cinch." Ha! Maybe things would be much smoother if we could simply remove the people from the equation. And live in a vacuum. But this probably wouldn't work very well. Or be truly desirable. Because of course people are what ministry is all about! Serving them is our purpose. Our delight.

Rest assured, we gather together in our services first and foremost to worship and celebrate God. But as lead worshipers, we do so with a two-fold purpose: 1) to grow together in our relational connection with God, and 2) to build His Kingdom by sparking a genuine community of faithful Christ followers.

Love God. Love people.

We aren't in a competition to see who can compile the longest list of disengaged "members." People who stop by the church one or two Sundays per month. Some sort of country club. No. We're looking to build a family of people who are passionate about serving God and who want to do life together—an ocean of God's creation—all joined together to love and fellowship with Him. To love and serve each other. All united as one. This is what God desires. This is what we should desire.

In fact, would you permit me to speak something revolutionary? *God loves people more than God loves worship.*

Pause. Breathe.

I know. For some of us, this is very odd to hear. We've been taught over and over not to run in church and not to be too loud in church and to always act *just so* in church. In the house of God, that is. All with the idea that God gets mad if we misbehave in church.

In the Deyo family, "love God, love people" is simple. It applies both to musical worship *and* to the areas of our lives outside musical worship. But, to my surprise, the Spirit of God instructed me a few years ago to stop omitting this concept when it comes to worship leadership.

Obviously, it's fitting to be respectful to God—and to each other—during church services (and at all times, of course). But did you ever consider that God asks us to gather *together* for a very special purpose? I mean, He could simply invite each of us to worship Him at home alone. In our own little corners. In our own little worlds. And yes, He does. But He also commands us to worship Him *together*. In families. In community. Side by side. Across social and generational barriers. With friends. With neighbors. With strangers. As part of the great multitude.

LOVING WHAT GOD LOVES

Question is, how exactly do we expect to lead people in these "together gatherings" if we refuse to sincerely love them? If we continue to put the sole focus of worship leadership on loving God and never let our love for God steer us toward loving people, how will we keep from receiving the same rebuke from Jesus as the church at Ephesus (see Revelation 2:4)?

"But Jeff, the Bible clearly defines our purpose in John 12:32: *And when I am lifted up from the earth, I will draw everyone to myself.*' You see, our job is to lift up Jesus, and then God will draw all people to Himself."

I get it. This is an important verse. But we can't put this one verse on an island and declare eternal purpose. How many times does the New

Testament tell us that Jesus has given us a new commandment? To love one another. To serve one another. To help one another. Over and over again.

This is worship leadership.

Love God. Love people.

It dawned on me. The "consequence" of loving God *first* is that we subsequently increase in our love for what He loves. And what does He love? What is His greatest passion? What in all of creation is the object of His greatest affection? People.

I wondered then, *If God loves people so much, why is it that we spend so much time during musical worship—as leaders—ignoring the very ones He loves instead of helping them love God?*

Interesting question

Don't roll your eyes just yet.

It's true. As a leader, I simply can't lead or serve people I don't love. That's why I resonate so strongly with the practical advice Paul Baloche gave our NCU Worship Leading class in a Skype session a few years back.

He shared how he often ventures into the sanctuary of his local church when no one is around. After positioning himself at the front of the empty room with his guitar, he pictures families from his church in each section throughout the sanctuary. Each one sitting in their usual spot. Some he knows. Some he doesn't. Some he's naturally drawn to. Some he's naturally resistant to. And he sings. And prays. Over each family. Until his heart begins to soften toward each one. He sings the songs of God over them, standing in the gap for them concerning the difficulties of life. Trusting and believing for deliverance and healing and tangible spiritual growth in whatever areas are needed. All by faith.

Then, as he steps to the stage the following Sunday morning, he finds he has begun to cultivate a truer heart of love toward God *and* toward those in the pews. Even toward those who don't fancy him as a leader. Or embrace his methods. Or his song choices. In this way, he's able to serve each family more authentically. No matter their feelings toward his style, his set list, or his personality.

Worship leading is first about loving God. No question. (And yet there are plenty of worship leaders who still don't grasp this sincerely.

They make it about influence, or the joy of the music, or even about exploiting their talents to build their own kingdoms.) Even so, this isn't an either/or issue. We can't separate loving God from loving people. They both sit right at the heart of worship leading. John 4:20–21 brings it home: *"If someone says, 'I love God,' but hates a fellow believer, that person is a liar; for if we don't love people we can see, how can we love God, whom we cannot see? And he has given us this command: Those who love God must also love their fellow believers."*

GETTING BEYOND THE LEADERSHIP TRAP

Let's back up and talk a bit more about leadership in general. To be honest, I'd say we've veered off the Kingdom path in several dangerous ways.

If I asked you to write down your best definition of leadership, what would you write? How would you describe it? Take a few minutes in the lines below to put it on paper.

_____

_____

_____

_____

_____

I honestly hesitate to broach the subject of leadership. Certainly, there have been many more qualified leadership experts than me. I dare say, leadership is probably *the* most talked about, written on, and researched subject on the planet these days. That's not bad. Mostly. But I'm compelled to help us tweak our leadership definition a little and our leadership practice a lot.

Ever wonder why leadership has become such a popular topic? Ever bother to ask why leadership books, podcasts, and conferences are being consumed so vigilantly? To me, it's pretty obvious.

Leaders win. And leadership sells.

I mean, who wants to be a follower? Especially when they can be a leader? Leaders are in charge. Leaders have power. Leaders have money. And leaders have another highly coveted trait. *Influence.*

We all desire influence, but let me say right up front that influence must never be the focus of biblical leadership.

Look, I desperately want to grow in my ability to lead, just like the next guy. I've studied and read and studied and read some more, attempting to key in on the ways "successful" businesses and business leaders operate. I do believe God has called me to lead, and I want to make sure I'm not living out on the corner of a roof somewhere. But it's quite a balancing act to walk the line between worldly leadership and Kingdom leadership.

WHAT IS LEADERSHIP?

If leadership isn't *influence*, what is it?

What does Jesus say? *"In this world the kings and great men order their people around, and yet they are called 'friends of the people.' But among you, those who are the greatest should take the lowest rank, and **the leader should be like a servant**. Normally the master sits at the table and is served by his servants. But not here! For **I am your servant**"* (Luke 22:25–27).

Based on these verses, it's perfectly clear what Jesus is getting at. First, He makes a clear distinction between worldly leadership and Kingdom leadership. He makes no bones about presenting a different definition of leadership than most heralded leaders of His time. In fact, I'd argue He's laying out a definition of leadership that is a full 180-degree about-face.

He doesn't beat around the bush. He cuts to the chase; "Leadership is service. And I'm the head servant." Jesus is known for this. Flipping everything on its head. And we're largely uncomfortable with His approach. It messes with our natural sensibilities. It upends our systems and our protocols. But there's no getting around it.

Of course, this passage doesn't exist inside a vacuum. Jesus presents many similar expressions. Take John 13, where Jesus washes the disciples' feet. Here, Jesus invites us to stop racing to the front of the line and intentionally race toward the back. To purposefully seek out the position nobody else wants. The servant role. The one where we have to get our hands dirty. The one where our posture bows low before the others in the room. To be vulnerable. To be humble. Even if we're the only one.

Jesus tells the Pharisees in Matthew 23:11, *"The greatest among you must serve."* Not *should* serve. *Must* serve. You see, much misunderstanding surrounds our modern-day leadership philosophies. Take these three doozies:

1. **Kenneth Blanchard:** "The key to successful leadership today is influence, not authority."[1]

   At first glance, it appears flawless. I mean, who doesn't prefer influence over authoritarianism? But what if this quote fails because it assumes there are only two possible options. What if there is another, better third option? And what if influence is not actually the opposite of authoritative leadership, after all? What if servitude is?

   How about this one?

2. **General Dwight D. Eisenhower:** "Leadership is the art of getting someone else to do something you want done because he wants to do it."[2]

   Beware. This one can work, but it also quickly morphs into manipulation. We walk a fine line. Many leaders pride themselves on being enormously crafty in the way they assert power over people to get their way. Though it's subtle, this style of leadership is often rooted in arrogance, especially when the Bible makes it clear that God alone is the one who raises people up and brings them down (see Psalm 75:7, Daniel 2:21).

   Another dangerous ideology I've heard out there goes a little something like this:

---

1 "Ken Blanchard Quotes," Brainy Quote, https://www.brainyquote.com/quotes/ken_blanchard_307860.

2 "Dwight D. Eisenhower Quotes," Brainy Quote, https://www.brainyquote.com/quotes/dwight_d_eisenhower_101562.

3. Your best answer to your critics is success.

Truth is, we're as capable of achieving success on our own—in order to prove someone wrong—as we are of causing our own heart to beat. On top of that, this idea is rooted in a demonic "I'll show them" spirit that should never enter our thoughts or motivate our work. Honestly, if we did want to "show them" anything by our lives, it shouldn't be success. It should be the blood of Jesus, the denial of self, and quiet, godly living (see 1 Thessalonians 4:11).

Paul is abundantly clear: ***"Don't copy the behavior and customs [leadership included] of this world***, *but let God transform you into a new person by changing the way you think. Then you will learn to know God's will for you, which is good and pleasing and perfect"* (Romans 12:2).

With God's help, we can stop emulating the world's tactics and change the way we think about leadership.

SUCCESS EQUALS SUCCESSION

I once heard the marvelous Paul Anderson speak these powerful words in a North Central University chapel: "The key to success is succession; that is, fathering, mentoring, and pouring into the next generation. The Old Testament is full of good leaders but horrible fathers!"[3]

Do you want to lead? Begin by loving the people around you. Father (or mother) them. Mentor them. Pour into them. Support them. Be there for them. *With* them.

Do you want to lead? Start serving. I know. Books on serving don't sell nearly as well as books on influence. Just as books on followership won't steal the hearts of readers quite like books on leadership. Yet, the best leaders cut their teeth by learning to follow—and follow well. What do I mean? Paul said it best: *"Follow my example, as I follow the example of Christ"* (1 Corinthians 11:1).

Isn't this what we're called to? Isn't this where Kingdom leadership begins—with following? Even the greatest leaders like Paul are told to follow the example of Christ. Even Jesus didn't do anything until His Father directed Him to.

---

3   Paul Anderson *North Central University* chapel (April 12, 2017).

Maybe we have it backwards. Maybe it's:

- Not so much leaders, but followers
- Not so much motivators, but modelers
- Not so much influencers, but servants
- Not so much pied pipers, but psalmists
- Not so much convert makers, but disciple makers
- Not so much stars, but fathers and mothers

THE ULTIMATE GOAL OF LEADERSHIP

What is the end goal of leading our teams and our congregation? Is it to trick them into doing as we please so they will do the work we don't want to do. Or is it to help them to become something beautiful? Something revolutionary. Something Kingdom.

According to God's Word, the way we assess whether we're leading properly or not is to determine whether or not we're bearing fruit. So what does that look like? I'd say, it's better known by another name—making disciples. This is the second most important responsibility of every believer after cultivating our own vibrant relationship with God: *"So, my brothers and sisters, you also died to the law through the body of Christ, that you might belong to another, to him who was raised from the dead, **in order that we might bear fruit for God**"* (Romans 7:4). *"You did not choose me, but I chose you and appointed you **so that you might go and bear fruit**—fruit that will last—and so that whatever you ask in my name the Father will give you. This is my command: Love each other"* (John 15:16–17).

If the ultimate goal of leadership is to bear fruit, we might begin to wonder, *How exactly do we do it?* By planting seeds, of course.

Sadly, many folks are more interested in taking shortcuts than actually doing what it takes to bear fruit. Who wants to do the work of pulling back the dirt in order to put a tiny little seed in the ground? I mean, planting and watching over seeds until they produce good fruit is *way* too much work. Who has the time?

Even so, there are no shortcuts if we want to spark something God-drenched in our churches. We must begin by planting seeds. Three seeds, to be exact.

1. The Seed of Encouragement

This was a huge one for me, because I didn't have a clue. Trust me when I say I was the worst encourager on the planet. I was the guy who focused on all the mistakes. Seriously, we could have just finished an incredible, Holy Spirit-filled night of worship, and yet I was fixated on one or two small things that went wrong.

God did give some of us a heightened hunger for excellence for good reason, but, as with all good things, this hunger can quickly become toxic when taken to the extreme. I had to learn the balance of these things the hard way.

I remember working through the pain of this as different band members began to walk away out of frustration over my overly critical leadership style. One of them finally confronted me in love to let me know how badly I was hurting them. I was forced to take a long look in the mirror.

I wasn't out to hurt anyone. I simply found myself battling insecurities that worked their way into my leadership. It was crazy. I somehow thought that encouraging them regarding the 98 percent they played right would keep them from working on the 2 percent they played wrong. So I failed to encourage them at all. Fear-based leadership was killing me. And I didn't even know it.

As a result, I picked up John Maxwell's book *Developing the Leader within You*, and it changed my life. I finally began to understand the power of encouragement. This may seem terribly obvious to some, but for others, you may be taking a good look in that mirror right now.

As a result of that book, I started on a journey that's still in process today. I began to encourage those around me. But it didn't come easy. Making the transition was painfully awkward. I would open my mouth to encourage someone and feel like the biggest faker. Like everyone in the room knew I had just read a book on the importance of encouraging peo-

> We cannot simply tell people *where* to go. We must *tell* them, *show* them, and then go *with* them on the journey.

ple. Like I was only encouraging people "because I had to."

Still, I kept at it, and a funny thing began to happen. Little by little, my heart began to wake up. I asked God for help too. Even as I practiced encouraging people "because I had to," I started loving the way it made people feel (*and* how it made me feel), which caused me to encourage people more and more "because I wanted to." This gave me more practice, which allowed it to become more natural. The more I encouraged people, the more it became an authentic part of who I was.

I was finally discovering what Jack Welch knew all along: "Before you are a leader, success is all about growing yourself. When you become a leader, success is all about growing others."[4]

2. The Seed of Equipping

Planting the seed of equipping in others is imperative if we are to lead them graciously and effectively. This idea is all about showing others the path. Showing them a better way of doing things and inspiring them to believe they, too, can grow into it with a commitment to learning, hard work, and listening to the Holy Spirit.

Becoming a Kingdom leader starts with embracing this classic Latin Proverb: "It is absurd that a man should rule others, who cannot rule himself."

The seed of equipping begins with leading by example, but it also requires that we take people with us. This means mentoring and fathering those under our care and also being the first to pick up a machete to cut through the great challenges of life's jungle. We cannot simply tell people *where* to go. We must *tell* them, *show* them, and then go *with* them on the journey.

If we're going to equip others to become the worshipers God desires, we're going to have to embrace coaching. This is ironic, because if you had told me fifteen years ago that I would need to coach other worshipers, I would have assumed you meant only as I led by example. I wasn't prepared to be a coach. I didn't want to be a coach. I liked being a player too much. Back then. But now I'm learning to be an authentic worship leader *and* an inspirational worship coach.

---

4   "Jack Welch Quotes," Brainy Quote, https://www.brainyquote.com/quotes/jack _welch_833427.

Coaching is the process of intentionally giving away what we have. Some are afraid to pass on their secrets for fear that others might surpass them, but mature leaders long for this. To reproduce themselves and—if possible— make a way for those under their care to do above and beyond what they could ever do.

When I came to NCU, I had a fairly good idea of how to be a passionate worshiper, an effective worship leader, and an exceptional songwriter. But could I learn to communicate to others in a way that would equip them to do the same? Could I develop a system that thrived on taking everything God had taught me and transferring it to others?

This is exactly what we need the Spirit of God to help us do.

3. The Seed of Empowerment

According to Bill Gates, "As we look ahead into the next century, leaders will be those who empower others."[5]

No matter what you think of Bill, I do believe he's correct in this instance. The obvious next step for leaders is moving from equipping to empowering. If *equipping* is playing our part in the transference of knowledge, understanding, and know-how, *empowerment* is playing our part in assisting people with the application of all they've learned. This is *not* easy. But it's *not* hard either.

It all starts with setting others in motion. That can be tricky, because it's difficult for leaders to move from doing everything to delegating. It can feel like we *and* they are never quite ready for this power transference. And yet, ultimately, the risk has to be taken on both sides. The leader must be willing to step aside while inviting others to step up. And the people must be courageous enough to leave the bleachers and take part in the game.

Maybe it's a bit like a momma bird preparing for her babies to fly the coop. Are they ready? No. But it's time. And they must take a leap of faith. Is there potential for disaster? Sure. Might they fail? Possibly. But

---

5   Natasha Wallace, "Bill Gates: Tomorrow's Leaders Will be Those That Empower Others," RealLeaders, December 19, 2019, https://real-leaders.com/bill-gates -tomorrows-leaders-will-be-those-that-empower-others/.

they can't stay in the nest forever. Their true potential can only be realized when they spread their wings and catch the wind. Mature leaders understand they need to give their people a little push if they want to see them rise to the next level. In this way, we help them see, and we help them believe. This is the spark!

MOVING FROM MANIPULATION TO MULTIPLICATION

As we know, the enemy has set a clever trap. Most of us strongly crave influence and can easily fall prey to pursuing influence over serving our teams. Of course, we mostly chase influence in order to help our people know God through Jesus Christ and to walk with Him through the Holy Spirit. But we must be cautious.

When we have influence, we have power. When we have influence, we are loved by people. When we have influence, others are impressed with us. When we have influence, we are nearer the top. And this, of course, affords us many things, not the least of which is more stuff.

> Authentic leadership really does *end* in influence. But it doesn't *start* with influence.

When we believe leadership *is* influence, we begin to *aim* for influence, because we believe this is the best path toward becoming an effective leader. And rightly so. Correct? If influence is the full embodiment of leadership, we should—by all counts—seek influence. Unfortunately, this is like attempting to pick the fruit of an apple tree without ever having planted the seed. There cannot be fruit (influence) without a tree (leadership). And there cannot be a tree (leadership) without a seed (service).

Do you see it?

The big mistake we make is believing that influence is the seed. Influence is not the seed. It's only one of the fruits of good leadership. But we can't start with the fruit. We can't even start with the tree. We must start with the seed.

The reason this can be so tricky is because authentic leadership really does *end* in influence. But it doesn't *start* with influence. Authentic leadership starts with a seed, and after much work and patient cultivation of that seed, it grows into a healthy tree that produces healthy fruit. That of Kingdom influence.

Healthy influence is only the result of a healthy tree, and a healthy tree is only the result of a healthy seed. A seed that has been lovingly nurtured and cared for.

Service is the seed. (Well, actually the *servant* is the seed.)

What do I mean? It's about what we aim for. What we have in our sights. When we aim for influence, we do things backwards. We attempt to "plant" our talent, our giftings, our expertise, and our agenda as the main means of growing our ministry rather than simply planting ourselves for the benefit of others—through *service*. By planting ourselves, we do what all seeds must do. Die.

Sounds fun, right?

Ironically, God's Kingdom methods always behave differently. Oppositely. In His world, we are asked to give up the thing we want for ourselves in order to achieve the thing we want for the whole. In this case, aiming for influence allows one person to rise to the top alone, affirming a model where everyone is now dependent on that person. But aiming for service allows one person to die at the bottom, paving a way for many people to rise together to accomplish the heartbeat of heaven. God is asking us to do the unexpected and move from the leadership of manipulation to the leadership of service in order to spark multiplication.

"I tell you the truth, unless a kernel of wheat is planted in the soil and dies, it remains alone. But its death will produce many new kernels—a plentiful harvest of new lives" (John 12:24). A plentiful harvest of new lives—now that's Kingdom influence.

This is the very thing we wanted from the beginning—but we were going about it backwards. Poignantly, we can't gain true influence when we aim for it. And we won't serve people simply by attempting to lead them well. We will only produce the fruit of Kingdom influence when we aim to serve people well, laying down our lives to yield an abundance of life. Even as God handles the miracle of growth.

WE SOW AND GOD GROWS

Have you considered whose job it is to grow things? Seems like we often beat ourselves up too much when things don't grow, and we pat ourselves on the back too heartily when things do. Many seem to accept the false notion that we're responsible for growth, when the truth is we don't grow things at all.

I planted the seed in your hearts, and Apollos watered it, but it was God who made it grow. It's not important who does the planting, or who does the watering. **What's important is that God makes the seed grow.** *The one who plants and the one who waters work together with the same purpose. And both will be rewarded for their own hard work. For we are both God's workers. And you are God's field. You are God's building.* (1 Corinthians 3:6–9)

We can do things that provide an atmosphere for growth. We can cultivate the soil, water the seed, pull the weeds, etc. But the miracle of growth is entirely in the Lord's hands. The difference is subtle but significant. Think about it. Even though we understand the science of plant growth, is it us who makes it happen? Of course not. Think of how God often caused famine to overcome people in the Old Testament. The Israelites could do everything a good farmer should, and yet, without the Lord, there was no harvest.

Same goes for us.

In essence, by attempting to provide our own seed (something only God can do), we recklessly discard the seed He's given us, that of service (or the servant). Blindly, we attempt to plant an empty shell of talent and gifting, which is hollow and without substance. It can't "die" in the ground and will therefore fail to produce any good fruit. Only the seed of service can die. You and I are that seed—the *servant*—meant to die so that others might spark the production of the fruit of the Kingdom.

The twist? When we aim for influence, we harvest things like comparison, manipulation, and division. And the heaviness of the work increases. But when we aim for service, the sky is the limit. And the joy of the work increases.

EVERY CHURCH SHOULD BE FRIENDLY TO SEEKERS

Speaking of aim, let me share a profound thought I received from the Spirit: If leadership starts with love, every church should aim to be seeker-friendly—that is, aim to truly love the unbelievers who walk through our doors.

Now, before you applaud madly and/or consider stoning me, hear me out.

The church growth movement began surrounding the publication of Donald McGavran's book *The Bridges of God* in 1955. Megachurches, as they have come to be known (like Willow Creek, Chicago, Illinois) and Saddleback (Lake Forest, California), helped us—largely unintentionally—back in the 1990s to increase the popularity of the terms *seeker-friendly* and *seeker* (roughly defined as unbelievers searching for answers to the question of human origin surrounding the existence of a supreme being). (Interestingly, many twenty-first century young people—college age and under—are unfamiliar with these terms. For their sake, I'll offer a little history before explaining myself.)

A revolutionary idea began to gain momentum. The thought was, if we want to reach "seekers" for Christ—and we believe getting them to church is the best way to do this—it makes sense to rethink our methods. The question was: what if we stopped designing our services for the people who are Christians and started designing them for people who are not? For the seeker? For those with the greatest potential of coming to Christ?

Instead of planning church services around believers, some churches began turning their focus to the interests of "pre-Christians." They began designing their programs to attract seekers—utilizing popular music, entertaining dramas, and shorter, simpler messages. From there, they began to rethink just about every aspect of their services. From the way we dress to the quality of the coffee we serve. All with a compassionate heart to reach the lost.

Seems logical. And hospitable.

Up and coming leaders began to consider the idea that some of the most traditional elements of our local gatherings might actually be preventing unbelievers from coming. This fact alone could be preventing us from ministering to hundreds and hundreds of "seekers," and ultimately touching fewer and fewer lives for the gospel.

Pastors began to ask, "What needs to go?"

Things like extended musical worship. Uncomfortable altar calls. Fiery, convicting preaching. Physical expression in musical worship. And certainly, the greatest barrier of all—the utilization of spiritual gifts. Things like prophecy, messages in tongues and interpretation, miracles, and, well, anything that could make people feel uncomfortable. Either that, or we needed to curb these expressions—especially on Sunday mornings—in order to increase the potential of luring seekers into the house of God. (Or better said, to keep from scaring them away.)

Tracking with me so far?

I really love the heart behind this, because it displays an insatiable desire to continually reevaluate our methods as well as of showing love for all people.

Only one problem.

REMOVING THE SUPER FROM OUR SERVICES

In an attempt to make church services more relevant and "friendly" to the unsaved—a truly noble idea—we mistakenly begin by eliminating the very elements that so often touch them the most. The supernatural ones. The *God* ones. As you can imagine, this leaves us with little more than the techniques and talents of man, something most people already enjoy outside of church. On a frequent basis. In concert halls and comedy clubs, at shows and in bars.

Bottom line: There is nothing we need more than the supernatural help of God's Spirit if we hope to make a difference in an unbeliever's life. But, instead of loving seekers in a way that creates an atmosphere for more potential God encounters, we strip our services back to keep from frightening or offending them. Doing them more harm than good.

Regrettably, we misidentify the seekers' needs *and* desires, attempting to hook them by giving them something they already have. More of *us.* Strangely, we believe our organizational aptitude and skillfully crafted church rendezvous are just what the doctor ordered, when, in reality, these amazing seekers are after something else entirely. Something no human alone—even the best of us—can provide.

Recently, a pastor friend told me, "When it comes to music, we've discovered that people are attracted to excellence in worship, so that's what we focus on." I thought to myself, *Yes, people are attracted to excellence, but people are transformed by anointing.* Excellence is wonderful, and we should do most anything in our power to present our music with excellence, but when excellence is presented apart from anointing, it does more harm than good. And we cease to rightly love the very ones we're trying to bring to Jesus.

Imagine the unbeliever's frustration. They slip into our church hoping for something profound. Something life-changing. Something besides rules and religion. They're desperate for something beyond themselves. Something beyond man. Something more than they've encountered in pop culture. Likely, they're hoping for God Himself, though they may not know it.

> In attempting to love seekers the wrong way, we actually end up hurting them instead.

In the end, they aren't seeking what man can offer. Talent. Programs. Hype. Music. Christian clichés. Nice facilities. Clever speeches. No. They're overrun with all of this already. And yet, we spare no expense in giving it to them anyway. With more strings attached. Something the world can do a thousand times better.

Not surprisingly, in attempting to love seekers the wrong way, we actually end up hurting them instead.

Even with our grandest efforts in the areas of drama, music, lights, and sound—with million-dollar budgets—we're still offering them a lesser version of Broadway? They've already rubbed shoulders with the most talented speakers and singers and actors the world has to offer, and yet they remain unsatisfied. And still, they are seeking. Because something is missing. And this should greatly excite us, knowing we can give them what the world can never offer.

ANOINTING—WHAT THE WORLD CAN'T OFFER

People often look longingly to the Church to provide something the world cannot. Yet, time and again, they come up empty. Why? Because we're doing our best—like mice on a running wheel—to compete with all the world has already mastered.

Thankfully, we don't need to. Compete, that is. Truth is, we have something the world doesn't. Something powerful. Something beyond compare. Something terrifying and beautiful at the same time. Something that defies description. Something raw and gut-wrenching. Something many leaders are afraid to let loose. Ironically. Because of seekers.

It's called the anointing—the power of God flowing through His people in the form of His Spirit.

Talent alone has never changed the human heart. In fact, the overemphasis of natural gifting regularly leads people astray in large numbers. Ironically, exposure to the anointing of the Holy Spirit does quite the opposite—softens the hardest of hard hearts every single day.

We've all witnessed some highly sought-after leaders work tirelessly to keep their church "safe" by filtering out the "weirdoes." By removing the offensive language in our songs and preaching. By taming the fanatics with their flags and their dancing. By working diligently to produce slick, down-to-the-second services. By making sure nothing—*nothing*—would ever make someone feel uncomfortable.

It's crazy. I'm aware of a real church that refuses to let their pastors speak the word *blood* from the pulpit. I've also heard of pastors who tell their worship singers to stop raising their hands during musical worship. I know of specific churches who silence shouts of praise from their core members in order to keep from making others uncomfortable.

All the while, unbelievers attend concerts and sporting events where people act like this all the time. Raising their hands, shouting, and screaming out passionately—going cuckoo "crazy"—dressing up and painting themselves with bright colors and hollering at the top of their lungs, even dancing wildly when their team scores or when their favorite recording artist pops through a trap door in the stage.

Then they show up at church, and we silence our most zealous Christ-followers for fear that seekers might be caught off-guard. This is insanity! Heaven forbid unbelievers observe believers expressing real passion for God—a far more wonderful purpose than cheering on talented singers and athletes!

Truthfully, I see it the other way around. Heaven forbid unbelievers never observe believers responding passionately to the very God who transforms their lives. Heaven forbid seekers never rub shoulders with believers who are excited and expressive in their love and devotion to the One who destroyed the power of sin and death.

Heaven forbid.

SELF-FEEDERS

This explains why Willow Creek pastor Bill Hybels had "the wake up call of his adult life" after spending thirty years creating and promoting a multi-million-dollar organization driven by programs and measured participation—all while convincing hundreds of other church leaders to do the same.

Ponder these thoughts from his lips: "Some of the stuff that we have put millions of dollars into thinking it would really help our people grow and develop spiritually, when the data actually came back, it wasn't helping people that much. Other things that we didn't put that much money into and didn't put much staff against is stuff our people are crying out for."

Hybels continues, "We made a mistake. What we should have done when people crossed the line of faith and became Christians, we should have started telling people and teaching people that they have to take responsibility to become self-feeders. We should have gotten people, taught people, how to read their Bible between services, how to do the spiritual practices much more aggressively on their own."[6]

In other words, Hybels discovered that spiritual growth for our congregants doesn't occur by leading them to become dependent on elaborate church programs and put-together people. It happens via the age-old spiritual disciplines of personal prayer, Bible study, musical worship, and genuine relationships. In the process, he also realized that

6   "Willow Creek Repents?" Christianity Today, October 18, 2007, https://www. christianitytoday.com/pastors/2007/october-online-only/willow-creek-repents.html.

empowering others to excel in these basic disciplines does not often require multi-million-dollar facilities with hundreds of staff to manage.

I have personally led worship at several well-known megachurches with traditional "seeker" models, and the reaction has always been the same. Secretly, staff members approach me afterward to tell me how refreshing my "deep worship" is—to admit that they and other core leaders are starving for spiritual depth. All because the spiritual focus of these types of churches is often down near the shallow end of the pool.

Honestly, many of these so-called seeker-friendly churches are a mile wide (boasting incredible numbers) and yet barely an inch deep (failing egregiously in producing self-sustaining, mature followers of Christ).

THE CLASH OVER DEEP AND WIDE

Unfortunately, it seems we as leaders are often forced to choose between growing deep (spiritual growth) and growing wide (numerical growth), sacrificing one to gain the other. Of course, we all pray and believe for both, yet we must never sacrifice much depth to gain much width.

Look at Jesus' ministry. The deeper He went into spiritual things, the leaner His numbers became, yet that is exactly what He did. As many pastors commonly report, the crowds were vast at first, and yet as Jesus started insulting church leaders, sending away seekers, casting out demons, healing the sick, raising the dead, calling out His twelve disciples, and demanding people eat his flesh and drink his blood (John 6), many people gave up and deserted him (see John 6:66).

Jesus (though He is love) is extremely offensive. To our flesh. To our pride. To our sin nature. While ministering to unbelievers, Jesus seems to avoid political correctness altogether. He goes straight for the jugular. Think of how he "ministered" to the women at the well, exposing her infidelity through a prophetic word. Think of how he sent the rich young ruler packing (with all his potential tithe). And yet, astonishingly, we work overtime in our services

> Astonishingly, we work tirelessly in our services to appeal to unbelievers via the natural rather than via the supernatural—by the Spirit.

to appeal to unbelievers via the natural rather than via the supernatural—by the Spirit.

Here's the point.

In the end, the most troubling downside to a traditional seeker-friendly church is that it is not friendly (loving) to the seeker after all. It's true. By appealing to unbelievers in the natural, we actually diminish their chances of giving their hearts to Christ. Why? Because we teach them that church is about an event rather than about a Person. About feelings rather than about faith. About a building rather than about community.

By sticking with our relatively Spirit-less church service orders, we shout from the rooftops that Christianity amounts only to attending a lengthy, man-produced "show." A lesser version of the entertainment they already enjoy elsewhere. And yet, one where they can't drink beer, shout out, or do much else besides drink coffee and stare at the back of the guy's balding head in front of them. Thank goodness it's only once a week.

What the seeker needs from us is a full on, face-to-face encounter with God. What they don't need is for us to give them what we think they want—an impressive, slickly perfected program designed for spectators. One where they can applaud our efforts and be impressed with our knowledge of Jesus.

Like good parents, loving our "children" means giving them what they need rather than what they want. This is the most loving and friendly thing we can do—give "seekers" every opportunity to come into direct contact with God's overwhelming power and love. Not with our program. Not with our production. Not with our ingenuity. But with everything Jesus brought to the table. Relationship. Truth. Deliverance. Healing. Freedom. Power. Guidance. Fruits of the Spirit. Gifts of the Spirit. All of the above.

It begs the question; which approach is most friendly to the seeker? The one where leaders attempt to entertain congregants—doing everything possible not to offend them—or the one where leaders go rogue, fully exposing congregants to all they so desperately need—the transformational, uncomfortable, and supernatural presence of God? Ironically, when we love unbelievers the way Jesus did, we become more seeker-friendly than the ones who coined the term to begin with.

Chapter Highlights

1. Though it may seem counterintuitive, loving people *in worship leadership* is just as important as loving God. Clearly our first priority must be to bring glory to God, but if we're truly serving the Lord, we should love what He loves. He loves people, and when we love His people, we bring Him great glory.

2. When we struggle to love the people God has placed in front of us, we miss the point of serving God and serving people. Fact is, we can't lead people if we don't love people.

3. Many popular quotes aren't as true as they seem. We must be clear on this. Biblical leadership is not influence. Biblical leadership is service (see Luke 22:25–27).

4. Success in the Kingdom often looks very different from success in the world. God doesn't measure the impact of your leadership in numbers alone, but in fruit. At the end of it all, success in the Kingdom means succession—through fathering, mentoring, and discipling—no matter how many people your ministry is touching.

5. The term *seeker-friendly* has been around for a few decades, and it has long been defined as an intentional effort to plan and produce our weekly church services in a way that prioritizes unbelievers over believers. Ironically, when we do this, we hurt unbelievers. By aiming to give them what we think they want, we fail to give them all they need. If our churches are to become truly seeker-friendly—and I believe they should—we will need to plan our services in a way that allows them to become as friendly to seekers as possible. This means refusing to remove the supernatural from our services and instead creating a communal atmosphere where they can directly encounter the full-on power of God. This is truly what it means to be "friendly" to seekers.

Chapter 13

THE PERFECT UNION: A MARVELOUS MARRIAGE OF THE SCRIPTED AND THE UNSCRIPTED

Lie #13

*"We've done just fine without spontaneous worship,
so there's no good reason to run people off
by incorporating it now."*

W e have chapel services at NCU five days a week. For some, this may seem a bit excessive. I get it. Requiring today's modern-day university student to attend chapel every day seems like it could easily backfire by increasing the potentiality of spiritual numbness.

Yet, we have experienced just the opposite. Go figure.

Of course, I'm not suggesting that our students gleefully bound out of bed each day, run to chapel, and seek God passionately Monday through Friday. Shoot, I don't even do that! Still, what we've intentionally cultivated—by the grace and power of God—is a vibrant, God-seeking community that defies the odds of what typically happens at a normal Christian university. I'd love to help you do the same within your local body of believers.

THE DAY IT ALL BEGAN

Four years into my time at NCU, something shifted. I was standing in my normal spot in our sanctuary—stage right, front—worshiping the Lord, when our student worship leader began to sing spontaneously.

All was glorious. At first.

I waited. And waited. A forever ten seconds went by. Hearts were open. Instruments were soaring. But the worship leader wasn't doing his job. Frustration crowded my mind. We had discussed this many times in class. I had modeled it. I had taught it. I had asked them do it in their assigned worship leader presentations. But nothing.

Then, suddenly it didn't matter.

What I had waited for for years was finally happening. Right before my ears. Holy cow. Could it be? Was this real? Was I making it up?

No, it continued.

With absolutely no instruction from the worship leader or the worship team, our students began to lift up their own song to the Lord as the band played instrumentally. It was a sacred spontaneous song from their hearts to the Lord.

Truthfully, there was no real reason the congregation should be singing. In the natural. No one had invited them to sing. We weren't in a specific part of a known song. There were no lyrics on the screen. And yet they began lifting their voices to the Lord spontaneously anyway.

This may seem like no big deal, but you must understand. We had been slowly introducing the biblical culture of spontaneous worship at NCU for four years. We'd certainly had some nice moments when everyone joined in. But never without instruction.

I had drilled it into my worship leaders: "Always plan for space in your songs—in the beginning, middle, or near the end—so that our community can lift their voices to God in spontaneous worship. When the moment comes, simply vamp on a simple chord progression (usually from the chorus or bridge) and invite the congregation to lift up their own song to God."

I had said it a hundred times. Maybe more.

But the one thing I asked them *never* to do is linger in a long instrumental section without giving any instruction. (Of course, if you're from a church where singing spontaneously is part of the culture already, you may be thinking, *Why would you need to do that?* The simple answer is, because spontaneous singing wasn't a significant part of our culture at NCU. At least, not yet. You see—and this is key—if you hope to transition your church culture from one thing to another, you must provide clear and concise teaching on *what* you want people to do as well as *why* you want them to do it.

> If you hope to transition your church culture from one thing to another, you must provide clear and concise teaching on *what* you want people to do as well as *why* you want them to do it.

Simple.

Typically, when singers flow in long instrumental moments, without purposeful instruction, people disengage. *Why are there no lyrics on the screen? What is the band doing? What do they want me to do? Is the lyric operator lost? Hmmm, what are we having for lunch?*

Of course, this is exactly what we don't want.

But today was different.

UP CAME A SHOOT

Today, something happened that had never happened before. The culture of spontaneous worship began to peek its little head up through the soil. After planting many seeds of spontaneous worship into the soil of our little collegiate congregation, and after watering, nurturing, and cultivating these seeds over and over again, the moment finally arrived.

Remember in fifth grade how you planted those lettuce seeds and waited for them to come up? Day after day after day. Nothing. But then, when you least expected it, you peeked down into your little soil-in-a-Styrofoam-cup experiment, and, lo and behold, protruding out of the moist dirt was a tiny little sprout. A sign of life.

That's what we were experiencing.

A sign of life.

After several years of teaching in the classroom, leading in our daily chapels, working in our rehearsals, and giving our worship leaders spontaneous worship assignments, a little sign of life was beginning to show itself.

This is how we know new culture is taking root. When it begins to show signs of sustainable life. In this case, despite the fact that my worship leader totally forgot to invite our community to lift up a spontaneous song, they sung one anyway. All by themselves. Not reservedly either. And it gave us real proof that the hard work of teaching and nurturing was finally beginning to pay off.

Can you grasp the significance of this moment in the realm of culture building? This is what we are working toward. Our Christ-following community was beginning to embrace an aspect of biblical worship they had never embraced on their own before. The culture was shifting. The culture was growing. The culture was maturing.

WHAT IS SPONTANEOUS WORSHIP?

Spontaneous worship is simply this: the utilization of impromptu, previously unwritten songs within the musical worship context. I've found these impromptu songs typically arrive in two forms:

1. **Prayers set to music** – Different songs sung by each individual worshiper throughout the congregation. Songs that meander like a river and have no intentional rhythm or rhyme—much like a prayer.
2. **Songs for the body** – Songs that initially burst forth from an individual leader—as led by the Spirit. Songs that are spontaneous and yet more "structured" regarding rhythm and melody and that are intended for the entire congregation to sing together.

Spontaneous song lyrics are often spin-offs from normal corporate song lyrics or are inspired by a prophetic nudge from the Spirit. They may even erupt directly from certain Scripture verses we've hidden in our hearts. They often spring up during instrumental moments (quiet or loud) and can range from intimate to declaratory in tone. Ultimately, spontaneous songs serve to motivate congregants to step into deeper levels of personal connection with God's Spirit, empowering each person to engage more vibrantly and intentionally with their Creator.

Spontaneous worship is entirely biblical (which we will discuss in a moment) and relatively easy to incorporate (which I will explain). It can be woven right into the fabric of the musical worship we're already doing in our services. One thing is for sure: introducing spontaneous worship to your congregation will set off a chain reaction of spiritual and relational growth that we could have only dreamed of previously.

Amazingly, spontaneous worship is one of our most effective strategies to help break the cycle of spiritual immaturity in the everyday believer. Think of it. By inviting our congregants to lift up their own songs to God—in congruence with the corporate songs we already sing—we are essentially taking off the training wheels. This is an invaluable leadership strategy, because it empowers each person to cultivate a language of authentic worship all their own, which, of course, decreases the congregation's dependency on the worship leader and accelerates their own personal connection with God.

No longer must we plead with people to worship the Lord, because we have, in essence, handed them the baton to *lead themselves* into God's presence from Sunday to Sunday.

CREATING SPACE FOR GOD

Spontaneous worship is one of the most—if not *the* most—overlooked transformational strategies in the Church today. Let me say it again. Across the board, there is simply no greater, more potent missing element in our church services than this one thing. Spontaneous worship. It cannot be overstated, and it must not be omitted.

Be sure: I'm not suggesting that spontaneous worship is the *most* important element in worship. That would be exaggeratory. But I am suggesting that—of all the foundational, impactful elements needed in corporate (and personal) worship—spontaneous worship is the most overlooked. When we consider other foundational worship elements like authenticity, engagement, passion, humility, preparation, community, love, excellence, relationship, etc., it's clear that most churches incorporate, or attempt to incorporate, most of these. All but spontaneous worship.

And it's time to change that narrative.

One of the very first things God told me to do when I arrived at NCU on January 11, 2010, was to create more space for His Spirit in our chapel services. He told me we'd been cramming too many things into our services, and, as a result, we were, in a sense, pushing Him out. This launched us into a four-year journey that would move us—slowly but intentionally—from planning four songs for eighteen minutes to planning two songs for eighteen minutes. Gradually but dramatically, this began to revitalize our services.

Spontaneous worship was not something we were utilizing at NCU when I arrived, and it's still not something found in most modern churches. Even so, I advocate strongly that if we sincerely desire to emulate biblical worship (which I know we do), and if we have a genuine passion to quicken the connection between the worshiper and God (which I know we do), we must incorporate spontaneous worship into our services moving forward.

To be sure, there were already incredible things happening in our daily fifty-minute chapel gathering. Long before I came. But, as you might guess, God still wanted more. He always does. And I was compelled to implement whatever strategy His Spirit would give us so we could grow our beautiful gathering into something even more beautiful.

DRAWN TO THE SCRIBBLES

About fifteen years ago, the Lord gave me an analogy to help explain what I'm about to present to you. Following that, He began teaching me the truths of these things from His Word—which, of course, is vital. It goes like this.

Have you ever gone to a store to buy a card for someone? Of course. I've often done this for family and friends (at $8 a pop, I might add). Imagine I spend fifteen to twenty minutes reading card after card until I find just the right one for Martha's birthday. The cover is touching. The poem is peach perfect. And it has just the right balance of romance and humor.

I take the card home and scribble a few heartfelt thoughts inside to express my sincerest love for her, and then I place the card in the envelope, attempt to write a fancy version of her name on the front, lick it, and seal it.

The moment of truth comes.

Martha opens the card. She reads the message on the front. She reads the poem inside. But then she lingers on my personal note—you know, the part I wrote with my own hand. The words I crafted especially for her. From me. The one who treasures everything about her.

She smiles.

You see, there's something extra beautiful about a person's personally written words that touch us even more deeply than the calculated, professionally written words found in the cards we purchase. Could it be that God feels the same way about spontaneous worship?

Scott Hagan, president of NCU, shared a similar analogy in chapel a couple of years back. He talked about how he would often receive birthday cards from his kids when they were little, and how he would always gravitate toward their crayon-scribbled notes. Sure, they wrote things like *I luv yew* with a backwards "y," but it didn't matter. In fact, it didn't matter if it didn't rhyme or if there was missing punctuation. It didn't matter if the words were misspelled or if the grammar wasn't just so. It was from them. From their little hearts. From their little minds. From their little hands.

This isn't to say that the pre-written words in a card (or in a song) have no value. In fact, as I mentioned, many people spend a great deal of time treasure hunting for just the right card that says it just the right way. This can be very meaningful. But rarely is it as meaningful as our own heart-written words.

Could it be God feels the same way about songs? Could it be He's longing to hear a personally "written" song of love from each and every son and daughter, even if it isn't crafted perfectly, pitched flawlessly, or sung professionally?

This is spontaneous worship.

THE BIG QUESTION

You might say, "Jeff, we know all about spontaneous worship. We've heard Bethel, Hillsong, and Elevation do it a ton." Great. But that's not the question. The question is, are *you* implementing spontaneous worship in your church? Regularly. Effectively. Intentionally. Not only in your Wednesday or Friday night services, but also in your Sunday morning services?

It all begins as we (the leaders) step up to invite our worshiping communities to step in, even as we step back. More than any other strategy you aren't already implementing, intermingling spontaneous worship with corporate worship will help you take your church family to the next level. Why? Two simple reasons:

1. Spontaneous worship equips and releases people to engage from their hearts with greater intentionality and authenticity, and…
2. Spontaneous worship increases the leader's ability to excel in the single most effective form of leadership known to man—empowerment of people.

So, what about it?

Are you regularly sharing biblical teaching on spontaneous worship with your teams and your congregation? Are you creating deliberate space for spontaneous worship in your service orders? Are you intentionally inviting people to lift up their own songs to God as part of your Sunday services? If not, you, your teams, and your church are missing out on the fullness of biblical worship.

No exaggeration.

Sure, today's churches are moving less and less toward the unscripted and more and more toward the strict scripting of their services—down to the second. Why? Most rationalize that any other approach could scare away potential unbelieving visitors. They reason: the tighter the ship, the greater the crowd. The greater the crowd, the greater potential for unbelievers to be saved.

Okay. Maybe.

Maybe not.

I want to suggest a paradox here. What if a tight ship is not what unbelievers are looking for after all?

Ask yourself, as it relates to structured ministry:

1. Is this what we find in the Scriptures concerning Jesus' approach to ministry? Scripted, neat, and tidy?

2. Are we willing to consider the possibility that unbelievers are actually searching for a more authentic version of "religion"? Something beyond the mind-blowing, scripted movies, shows, and concerts they already enjoy outside of church?

With many churches attempting to grow their online communities by streaming their Sunday services online, it's completely logical to assume that tightening up the service order is the way to go. Even so, what if it simply isn't true?

Do we really believe unbelievers are attracted to organization and structure over anointing and authenticity? What if unbelievers (and believers alike) aren't as impressed with our manicured service templates as we think? Don't they already have unlimited access to "entertainment" like this every day? And with much more robust budgets? What if unbelievers are really searching for something supernatural? Something beyond what man can offer.

> Do we really believe unbelievers are attracted to organization and structure over anointing and authenticity?

PLANNING GOD OUT OF THE SERVICE

If you look closely with spiritual eyes, you may notice that many churches are planning God right out of the service. "What? How can you say that?"

I know. It's terribly bold. And I do mean it to be. It's like we're playing with fire.

Chris Dupré warns us in *The Lost Art of Pure Worship*, "This truth [that it is impossible to love God without a profound revelation of His love] and the corresponding process of growth is so important for the believer to grasp. *Otherwise, we slowly learn how to do this thing called 'Christianity' until, after a few years, we have got it down so well that we have no need of God.*"[7]

---

7   Chris DuPré, *The Lost Art of Pure Worship* (Shippensburg, PA: Destiny Image, 2012), page 28.

Isn't this the grand deception? To believe we have the ability to "do church" in our own power? As if anything we could ever do on our own could make an eternal difference?

A. W. Tozer attempts to shake us awake: "I remind you that there are churches so completely out of the hands of God that if the Holy Spirit withdrew from them, they wouldn't find it out for many months."[8]

Wow. Double back on that.

We often dismiss this type of radical statement, assuming it doesn't apply to us. But please remember, churches that fall into this category are largely unaware of it. (Just as Samson was entirely unaware that the Lord had left him in Judges 16:20).

Ask yourself, *Have I seen it?* Our tendency to program God out of our lives—with our busyness? Out of our services—with our agendas? Out of our musical worship—with our fear of man?

This is serious stuff and is certainly one of the most known tactics of the enemy. If he can get us to believe we've mastered Christianity—even church—so completely that we slip back into the driver's seat, he wins. It's subtle. Yet, he knows we crave this type of control. Subconsciously. We really do resist a "religion" where we must completely depend on God. We crave a god who can be figured out. Programmed. Reproduced. Manufactured. Arrive and coast. It's much easier. Much easier than listening to the Holy Spirit. Yet much less productive.

God, in his kindness, is continually leading us to the place where we are forced to recognize our desperate need for Him. Where we must tune our ears to His Spirit in every moment of our lives. In every moment of our services. In every moment of our songs. This is precisely why leading spontaneous worship is so important. It helps us fight our natural tendency to take the reins and push away the Holy Spirit.

NAVY SEALS, BORN TO ADAPT

Chris Dupré helped me understand the beautiful marriage of the planned and the unplanned with this metaphor.

---

8 "A.W. Tozer>Quotes>Quotable Quote," Goodreads, www.goodreads.com/quotes
/567366-i-remind-you-that-there-are-churches-so-completely-out.

Navy SEALs are, no doubt, meticulous when it comes to planning their missions. Of course. Down to the last detail. Crossing every "t" and dotting every "i." There's no room for error. No room for mistakes. No room for unpreparedness. Lives are at stake. With every mission.

The team consults the higher-ups. They meet and discuss every possibility. They devise a plan to accomplish the mission—one they believe will help them overcome the enemy.

That said, it wouldn't surprise anyone to know that Navy SEAL missions rarely go 100 percent according to plan. But this is what makes them so special. This is why they're sent on the most dangerous missions. They adapt.

These men and women have been so highly trained that when something changes, they don't blink. They adjust. When something goes wrong—something they didn't see coming—they don't freeze. They don't give up. And they most certainly don't stick to the original plan. They adapt. They lean in hard on their training and do whatever must be done to accomplish the mission.

> Sadly, many worship leaders and worship teams are more committed to the plan than they are to the mission.

Please, hear this. Their mission was never to accomplish the *plan*. Their mission was to accomplish the *mission*. With or without the help of the plan. If the original plan helps them accomplish the mission, great. But the plan itself was never the end goal. It simply represented one possible path toward accomplishing the end goal. The mission.

The set list (and service order) is our plan, but connecting people with God is our mission. Sadly, many worship leaders and worship teams are more committed to the plan than they are to the mission. (Either that, or they haven't planned for the unplanned and are therefore unprepared—despite their willingness—to adapt. Note: I discuss the practical sides of planning for the unplanned in the pages ahead.)

We are at war, people! And we had better be prepared to adapt. Our congregants' souls are at stake, and spontaneous worship helps us flex in order to keep the mission in our sights. God is not looking for a bunch of robots with plastic routines and programmed worship techniques to lead His people. He made us to ebb and flow. To react and interact. To breathe and to move. Just like Navy SEALs.

THE BIBLICAL PRECEDENT FOR SPONTANEOUS WORSHIP

Once God began opening my eyes to the transformative power of spontaneous worship, I immediately started to educate our teams and our community on its biblical origins. If there was any hope of grafting spontaneous worship into our worship culture, we would need to establish relevant biblical direction right from the get-go.

The following are some of the foundational biblical truths I've discovered:

1. The *Tehillâh* Praise – One of the first things I began to teach our NCU community is the seven Hebrew words for *praise*. As you now know, the word *Tehillâh* is a Hebrew word that means "to sing with songs or hymns; laudations of the spirit. The song of the Lord; spontaneous song to the Lord." It's used frequently in the Bible, including in Psalm 22:3, where we learn that God inhabits—or "lives together with His people in"—the "*Tehillâh*" (spontaneous) praise. *Inhabits* could literally be translated "God will join Himself to our praise." The Amplified Bible reads, "But You are holy, O You Who *dwell* in [the holy place where] the praises (Tehillâh) of Israel [are offered]." This is the type of biblical expression we're missing so much in our Western churches.

2. Like the Wind – Another biblical concept we must embrace is the way in which God's character informs our worship. If spontaneous worship really is a "thing," it would most certainly spring out of who He is—from His character. He never directs us to lead His people in ways that are contrary to His own nature, especially as He invites us to become more and more like Him. The revelation of "God, like a rock" is certainly one of the most foundational metaphors we have concerning God's character. It establishes our God as One who is unchanging, orderly, reliable, and secure—qualities that are important in life and in worship (see Psalm 18:1; 1 Samuel 2:2; Deuteronomy 32:15; Exodus 17:6). Even so, we must equally grasp the metaphor of "God, like the wind." Here, we are reminded that our God is the God of newness, creativity, surprises, and freedom—also qualities that are important in life and worship (see John 3:8; 2 Samuel 22:11; Job 38:1). God is *both* a rock and a wind, and our worship leadership should embody both metaphors—the scripted (the rock) *and* the unscripted (the wind).

3. The New Song – A third phenomena we simply cannot ignore is the Bible's incessant use of the term *new song*. In fact, in *The Lost Art of Pure Worship*, fellow author Sean Feucht informs readers that the phrase *sing a new song to the Lord* is repeated eighty-seven times in the Bible. This is compelling when it comes to resisting our tendency to regurgitate the same old songs again and again. Bob Sorge's teachings also aim to keep us in balance. He often reminds us that old songs gather, and new songs propel. (Of course, God's command to *sing a new song* doesn't refer only to spontaneous songs, but also to adding new corporate songs to the set list as well, even as we enjoy older, familiar songs.) What we discover is that "known songs" and "spontaneous songs" actually work hand in glove. "Known songs" serve to launch us beautifully into uncharted spontaneous worship, only to return us, full circle, to the songs we already know—but this time, the songs we already know take on a brand-new life.

4. Singing in the Spirit – When it comes to the New Testament, significant encouragement on spontaneous worship can be gleaned from Paul's writings in 1 Corinthians 14:15: *"Well then, what shall I do? I will do both. I will pray in the spirit, and I will pray in words I understand. I will sing in the spirit, and I will sing in words I understand."* While this passage doesn't specifically tell us that Paul is singing spontaneously, we shouldn't imagine he would be doing anything else if he is singing in the spirit (singing in tongues). How else would you sing in the Spirit? There are no pre-written phrases to learn, only unrehearsed, free-flowing unctions from the Spirit of God. Beautiful!

5. The River Hunter – One final in-depth scriptural example comes from best-selling author and pastor, Bob Sorge, from his book *Following the River*. He derives his "River Hunter" concept from Ezekiel 47, a chapter that unveils a metaphorical river flowing down from the temple of God bringing healing to all. The river doubles as a metaphor for God's presence, reminding us that there are deeper and deeper depths of relational connection with God.

Sorge invites worship leaders to become "River Hunters" as they seek to fulfill their assigned biblical task of "hunting" or "seeking" diligently for the river of God's relational presence on behalf of the people. He reveals that many leaders fail to lead people into God's presence because they are determined to stick to their planned lists (straight paths). They do so rather than becoming "hunters" of the largely unpredictable, twisting and turning nature of God's supernatural love, exemplified by the meandering river (God's Spirit).

Some lead worshipers may happen by the river at certain points in a service, yet their inability to recognize it and change course renders them incapable of joining the flow. Have you been there? Suddenly, a powerful Holy Spirit moment occurs, and one of two things happen: 1) It passes us by, because the band is ill-prepared to be anything other than a late-night cover band, or 2) another pastor steps up and utters those infamous five words, "You may now be seated."

Our job as worship leaders is to search for the Lord, to listen for His voice, and to lean in to His heart. On behalf of our congregation. We "hunt" for the "sweet spot" in God's presence and direct the congregation to join Him in the flow. At our 2016 Pure Worship Institute conference, Sorge appealed vehemently to us, "People don't come to the house for your list. They come for the river!" As difficult as it may be for some to swallow, we must move away from a traditional "set list only" model and toward a model that balances the scripted with the unscripted.

PLANNING FOR THE UNPLANNED

You might be starting to wonder, *Are you saying God is uninvolved in the planning of our songs, set lists, and service orders?* Of course not. In fact, we should always engage with God as we plan for our services. (Hopefully we're actually doing this and not just saying it.) God wants to guide and direct us through the entire planning process—days, weeks, and even months in advance. Yet, He also wants to guide and direct us by speaking and moving in real time in each and every moment of our services.

This means we must diligently plan to incorporate specific space for these moments within our sets. In this way, we find ourselves planning for the unplanned. Like the Navy SEALs, we must stop assuming everything is going to go as planned and actually begin to realize that God is going to nudge us this way and that in every service. Why? For two reasons: 1) To discover whether we're actually engaging in real time with Him or just "doing church." He tests our obedience in this way, just as He tested Abraham's worship when it came to sacrificing Isaac. 2) To teach us to adjust on the fly as part of His secret battle strategy. Yep, He knows the enemy is also eyeing our plans and has a much harder time disrupting them when he can't predict everything we're going to do. God keeps some of His plans close to His vest and reveals them only on a need-to-know basis.

Not surprisingly, good preachers use these same techniques when they preach and teach. They spend hours creating outlines, planning analogies, rehearsing jokes, and constructing scriptural proofs. But then, in the midst of sharing the message, they listen to the Spirit to discern whether He wants them to add or subtract any additional thoughts. This is the beauty of working together with God. It's the ultimate partnership.

Remember, when we plan for the unplanned, we're not simply saying we're willing to change things *if* God happens to show up (lip service). We're planning ahead by making *space* in our worship services, believing full well that God *is* going to move in unplanned ways during our services. Dr. Amy Anderson, a highly regarded professor of New Testament and Greek at NCU, shared this thought in her book *When You Come Together*: "Plan as if there is no Holy Spirit, and enter into the worship gathering as if the Holy Spirit is all there is."[9]

Practically, this means planning for fewer songs as well as planning for more possible spontaneous moments. It means purposefully writing in a few minutes for Holy Spirit moments on our PCO service order. Of

---

9   Amy Anderson, *When You Come Together: Challenging the Church to an Interactive Relationship with God* (Being Church, 2011), 142.

course, we don't have to write it in like this: *HOLY SPIRIT MOMENT: 5 minutes.* We can accomplish the same thing by adding three or four minutes to a couple of the songs to allow for more freedom within the songs themselves. Like this:

- 7:00   Raise A Hallelujah (normally 5:00)
- 9:00   Build My Life (normally 5:00)
- 10:00   Waymaker (normally 7:00)

This can be scary at first. But we must realize that when we cram too much into our services, we essentially push God out. Consequently, we must fully commit to following the Holy Spirit, anticipating—based on Scripture—that He is very likely to change the plan. Even the plan He gave us at first.

This requires rehearsal.

REHEARSING SPONTANEOUS WORSHIP WITH YOUR TEAMS

There's only one way to grow personally in leading spontaneous moments, and that is to rehearse them. It's like anything else. Rarely do people excel in things they don't practice. Spontaneous worship is no different. I understand. It may seem ingenuine of me to speak of rehearsing spontaneous worship. But, alas, we're not talking about faking the spontaneous. We're talking about excelling in it.

> The more we practice spontaneous worship, the more comfortable we become being uncomfortable with it.

Rehearsed Spontaneity

It's simple. We must rehearse the spontaneous, both in our time alone with the Lord and in our team rehearsals (and, of course, this is *not* a burden but a pleasure).

Rehearsing the spontaneous helps us grow, personally and as a team, in our relational connection with God. Of course, it also helps us learn to steward these moments "effortlessly" as we lead our congregations from week to week. Not surprisingly, the more we practice spontaneous worship, the more comfortable we become being uncomfortable with it. Likewise, the more we step into the unknown, the more known the unknown becomes.

All by faith. All by God's Spirit.

Of course, it would be easy to give this whole thing a try one random Sunday morning (because Jeff Deyo said so) and then—when it fails miserably—to chalk it up to "our congregation just isn't ready" or "spontaneous worship might be good for some churches, but not for ours." Please don't do this.

We must take baby steps as we begin slowly grafting this culture into our current church culture. This happens when we begin with getting our teams on the same page by practicing flowing in the spontaneous in our rehearsals—long before we ever attempt to bring our congregations along for the ride. (This is especially true if spontaneous worship already makes you feel like a fish out of water. If it doesn't, you may find yourself ready to begin teaching it to your congregation and your band simultaneously, working in a little at each rehearsal and in each service).

Here's what it might look like to introduce singing and playing spontaneously to your teams in rehearsal:

1. **Repeat a known chord progression.** Start by picking a repetitive chord progression from a song you already know (typically the chorus or bridge progression). Get everyone vamping on this progression while the singer sings the normal lyrics.

2. **Ask the band to improvise.** After repeating this section several times, instruct the singer to stop singing so the band can improvise instrumentally, taking turns playing "new" melodies that are "fresh" but don't completely depart from the original vibe of the song.

3. **Ask the singers to sing spontaneously off the mic.** While the band improvises on the same chord progression, ask the singers to sing to the Lord spontaneously off the mic. This is simply like singing your prayers and does not require a repetitive rhythmic pattern. They should simply sing to the Lord whatever comes to their hearts.

4. **Ask the singers to sing spontaneously on the mic.** After a few minutes (and possibly after a demonstration from you), invite one singer at a time to begin singing spontaneously on the mic. This builds confidence as they get used to hearing themselves sing this way. If they can't think of anything to sing, give them a simple biblical or worshipful phrase (like "You alone are my God") and have them craft a melody to it.

5. **Let everyone experiment.** The band should continue to play spontaneously, experimenting with little spin-off melodies and rhythms that inspire each other. This is an incredible time of fun and creativity for the band (and for the singers) as they learn to play off one another, utilizing improvisational melodies and lyrics—all inspired by the Spirit of God.

6. **Instrumentalists are important too.** Instrumentalists must be reminded that they, too, play a vital role as they prophesy on their instruments, either by coming into agreement with the vocalists or by soaring high on a prophetic melody during an instrumental section. Often, the band may begin to build in intensity in response to what they're playing or in response to specific direction or impressions they're receiving from the singer and/or from the Spirit. Let it all happen.

7. **Identify when not to play.** The band must be careful not to step on each other's toes (or on the singer's toes), but to play off of each other, complementing each other as they go. (This typically involves sensing when *not* to play as much as sensing *what* to play.)

8. **Encourage patterns and motifs.** The guitarist may begin playing a melodic motif that is picked up by the keyboardist and bassist. It may even impact the rhythms the drummer is playing. Eventually, the vocalists may jump on board and begin adding lyrics that are inspired by the guitarist's melody.

9. **Play and sing in the Spirit.** You'll need to remind everyone that spontaneous playing is not the same as playing a traditional instrumental "solo" but involves playing an instrument as directed by the Spirit (for the Spirit), not for show but to express honor, worship, and adoration to God. Ask the singers to listen to the

Spirit as He highlights certain phrases along with unique melodies—either something biblical or a spin-off lyric from the known choruses we've already been singing.

10. **Keep an ear out for corporate spontaneous songs.** As the singers sing out random prayers set to music, ask them to listen for phrases that could be sung by the entire congregation. When they land on a short repetitive phrase—one they believe could be sung by all—they should sing it on the mic in a way that would encourage a congregation to join them. (When something like this hits, they might sing on it for quite a while, even adding slight alterations to the lyrics as they go. For example, a lyric that begins as, "We need you," can easily morph into, "We seek you," or "We love you," utilizing the same melody.)

11. **Return to the known song.** As everything crescendos, direct your teams to consider returning to the corporate song they started with. This is where things can go "next-level." By meandering away from the normal song—and then returning to it after introducing something spontaneous—we breathe a freshness into the "old" song.

12. **Repeat the corporate spontaneous song.** It works the other way too. After returning to the known song, the congregation will often forget about the corporate spontaneous song they already sang. Have the team consider bringing it back again toward the end of the known song, possibly at a lower dynamic level. It will be new all over again.

13. **Reaffirm the new culture.** As your team grows in these endeavors, remind them that you are all in the process of instilling new culture together. This culture typically utilizes the chord progression of a known chorus or bridge and flows back and forth between the two with known lyrics *and* spontaneous lyrics. While playing either chord progression, we can slip off into spontaneous worship for any amount of time, flowing up and down dynamically, and even rocketing into drums-only moments.

14. **Use signals to communicate.** This is a must. As always, we use a combination of hand signals, vocal cues, and body language to signify directional changes to the team, to the lyric presenter,

and to the congregation. Devise simple signals to tell your band when you want to navigate to the chorus progression, to the bridge progression, and vice versa. (Refer to chapter 7 for specific instructions on easy-to-use hand signals that will help your band flow effectively in the spontaneous.)

INTRODUCING SPONTANEOUS WORSHIP TO YOUR CONGREGATION

Now that we're truly understanding the potency of spontaneous worship, as well as the importance of rehearsing it with our teams, we're ready—potentially—to introduce it to our congregation. Slowly but surely.

At this point, you may say, "Jeff, I know my congregation, and spontaneous worship is never gonna fly in our church." I beg you not to think like this. This is not Kingdom leadership stratagem. We cannot allow ourselves to make culture-transforming decisions based on what we believe is—or is not—possible in our local church.

Kingdom leaders simply study God's Word, identify Kingdom principles, and follow the leading of the Holy Spirit to slowly and intentionally shift and build Kingdom culture, implementing the principles He has established. There is no *can't* when it comes to establishing Kingdom culture. When God gives us biblical examples of healthy Church culture, we have a clear mandate to lead our church family into these endeavors regardless of whether or not we think they will be accepted. (Normally, I would be tempted to insert a verse like Luke 1:37, *"For with God nothing will be impossible,"* but I won't do that.)

Step By Step

I have spent ten years slowly introducing spontaneous worship to our NCU community, which means I have spent ten years learning the right and wrong ways to do so. Let's look at the progression I often use:

1. **Model it.** I begin by leading one or two short Spirit-directed spontaneous worship moments every time I lead so I can model its power and effectiveness to our community.

2. **Teach it.** We must regularly teach on the subject of spontaneous worship surrounding the times we lead it in our services (either using the greeting card analogy or additional instruction on the "*Tehillâh*" praise, etc.). This can happen before inviting everyone to sing spontaneously while the band vamps quietly on a known chord progression.

3. **Pray about it.** I ask our worship teams to prayerfully pick one or two moments in every set list where they believe God might want to do something spontaneous (possibly at the beginning of a song, between the second chorus and the bridge, or in some other obvious spot). The Lord will continually give us anointed, creative ideas, especially as we ask Him.

4. **Try it.** After practicing together regularly behind closed doors, we're ready to introduce spontaneous worship in our services. As we approach these potential spontaneous moments—instead of charging ahead with the known part of the song—the band simply repeats a particular "planned" chord progression without singing the known lyrics. This serves many purposes, but primarily, it 1) opens up a space for us to sing spontaneously to God, and 2) reminds us to pause and listen to the Holy Spirit to discern whether He wants to redirect our path.

5. **Verbalize it.** Whoever is leading is taught to give verbal instruction on the mic, saying something like, "I want to encourage everyone to begin singing your own song to the Lord." (As mentioned at the beginning of this chapter, a directional phrase of this sort is critical, since the congregation will immediately begin to disengage if the band plays instrumentally and the singers deviate from the known song lyrics. Without instruction, the congregation typically assumes their role is to observe rather than to participate, especially if there are no lyrics on the screen or if spontaneous worship is not a "normal" part of the culture.)

6. **Teach it again.** As always, it is very important to present short biblically based teachings on spontaneous worship. Repetition in teaching is vital as we establish new culture. It can easily take twenty to twenty-five clear and concise teachings over many months for people to embody "new" truth and to embrace "new" culture.

7. **Increase it.** After continually incorporating bite-sized spontaneous moments again and again, gradually begin increasing the amount of time spent in these moments, encouraging the congregation multiple times over to "sing out a new song to the Lord" or to "sing out your prayers to God." We must be aware that our congregations continually test us subconsciously to see if we are "serious" about this invitation to sing spontaneously. They may sing out a little at first but then quickly draw back unless we encourage them to continue. They learn through repetition that we actually mean business, and in this way, we empower them to step into spontaneous worship with more confidence and freedom.

Slowly But Surely

Admittedly, the first few times I tried leading these spontaneous moments, there wasn't much response. A few eager students sang out, but most held back, unsure. Even so, we remained persistent (and ignored discouragement), and slowly but surely our community began to step in. As we continued to identify our biblical and supernatural intentionality, they would sing a few bars and then grow quiet. We would fan the flame, encouraging them to keep going. It took multiple times—over many weeks—for them to realize it was safe to "let go" in this new "spontaneous worship thing." It was like they wanted to make sure we weren't going to pull the rug out from under them.

As our teams continued to provide meaningful unscripted moments, all while growing in our ability to confidently and effectively steward these moments, our community began to increase in their comfort level. They became more and more engaged. More and more passionate. More and more expectant.

It was as if our community had been longing (without realizing it) for just such a space to express themselves to God, just hoping a fearless, Spirit-led leader would "give them permission" to chase after God more fervently. (Incidentally, I believe this is the truth. Nearly every person on the planet is waiting—unsuspectingly but desperately—for someone to release them into meaningful, transformative, worshipful connection with God.

That role is yours. Embrace it. This is the joy of every worship leader and every worship team.

CRITICAL STRATEGIES

As you begin introducing spontaneous worship to your congregation, you'll inevitably stumble and fall. No worries. Simply consider these additional strategies as you jump back in the saddle:

1. **Plan a couple spots in nearly every song where "anything goes."** Start with one moment in one song and gradually add more as everyone grows accustomed to this new culture. The goal is *not* to attempt to insert a spontaneous worship moment into every song, but to give ourselves *options* so we can respond as the Holy Spirit directs. (Note: Always avoid asking people to sing spontaneously for less than thirty seconds. This will backfire as people hold back, realizing we aren't going to give them enough time to really step in.)

2. **Assume that some songs are going to go entirely according to plan.** There are certain songs that don't really lend themselves to spontaneous worship, so we can mark these off the list. Others may only have one spot that works. Of course, the band should be made aware of potential spontaneous worship "off-ramp locales" ahead of time, so they can make sure to have their eyes open for direction from the worship leader upon approach. We shouldn't leave each and every song and section open for spontaneous worship, because that would force the band to frantically watch the worship leader for cues at all times. (Note: I don't recommend leading long sets where absolutely nothing is planned. Again, God is like a rock *and* a wind, so this would fly in the face of His character. Plus, I've found that if it's a complete free-for-all—where everything is spontaneous—things are usually too confusing for the band and the congregation. That said, feel free

> Nearly every person on the planet is waiting—unsuspectingly but desperately—for someone to release them into meaningful, transformative, worshipful connection with God.

to follow the Spirit, especially if you have an extremely gifted band and you've been flowing in the spontaneous with your congregation for years.)

3. **Raise your spiritual antenna so you can discern where the Spirit of God is leading.** As you approach specific predetermined spots in your songs that *could* turn into spontaneous moments, remember to attune your ears to the Spirit so you can sense His nudging one way or the other. This is another reason rehearsal is so important. When we're unrehearsed, it is much more difficult to focus on God's voice, because we're too preoccupied with remembering the chords and lyrics. Diligent rehearsal also builds up skill and muscle memory so we can develop the physical skill set (with hands, feet, and vocal technique) to follow wherever the Spirit of God is leading. He is generally only "limited" by our limitations—in accordance with how much we have either prepared or failed to prepare to follow His lead.

4. **Continue to ebb and flow between different repetitive sections of your known songs and spontaneous songs.** Once you get the hang of moving unhindered between corporate and spontaneous songs, you'll find the possibilities of expressing yourselves musically and lyrically to God are virtually limitless. You can swell up and down dynamically, sing near-endless spin-offs of the known songs on your set list, dive in and out of instrumental sections, and then flow seamlessly into songs further down on the list. This is not only fun and exciting, but it equips your team to grow spiritually and musically together, all while empowering your congregation to express themselves more authentically to their heavenly Father as they worship in faith.

5. **Remember, spontaneous worship songs are not inherently more spiritual than planned corporate songs.** Just as the characteristics of *God, like a rock* and *God, like the wind* are equally important, spontaneous songs and known worship songs have their own intrinsic significance as well. It's only when we attempt to consume a steady diet of one or the other that we trigger spiritual indigestion. Continually feasting on both goes a long way toward maintaining a healthy balance in our expression to God.

A HOLY SPIRIT REBUKE

As our spontaneous worship moments continued to increase, we discovered a growing desire for a better balance between known songs and spontaneous songs. As you know, we continued to trim back the number of known worship songs in our eighteen-minute set from four to three and a half, to three, then two and a half, and so forth, over two to three years' time. (Note: It has never been our goal to get rid of the known songs, but to purposefully engage in both known songs *and* spontaneous songs.)

Interestingly, removing songs from my set to make space for the Holy Spirit would never have dawned on me twenty years ago. Back then, I was the guy who often rebelled against time limitations in worship. I burned many a bridge by leading a forty-five-minute set after being asked to lead a thirty-five-minute set. I reasoned we shouldn't put limitations on the Spirit. And while this approach may have some validity, the Holy Spirit gave me this important rebuke: "Maybe the problem isn't that you need more time, but that you need to make better use of the time you've been given." What a thought! He expounded, "Maybe you should consider taking a few songs out of your set list to make more room for more of me." (Of course, when He said *maybe*, He was instructing, not suggesting.)

I had never thought about it that way before. But I was thinking about it now. Whoa. Could I have been going about it all backwards? Could it be that all I needed to do—instead of constantly pushing for more time—was embrace a "less is more" mentality in order to make the most of the time I had been given?

This is exactly what I was processing when I arrived at NCU.

Most churches simply do the math. Many popular worship songs are about 4.5 minutes long, so 18 minutes divided by four equals 4.5 minutes per song. Simple. Pick the songs, cover them like the album, and boom, you're good to go. With a slick, perfectly timed worship set.

But God wanted more for us. And I believe He wants more for you too.

So we turned up the heat.

Note: For a full breakdown of the assignment I give each year to our NCU students to lead 1 song for 18 minutes, check out the addendum.

KEEPING YOUR CONGREGATION ZONED IN

If you're like me, you can unintentionally find yourself zoning in and out as you sing songs you've already sung a million times ("Reckless Love," "What a Beautiful Name," etc.). We don't mean to, but we get distracted, thinking about lunch or the person wearing the curious outfit in front of us. Everyone has moments like these—even worship leaders—where we disengage as a result of familiarity.

Here's the thing. As we invite our congregations to lift up their own songs to God, we immediately make it easier for them to *stay* engaged. Why? Because instead of thinking about what we're doing after church or wondering why the bassist hasn't trimmed his beard, we're all rocketed back into purpose through spontaneous worship. Incapable now of simply regurgitating lyrics we've already memorized, we're "forced"—with heightened awareness—to engage our hearts a little bit more than before in order to bring forth an authentic song from our hearts.

Score!

It all happens as a result of a leader inviting us to begin forming our own words of adoration to God. What we discover is both significant and wonderful. Familiar songs projected onto a screen—even those in a book—have all the potential to be helpful at first, and yet they can turn sour over time. Even so, fascinatingly, the risk of disengagement with familiar songs decreases dramatically when they're paired with spontaneous songs. In fact, there's no better way to reinvigorate songs like "What a Beautiful Name" than to couple them with spontaneous worship.

A JOYFUL NOISE

Of course, some congregants find it difficult to sing spontaneously at first. Not everyone is a gifted songwriter. How is it, then, that we expect our church family to pen words more profound than the ones of the great songwriters? They may feel like they're writing in crayon while the professional songwriters are using a calligraphy pen. Even so, when we sing our own songs to God, we sing straight to Him from our hearts—without a script—and it hardly matters whether we're singing in pitch or with great profundity. All that's needed is an openness to love the Lord and to step into a moment where we express our sincere adoration to Him.

"But Jeff, I'm not a singer!" That's okay. God isn't looking for "professionals." He's looking for a people who are willing to make a joyful *noise*.

> **The number one job of a worship leader is to work oneself out of a job.**

This is top-tier leadership, because we're aiding people in moving to a higher, more personal level of connection with God by teaching them to communicate directly with Him for themselves rather than simply echoing what others are saying. We're helping them to move from simply regurgitating someone else's words—which is not a bad place to start—to birthing worshipful declarations of their own.

In the end, the number one job of a worship leader is to work oneself out of a job. And when we lead in a way that empowers others to lift their own voices and hearts to the Lord, we are well on our way.

CAUTIONS CONNECTED TO SPONTANEOUS WORSHIP

As you grow in your passion to introduce the culture of spontaneous worship to your congregants, there will naturally be increased excitement over the many ways in which your church family begins to mature spiritually. Of course, as with any new additions to culture, we can assume there will be a significant learning curve and some hurdles along the way. In order to minimize the struggles, I encourage you to consider the following:

1. Get rid of fear. Fear is the biggest hindrance we face in building the supernatural Kingdom culture God desires. It can be daunting to raise our spiritual antennas a little higher, believing we should begin to hear from Him more often in every service. At the same time, it's very freeing. Why? Because we no longer carry the burden of trying to do God's job. Our job is to 1) prepare, and 2) listen to the Spirit. His job is to do what only He can do: transform lives. This relieves the pressure we often put on ourselves to "make something happen." Of course, it may seem easier to skip all of this and stick with the 4.5-minutes-per-song math. But what are we missing when we do? What growth and increased fellowship are we keeping our congregations from in the process?

Spontaneous worship may seem awkward or odd to some at first, but only because of the way we were raised. Not because it actually *is* strange. In fact, based on the biblical and practical evidence we've gathered in this chapter alone, we could argue that it's even stranger that more churches are not operating in the spontaneous. I know that it *is* strange to God!

Do we really believe we'll lose attendees by leading our church family into refreshing, biblical forms of worship? God sees. And He sees your desire to obey Him no matter what other "successful" churches are doing. He would plainly tell you to cast off all of the what-ifs. Things like:

- What if I mess it all up?
- What if nobody sings when I ask them to?
- What if I don't hear the Spirit?
- What if unbelievers think we're weird?
- What if the band has a train wreck?

The consequences of messing up in spontaneous worship are much less than the consequences of *not* doing spontaneous worship. Are you going to get it perfect every time? No. Have I ever sung weird phrases or words that accidentally popped out of my mouth and embarrassed me? Yes. But I've also sang and played many things with my teams in spontaneous worship that have blown the supernatural doors off. Don't worry. Just trust God to make up the difference concerning our humanity as we allow our natural to collide with God's supernatural.

2. Get into the flow. It's all about purpose. Meandering aimlessly in spontaneous worship with no purpose or direction from the Holy Spirit is ill-advised. This will do little for you as a worship leader except get you in trouble with your pastor, frustrate your band, and help you lose the congregation. Perfect! Remember, it's the ebb and flow of the scripted and the unscripted that helps keep everyone in the river. Lingering too long in the unscripted can work against us in the same way as depending too much on the scripted.

My advice is to maintain balance by not moving on too quickly from spontaneous worship, and yet also refusing to beat the "sweet spot" to death. If you feel led to linger a little longer in the spontaneous—despite your congregation's lack of engagement—you'll need to bring extra exhortation or teaching in order to encourage them to re-engage. Discernment is key.

3. Get more out of your altar music. One of the incredible benefits of spontaneous worship is the way it augments your post-preaching music. Let me share this quick story.

I was leading worship at a large youth conference with four general sessions over three days, all with lengthy altar call response times of thirty to forty-five minutes or more. Quite honestly, I was beginning to run out of relevant "altar tunes." I had already recycled several songs as I stepped back onto the stage for the final altar-response moment. The speaker was wrapping up his message, and though I still didn't know what song I was going to lead, I instructed the band to begin vamping on the chorus of my old standard, "Jesus, I Surrender."

Out of the blue, something exciting happened that forever changed the way I approach these moments. The speaker had been preaching a powerful message entitled "It's a Good Day to Die," and he repeatedly asked the students to shout this phrase. Suddenly, I realized the spontaneous melody I was humming (off the mic) was perfect for these words, so I began singing them under my breath. As the speaker motioned for me to begin leading the students, I began singing the words he had just been preaching—to his (and my) surprise—inviting the students to join me.

Several things happened all at once. 1) Two thousand teenagers suddenly leaned in expectantly to this spontaneous, Holy Spirit-inspired song. 2) The speaker did a joy-filled doubletake over what he was hearing. 3) The Holy Spirit began moving in students' lives in supernatural ways. As a result, these students not only had the opportunity to *hear* a powerful message, but they were now also able to sing it out boldly as a worship song to God, deepening its impact on their lives. Meanwhile, the band and I were able to flow back and forth between this new spontaneous song and "Jesus, I Surrender," which was now teeming with new life.

Needless to say, when I got back to the green room, the speaker sought me out, saying, "Bro, where did that song come from?" Of course, I told him the Spirit of God led me to sing it in the moment. He was extremely grateful for our commitment to hearing the Holy Spirit and to refusing to sing whatever random song was on the set list. I was reminded that leading spontaneous worship not only serves the congregation well, but also bolsters our pastor/worship leader relationships.

CATCHING THE CURRENT

Gifted teacher and leader Chuck Porta shared a profound metaphor at our Pure Worship Institute conference in 2016. He explained it this way. The bald eagle has the most powerful wings of any bird, and yet his goal is not to use them. What? Seems odd. They can span up to 7.5 feet across, almost as wide as a grand piano is long.

Nevertheless, the eagle only flaps his ginormous wings if he has to. As little as possible. He'll leave the nest, using his wings to climb high into the thinning atmosphere. Even above mountaintops and low hanging clouds. But he only does so because he's searching. Searching for the current. And when he finds it, he begins to do what he was created to do. Soar. The ultimate goal of the bald eagle is not to flap his wings but to catch the current and glide through the sky effortlessly on the wind.

Are you seeing how this applies to worship leadership?

The flapping represents human effort. Human plans. Our work. Our set lists and service orders. Our preparation. This is all fine and good. Eagles have wings for a reason. Their wings are a part of their natural existence. An important part of how God created them. Similarly, our work is part of our natural existence as well. No apologies. It is expected and effective when we flap our wings in worship leadership in order to get things going. But—like the bald eagle—the ultimate goal is to soar. Wings spread wide, head lifted high, riding on the wind. Abandoning the efforts of man to glide with the current of the Spirit.

Clearly, these two exist in beautiful harmony. The effort and the soaring. Yet, the ultimate aspiration is to abandon the effort—when possible—preferring the soaring. Why? Because the soaring is where we become one with God. Completely. Where we fully open our lives, tap into His power, and allow Him to take us wherever He pleases.

Imagine. The eagle rises high into the big blue and begins to catch the current. He follows it wherever it takes him, negotiating the ebbs and flows and the many unknowns, on the ride of his life. It turns him this way and that, and at times lifts him even higher than he started. It dies down for a bit, and the eagle swoops low and deep. He digs in for a few mighty flaps—just enough to navigate over to another current—only to do it all over again.

This is the power of leading spontaneous worship. We utilize everything at our disposal—all the Lord has given us—to plan and prepare and work to serve God's people. But then we watch and we wait—in great expectation—for a place where we can rise up to join Him in the relational flow of His Spirit. For His purpose and for His glory. For relational communion.

It's an exciting journey through uncharted skies that keeps things fresh and exhilarating for us, our teams, and our congregation. We never know exactly what He might do or where He might take us. The lid is off and we're completely—and gladly—subject to His whims and desires. Even as we lead His people out of spiritual infancy and into spiritual maturity.

Chapter Highlights

1. It is troubling that so many churches don't employ one of the most powerful biblical strategies given by the Holy Spirit. And yet, teaching your congregation and your teams to operate in spontaneous worship—within the context of normal congregational singing—is just that powerful. Spontaneous worship is simply the utilization of impromptu, previously unwritten songs within the musical worship context.

2. One of the reasons it's so important to marry known corporate songs with spontaneous worship songs is that each serves the other by amping up the impact of the other. Corporate songs help us get our feet wet in communal worship while spontaneous songs launch us out into deeper places of relationship with God. Ironically, spontaneous worship also breathes new life into the known songs we've grown numb to.

3. Spontaneous worship is beautiful, much like the handwritten notes on birthday cards. Though these heart-felt expressions are not always sung in tune or written professionally, they are straight from our heart to God, and they mean the world coming from you.

4. One incredible feature of spontaneous singing is the way it helps our congregations stay engaged. If we're honest, it's easy to disengage unintentionally during worship when we're singing a song we already know. But when we're invited to sing a simple song from us to God, we're more likely to think about what we're singing, much the same way we would if someone asked us to pray spontaneously.

5. Unbeknownst to some, spontaneous singing is not just for emotional believers looking for a way to break the mold. The Bible is full of passages that support the idea of spontaneous singing for all believers, not the least of which is the Hebrew word for *praise*, *Tehillâh*. This little word is sprinkled throughout Scripture and most often refers to singing spontaneous songs to the Lord.

6. Planning for the unplanned aids the worship leader in intentionally incorporating spontaneous singing into their Sunday services a little at a time. It typically involves planning less songs in the set while purposefully leaving room for spontaneous singing. It also means rehearsing spontaneous playing and singing with your teams behind closed doors.

Chapter 14

BONA FIDE BABIES AND BRACKISH BURNOUT

Lie #14

*"Church leadership is lonely and exhausting,
and that's just the way it's going to be."*

Houston, we have a problem. Have you noticed? Our churches are filled with milk-sucking infants and gloriously burned-out pastors and leaders. Whoa. Did I just say that aloud? It's true. And it's a culture we as leaders have largely built *and* perpetuated, often without realizing it.

Something's gotta give.

We—all of us—have bought into the erroneous idea that it is the layperson's job to attend church and the pastor's job to study the Bible and get people saved. This is not biblical.

But before we break it all down, I'll make a bold statement: If we don't do something with the information I'm about to share in this chapter, the Church body as we know it is going to implode, along with its pastors and leaders.

Sure, I know I sound like an alarmist. "Certainly, God can handle His Church. It's not like He's going to sit by and let it fall to pieces." At the same time, Jesus warns of the numerous believers who are going to fall away in these days: *"And many will turn away from me and betray and hate each other. And many false prophets will appear and will deceive many people. Sin will be rampant everywhere, and the love of many will grow cold"* (Matthew 24:10–12). How else would this come about unless our pews were filled with baby Christians and our platforms with exhausted, often immoral leaders?

Hear me, please. It is paramount that every worship leader on the planet join together with their lead pastor with one main goal in mind: to begin championing God's "kingdom of priests" model so we can flip the script on this epidemic.

WORSHIP LEADERS, CLIMATE SETTERS

"How does all of this apply to the worship leader?" you ask. Great question.

Here's the thing. While worship pastors don't ultimately control the spiritual climate, we are often the second-most-influential leaders in our churches. We're on stage nearly as frequently as the lead pastor, and everyone is keenly aware of the power of music. For better or worse.

We must embrace the responsibility of the enormous role we play in the overall growth and maturity of the body, sparked by everything we do, on and off the stage. From what we wear, to what we say and sing, from the songs we choose, to how we treat our teams and our own family, we are either helping or hindering our congregants as they attempt to step toward their Maker.

> The "pressure" is on God to accomplish His Word. All we need to do is listen and obey. He does the heavy lifting as we stay yoked to Him.

Wow, so much pressure.

Not really.

The "pressure" is on God to accomplish His Word. All we need to do is listen and obey. He does the heavy lifting as we stay yoked to Him.

Before we take a look at some of the foundational things the Bible has to say about our role in equipping the body of Christ, I'd like to ask you to brainstorm a bit concerning the things we can do (or stop doing) as leaders to empower our church family to grow in maturity and passion. Go ahead and make a short list here.

_____

_____

_____

_____

WHOSE JOB IS IT, ANYWAY?

Over time, pastors have become increasingly frustrated with the lack of enthusiasm oozing from their constituents, so they've done the only thing they know to do. Do the work for them.

It goes like this. If churchgoers aren't going to read their Bibles, pray fervently, spend daily time with God in musical worship, strive to hear the voice of the Lord, operate in spiritual gifts, worship with freedom of expression, or share their faith, the pastor has no other choice. He'll simply have to wear all these hats on behalf of his sheep. Isn't this what we pay the pastor for, anyway—to study the Bible, to be spiritual, to hear from the Lord, and to win the lost?

All it takes is a quick look at Ephesians 4:11–12 to set us straight concerning the specific roles of pastors and leaders in the Church: _"Now these are the gifts Christ gave to the church: the apostles, the prophets, the evangelists, and the pastors and teachers. Their responsibility is to equip God's people to do his work and build up the church, the body of Christ."_

It's so simple, we almost miss it. The role of the leaders in the church—the five-fold ministers—is not to _do_ the work of the ministry but to _equip_ the body of Christ to do the work of the ministry.

Of the many pastors and leaders who are familiar with these verses, few truly embrace them in such a way as to fully implement them through faith. But why?

Here are a few possibilities:

- They've grown tired of begging their lay people to do the work of the ministry (understandably), so they see no other recourse but to do God's work by themselves.

- They don't truly understand their role as the Bible lays it out in Ephesians 4:11–12 and therefore perpetuate the wrong approach out of ignorance.
- They enjoy receiving credit for doing God's work and constantly being needed by their infant congregations.

The good news is these biblical ideals are made clear to *help us* as leaders, not to *hurt us*. No matter how strong we are, we're all subject to the same struggles and temptations. Certainly, the precautionary measures laid out are here for our protection. Apparently, from God's perspective, this is the best system. A system where pastors and leaders pour into their congregants to build them up into spiritual maturity *so that* the weight of the ministry is spread over the entire body rather than over just a few.

Makes total sense.

But for our egos.

Unfortunately, in attempting to do the work of the ministry on our own, we have contributed to the breakdown of the body of Christ by increasing the likelihood that 1) we'll burn out and that 2) our congregants will continue as spiritual infants. Apparently, this was a common theme among early Christians as well: *"You have been believers so long now that you ought to be teaching others. Instead, you need someone to teach you again the basic things about God's word. You are like babies who need milk and cannot eat solid food. For someone who lives on milk is still an infant and doesn't know how to do what is right. Solid food is for those who are mature, who through training have the skill to recognize the difference between right and wrong"* (Hebrews 5:12–14).

Can you see the dilemma of many leaders? *What to do? The people in my church are spiritually immature. But I dare not push them too hard or they might leave. Guess I'll have to coddle them and do my best to win as many folks to Jesus as I can.*

FRIENDSHIP SUNDAY

I remember an evangelism tactic we used in my home church growing up. It seemed good enough. Once a month, we'd do something we called

Friendship Sunday. The pastor would appeal to everyone in the congregation—for three weeks out of the month—to make efforts to invite an unsaved friend to church for the fourth Sunday of the month. This service would be a special service designed to reach those for Jesus who would not normally attend. Your church may do something similar.

While this seems like a decent way to reach the lost, it perpetuates a long-term philosophy that's been hurting our churches greatly over time. It's a philosophy that wrongly affirms the idea that the only role in evangelism for the everyday believer is to bring their unsaved friends to church. This couldn't be more contrary to God's Word. Can you imagine the number of people who could be saved if the pastor would stop trying to do all the "saving" and simply put his energy into equipping his congregants to share the gospel? I mean, which is a greater force for the Kingdom: one man reaching a few hundred or a few hundred reaching (and discipling) a few thousand?

God wants each person to share in the work of the Church. God wants each person to grow as an authentic witness for the gospel. God wants each person to reach those in their sphere of influence.

SHEPHERDS VS. TROUBADOURS

As worship leaders, we're charged with caring for God's sheep. We're shepherds right alongside our lead pastors. Don't miss this. Our role is to shepherd our teams first and foremost and then to take part in shepherding the entire flock (with the help of our teams) under the direction of our lead pastor—who is the lead shepherd under the Head Shepherd, Jesus.

Singing is something we *do*. Pastoring and shepherding is something we *are*.

Truth is, many of us misunderstand the shepherd/sheep analogy entirely. Unintentionally. Yet, this goes right along with living out Ephesians 4:11–12. I'm no sheep expert, but it doesn't take one to realize the main job of the shepherd is *not* to feed the sheep. Only the weak and orphaned sheep need this type of care, and then only until they're strong enough to graze for themselves.

The job of the pastor is *not* to feed the sheep but to guide them to new pastures. *"The Lord is my shepherd; I have all that I need. He lets me rest in green meadows; he leads me beside peaceful streams. He renews my strength.* **He guides me along right paths,** *bringing honor to his name"* (Psalm 23:1–3).

> Many worship pastors baby their sheep by keeping the musical worship expectations low while avoiding— at all costs— making anyone feel uncomfortable.

Though many a disgruntled church attendee has been quoted saying, "I'm just not getting fed at church these days," there's a profound reason why. Plain and simple. It has never been the job of the pastor to feed the sheep, but mature and healthy sheep (even the very young) are expected to feed themselves. If people aren't being fed, it's simply because they refuse to eat. *"Lazy people take food in their hand but don't even lift it to their mouth"* (Proverbs 19:24). (Of course, this fascinating verse is talking as much about spiritual laziness as it is about physical laziness.)

Sadly, many pastors continue bottle feeding their sheep each week. Likewise, many worship pastors baby their sheep by keeping the musical worship expectations low while avoiding—at all costs—making anyone feel uncomfortable.

Studying the Word of God for ourselves with the guidance of the Holy Spirit is how we grow. Inviting people to step outside their comfort zones in worship is how they learn to let go of paralyzing insecurities in order to live more fully in God's presence. It's how we learn to recognize His voice. By feeding on the Word of God and fellowshipping with the Spirit of God.

Imagine only communicating with God through the pastor or worship pastor. (Incidentally, this is exactly what they did in pre-Jesus days.) This would be like only speaking to your mom through a friend or a stranger your entire life. You might be able to understand your mom's heart from a distance, but you would never be able to recognize her voice. You wouldn't know her perfume, her tone, or her smile. You would have no personal connection with her. No face-to-face relationship. Only formalities and surface-level communication through a third party.

This is how many people live their days with God. Through a middleman. There's little to no direct connection. They may have some understanding concerning what God says in His Word (through the messages of their pastor or others), but they rarely study the Bible for themselves, and, when it comes right down to it, many don't *really* know what it says. They only know what their pastor says it says.

This is incredibly dangerous, especially since one of the distinctives of God's children is their ability to hear His voice. It's something we must help facilitate in the way we lead worship. *"My sheep listen to my voice; I know them, and they follow me. I give them eternal life, and they will never perish. No one can snatch them away from me"* (John 10:27–28).

The Shepherd gives them eternal life because they know His voice. As a result, they're able to follow Him. This also tells us that He *doesn't* give eternal life to those who don't know His voice, because they're incapable of truly following Him.

As worship leaders, we must do everything we can to facilitate a direct connection between God and His people. It's vital that we keep from becoming the middlemen.

WHEN WE COME TOGETHER

If you were to place me and Dr. Amy Anderson side-by-side, few would believe we hold similar ideals when it comes to musical worship in the Church. But the truth is, her wonderful book, *When You Come Together*, based on 1 Corinthians 14:26, helps lay a sure foundation for what all ministry in the church should look like.

> *"Well, my brothers and sisters, let's summarize. **When you meet together**, one will sing, another will teach, another will tell some special revelation God has given, one will speak in tongues, and another will interpret what is said. But everything that is done must strengthen all of you."*

Most theologians agree that chapters 12 to 14 of 1 Corinthians were written by Paul to help the early Church understand the strategies that should be realized, primarily, as God's people gather together corporately. If this is true, 1 Corinthians 14:26 is a short summary of all three chapters, clearly laying out much of what we should do in our gatherings. In one simple sentence.

Only thing: many churches are not structuring their services based on these biblical directives. In fact, in many ways we have almost entirely moved away from these strategies. What strategies? Well, for starters, the idea that everyone has something to bring to the gathering.

I love how these verses read in the New King James Version and *THE MESSAGE*.

> *"How is it then, brethren? Whenever you come together, **each of you** has a psalm, has a teaching, has a tongue, has a revelation, has an interpretation. Let all things be done for edification"* (1 Corinthians 14:26 NKJV). *"So here's what I want you to do. When you gather for worship, **each one of you be prepared** with something that will be useful for all: Sing a hymn, teach a lesson, tell a story, lead a prayer, provide an insight"* (1 Corinthians 14:26 MSG).

Again, many people—church leaders and churchgoers alike—still hold to the false notion that church is a place where weary believers drag themselves into a service after an arduous work week in order to be encouraged and strengthened, only to go back out into the world to be bruised and battered all over again. Only to drag themselves back to church with hopes that they can be convinced not to give up on God or themselves, only to do it all over again. And again. And again.

This approach is rooted in the same errant ideology we spoke of earlier. One where the bulk of the weight is on the pastors to help the poor laypeople snag a quick bite on Sunday's so they'll have just enough sustenance to survive the challenges of the other six days of the week. It's like we've long since discarded any hope of helping our church family grow as Spirit-filled believers and simply settled for making it through another week.

What if, instead, we raised the bar on Sundays while also empowering people to grow during the week? What if people came to our services already filled up after a week of spending daily time with God and were primed to join together as the body to celebrate our Creator and to hear what He has to say? What if each person was taught to arrive on Sunday believing that God might want to speak or move through them for the benefit of the entire community? What if everyone showed up filled up and ready to encourage the body instead of always showing up as needy, powerless leaches?

> We perpetuate comfort and coddling instead of fire and passion, believing we are doing our people a great service. All the while, we're killing them softly.

Could this change the way we gather? Would this lift the load of a weary pastor who feels like he's the only one seeking God through the week? Would this also make for a much more engaging and passionate time of musical worship?

Of course it would.

Unfortunately, our musical worship often perpetuates spiritual immaturity among those who attend our services, as we strive to avoid—either out of obedience to our lead pastor or otherwise—reflective songs that encourage repentance, humility, or spiritual growth and instead enlist superficial, emotionally shallow songs that fail to deal with the real issues of the heart.

We also add to our potential problems by creating a concert-like atmosphere where attendees are encouraged to "sit back and enjoy the show." We perpetuate comfort and coddling instead of fire and passion, believing we are doing our people a great service. All the while, we're killing them softly.

THE ACTIVATION OF ALL

Depending on the church culture you were raised in, you may not have realized how far we've fallen from the true culture of the Kingdom in our church gatherings. Simply put, our job as worship leaders is to activate the body. The entire body. Yet, sadly, we often play the role of the helicopter mom who does everything for her child for fear that they might be forced to endure difficulty or hardship in their lives. We protect our flock from the very things they need. The very things that will help them mature. Pain. Struggles. Challenges. Discomfort. Trials. Etc. Ironically, this *seems* like loving leadership, but ultimately, it's the kind that hurts us long term.

According to Amy Anderson, "When the saints are not equipped for ministry by their leaders, what do they do? They might just stay babies, needing to be fed, pampered, and diapered for the rest of their lives."[10]

The activation of the entire body is expressed in a biblical concept we often refer to as "the kingdom of priests." This idea flies in the face of our typical understanding of Old Testament philosophy where only the priests had direct access to God while everyone else was instructed to stay away. As you know, this all came to a screeching halt when the veil was torn, as Jesus breathed His last. The tearing of the veil reaffirmed God's heart from the beginning—that *all people* would be able to freely approach Him and have relationship with Him without a middleman (that is, except for Jesus). Each and every individual.

Ironically, Moses himself prophesied God's ultimate plan for His people hundreds of years before it became a reality in Exodus 19:5–6:

*"Now if you will obey me and keep my covenant, you will be my own special treasure from among all the peoples on earth; for all the earth belongs to me. And **you will be my kingdom of priests, my holy nation**.' This is the message you must give to the people of Israel."*

Many are aware of Peter's sanctioning of this beautiful activation of the Church, but few realize it was God's heart from the beginning. *"But you are not like that, **for you are a chosen people. You are royal priests, a holy nation**, God's very own possession. As a result, you can show others the goodness of God, for he called you out of the darkness into his wonderful light"* (1 Peter 2:9). This wasn't a New Testament idea, but a reverberation of an ancient Exodus 19 idea that never took root. Ironically, the people of Israel rejected this beautiful offering in Moses' day, just as many in the

10 Anderson, *When You Come Together*, 58.

Church reject it now, preferring to live in a world where we keep some sort of figurehead between us and God.

This is not God's heart, and we must work diligently to find ways to lead our church family boldly while continuing to step out of the way.

EXPECT GREAT THINGS

Consider these things. What if the end goal of leading worship is not to be loved by the people, but to help the people love God? What if the end goal of leading worship is not to make people feel better, but to provide an atmosphere where people can come face-to-face with God? What if the end goal of leading worship is not to stir up our emotions, but to provide a space where God can pour out His love on us as we give Him glory? What if the end goal of leading worship is not to prepare us to hear the Word of God, but to allow our congregants to encounter the beautifully ferocious God of the Word?

What if we used 1 Corinthians 14:26 as a guide, allowing it to increase our awareness that everyone in our spiritual family—not only the leaders—are meant to bring something to the gathering, with the potential of sharing it publicly or privately in order to build up the body?

The list in 1 Corinthians 14:26 is not exhaustive, but it's a great place to start:

- Sing a hymn
- Teach a lesson
- Tell a story
- Lead a prayer
- Provide a spiritual insight

It's a different mindset. Imagine if everyone in your congregation arrived from week to week with a great openness to being used by the Holy Spirit to encourage their fellow believers in these ways. This one small shift would drastically change the mentality, the culture, and the potency of our church meetings?

When I first talked with Amy about putting these things to work in our services, she gave me a few ideas to get the ball rolling.

1. **Provide a moment of "popcorn" participation.** This can be achieved in several ways, including inviting congregants to read Scripture aloud or pray aloud. This challenges people to lean in to what the Spirit is saying and doing and helps them gain the courage to speak up spiritually. It also reminds them that God wants to use them as part of the whole body to encourage the whole body. Simply ask a few congregants to spontaneously share three or four short passages of praise or to shout out a few short prayers of thanksgiving from their seats. Make sure the music underneath is not too loud and that each person speaks out boldly for everyone to hear.

2. **Give the congregation a voice.** Use every opportunity to engage people who are not on the leadership team to help in small ways in the service. If a Scripture passage is to be read, or a prayer prayed, etc., have someone from the congregation do it. They might volunteer in the moment, or you could ask them a few days ahead of time. Call them up to the mic in such cases.

3. **Encourage transformative testimonies.** These are typically best shared on a mic with a fair amount of pastoral oversight. Provide the topic and ask those sharing to be brief (possibly even hold the mic for them). Watch out for inappropriateness (sharing something that is too private, unless it's been talked through ahead of time). Topics can center around things like: How did you experience God's healing this week? Has God brought you through a tough season recently? What has it been like growing up in a Christian (or non-Christian) home all of your life? How did you decide to surrender your heart to Jesus? Tell us about a vision for ministry that God is stirring in you. One of these short testimonies can be shared right before the musical worship, since it will inspire others to give glory to God for the way He has touched that person's life.

4. **Include a moment of silence.** With so much stimuli in our world, providing a moment of silence in worship (to rest and listen to the Spirit) can turn into a coveted expression. The idea is to encourage everyone to wait in silence with no expectations of anyone sharing or singing or playing. Just to be still before the Lord. Together. No instruments at all. Just silence. A couple of minutes is good at first,

but more time can be beneficial as the congregation begins to become more comfortable in these moments. Be sure the congregation knows that we are intentionally waiting on God, and that we're okay with a few potentially awkward moments. This helps everyone relax and not be afraid to embrace the silence.

What if we stopped trying to do all the ministry ourselves? What if we created an environment where people are inspired to hear from the Lord for themselves? To step out of their comfort zones? To minister in ways they never thought they could?

What if we created space in our services where people—directed by the Spirit—could sing, teach, prophesy, tell a story, share a testimony, bring a message in tongues with an interpretation, and more, all for the strengthening of the body, and for the glory of the Lord?

Pretty risky, right?

Sure, it is!

But which is riskier, after all? Empowering our people to do what the Word says and risking them saying or singing something inappropriate, or allowing them to continue as life-long spectators while the pastors and leaders do all of the spiritual heavy lifting? Which is worse? Opening ourselves up to the possibility of a congregant prophesying something that was *not* directed by the Spirit, or refusing to give the Spirit of God the opportunity to speak through His people at all, as the Scriptures mandate?

WHAT IF SOMETHING GOES WRONG?

When pressed, most leaders won't deny that God wants to speak through His people, but in our modern-day churches, few allow space for such a thing. Why? Because of fear. What if something goes wrong? What if someone does something crazy? What if someone speaks out of turn? What if someone speaks a word that is "not from God"?

No problem. When these things happen, *and they will*, it simply provides an incredible opportunity to bring further clarity to the appropriate biblical procedures—through teaching *and* correction. We could even say the very opportunity to bring correction—in response to a congregant moving outside of the Spirit's leading—is the perfect chance for personal and congregational growth. This is the type of growth we won't enjoy if we discourage people from stepping out in faith for fear they might "miss it."

What if we started imparting the principles from 1 Corinthians 14:26 within our community of faith? What if we invited our congregants to meditate throughout the week on the things God might want to say to the rest of the church on Sunday? What if we also encouraged everyone to be prayerful during our services concerning what the Lord might want to do through them?

What if we stopped being afraid of what might happen and started being more afraid of what might *not* happen when people are kept from responding to the Spirit's nudges? What if we also stopped hoarding the spiritual leadership opportunities, presuming we're the only ones God can speak through? Pastors and leaders are *not* the only ones God uses in public church ministry. His Spirit aims to empower every member of the body of Christ to encourage many people in many ways. Pastors and leaders are simply the instigators and overseers of what happens when.

You might say, "Jeff, no one ever speaks in tongues or prophesies in our church, so there's no reason to believe they're going to start now." Okay. But have you considered the possibility that the reason they don't do many of these things—sing a hymn, teach a lesson, tell a story, lead a prayer, provide an insight (through the Spirit)—is because we've never made this a clear part of the biblical norm for our church? Maybe we've simply never affirmed a culture where this type of thing is encouraged or expected. Or welcomed.

So let's change that!

Here's what we did. With the Spirit's help:

- We started using Scripture to build the faith of our congregants concerning the movement of the Spirit in our services (see Romans 10:17).
- We invited our community to make their way up to one of our leaders during musical worship when they believe they had a message from the Lord to share.

- After sharing the message with a leader, the leader would discern whether or not the message was fitting for the entire body as well as if the timing was right.
- At the appropriate time, the leader would bring the person to the stage to share on the mic during a "flowing moment" in the musical worship.
- The person was instructed to keep things short and sweet and to only share what they believed the Lord was saying. Nothing more.
- If the leader determined the message wasn't appropriate for that particular moment (timing) or that it didn't seem to be aligned with Scripture, it was communicated to the person in love, and they were sent back to their seat.
- Of course, we had also spent many months prepping our musicians and singers to be flexible and to watch for moments like these so they would know how to adapt musically and would not be offended by these Holy Spirit "interruptions."

HOLDING LOOSELY TO YOUR SET LIST

In one of our chapel leadership meetings, it was brought up by a well-meaning leader that he wanted to respect the musicians and not "cut into" their time. The musical worship sets were relatively short already, so he didn't want to "take away" from our precious eighteen minutes.

My first thought was, *Yes, they finally get it. Thank you!* (I mean, how often does a pastor or leader come to the worship team and ask them to cut a song because something else has taken precedent in the service. Very rarely does the message get cut back for a baby dedication, communion, or some special announcement. For sure, when we cut the musical worship for other service elements, we display our priorities without saying a word.) Nevertheless, I was happy that he was taking the musicians into consideration.

> As we seek to instill a culture where we expect the Holy Spirit to "interrupt" our services, everyone in leadership must be prepared to hold loosely to their plans.

That said, as we seek to instill a culture where we expect the Holy Spirit to "interrupt" our services, everyone in leadership must be prepared to hold loosely to their plans. Musicians and pastors alike. (Remember, it's not that God is uninvolved in our planning before the service. He is, indeed. It's just that He is involved in *both* the planning and the unplanned. There are many times He gives us specifics for the plan and then calls an audible in the middle of the service.)

I had been coaching our worship teams in these things, but now it was time to let our leaders know they needn't worry about "taking time away" from the musical worship portion of the service for a Holy Spirit interruption, as long as we all agreed to lean in and really hear from the Lord during all parts of the service.

Ironically, I had the chance to prove my willingness to "hold loosely" to my own sermon when I was scheduled to preach on October 29, 2018. You see, God began moving so powerfully among our students that day, that we kept going in worship and prayer right past the time I was supposed to preach. This was a big deal, since it had never happened before and because I'm usually only scheduled to preach once each semester. Who better to be asked by the Holy Spirit to hold loosely to his plans than the one lobbying for greater flexibility from everyone else?

You see, when God asked me to "create more space" in our gatherings for the Spirit (upon my arrival at NCU), I didn't fully realize that He was also doing it to make room for a "Kingdom of priests" ideology. An ideology where two or three people from the congregation might share unplanned prophetic messages from the Lord. I'd assumed we were simply making space for people to worship spontaneously, but He had that and so much more in mind.

As with all things, there is balance. We definitely don't want to create a culture where we stifle the move of the Holy Spirit, but we also don't want to allow for so many "words from the Lord" that we never have time for musical worship and preaching. The Bible is clear. The Holy Spirit will typically only interrupt our services a couple times with things like a prophecy or a message in tongues. But this type of thing should be normal.

No more than two or three should speak in tongues. They must speak one at a time, and someone must interpret what they say. But if no one is present who can interpret, they must be silent in your church meeting and speak in tongues to God privately. Let two or three people prophesy, and let the others evaluate what is said. But if someone is prophesying and another person receives a revelation from the Lord, the one who is speaking must stop. In this way, all who prophesy will have a turn to speak, one after the other, so that everyone will learn and be encouraged. Remember that people who prophesy are in control of their spirit and can take turns. (1 Corinthians 14:27–32)

As we discussed the logistics of these cultural shifts with our leadership team, I let them know that we had been teaching our musicians ahead of time to hold loosely to their set lists with the purpose of allowing the Spirit to interject and guide our services as He pleased. Fewer songs and more "flowing" musical moments were helping to facilitate this nicely. Heaven forbid we miss or ignore an opportunity to hear from the Lord, simply because we were determined to finish our set list.

Of course, it's taken some time to shift our mentality (and we're still working on it). Many musicians and singers are easily offended or hurt if they don't get to sing or play a song they've been practicing all week, especially if it is one where they are featured.

"Oh, baby! That's not fair. We worked hard on this set all week, and I didn't get to play my guitar solo!"

What if one of our worship leaders was only scheduled to sing one song, and that song is the one that gets cut? At first glance, this seems terribly unjust, and yet this is exactly the type of mindset we must eradicate. Again, we cannot hold so tightly to the plan that we fail to accomplish the mission; the mission of letting the Spirit of God do whatever He sees fit in order to connect His people relationally to God. We must avoid, at all costs, placing our desires above the Spirit's desires. This goes for the band, the pastor, and every other person involved in leadership. We must all hold loosely to our personal agendas in order to remain spiritually flexible regarding moments where God's Spirit wants to go "off-script."

A KINGDOM MODEL

I remember it like it was yesterday. I was lost in worship in chapel in March of 2018, when our Vice President of Spiritual Life, Dr. Doug Graham, was approached by a student who had something from the Lord to share with the rest of us. After hearing what the student had to say, Dr. Graham discerned its appropriateness and brought him to the stage in an opportune moment during the musical worship. This was becoming more and more commonplace.

> We have encouraged our spiritual community to stop coming to our services with a "feed me" mentality, and to start coming with a "flow through me" mentality.

Let me preface this by reminding you that we had also been working to remind our congregation that those of us in leadership expect God to move through them just as much as we expect Him to move through us. We had also been repeatedly teaching them about the "Kingdom of priests" model and had encouraged them to listen for God to speak throughout our services.

In essence, we have encouraged our spiritual community to stop coming to our services with a "feed me" mentality, and to start coming with a "flow through me" mentality. This simple shift in expectation has dramatically altered the way our community comes to chapel. Let me explain.

As the team stopped singing and kept flowing softly, Dr. Graham told us the student had a message in tongues to share. I just about fell over dead. Why? Because up to this point, we had not had a message in tongues—in our Pentecostal university—during chapel in about five years.

My heart raced.

The student clutched the microphone and began to speak in tongues. Now if you know anything about the gift of tongues, you know this can turn into a make-it-or-break-it moment, especially since close to half of our students do not come from Pentecostal churches. On top of this, sadly, most of today's "Pentecostal" churches have moved away from allowing the gifts of the Spirit to operate in their Sunday morning services. This meant few of our students had ever even heard a message in tongues in a service before.

It seemed like an eternity. The student continued for what must have been two minutes or more (all the while, I was lying on the floor weeping quietly). I'm guessing he sounded, to many people, as if he were talking in some sort of extraterrestrial language, which in a sense, he was. He spoke boldly in the language of the Spirit.

You could feel two things in the room: a powerful move of the Spirit, and lots of curious students.

Why was I weeping on the floor? First, because of the power of the Spirit, but mostly because I had waited for years for something like this to happen again. I and others had been teaching and modeling and sharing Scripture passages for months, believing that God would eventually pour out a harvest of Holy Spirit activity in our services again. It was finally happening, and I couldn't contain my joy in that moment.

I'm convinced that many churches operate from week to week in an atmosphere of human effort and man's tradition, an atmosphere devoid of God's Spirit. And yet we were determined to demonstrate our desperate desire to let the Lord have His way, even if it meant we had to adjust our plans or sacrifice a bit of our manicured agendas.

We all listened with bated breath as the student finished and handed the microphone back to Dr. Graham. And we waited. And waited some more. For the interpretation. And then it came. One of our professors stepped up and shouted it for all to hear. Powerful. Incredible. Supernatural. And yet, it shouldn't be *that* incredible (or *that* rare), since this type of thing is normal according to Scripture.

Some might argue, "But what about the unbeliever? Won't they be freaked out?" Probably. I hope so. I hope we're *all* freaked out a little bit. Freaked out enough to stand in awe of the way God can speak supernatural things through natural beings. Freaked out enough to realize that He sees fit to cut through man's manufactured spirituality. Honestly, this is exactly the type of thing the unbeliever is looking for—something beyond themselves. Something beyond the powers of man. Something truly supernatural.

A person who speaks in tongues is strengthened personally, but one who speaks a word of prophecy strengthens the entire church. I wish you *could all speak in tongues, but even more I wish you could all prophesy. For prophecy is greater than speaking in tongues, **unless someone interprets what you are saying so that the whole church will be strengthened*** (1 Corinthians 14:4–5).

Basically, a message in tongues becomes a prophecy once it's interpreted. It's just another way that God likes to speak. Through His people. Through His Spirit. Truthfully, increasing our expectation for supernatural "interruptions" is exactly the type of thing that perpetuates spiritual growth within each individual and within the entire Church. With slow and intentional alterations, we can easily move to the point where this type of biblical culture takes root.

EVERYONE BRINGS SOMETHING

The ultimate idea here is that we want our "gathering culture" to perfectly emulate "Kingdom culture." Don't we? If our church culture is "off" even just a little bit from the culture of heaven—which it probably is—we want to continue to shift our culture a little each week until it is as closely aligned to Kingdom culture as it can be.

Funny thing is, this process is never really complete. Even once we find ourselves operating in our gatherings in total congruency with God's ways, if left to themselves, they will begin to erode. Almost overnight. It's true. This is why spiritual oversight is so important. Our job as leaders is to continually encourage and challenge our spiritual community to stay as close to God as possible, even as the enemy of our souls is working feverishly to do just the opposite.

As discussed in chapters 10 and 11, the best way to do this in our services is to continually raise the bar with modeling, teaching, and doing moments, all within the context of musical worship, and all led by the Spirit. We no longer buy into the idea of pampering our spiritual family. No. We expect great things from each and every believer. Even from those we might call "pre-Christians."

- We're asking each person to spend time with God throughout the week so they're more inclined to hear from Him on behalf of the whole church.
- We're asking each person to bring something from the Spirit as we gather together, and not simply attend as spectators.
- We're asking each person to grow up spiritually so that the entire church can do the work of the ministry and see our communities won for the Lord.

The bar is set high because we have the Most High living within us. And He has promised to work through each and every believer—not only the rich, the talented, or the beautiful—but each individual, from every nation, tribe, people, and language. Praise the Lord!

Chapter Highlights

1. One of the biggest issues we face in the body of Christ today is the growing immaturity of our attendees resulting from a false belief that our pastors exist primarily to seek God and do the work of the ministry in our stead. This leads most "believers" to feast on a regular diet of regurgitated Word, shared with them by their lead shepherd. The same thing happens as we perpetuate—sometimes unintentionally—the atmosphere of a concert in our worship settings. Baby Christians sit by unengaged, drinking coffee, as they watch us perform. This must change.

2. The ultimate goal of a worship leader is to work himself/herself out of a job. When we get to the place in our leadership where the congregation no longer has to be poked and prodded to seek the Lord—to the point where they nearly "take over" the service—we'll know we've cultivated a biblical culture of worship.

3. These days, people often drag themselves to church completely empty after a hard week of work, hoping to find solace in reconnecting with God in His "house." But what if we created a culture where people spent time with God all week and came to church filled up and ready to celebrate together? This is our job as leaders.

4. Since we now live in a "Kingdom of priests" era—where everyone has access to the Word of God and the Spirit of God—we must continue to lead in a way that affirms this culture rather than leading in a way that affirms a pre-death-and-resurrection era where the veil is not yet torn. We must help people understand they have full access to God for themselves and are expected *and* invited to engage with Him directly. This philosophy flies in the face of the spoon-fed church culture we have often perpetuated.

Chapter 15

THE FUTURE
OF MUSICAL WORSHIP
IN THE CHURCH

Lie #15

*"As a worship leader, my primary role on
Sunday mornings is to sing songs and worship God,
nothing more and nothing less."*

CHAPTER NOTE: *When writing a chapter on the future of musical worship in the Church, you might assume we'd cover things like learning to lead
worship at a multi-site campus or in a multicultural setting, but this is not
my approach. Though I do touch on some important issues concerning multicultural worship in this chapter, we already covered many of our modern
worship issues in chapter 8. I want to think bigger and broader while helping
us understand the direction God's Spirit is moving so we can serve our congregations biblically and responsibly in the coming days.*

Back in the day, I took yearly trips to Christ for the Nations (CFNI)
in Dallas, Texas, to lead at their Youth for the Nations conferences
as well as to partner with Marco Barrientos at his Aliento conferences.
I'll never forget the Kingdom impact these gatherings had on me as a

worshiper and as a leader, especially as we consider the future of musical worship in the Church.

Leading worship is about empowering people. It's not about gaining power. It's about releasing people in the power of God. For what purpose? So they might become all that He wants them to become in His refining, healing presence. That is, to love Him richly, to live with Him closely, and to walk in holiness and unity with all of His people for all time.

> Leading worship is about empowering people. It's not about gaining power. It's about releasing people in the power of God.

Sadly, too many leaders lord their power over their people. Why? Because they love the rush they get in return. It's sad to say, but many leaders still love power more than they love people (which means they also love power more than they love God).

True Kingdom leadership culture—the kind that will meaningfully spark the future of musical worship in the Church—is entirely uninterested in positional power, but is, without a doubt, utterly consumed with activating people by the Spirit. Let me say it again: *The number one job of a worship leader is to work oneself out of a job.*

What do we mean? Well, again, it's about finding a way to pass the baton to those in the stands. This is the picture of a preferred future—the one I began telling you about in the intro of this book. Truthfully, the most compelling moment in a worship service for a Kingdom worship leader is not listening to her own voice on the microphone, but listening to the unified voice of the multitude giving all glory to Christ as she steps back from the microphone.

If this is true, we must uncover all possible means by which we can spur on more Kingdom moments like these for our congregants. No matter what it takes. If it means singing louder or softer, or leading them in a moment of complete silence. If it means changing songs, singing spontaneously, or sharing a Scripture passage in the middle of musical worship. Whatever it takes—in obedience to the Holy Spirit—in order to increase the possibilities of stirring up the hunger of God's people for greater intimacy and fellowship with Him. This is the joy of our mission.

HORRIBLY BEAUTIFUL

As bold of a worship leader as I am, I can't forget the feeling of utter incompetence I felt when I first stepped onto the stage with my band at a Christ for the Nations event. It was a feeling of complete awe one minute and absolute insecurity the next. I was quite familiar with traveling to places where it was like pulling teeth to get people to respond in worship. I was used to visiting Christian universities where students sat with their arms folded, daring anyone to provoke them. I was used to leading in sanctuaries where people seemed more interested in their Apple Watch than in the person of God.

But this was not that. Definitely. Not. That.

Before we even had a chance to get to the first chorus, the congregation was shot out of a cannon in fervent expression and worship to the Lord. It was wild. It was backwards. We, the band, were used to being the passionate ones, and now we suddenly found ourselves playing "catch up" to the congregation.

We felt the congregation tugging on us. Pulling us deeper into worship. Daring us to believe more. Seek more. Release more. Love more. Wow. What a horribly beautiful thing. Horrible because it was driving us out of our comfort zone. Out of our *coasting* zone. And beautiful because we were being challenged to trust God's Spirit to lead through us, rather than attempting to manhandle the whole thing. I hated and I loved it all at the same time.

LEADING YOUR CONGREGATION TO LEAD THEMSELVES

Bob Sorge would cheerfully interject here to inform us that God is calling His Church to gradually gravitate from what he calls "platform-driven worship culture" to "multitude-driven worship culture." Multitude-driven worship culture is the culture of heaven—the culture we should be moving toward—while platform-driven worship culture is currently the culture of earth—the culture we should be moving away from.

"Fear not. It is what it is," Bob would say, referring to the current dilemma of platform-driven worship culture. We must identify the type of culture we've inherited if we're to understand the type of culture we need to build.

Platform-driven worship culture is the kind where everyone arrives precisely when the platform people tell them to arrive, wearing exactly (or mostly) what the platform people have "suggested" they wear. Then, the non-platform people gather in chairs facing the platform, waiting for the platform people to step onto the platform. Once this happens, the platform people provide step-by-step instructions concerning what the non-platform people are supposed to do as they face the people on the platform.

The platform people undoubtedly ask the non-platform people to do a variety of things, including but not limited to standing, singing, lifting their hands, clapping, praising, worshiping, and shouting. Following this, the non-platform people may be asked to sit again or to mingle and fellowship with other non-platform people. The platform people may also encourage the non-platform people to participate in an offering or take communion, and most certainly to listen to a message authored by one of the foremost platform people.

All of the non-platform people sit neatly in their seats listening intently until one of the platform people sees fit to excuse them. They're now on their way, hopefully entirely equipped to accomplish all that the foremost platform person has challenged them to accomplish. All throughout the week. Until next week, when they will again gather to do what the platform people invite them to do.

Whew. You get the gist.

Sadly, this style of leadership only *seems* to be going somewhere. But we begin to wonder if it really is as fruitful as we thought. Why? Because this style of leadership fails to activate people, to move them beyond where they currently are. It simply invites them to go through the same ritual over and over and over again. Like little preprogrammed worship robots.

This is where many church folk live, as a result of uninspired leadership. But this is not where God is calling us to stay. He is calling us to move gradually away from a platform-driven worship culture and toward a multitude-driven worship culture, the culture of heaven. Think of it. Once in heaven, we'll have no need for the traditional worship leader.

Why? Because the physical presence of Jesus will be right there among us. They'll be no need for anyone to point Him out. Every knee will bow, and every tongue will confess that Jesus Christ is Lord.

The whole point of the worship leader is to serve as a connector of sorts. Yet, with Jesus standing there "in the flesh," the congregation won't need any additional inspiration. We'll respond immediately. Involuntarily. Each one. We'll be compelled—not coerced—to engage in the most fitting, passionate worship.

Thing is, we're not there. Yet.

Even so, we must be on our way. Moving slowly to a point where our congregants have less and less need for the platform people to instruct them in how, when, and why to worship. With every additional revelation gathered from the Word of God and the Spirit of God, they should steadily be transitioning—with our help—out of a platform-driven worship culture and into a multitude-driven worship culture. Most importantly, our worship leadership ought to be defined by an increased move toward empowering people to worship God on their own rather than prodding people to respond at our command.

As we continually invite our church family to engage with God on their own, they should be increasingly compelled to worship Him with greater passion in the public place. As a result, they should also grow in their hunger to explore the deeper depths of God in the secret place. And round and round we go. (Ironically, this highlights again the importance of spontaneous worship to help us empower our church family to worship God with their own words.)

Side note: Don't worry. Our end goal is not to get rid of worship leaders this side of heaven. There will always be a continued influx of unbelievers and new believers who need us to stir and teach them. Yet clearly, as the majority shifts to a multitude-driven worship culture, there is a decreased need for worship leadership as we currently know it. This is our hope!

WHO'S LEADING WHO?

For ten years, I hosted the Pure Worship Institute conference, affording us the incredible opportunity of building our worship culture from scratch. Since we worked hard over many years to implement the things I discuss in this book, our attendees rarely had to be pleaded with to worship the Lord with authentic enthusiasm. Much like those at Christ for the Nations.

Interestingly, one of the bands we hosted a few years back was not familiar with this type of culture. They're a well-known band with well-known songs, but their approach is one where you play-the-song-like-the-album and then move on to the next song. Don't get me wrong. They were super authentic and pleasantly anointed. They just didn't operate with the type of spontaneous, creative flow that our attendees were used to.

Until tonight.

It seemed, as the band approached the end of one of their popular worship songs, our naïve worship attendees missed the message. They didn't realize they were supposed to stop worshiping when the song ended. So, as the band played the final chord—with that just-like-the-album finality—our congregation kept right on singing. Not out of rebellion or attempted mutiny, but out of unrestrained delight for God.

You should have seen the look on those band members' faces. They were completely taken off-guard. With nervous glances (and a slight skip in the music) they adjusted and continued playing the chorus progression. As our attendees led the way.

It was beautiful. I couldn't help but smile. Not because we had made the band uncomfortable, but because we were literally watching multitude-driven worship culture be sparked right before our eyes.

More, Lord!

You may wonder what all the fuss is about. What's so wonderful about the congregation continuing to worship when the band was planning to stop? Fair question. Here's the reason this is so beautiful: if the number one job of a worship leader is to work oneself out of a job—to pass the baton to the congregation—their response equates to an enormous step in the right direction. The moment they understand they no longer need to be told how or when to worship; *this* is the moment we know they're beginning to embrace Kingdom worship culture. *This* is the moment they stop worshiping like puppets on a string and start pursuing God for themselves. *This* is the moment they stop sitting in the bleachers and start getting out onto the track.

This is what we've been longing for.

UNLOWERING THE BAR FOR YOUR CONGREGATION

Can you imagine—if people began to catch on? What if they began to realize we don't have to come to church to worship—or, better said, what if they began to realize church isn't the *only* place we can worship? What if we helped them grab on to a truly biblical model of worship that empowers them to worship inside *and* outside the walls of the church, and to forever "unlower" the bar on musical worship?

Ironically, that's exactly what we were hoping to accomplish with the release of the first Sonicflood CD. Even back then, God was beginning to show us some new things (actually, old things) about the kind of worshipers He seeks—the kind of worshipers He wants *His* leaders in *His* church to help *His* people become.

"But the time is coming—indeed it's here now—when true worshipers will worship the Father in spirit and in truth. The Father is looking for those who will worship him that way" (John 4:23). The NIV ends this verse with *"for they are the kind of worshipers the Father seeks."*

Think about that. There is a type of worshiper God seeks and a type of worshiper God rejects. Wait. What? I know. That stings a little. But it's true. I don't know how else to say it. If there's a type of worshiper God desires, then it's only logical to assume there's also a type He dismisses. The only question is, which one are we?

He is literally probing the globe, our nation, our states, our neighborhoods, and our homes to see if He can pinpoint any true worshipers. Non-lip-service worshipers. Non-fake-it-to-make-it worshipers. Non-sing-the-song-but-don't-live-the-life worshipers. Non-try-to-do-it-in-my-own-strength worshipers. And for us, He wants to know if there are any leaders who will train His people to be the kind of worshipers He seeks.

This excites me, because I believe God is raising up a generation of fiery worshipers for such a time as this. And—as you might expect—there are a few very important characteristics shared by these authentic, Christ-following worshipers. Characteristics that we, worship leaders, must encourage and champion again and again. (Don't misunderstand. This is not an exhaustive list. This section focuses primarily on equipping our congregations in the area of *corporate musical worship*.)

Let's take a peek.

1. The kind of worshipers the Father seeks are those who don't require a worship leader.

Isn't this what we want? Maybe. Maybe not. Who knows? Maybe if we instilled this type of culture in our churches, we'd realize we don't really like it, because it could rob us of what we crave more than our congregation's transformation. Recognition. For better or worse, when the congregation takes the wheel, it means I have to let go of it. And something else. Control.

The irony is, people are dying to be set free to express themselves to God. After all, they/we were made for this. Yet, we seem to hold to the idea that people are holding back, refusing to truly worship God. It's frustrating. But sometimes I can't help but wonder if they're not holding back as much as we're holding them back.

It's like we're afraid they're going to grow up and not need us any longer. Heaven forbid. So we keep the leash on. It's like we're afraid they're going to discover the real freedom they have in Christ. So we tighten up the training wheels. It's no wonder insecure leaders avoid empowering church people. They're often afraid that the people will learn to "worship" on their own and won't come back to church.

But this is not true.

We will never hurt our church attendance by raising up our everyday congregants. Worshipers who continue to need worship leaders less and less only serve to make our churches stronger and stronger.

Don't get me wrong. I'm not implying that worship leaders aren't important or that churches should slowly begin replacing them. Even so, as I continue to mention, the best worship leaders remain committed to working themselves out of a job. One person at a time. One family at a time. Developing our congregants into the kind of worshipers who can worship God passionately and consistently with or without us—with or without a worship leader.

The kind of worshiper God is looking for is next-level. Uncommon. They're the kind of worshiper who doesn't require a cheerleader to get them all riled up. The kind of worshiper who doesn't need to be coddled or pampered. Mature worshipers have already been developing a close relationship with God, and they don't need someone to reintroduce them to their Creator every Sunday. They are flowing with Him regularly in the secret place as well as passionately in the public place. They're on a first name basis, and are experiencing vibrant fellowship with Him throughout the day, much like Moses did, speaking face-to-face with Him as a man speaks with a friend.

> Mature worshipers have already been developing a close relationship with God, and they don't need someone to reintroduce them to their Creator every Sunday.

Here's a question. What if we set our hearts on commissioning each and every person to become a worship leader?

Whoa, pump the brakes. What did you say?

Let me explain.

Ultimately, our greatest passion in worship leadership—besides loving God with our entire being—should be to lead people to become their own worship leader. See, I can't actually make anyone worship God (nor do I want to). I can only show them the door. I can only point them to Jesus. I can only invite them to lift up their songs to the Almighty. And I should. But I cannot force them to seek the Lord with all their heart, soul, mind, and strength. I can only hope to inspire them biblically to this end. This is what leadership is—service that endeavors to inspire others to step into action.

I remember when God dropped a bomb on me. I was leading worship in a large church, and the Holy Spirit directed me to commission everyone in the place to be a worship leader. *But why, Lord?* I thought. *Not everyone is called to lead worship. Won't this only complicate matters?*

"Yes, it might. But I'm not asking you to commission them to lead worship for thousands. I'm asking you to commission them to lead worship for one. Themselves. You see, ultimately, each person has to decide according to their own will. 'Will I open my mouth? Will I lift up my hands? Will I surrender to my Maker?' You can only do so much, Jeff. You're doing great, but, in the end, it is not your responsibility to *make* them worship. It is your responsibility to *invite* them to worship. They must decide for themselves."

Wow.

So I brought the music down and shared the new revelation, and it was as if the place turned on its head. Suddenly, everyone was operating on a higher plane with a brand-new understanding of what it means to worship the Lord—for themselves. This raised the bar across the entire room as people stopped depending on the platform people to inspire them and began leading themselves into God's relational presence.

The kind of worshipers God is raising up are the ones who don't need to be coerced or begged. They can worship God just fine whether there's a talented, anointed worship leader on the stage or not.

2. The kind of worshipers the Father seeks are those who don't require lyrics on a screen.

Once again, no one is suggesting that lyrics on a screen are bad or that we should take down our sanctuary projectors and sell them on Facebook Marketplace. It's just that true worshipers—the kind the Father seeks—don't need a "cheat sheet" in order to worship their Creator. They know the words already, because the words emanate from hearts that worship Him all day long.

Nothing much bugs me more than when I hear people talk about running out of things to say to God after praying for two minutes. What? True Christ-followers can talk to God—and listen to Him—for hours at a time without the conversation going stale. It's what close friends do.

I remember my first real conversation with Martha, who is now my wife of twenty-eight plus years. We were juniors at Anderson University in Anderson, Indiana. I was studying on a bench one day after class, waiting to go to my hour-long private piano lesson. Out of nowhere, an angel came floating down the hallway. I was simply minding my own business when she spoke my name. I looked up and there she was. We began talking. And talking. And talking. She would sit down on the bench and then stand up again, wondering if she should leave me alone to study. But I closed my books and gladly encouraged her to stay.

When she first approached me, it was forty-five minutes before my private piano lesson. Then it was fifteen minutes before. Then five before. Then five after. Oh man, I could be a little late. Then it was fifteen minutes and then twenty minutes after. Ahhhhh! Too late. Oh well. This conversation was going too good to worry about my lesson at this point. I wasn't about to miss this moment. Not for anything. Our conversation flowed effortlessly.

We were so drawn to each other that there seemed to be endless subjects to entertain us. Endless reasons to carry on. Endless joy in every word. At the sound of her voice. At the flip of her hair. And nothing else could compete for her attention. It was magnificent! (Dramatic pause for a moment of pure gratitude.)

"The message is very close at hand; it is on your lips and in your heart" (Romans 10:8).

Where do the lyrics for spontaneous worship originate? From within. For believers. We draw on the very words God has written on our hearts. Words that were put there by Him for Him—words that can be drawn out from the reservoir that God created deep in our hearts. But if we don't know Him, we won't know the words. And we quickly run out of things to say.

Trust me. I'm not suggesting the time of the known song is coming to an end—that we should only sing spontaneous songs or that the congregation should somehow memorize all the lyrics. I'm simply saying that for those who want to be the worshipers the Father seeks, there shouldn't be a shortage of ways to express our adoration to Him. And we shouldn't fear shutting down if or when our church projectors shut down.

The words of *praise* and *worship* are alive within our hearts as we continue to seek Him daily. Think about it. We don't require a script to pray when someone asks us to speak to God to close a meeting. Likewise, the worshipers the Father seeks have no issue worshiping God just as passionately with or without lyrics on a screen.

3. The kind of worshipers the Father seeks are those who don't require a band or music.

How did you feel in chapter 11 when I said, "The presence of God isn't in the music"? You probably nodded your head. You knew that. But quite possibly, it was something you hadn't put voice to yet.

It's true, though. We get it. Whether or not we have professional experience in this arena, it's easy to understand that when the music stops, God doesn't disappear. It's not as if, just after the band plays its final chord, God is suddenly inaccessible. As if His ability to engage with His people depends on soft, flowy, piano music. Ha! God's presence is available to us whether we have the perfect music emanating from the keyboard or not.

We used to jokingly refer to the quiet, warm pad sounds on our keyboard as "the Holy Spirit," because it was almost as if when we began playing these sounds, God's ability to move (or our ability to sense His movement) increased exponentially. As if God only touches people when this type of music is playing.

But no. He is with us when the music is playing and when the music fades. God's presence is not found in the music, but is increasingly realized as we engage with Him in close fellowship. In real-time relationship. This is where we find ourselves basking in His manifest presence.

God's presence is not found in the music, but is increasingly realized as we engage with Him in close fellowship. In real-time relationship.

It's scary to think, but it *is* possible to sing the songs, enjoy the band, feel the music, and still miss out on encountering God. His presence. Personally.

I even wonder sometimes if the simple joy of having a great band can backfire. It's a catch twenty-two. People might enjoy our music so much that they forget to enjoy God—the One who made the ones making the music. Of course, this doesn't give us permission to encourage the band to stop playing with excellence or with creativity (or entirely), because the opposite can be true as well.

Even so, let's forget about the band for a minute. The kind of worshipers the Father seeks can worship just fine with or without a band—no matter their skill set—simply because they've discovered that the music isn't the point. They aren't focused on the music itself so much, because they see it for what it is: a tool. A tool to help them connect with their heavenly Father, as well as further proof that the Creator of the universe deserves beautiful praise for dreaming up this thing we call music.

Part of our role as the worship leader is to help our church community become aware of these important under-the-radar truths through teaching. In this way, we spur them on to maturity.

4. The kind of worshipers the Father seeks are those who don't require a church service or a trendy conference.

Have you noticed we've made a bit of a return to the church of old? Whether forced upon us or simply misunderstood, many churchgoing Christians have bought into the idea, all over again, that there is a certain *physical place* where God can touch us better than others—that God's healing or prophetic touch is tied to a location, a place often referred to by many well-meaning leaders as "God's house."

Jesus addressed this idea with the woman at the well in John 4. She, too, was convinced the issue was a "where" issue when she asked Jesus to clarify which place was better suited for worship, Mount Gerizim or Jerusalem. Yet, as Louie Giglio puts it in his book *The Air I Breathe*, "Jesus took the subject to another level, answering her simple 'where' question with a riveting 'who' answer."[1]

Post-resurrection theology erases the idea that worship is connected to a *place* and helps us understand instead that it is connected to a *person*. The kind of worshipers the Father seeks realize the poignant truth from Acts 7:48: *"The Most High doesn't live in temples made with human hands."* They understand that God's power isn't available to us more readily in one building over another, or only in certain revival services in certain parts of the world. They realize the truth: that God's power is tied to His people, because His people are His temple—the Temple of the Holy Spirit—and He lives in His people, not in a church building.

---

1   Louie Giglio, *The Air I Breathe* (Colorado Springs, CO: Multnomah Books, 2003), page 41.

The church building is not God's house. We are. And while this may be a tiny deception, it is one that needs to be expunged—once again—from the hearts of many misinformed churchgoers. *"Don't you realize that all of you together are the temple of God and that the Spirit of God lives in you? God will destroy anyone who destroys this temple. For God's temple is holy, and you are that temple"* (1 Corinthians 3:16–17).

Wow. Beautiful.

What are you saying, Jeff? That people don't need to go to church?

Of course not.

I'm just echoing the words of God to remind us that He is not limited only to moving within a church building. His presence isn't housed within a temple or contained within the structure of a perfectly ordered, perfectly crafted worship service. He is not limited to our attempts to confine Him, and we must help our church family recognize this fact. He is in the street. He is in your house. He is in your car. He is at the beach. He is on the plane. He is in your office. Why? Because He is in you wherever you are.

The next-level worshipers God is raising up are those who understand they can worship very well in a church building or on a field. On a mountain or on a train. In an eight-hundred-year-old cathedral or at a ball park. In a cubical or in a jail cell.

All of the above.

Here's the real question. What if the day comes where people are thrown into prison for following Christ? In the USA or a similar country? This, of course, is already happening in many places around the world. Why not here? What will we do if there aren't any video projectors, worship leaders, bands, sound systems, or services in these prisons? How will we function? How will we seek His face? How will we worship Him?

This might be hard to fathom. But is it really that inconceivable?

Shoot, we experienced a microcosm of this in 2020 with COVID-19, didn't we? Many of our families struggled significantly to engage with the musical worship in their homes in the same way they do at church? Doesn't this reveal a little something about where we are?

In these situations, Jesus finally has us where He wants us, fully exposed—and fully liberated from empty man-made traditions where we exalt the methods, manner, or means of worship. Where we can now exalt the King Himself. Then and then only is the worship bar "unlowered" to the place it was originally intended to be.

CHASING CULTURE AND STYLE

5. The kind of worshipers the Father seeks are those who don't need their cultural or stylistic preferences catered to. (Fair warning: This one's going to take up a few more pages than the first four because of its relevance.)

Diversity has become a serious buzz word in our world, especially in the last ten years. And of course, this means the Church has largely wrestled with its definition (as it should) in light of the Kingdom.

Let me say up-front that diversity itself is an incredibly beautiful thing. The gathering of people from every nation and people group to worship and unite together in the Lord is something we want both now and in God's heavenly Kingdom forever and ever. Each culture and race are equally valuable and make up a significant and wonderful part of the body of Christ that is truly irreplaceable.

That said, achieving diversity should not be our main focus and should not be something we are chasing as leaders in the body of Christ. As crazy as this may sound, to do so will not yield the desired results—results that include people of every tribe, culture, and tongue at the throne of Christ.

Let me explain.

Unity is a much higher goal than diversity, and it must be understood that these two are not one and the same. In fact, if we're not careful, we can achieve great diversity and still have virtually no unity. Just because people of different cultures and colors attend church gatherings together (diversity) does not mean we have Kingdom agreement with each other (unity). Additionally, walking in diversity alone doesn't guarantee that our church is walking in Kingdom ways. Maybe yes. Maybe no. But let's

> Diversity is not the mark of a healthy church. How do I know? Simple. Because hell is going to be just as diverse as heaven.

not be fooled. Though diversity is wonderful, it is still not among the very highest of Kingdom goals.

Buckle your seat belts. I'm going to shake things up a bit. Not for fun, but as we aim to be the most effective, godly leaders possible. Here goes. Diversity is not the mark of a healthy church. How do I know? Simple. Because hell is going to be just as diverse as heaven.

Think about it. We'll circle back shortly.

One afternoon a few years back, as I sat chatting with our beloved (now former) president of NCU, Dr. Gordon Anderson, I learned something new about our God-fearing leader. He really loves music. He spoke in great detail about some of his favorite artists and even about the abundant joy he receives from playing his '75 Ovation acoustic and his '70 Gibson Les Paul electric. After all these years, I couldn't believe he'd been holding out on me.

He asked if I was familiar with any of the songs or artists he deemed inspirational, but I was not. He then expressed a desire to let me sample some of his favorites at some point in the near future. Bursting with curiosity, I said, "How about now?" After a bit of coercing, he agreed to take the short walk from his office to our NCU sanctuary where our cherished Steinway grand piano sat. I bubbled with anticipation.

What happened next opened my eyes.

He sat at the piano playing chords and singing melodies from years gone by— unnecessarily excusing his supposed rudimentary piano skills—all the while, glancing at me with eyes and face aglow, giddy like a school boy.

I was beyond enthralled. In awe. Not so much by the music, but certainly by his skills, his passion, and the poignancy of the moment. He kept looking at me as if to say, "Don't these songs just take the cake?" And while I was deeply fascinated—feeling great *appreciation* for the music emanating from those ebonies and ivories—I didn't personally connect with it stylistically in the same way he did.

Funny thing is, I started getting my own ideas. Ideas of sharing a little of *my* favorite music with him. After all, I'd recently written some instrumental-movie-score-type tunes I was dying to share. (NOTE: For those who might be interested, I've recently released these five piano instrumentals on all streaming platforms in an EP entitled, From Eternity.)

We switched places.

Amusingly, I began behaving in the same manner he had. Playing passionately, looking up at him with that same gleeful grin—the one that said, "Now, *this* is real music, eh?" Yet, to my astonishment, he appeared to be distracted—just as I had been when he was playing. He began to show signs of disengagement, as if he might burst out at any moment, "Oh, no, look at the time. Is that my admin calling?"

I was intrigued. And then the Holy Spirit downloaded some invaluable thoughts on why chasing diversity in our church worship culture is almost certainly a set-up for disaster.

Fact is, just as the worshipers God seeks in John 4:23 are adept at worshiping with or without lyrics, with or without worship leaders, with or without music, and with or without special services, the type of mature worshipers the Lord seeks are also largely unmoved by the issues of style. They are able to worship God unconstrained regardless of the genre of worship music emanating from the stage. Whether it fits their personal preferences or not.

The New Denomination

Have you noticed? Style of worship music has become the new denomination. Sure, traditional denominations still exist, but nowadays people tend to gather together in churches with those who worship musically in the same way they do (with the same instrumentation and/or the same level of expression) rather than with those who share the same theology.

Interesting.

Some prefer piano and organ with hymns. Others lean toward gospel music with choirs and lots of musical/lyrical repetition. Some tend toward acoustic instruments like guitars, ukuleles, and percussion and prefer to sing in the round. Still others connect with a more youthy, synth-driven, high-energy genre.

Meanwhile, for better or worse, the cry for diversity has been challenging pastors to rethink their method of attracting folks of different cultures to their churches—mostly as a result of the prevailing notion that the church with the most nations wins. This, of course, often leads pastors to encourage their worship leaders to incorporate as many different styles as possible in order to appeal to as many different people groups as possible.

This is an error, because it assumes—devastatingly—that incorporating a diverse style of music is the key to building a diverse church. This in turn places the emphasis—a tiring effort—on chasing styles in order to please and gain attendees. A truth that is not very true at all.

Let me say it this way: I believe deeply that the "problem" of attracting people from different nations to worship in our churches will never be "solved" by diversifying our styles of music. This is surely as illogical as it is dangerous. Even worse, it flat out doesn't work. Yet, unfortunately, if we find in some small way that it *does* seem to work, we'll surely work tirelessly in an attempt to incorporate each of the culturally unique musical expressions that fill the earth.

Population Demographics

Do you believe building a culturally diverse church is important? That it is scriptural? Do you believe that incorporating just the right amount of everyone's individual styles and preferences is the answer to growing a diverse church? A healthy church?

So many questions.

If building a diverse church is indeed of premium importance, we must first ask how we might accomplish it? Which people group should we appeal to first? Which culture? Which genre of music? And which genre within that genre?

I find it interesting. Often, those who talk the most about diversity in worship music really only intend to incorporate two distinct styles. Pop-sounding White music and Black gospel music. There you have it. Tada! We've achieved it! Diversity. Honestly, this type of thinking makes us appear arrogant (or ignorant). How can we claim to have achieved "diversity" when we're representing only a fragment of the world's musical styles while excluding so many others?

I suppose we could study the population demographics of the neighborhoods surrounding our churches and attempt to diversify our music styles accordingly. According to a 2019 census,[2] it was reported that the city of Minneapolis, MN is approximately 19.2% Black, 9.6% Hispanic or Latino, 60% White, 5.9% Asian, 1.4% American Indian, 0.0% Hawaiian or other Pacific Islander, and 4.8% two or more races. If we subscribe to this rationale, we'll need to divide up our standard twenty-three-minute Sunday morning worship set in like manner. Approximately.

We'll need to incorporate 19.2% Black music, 9.6% Hispanic or Latino music, 60% White music, 5.9% Asian music, 0.0% Native American music, and 4.8% other music. In this way, we'll assure a diverse congregation. Correct?

It's tough. I truly understand why certain leaders buy into chasing style, assuming this is the best way to corral people from different cultures. Yet, if we start down this road, we'll never find an end to it. Even worse, we'll never actually reach our intended destination.

This Could Get Complicated

Believe it or not, when I was in college, I began listening to a little rap music—some dc Talk as well as some popular rap tunes on the radio. I loved the groove and the rhythmic aspects as well as the way the artists explored controversial issues within their lyrics.

Soon I began enjoying rap music so much that I started writing my own rap songs. I even recorded two rap CDs (*Another Alternative* and *Go the Distance*). Yes, you heard me right. Two rap CDs. I wore baggie clothing, backwards ball caps, extra jewelry, and Nike high-tops. What can I say? It was the early '90s.

Here's the thing. As I traveled to different churches and youth groups, performing, people had different responses. But I'll never forget the night a tall, lanky fella in cowboy boots and a cowboy hat walked up to me and said with a thick Southern accent, "Hey, man. I don't usually like that rap music, ya hear. But there was just something about your anointed performance and the way you spoke about God that really touched me tonight."

A few years later, I followed the trends and started writing and

---

2   www.census.gov/quickfacts/fact/table/minneapoliscityminnesota,US/PST045219.

singing alternative rock music. Similarly, one Sunday morning, an elderly lady approached me, pulled out her ear plugs, and said, "Well, son, I don't usually like that rock-n-roll music, but there was something about your anointed singing this morning and the way you shared your heart that really touched me. Thank you."

Wow.

I had spent years trying to appeal to different people groups by singing a little something for everyone. A little rap for the hip-hop kids. A little rock for the alternative kids. A ballad or two for the young married couples. And a hymn for the older folks. And yet, just like that, my theory was shot to bits.

Astonishingly, according to theguardian.com, Glenn McDonald reports that there are now over 1,264 total music genres and micro-genres in the world representing all cultures.[3] With this in mind, let's ask again. Out of the hundreds of cultures in the world with differing music styles, which one(s) should we aim to please? Just about the time we incorporate the right amount of one music style into our services, we realize we'd better consider scores of others, as well. Thing is, even if we simply consider the seven major culture categories from our government census, we still have an enormous amount of work to do.

I'm French *and* German. So which culture should we incorporate if we're hoping to get me to church? Especially since the French and the Germans have very different musical tastes? Maybe we assume all White people enjoy the same genre of music. Oops. Or maybe we think because White people are the majority in America, their style preferences don't matter. But then aren't we doing exactly what we don't want others to do to us? Lumping all like-skinned people together, assuming they're all the same—with the same musical preferences?

While we're at it, let's ask another important, but potentially volatile, question: Is the responsibility to diversify our church populations expected only of large White churches, or does that same responsibility rest on Mung churches, Latin churches, Filipino Churches, Black

---

3 www.theguardian.com/music/2014/sep/04/-sp-from-charred-death-to-deep-filthstep
   -the-1264-genres-that-make-modern-music

churches, Asian churches, and Messianic Jewish churches, etc.? If so, what percentage of differing styles should each of these churches mix in to their worship services on behalf of all other cultures?

Okay. This could get complicated.

Hell Boasts Great Diversity Too

Can you see how easily chasing style quickly becomes a distraction? Honestly, chasing style with the hopes of drawing greater numbers of diverse people to our services is a bottomless pit. A black hole. Plus, it backfires on us.

Which is more important, a diverse church or a spiritually mature church? Some might argue that our efforts to build a diverse church prove we are growing toward spiritual maturity, but this is an oversimplification. Being diverse accomplishes little by itself. Again, diversity is wonderful and desirable, but diversity is not the end goal. Unity is the goal. (One of the foundational goals of the Church, according to Jesus' prayer in John 17:21.)

Let me repeat the bold statement I made a few paragraphs back. Diversity is not the mark of heaven. How do we know? Because hell is going to be just as diverse as heaven.

Are you seeing this? Am I saying something that is untrue? Unbiblical? Consider the verse we often site to justify the idea of chasing diversity:

"After this I saw a vast crowd, too great to count, from every nation and tribe and people and language, standing in front of the throne and before the Lamb. They were clothed in white robes and held palm branches in their hands. And they were shouting with a great roar, 'Salvation comes from our God who sits on the throne and from the Lamb'" (Revelation 7:9–10).

Beautiful!

Here's my question, though: Is heaven going to be made up of people from every tribe, every tongue, and every nation? Yes, of course. And this should excite every believer. It excites me profoundly! But let me ask: Isn't hell *also* going to be made up of people from every tribe, every tongue, and every nation? Yes, of course. And if this is true, it can only lead us to one important conclusion: diversity is not one of the defining characteristics that distinguishes the people of God from the people of eternal destruction. Both groups will be diverse. Both groups will be made up of people from every culture. Those who spend eternity with God as well as those who spend eternity in hell will both be a part of a group that is highly diverse.

Trust me. This may be hard to wrap your mind around, and you may need to say it aloud—777 times: "Diversity is not the goal. Diversity is not the goal."

But if diversity is not the goal, what is?

We know.

Love.

Love is the goal. Love is ultimately why people come to church. It's why they stay at church. Not music style. We don't need to achieve an equal representation of cultural styles, musical preferences, or skin color—based on our current population demographic—to be known as an inclusive, loving church. We don't even have to enjoy the same musical styles to prove we love one another. In fact, it would be atrocious if we all preferred the same styles of anything. Music. Food. Clothing. Dance. Travel. Art. Books. Entertainment.

Here's the truth.

Growing a multicultural congregation (something we truly desire) is remarkably more about operating with a fusion of authentic love and Holy Spirit anointing than it ever will be about style.

Biblically Color Blind

This is the beauty of the Kingdom. It really is color blind. Not ignorant or insensitive to color or culture, mind you. But completely, 100 percent unbiased when it comes to our skin color or cultural backgrounds, and when it comes to the Kingdom value imbedded within every single person God created. Each person is equally and inherently valuable, no matter their culture or color, age or gender, economic status or IQ. Period.

Yet, in modern times, many have labeled this "color blind" phraseology inconsiderate. Mean spirited. Even racist. Meanwhile, it's entirely biblical:

*For you are all children of God through faith in Christ Jesus. And all who have been united with Christ in baptism have put on Christ, like putting on **new clothes**. There is **no longer** Jew or Gentile, [no longer] slave or free, [no longer] male and female. For you are all one in Christ Jesus. And now that you belong to Christ, you are the true children of Abraham. You are his heirs, and God's promise to Abraham belongs to you.* (Galatians 3:26–29)

This passage helps us grasp the truth—once and for all—that God no longer identifies or distinguishes us according to our outward appearances. Or by our race or culture—our "clothing," so to speak. Why? Because we are now a part of a brand-new culture. With brand-new clothes. A brand-new family. The family of Abraham. One culture. A Kingdom culture. No longer defined in the way things have been defined in the past. We are now one creation in Christ. Not Jew or Gentile. Not African or North American. Not Australian or Asian. Not South American or European. Not old or young. Not slave or free. Not even male or female, concerning our identity in the Kingdom. We have all become little Christs now, and the physical traits that once defined us (and often separated us) no longer apply in God's Kingdom.

We are all one big, beautiful family.

What unites us has now taken center stage over what separates us. That is, the Spirit of Christ. Alive within us. Each one.

Honestly, one of the biggest mistakes we make is overemphasizing our cultural differences. This is similar to identifying ourselves primarily by the "old man" and not according to Christ. This, of course, is not to say we shouldn't *greatly* appreciate and even *richly* celebrate our differences—skin color, hair, facial and body types, styles, and cultures. We ought! But it will *never* be our differences that unite us. It is our differences that make us beautiful, but it is our similarities—as children of God—that bring us together.

> It is our differences that make us beautiful, but it is our similarities—as children of God—that bring us together.

Breaking Through The Language Barrier

"Are you saying we should stop presenting diverse styles of music in our church services?"

Certainly not! I'm just saying we should stop believing this is the key to growing a healthy church. Here's the thing. As Dr. Anderson and I discovered, the issue is infinitely more complicated than we first thought. Even as we blindly consider race and cultural preferences, we nearly forgot about generational preferences. You see, music style is a language. A *cultural* language, as well as a *generational* one. There are countless dialects that represent all the diverse cultures of the world, as well as both genders, *and* the diverse age groups of the world.

This is why older people sometimes say things like, "These new songs are hard to sing." Not because they're *actually* hard to sing, but because they're written in a different musical language then when they grew up. A language that sounds "foreign" to that particular generation. It's the same reason young people think songs from the 1600s sound "old-fashioned" or "out of touch." It's all Greek to them. It just doesn't compute. Nor does it inspire. Lyrically and melodically. Not because it isn't quality music, but because it is written in a language preferred by older listeners that is virtually unknown to younger listeners.

Therein lies the barrier: a "foreign" musical language that can (if we let it) separate God's people. Yet, surprisingly, the solution comes not with attempting to cram a hundred and one new styles down people's throats. There's an approach that's incredibly more effective.

The Anointing Breaks The Yoke

"Fine. What is it, Jeff? What is it that's going to bring us all together in unity?"

Simple.

The cowboy and the grandma had it right from the beginning. It's the anointing. The heavenly language of the Holy Spirit. He is what (or *who*) unites us. His anointing is the thing that transcends every ounce of our style and cultural differences to bring us together. He is the One who breaks down the musical language barriers between His people (all without negating their own intrinsic value).

It is His presence—experienced through His person and His anointing—that weaves its way as a single thread to connect every believer on the face of the planet. Despite our style and generational differences and preferences. Hallelujah!

God's anointing is the "music" of all spiritual people. All born-again people. It's the anointing that breaks the yoke of bondage (see Isaiah 10:27). You can play me a nice song from the farthest reaches of the globe in an earthly language I've never heard, and you'll completely lose me. But I'm telling you, if you sing that same song under the anointing—in tandem with the powerful, universal, heavenly language of God's Spirit—my spirit will rise up to join with your spirit in explosive worship, even if I can't fully understand the words. We will be united in the supernatural in ways that are impossible in the natural.

Warning: Huge statement coming.

It's not that we should appeal to our congregation through their favorite styles of music, but that we should teach our congregation to worship God passionately regardless of the style of music. This is the solution. We must teach this. We must lead this.

God's people must learn to worship Him no matter the cultural style. No matter the generational style. No matter the music quality. No matter if there's a great band on stage or a few a cappella singers. No matter how we feel. No matter what the musicians are wearing or even how they're acting. No matter if we're singing our favorite songs in the right key or not. These things do matter to varying degrees, but they're all peripheral.

What many people miss is that chasing diversity puts us in a position to appeal to the fleshly desires of our church family, but chasing the anointing puts us in a position to appeal to their spirit. Additionally, chasing diversity often delivers exactly the opposite of what we desire. When we focus on style and preference, people learn that style and preference are king. But when we focus on the anointing, people learn that Jesus is King.

Truth is, we'll never create a church that has the perfect blend of music *and* the perfect balance of all cultures. And that's okay, because this has never been the objective. Ironically, when people attend a church that focuses on chasing diversity, they tend to grow angry at other churches who aren't focused on chasing diversity. But don't worry. Once people realize your church is chasing the Spirit of God, they'll stop worrying about the fact that you aren't chasing diversity. And when we chase the Spirit of God, He will do the work of drawing people from every tribe, nation, and culture to our churches and to Himself.

WORSHIP AS WARFARE

6. The kind of worshipers the Father seeks are those who understand that our spiritual battles are fought and won as we worship Him.

Whether or not we're prepared for this, God is expecting us to lead our congregations into a fuller understanding of spiritual warfare in worship. For many, this is frightening or simply something to disregard. Nevertheless, the kind of worship leader God is using to equip His people for the future is the kind who understands there's more happening during our musical worship than simply giving the glory to God.

Not many of us were raised in churches where we regularly came face-to-face with demonic activity. Deliverance, as many refer to it. And yet, this is clearly something Jesus empowers each of His followers to confront:

> *"One day Jesus called together his twelve disciples and **gave them power and authority to cast out all demons** and to heal all diseases. Then he sent them out to tell everyone about the Kingdom of God and to heal the sick"* (Luke 9:1–2).

Then, in Luke 10, Jesus chooses another set of seventy-two disciples and gives them similar instructions, apparently. How do we know? Because *"when the seventy-two disciples returned, they joyfully reported to him, 'Lord, **even the demons obey us when we use your name!**'"* (Luke 10:17).

Question: Are your team and congregation at the place where they're ready to grasp the reality of spiritual warfare, even in this modern age? Have you prepared them for the fact that we have been given authority over demonic powers and that God is overcoming the darkness on our behalf even as we worship and declare the Lordship of Jesus? Sounds like maybe we have some growing to do. (Of course, we must never boast when evil spirits obey us—but it's true: evil spirits must obey God's people because of the power and authority He has given us.)

The Battle Is Raging

Whether we admit it or not, a spiritual battle is raging, and it's critical that we pull our heads out of the sand to make sure that our church family is aware. Not to scare them, but to help them lean in with confidence to the reality of spiritual warfare. Otherwise, we leave them dangerously vulnerable.

Consider these verses:

"Stay alert! Watch out for your great enemy, the devil. He prowls around like a roaring lion, looking for someone to devour" (1 Peter 5:8). *"The thief's purpose is to steal and kill and destroy. My purpose is to give them a rich and satisfying life"* (John 10:10).

Often, when we read a familiar verse, we're tempted to gloss over it. But don't underestimate the devil. The Bible is clear. He isn't merely attempting to frustrate us with lost cell phones and cars that won't start. No. He is trying to kill us. His end goal is nothing short of putting you in the ground with six feet of dirt over the top of your head with the hope that you will join him in hell for all of eternity.

My friend Lou Santiago Jr. (drummer and physician's assistant) has a favorite verse for just such an occasion: *"Praise the Lord, who is my rock. He trains my hands for war and gives my fingers skill for battle"* (Psalm 144.1). Lou understands full well that part of his role as a drummer is to fight in the Spirit, leveraging the power and authority God provides to battle on behalf of God's people—with his hands, fingers, and feet—as he plays. As He worships. Though this verse is literally referring to God preparing His people for physical battles (fought with swords, bows, clubs, and spears), it's also referring to God preparing us for spiritual battles (fought and won in praise and worship).

Is your team aware of this? Is your congregation aware of this? If not, it's high time we raise their awareness to these facts: that 1) spiritual warfare is already happening in our services, and that 2) musical praise and worship is meant to be an extraordinary contributor in setting spiritually lost and oppressed people free.

Remarkably, ignoring this issue is like sending your team members and congregants out to the battlefield in shorts and a T-shirt—totally exposed!

Our Praise Exposes the Darkness

I remember stepping through a mob of student worshipers onto the stage in preparation to speak at a camp in Arizona under the direction of Griffin McGrath in 2014. The band had just led a powerful time of worship, and I was transitioning to speak. I began to stir the students in spontaneous worship as the band grew in intensity. Just then, a boy in the front, to my left, began screaming and seemingly convulsing. The students' eyes all shot in his direction.

I encouraged everyone to keep their focus on Jesus, even as I listened for direction from the Holy Spirit. Was this someone whose toe got stepped on? Was this someone overwhelmed by the conviction of the Holy Spirit? Or was this someone fighting demonic oppression (or possession)?

We discerned, relatively quickly, that the enemy was causing this young man to "cry out" in frustration and agitation, much in the same way demons did in Jesus day. *"And whenever the unclean spirits saw [Jesus], they fell down before him and **cried out**, "You are the Son of God,"* (Mark 3:11).

Here's the deal. Whenever demons who are possessing or oppressing people come in contact with Jesus (or the Spirit of Christ within those who are passionately exalting His name), they are highly agitated. Because of this, the demon(s) often cry out, unintentionally exposing themselves.

> The *praise* of Jesus stirs up the *presence* of Jesus, and the *presence* of Jesus exposes the enemy.

Shouldn't we think it odd that we rarely see—at least in the Western world—this type of raw demonic activity found so often in Jesus' day? We may even assume this type of thing isn't happening anymore. But I would suggest that demons are not disappearing, but merely attempting to fly under the radar. The last thing a demon wants is to be cast out, so they've adapted, doing much of their work unnoticed, subtly whispering lies into people's ears while pulling on their marionette strings.

When we sit idly by during the musical worship, the chances of demons exposing themselves (and freeing their victims) decreases dramatically. But, in presence-packed moments, they just can't help but show their hand. Out of pure frustration. Think of it this way: The *praise* of Jesus stirs up the *presence* of Jesus, and the *presence* of Jesus exposes the enemy.

Our Praise Pushes Back the Darkness

It's one thing to expose the enemy. It's quite another to push him back. And yet, this is exactly what we can expect as believers—as musicians and singers—when we face spiritual enemies in the power of Jesus.

> *"And whenever the tormenting spirit from God troubled Saul, David would play the harp. Then Saul would feel better, and **the tormenting spirit would go away**,"* (1 Samuel 16:23).

I truly wish every team member from every worship band from every church understood the supernatural power and authority they possess as believers when they play and sing. You see, the spiritual battle we're fighting consists largely of the devil and his demonic powers working overtime to lead as many people into spiritual darkness as possible. But we possess the power—through the blood of Jesus and the Spirit of God—to crack open spiritually blind eyes as we drive the darkness away with our praise and worship.

When people walk in spiritual blindness—a great epidemic in our day—they're incapable of seeing (understanding) God's truth. It could be staring them plainly in the face, and yet, they can't—or won't—see it. They have spiritually darkened eyes. Second Corinthians 4:4 reminds us of the enemy's role in this: *"Satan has blinded the eyes of unbelievers so they cannot see the truth of the Gospel."*

Satan blinds the eyes of unbelievers, keeping them from seeing the truth of the gospel, but he also blinds (deceives) the eyes of believers, keeping them from seeing (understanding) many peripheral truths, including issues with identity, mental health, confusion, fear, depression, etc.

Unfortunately, we're largely losing this battle, since we fail to realize that the battle has already been won through Jesus' actions on the cross. But it doesn't have to be this way. We simply need to agree in faith with the victory we have and recognize our God-given mantle to set people free. We are appointed to stand in the gap for believers and unbelievers alike so that their great enemy, the devil, might be derailed in his efforts to kill, steal, and destroy them.

John Piper says, "The enemies of God are thrown into confusion by the songs of God's people."[4] This is incredible. Do you agree? Does your team know this truth? *Really* know it? Does your congregation?

I picture it like this: As we exalt God, lifting up the name of Jesus with our voices and instruments, the demons are incensed and expose themselves. It's as if their demonic hands, once covering over people's eyes, are suddenly removed and placed over their own ears to drown out the wretched sound of our praises. In that moment, as the people of God declare the praises of God, the fog is lifted. The fog of depression. The fog of complacency. The fog of loneliness. The fog of disappointment. The fog of lostness.

For one incredible moment, the captives come to their senses in God's illuminating presence and begin to see clearly, possibly for the first time. They blink incessantly, attempting to use their spiritual eyes, ones that have long been tightly shut. In the light of Jesus' glory, they now recognize their own captivity and are able to choose the wonderful freedom in Christ that has been eluding them for so long.

And the chains break. And the prison doors swing wide. And the scales fall to the floor. All because of the great disturbance our praises cause our enemies.

Our Praise Defeats the Darkness

Now, just because the prison doors have swung open, doesn't mean the captives suddenly have the courage to step through them into freedom.

---

4   John Piper, https://www.desiringgod.org/messages/ambushing-satan-with-song

No. We have to take it one step further. Not only are we called to *engage* in spiritual battles with our praise, but—with God's help—we are ultimately destined to *win* them.

We know the story of King Jehoshaphat (the king of Judah) in 2 Chronicles 20. As it relates to music and worship, this is one of the greatest spiritual warfare tales in all of history.

Picture this. Things were cruising along nicely in Jehoshaphat's kingdom, when all of a sudden, the armies of the Moabites, Ammonites, and some of the Meunites declared war on Judah. This would be similar to us receiving news that China, Russia, and several other nations had mobilized their troops to descend upon the neighborhoods of America overnight. Whoa!

Jehoshaphat immediately did the right thing by seeking the Lord and calling the entire nation of Judah to fast and pray. The Lord then answered powerfully through one of His prophets, declaring:

"Listen, all you people of Judah and Jerusalem! Listen, King Jehoshaphat! This is what the Lord says: **Do not be afraid! Don't be discouraged by this mighty army, for the battle is not yours, but God's.** *Tomorrow, march out against them. You will find them coming up through the ascent of Ziz at the end of the valley that opens into the wilderness of Jeruel. But you will not even need to fight.* **Take your positions; then stand still and watch the Lord's victory.** *He is with you, O people of Judah and Jerusalem. Do not be afraid or discouraged. Go out against them tomorrow,* **for the Lord is with you!***" (2 Chronicles 20:15–17)

This is awesome. But also scary. Why? Because, had we been there with Jehoshaphat, we might have been disappointed by the fact that God didn't just tell us to stay home while He slaughtered the enemy by Himself. Rather, He invited the Israelites (as He does us) to "take up their positions" in worship.

In obedience, Jehoshaphat led the people of Judah toward the battlefield early the next morning. Then he did something odd. He appointed the singers to walk ahead of the army, singing to the Lord and praising

God. These were their lyrics: *"Give thanks to the Lord; his faithful love endures forever!"* (2 Chronicles 20:21).

Incredibly, this was the consequence of their singing:

> **At the very moment they began to sing and give praise, the Lord caused** *the armies of Ammon, Moab, and Mount Seir to start fighting among themselves. The armies of Moab and Ammon turned against their allies from Mount Seir and killed every one of them. After they had destroyed the army of Seir, they began attacking each other. So when the army of Judah arrived at the lookout point in the wilderness, all they saw were dead bodies lying on the ground as far as they could see.* **Not a single one of the enemy had escaped***"* (2 Chronicles 20:22–24).

Interestingly, the Hebrew word for *praise* in verse 22 is *Tehillâh,* so we know the people of God were singing spontaneous melodies centered around the lyrics "Give thanks to the Lord; his faithful love endures forever!" In reply, God went to work to destroy the enemy.

Who knew?

How odd is it to think of placing the singer types up near the front of the battle? Don't we normally put the fiercest, roughest, and toughest cats on the front lines? (Please forgive me for stereotyping my fellow singers!) But maybe Jehoshaphat knew something many people today don't know—that the anointed singers *were* the fierce ones. The fiery ones. The warrior ones. Spiritually.

Can you imagine if word got out to our people? What if we trained our teams *and* our congregations in these ways, reminding them that they were made to serve as spiritual warriors—to defeat the enemy in the name of Jesus—at the moment they begin to praise God?

> *"Let the praises of God be in their mouths,*
>   *and a sharp sword in their hands—*
> *to execute vengeance on the nations*
>   *and punishment on the peoples,*
> *to bind their kings with shackles*

and their leaders with iron chains,
to execute the judgment written against them.
   This is the glorious privilege of his faithful ones" (Psalm
149:6–9).

Praise the Lord!

Isn't this what so many worship songs are attempting to stir in us? Songs like "Surrounded," "Raise a Hallelujah," and "Rattle." Clearly, God doesn't ask us to fight spiritual Goliaths on our own. Instead, He would have us fight them in ways that are very odd indeed. He says to us, "I will fight your battles for you if you will lift up your songs and worship me with all of your heart, soul, mind, and strength." Our part in the battle is to praise Him. His part in the battle is to overcome the enemy.

Remember the tambourine lady in your church? Check this out: "*As the Lord strikes them, the Israelites will keep time with tambourines and harps*" (Isaiah 30:32). Yes! But please don't forget, as we seek to apply these Scriptures in our lives (post-resurrection), we're no longer worried about fighting *people*. People are not the enemy: "*We no longer fight against flesh and blood, but against evil rulers and authorities of the unseen world, against mighty powers in this dark world, and against evil spirits in the heavenly places*" (Ephesians 6:12).

As we exalt God through musical worship, we set the stage for Him to defeat the darkness and bring divine healing and deliverance to hurting people. Please realize, this strategy is growing more and more pivotal as we move closer and closer to the second coming of Christ. Of course, it's because of His grace that God has given us a prominent role to play in winning our spiritual battles. We're not suggesting that He *needs* us to praise Him in order to win the victory or that our primary focus shouldn't be to worship Him as we sing. It's just that He has invited us to partner with Him in overthrowing the enemy. With our praise. With our worship.

> Too often, our well-meaning intentions have left us drowning in survival mode rather than flourishing in revival mode.

A VISION FROM THE PAST FOR OUR FUTURE

As I begin to bring this book to a close, I want to take us back to the introduction, where I spoke of our great need to move beyond the all-too-common "tyranny of the urgent" leadership approach. Too often, our well-meaning intentions have left us drowning in survival mode rather than flourishing in revival mode. If we're honest, sometimes we're barely hanging on from week to week (living from spiritual paycheck to spiritual paycheck, in a sense). At best, we're scraping together a lovely little set list for our lovely little services.

But this is not where we're meant to live. This is not the visionary, ground-breaking, ground-taking approach that God has called us to. Nor is this the "yoke is easy, burden is light" philosophy He wants us to spark in our congregations. We are called to more. We've been given spiritual eyes to peer into the future to understand the wonderful things God has been planning for our spiritual family. We've been given spiritual ears to listen to the gentle but pervasive directives that flow from His heart. From His Word. From His Spirit.

Subsequently, we need to ask these questions:

- When was the last time we truly sought God for His plans over ours?
- When was the last time we really asked God about His long-term desires for our church?
- When was the last time we specifically made room for the supernatural in our services?
- When was the last time we celebrated the way God's Spirit orchestrated a "take-over" on a Sunday?

What type of church culture are we establishing as leaders—in word, in thought, in action? Are we building Kingdom culture, or are we simply preserving man-made traditions? Are we in sync with the Head of the Church, Jesus, and His vision for the body of Christ as revealed by God's Word and God's Spirit? Or are we always longing for something else? Something new. Something more…modern.

Of course, there's truly nothing new under the sun. Though we search for it. Hunger for it. Strive for it. In vain. Truth be told, we often drift wildly off course, seeking newness for newness' sake. Or maybe we do the opposite, looking back to Church history—one hundred, four hundred, or even a thousand years ago. Any resource besides the Word of God.

Intriguingly, if there are meaningful strategies to glean from churches of bygone eras (and I believe there are), we must assume that they originated from the Scriptures, too. If so, why not just go straight to the Word of God from the get-go to avoid the dangers that come with copying a copy?

WILDFIRE

It was April 5, 2018. We were in chapel at NCU, when suddenly God dropped a revelatory truth on our community through our president, Dr. Scott Hagan. One that has greatly impacted my perspective on church culture.

We were hosting my friend and anointed worship leader Jonathan Lee, and he was leading a new song he'd written with Dustin Smith and Johan Asgarde, titled "Wildfire." The whole place lit up as we sang words that invited the Spirit of God to come like a wildfire.

Near the end of the song, President Hagan stepped to the microphone and said something astonishing. He told us he had just returned from California where there were massive wildfires raging out of control. Many lives had been lost, and countless homes were destroyed. He reminded us that highly trained firemen often move out ahead of the wildfires to set controlled fires or 'controlled burns' in an attempt to put out the massive wildfires. The idea, of course, is that without fuel to consume, the wildfire will burn itself out when it reaches the area that has already been burned.

Then he turned everything on its head. He told us that though controlled fires are great for fighting destructive wildfires in California, Kingdom leadership works the other way around. When it comes to the wildfire of the Spirit, what we need are highly surrendered ministers engaged in stoking the fires of the Spirit rather than those who are attempting to control them or put them out.

All too often, we end up with ministers who move out ahead of the wildfire of the Spirit to set controlled burns, in an attempt to 'control' the supernatural fires they don't understand. These smaller, controlled fires appear to be real and potent, but they are counterfeits, only a shadow of God's genuine, all-consuming wildfire. They're typically set by well-meaning leaders who aim at manufacturing a "safe" spiritual atmosphere in order to keep things from getting 'out of control.' Unfortunately, this strategy is rooted in fear and is suffocating the supernatural move of the Holy Spirit within the Body of Christ.

Wow.

I had long sensed the same thing while watching some pastors and leaders demonstrate what seemed to be elements of a biblical Pentecostal church. All the while, they were operating in something closer to a "form of godliness, denying God's power" than anything resembling true fire. (Of course, it's one thing when church leaders act as if Pentecostalism is a sect or "cult" to avoid instead of a central element of the gospel. And still, worse yet are leaders who claim to be Pentecostal while attempting to contain or manipulate the *true* wildfire of the Holy Spirit.)

This type of cultural smokescreen must end. We must stop stopping the move of God's Spirit for fear that someone (believers or unbelievers) might be offended. Truth is, we know we're on the wrong path when we find ourselves more concerned with offending people by God's Spirit than with offending God's Spirit with the fear of man.

> We must stop stopping the move of God's Spirit for fear that someone (believers or unbelievers) might be offended.

Our congregations (each and every person) are desperate to be led into the "wild" things of the Spirit of God—even if they can't identify it as such. But all too often, we second-guess things, assuming they're not ready for the very thing God is saying He made them for.

Here's how I look at it:

- I didn't grow up lifting up my hands. But I read about it in the Bible, so I changed.

- I didn't grow up speaking in tongues. But I noticed it being highly encouraged in the Scriptures, so I speak out.
- I didn't grow up dancing or shouting. But I see it in the Bible, so I worship extravagantly.
- I didn't grow up feeling comfortable with the idea of "intimacy" with God. But I read the Song of Songs (and other passages), so I step into close fellowship with God.
- I didn't grow up listening for God's voice. But I see endless examples of Him speaking to His people in His Word, so I listen intently.
- I didn't grow up expecting to see miracles. But I read about it continuously in the Scriptures, so I pray and believe.
- I didn't grow up around prophecy. But I see God working through His prophets in the New and Old Testament, so I'm seeking to grow in my supernatural understanding (still in process).
- I didn't grow up casting out demons, but I read about Jesus giving all of His disciples authority in these areas, so I lean in and muster my faith.

In order for me to model, teach, and do these things in front of my church family—to spark this type of biblical "wildfire" culture for my team and for my congregation—I must first begin to walk in them myself. So what about it? In what areas from the list above do you need to grow?

_____

_____

_____

_____

_____

PROCEED WITH CONFIDENCE

With regard to the future of musical worship, there will forever be aspects of Kingdom culture that make us uncomfortable. But as long as we consistently see examples of these things in God's Word, we can follow His lead with confidence as He takes His Church to a place where:

- **Leaders** empower their people rather than lord over them
- **Team members** see themselves as more than just a back-up band
- **Congregants** grab the baton and understand their role in running the race
- **Leaders** dig the well of relationship with God so they can stop trying to lead people to a place in worship they've never been
- **Team members** see themselves as more than a karaoke band
- **Congregants** mature spiritually and begin to seek God on their own, Monday through Saturday
- **Leaders** wield creativity, technology, and excellence as tools to help spur on vibrancy in worship and un-numb their congregants
- **Team members** stop performing for people and start serving people
- **Congregants** stop worrying about what song styles are being led and start connecting with God no matter the song or the style
- **Leaders** learn to hunt for the Spirit's river in order to keep everyone moving together in the flow of God's presence
- **Team members** learn to lead and love their church family in a way that can be seen and felt from stage
- **Congregants** learn to sing spontaneous "joyful noise" songs to God in church and at home, just like writing beautiful handwritten notes to Him
- **Leaders** teach the scriptural *whys* behind our worship, allowing their congregations to become hearers *and* doers of the Word
- **Team members** grow in their ability to flow spontaneously together as a result of practicing these skills behind the scenes and taking intentional "risks" during the service

- **Congregants** learn to worship through the transitions rather than losing focus each the time the song changes

We must be careful. The corporate worship experience can easily gravitate toward an emotional, musical encounter designed for the "pleasure" of the worshiper instead of a genuine, intimate encounter designed for fellowship with the Father. Sadly, many modern churchgoers are still making it "all about me." All about my emotions. All about my preferences. All about my talents. All about my schedule. As it is, too many of us have made the corporate worship experience more about the "songs we sing" rather than "the lives we live as *expressed* in the songs we sing."

It's time for leaders to step up to impart the Father's vision of corporate worship—the one where all the people, the entire community—join together without reservation to worship the one true God of all the universe with all their heart, soul, mind, and strength.

> *"When **all the people** of Israel saw the fire coming down and the glorious presence of the Lord filling the Temple, they fell face down on the ground and worshiped and praised the Lord, saying, 'He is good! His faithful love endures forever!'"* (2 Chronicles 7:3).
>
> *"Then Ezra praised the Lord, the great God, and **all the people** chanted, 'Amen! Amen!' as they lifted their hands. Then they bowed down and worshiped the Lord with their faces to the ground"* (Nehemiah 8:6).

What a picture! Could this be the culture we're aiming for? Not a new one, but one that has been right under our noses throughout the history of the world?

STAYING POWER FOR NEW CULTURE

Honestly, building a biblical church culture in this modern age is a lot like being a parent. As parents, we are continually building the culture of our family, with every tiny decision, activity, word, and tradition. Understandably, attempting to make a significant shift in our family culture can be very daunting, especially if we've already established an unhealthy culture. No doubt, it's much more difficult to *change* our family culture than it is to start from scratch.

Most people just aren't willing to make the necessary sacrifices to transition a bad culture into a beautiful one, a lukewarm culture into a vibrant one. Too often, the enormous immediate challenges scare off the most well-intentioned parents (even though it rarely takes more than two weeks of pure anguish and focused, relentless love to bring an end to a child's rebellious habits).

The choice is simple. A little suffering now or years of suffering later. Taking the bull by the horns to stir things up a little bit more every week, or dangerously, comfortably sliding into that 'easy-chair' worship experience.

Yes, building Kingdom culture in our churches could be a bit more complicated than parenting a child. (Maybe.) Yes, it's going to be somewhat challenging to spark some of these "new" Kingdom cultural expressions in our churches. Yes, it's going to take hard work and tenacity. Yes, some people are going to get mad. Yes, some are going to leave as we begin shifting away from the comfort of what we know (often decades or centuries in the making) toward a grander vision of Kingdom culture (several millennia in the making).

But have no fear. Take comfort in knowing that you are obeying God. Take comfort in knowing that in obeying God, you are glorifying God. Take comfort in knowing that in glorifying God, you are serving, helping, and loving your congregants in the best possible way, all while giving yourself a true fighting chance of sparking the church God desires.

What's it worth to you?

Would you rather me leave you alone to sing, make music, and have a good time recording your new church EP, or are you ready to lead your church family into the Kingdom culture they were born to enjoy?

Do we trust the culture of heaven as revealed in the Word of God by the Spirit of God? If so, we're going to bear incredible fruit as we pour ourselves into sparking this beautiful culture of the Kingdom within the hearts and families of those in our church community.

Chapter Highlights

1. The best worship leadership is not rooted in position or power but in empowering others to grow in their passion to pursue God on their own. We must continually be about the transference of power in our leadership rather than about the acquisition of power. This is Kingdom leadership, and this is the future.

2. Our scriptural end goal is to move our church culture—with the help of the Spirit—from where it is, into Kingdom culture, no matter how short or long a distance that is. In this light, we must slowly and intentionally help our church family move from platform-driven worship—where everything is dictated by the leaders—to multitude-driven worship—where most things are driven by the fiery believing masses.

3. The most compelling moment in a worship service for a Kingdom worship leader is not listening to her own voice on the microphone, but listening to the unified voice of the multitude as she steps back from the microphone. When this happens, you know you've been used of the Lord to spark true worshipers in your congregation.

4. One of the most important ways we can help our church family get out of the bleachers and take the baton is to help them break free of the mentality that tells them they can only worship if everything is *just so*—with the perfect songs in the perfect style. With lyrics on a screen and a talented band on the stage. With a worship leader telling them what to sing and when to shout. With the perfect church people in the perfect church building. With our help, they can unlower the bar on corporate worship in their own lives so they can truly become the kind of worshiper the Father seeks (see John 4:23).

5. Many people live their lives believing they have to fight the devil and the world by themselves in order to stay afloat. The kind of worshipers the Father seeks are those who understand the battle has already been won by Jesus and that our role in the battle is not to fight the kingdom of darkness, but to simply worship. We have rarely seen the power and deliverance that will result from a church that understands worship is warfare.

ADDENDUM

FOUR THINGS GOD EXPOSED IN HIS CHURCH THROUGH COVID-19

I wrote the first half of *SPARK* before COVID-19 hit, but the rest of it was written in the midst of one of the craziest seasons in human history. A season where the entire world was shut down because of a pandemic, starting in late 2019 and continuing at least through the publishing of this book in 2021. Everyone I talked to said they never would have believed it if you had told them that America was going to go on lockdown, closing companies, schools, businesses, churches, stores, parks, vacation spots, and more, even while requiring everyone to wear masks in public—indoors, and often outdoors, as well. This has never happened on such a scale in America, let alone across the entire globe.

In response, I couldn't help but ask the Lord for a few things to share with you regarding everything He wants us to learn as church leaders and as followers of Christ. Lessons, I believe, we could not have learned apart from this most invasive and inconvenient trial. Here are four important things He showed me about how He used (and is using) COVID-19 to expose some very problematic issues within His Church:

1. Busyness. We've all been there. Too busy. Frantically juggling to keep up or simply pushing too rigorously in an attempt to preserve the momentum. As a result, pastors and leaders often suffer burn out and unintentionally fall into moral failure. COVID-19 provided a forced opportunity for rest and reset. But did we? Rest? Reset? No, we dug in and worked even harder, attempting to drown out our great worries and fears by bolstering our online service experiences. Music gear manufacturers were wonderfully blessed as churches raced to purchase digital consoles, new cameras, and improved internet packages. Isn't it wild? One of the very few positives that God was providing for His church, in the form of a pandemic, was a forced "time-out" of sorts. A protective discipline, designed for our good. But we would have none of it, and we pressed on in our own power, despite the warnings of the Spirit.

2. Talent over anointing. God was trying to reveal something to us by stripping away our sanctuaries, our cameras, our lighting, and our sound systems. You see, it's easy to hide the fact that we're relying on talent and production rather than anointing when we're in a big room with lots of people. But when we're standing behind a camera or on a stage in an empty room, it's much, much more difficult. Thing is. Talent can appear to cover a multitude of sins when anointing and authenticity are lacking. Especially when we're gathered in person. Have you noticed? Talent doesn't translate as well through a television screen or an iPad. But, do you know what does? Anointing, hunger, authenticity, and passion. These highly spiritual traits flow fluidly and powerfully through screens to a family of five attempting to worship God in their living room. Interesting. Maybe this is why many virtual churchgoers suddenly realized they could go elsewhere, to other online churches, if they were simply going to "watch" church. They could easily view more popular leaders online rather than continue to "attend" their own smalltime, hometown church. This needs to change.

3. False sheep. During COVID-19, we lost nearly one-third to half of our church family. Amazingly, God instigated a purging of the sheep through all of this. Many suddenly had the realization that going to church in their PJs, while sitting at home in their recliner around the big screen, was just as good as attending the service in a physical building. This showed us all something. Actually, two very important things. 1) It revealed that many who attend church don't really understand what church is; that it isn't something we attend, but rather something we are; something to take part in with real community, accountability, and iron-sharpening-iron friction. United with real flesh and blood people, rubbing shoulders, serving each other, loving each other, and walking together through the good and bad. 2) It also showed us that we have built our attendance numbers on very skewed calculations. Unbeknownst to us, we have been counting people as "members" who were not truly members at all. As explained in the parable of the sower (Matthew 13:20-21), many who initially received the message of God with joy (those who's seed had fallen on rocky soil), tend to fall away when faced with trials or persecution. These are the people we unintentionally encouraged, pre-COVID-19, to remain as spectators— rather than to grow into full participants—for fear that they might leave (or stop giving). If only we had challenged our spiritual brothers and sisters to grab the baton and become mature members of Christ's body. This way, when the winds blow and the storms come, they are less likely to rationalize their departure.

4. Inauthentic worship. The moment dads and moms were asked to worship together with their families around the same TV where unwholesome movies and violent video games are regularly viewed—something few families had done together pre-COVID-19—we were in trouble. You see, it's easy for non-worshipers to "hide" in a relatively full sanctuary with hundreds or thousands of other churchgoers. We can all sing along to the songs, and maybe even lift a hand, for a few minutes among a crowd of worshipers. There's a lot of positive peer pressure and a lot of good vibes to go around. No one stands out, especially since we've been taught as worship leaders never to make anyone feel uncomfortable. Fast forward to our living rooms (or to the classic man cave), and it's a very different story. Kids are suddenly put in close confines with parents who they've rarely seen praise God or shout to the Lord with much fervency. As such, they wouldn't be surprised when the church meeting around the family big screen becomes a very quiet one indeed; one where most family members sit quietly and uncomfortably watching the platform people on the screen sing and worship. Truth be told, it takes a lot of guts for parents to invite their families to boldly engage in worship when there are no other inspiring worshipers or worship leaders around, especially when we find ourselves in yoga pants and sweatshirts, lounging on our cozy couches. In this instance, parents were asked to become the worship leaders they were desperately ill-equipped to be.

From Chapter 3

USING THE LORD'S PRAYER AS A SPRINGBOARD TO TALK WITH GOD.

In chapter 3, I share some practical examples of how I spend time alone with God, including the many ways I speak with Him in prayer. Because Jesus presented the Lord's Prayer in Matthew 6 as a way to teach His disciples how to pray, I truly believe He gave us this text as a template rather than something we should pray by rote. With that in mind, here are a few ways I personally lean in to the Lord's Prayer as a guide when I talk with my Creator.

1. Hallowed be Your name. I like to expound on this single phrase, praising God for His power and might. His perfection and grandeur. His faithfulness and majesty. I echo other relevant Scripture passages: *"Holy, holy, holy is the Lord God, the Almighty—the one who always was, who is, and who is still to come"* (Revelation 4:8). I then remind myself again and again that Jesus is indeed coming back. Yes, one day the sky will crack open, the trumpet will sound, and the Son of Man will meet us in the air. There is no other God like our God. There is no other name with the power to save!

2. Your Kingdom come. I specifically declare God's Kingdom come and will be done in my life, in Martha's life, in our kid's lives, in our nation, in my neighbors' lives. It varies daily. But it could take two or ten minutes to get through it all, as I embrace His will over mine, His Kingdom over mine. Often, I follow Tommy Tenney's pattern and pray something like, "Lord, let your Kingdom come. Let my kingdom go. Let your will be done. Let my will be gone. Lord, I submit my will completely to yours."

3. Give us our daily bread. I use this opportunity to thank God specifically for all He has provided and continues to provide for me and my family. Cultivating a grateful heart toward God is so important. I also remind myself that I never have to worry about food or shelter, since God promises to take care of us (see Matthew 6:31). Sometimes I start thanking Him for random things around my office, for our house, for our cars, for my stapler, for everything. I may present some other requests here as well. Beyond my physical needs of daily bread, I also thank Him for the spiritual nourishment He provides. Nourishment that comes directly from His Word. I remind myself that everything I have comes from Him. Not just food. But breath. Life. Everything.

4. Forgive my sins. I repent of my sins just about every day. Specifically. Even ones I don't know I've committed. I list the sins I know about, calling them out as sin and humbling my heart before my God. (Some say we don't need to do this, but I see it as highly relational. We wouldn't stop asking forgiveness from friends and family members with each new transgression just because we know they'll forgive us. We would—and we should—continue to humble ourselves before anyone we've hurt. And God is no different. I love Proverbs 28:13: "People who conceal their sins will not prosper, but if they confess and turn from them, they will receive mercy." Don't forget that a huge part of forgiveness is receiving cleansing for your past through the blood of Jesus, but also receiving empowerment for your future (to stop sinning) through the Holy Spirit.

5. Forgive others. I regularly forgive those who have hurt me. Aloud. By name. Sometimes it's new people and new hurts, but I often revisit old scars to forgive, again, people who wronged me years ago. I don't want to hold bitterness toward anyone, and I don't want anyone to hold power over me because of painful wrongs they've committed against me. I genuinely want to offer them the same mercy and love God offers me. "If you forgive those who sin against you, your heavenly Father will forgive you. But if you refuse to forgive others, your Father will not forgive your sins" (Matthew 6:14–15). I regularly use the word *release* as I forgive people for money owed, malicious words, and hurtful actions taken against me.

I even forgive those who haven't asked for my forgiveness—those who don't "deserve" it—recognizing that my forgiveness doesn't condone what they've done, but simply means I refuse to let them keep me angry, callousing my heart.

6. Keep me from temptation. This is huge. Don't let this one slip by. We are tempted every day. And we desperately require the help of the Holy Spirit to resist temptation. We know the devil has no power to make us sin, and James reminds us that God never tempts us to sin. He clarifies, "Temptation comes from our own desires, which entice us and drag us away. These desires give birth to sinful actions. And when sin is allowed to grow, it gives birth to death" (James 1:14–15). Help us, Lord!

7. Deliver me from evil. I always ask God to deliver me from three types of evil: that of my own evil desires, that of the evil in the world, and that of the devil, dark forces, and principalities. I often plead the blood of Jesus over my entire family and thank God for His guardian angels who watch over our lives. I ask Him to deliver us from dangerous circumstances, and I release my fears of unforeseen sickness, tragedies, and disasters to Him, trusting Him to protect me and my family.

From Chapter 9

ALL THE PEOPLE

In chapter 9, we delved into the hidden treasure of the seven Hebrew words for *praise*. But, as you might imagine, there are actually more than seven of these little gems. It's wild. It's like we've been robbed by not being made aware of these incredible truths. Or maybe it's just that God often loves to bury the riches of His Word deep below the surface just to see who's intrigued enough to dig them up.

Here's the question: Is every single person on the planet really expected to worship God with every single one of the Hebrew words for *praise*?

Ponder that.

Then let's ask another.

How many times have we come across a passage in the Bible that reads like this: "And *most* of the people bowed down before the Lord," or, "And only the Israelites who were comfortable lifted their hands to praise God," or, "And all those whose personalities were compatible with God's command to sing, sang a new song"?

How many times?

None.

Yet, maybe the Bible is exaggerating. Maybe when it says "all the people" it really means *most* of the people. There are always a few stragglers, right?

Maybe. Maybe not.

Let's see.

Shouting and Praising

- Joshua 6:5 – *"When you hear the priests give one long blast on the rams' horns, have* all the people *shout as loud as they can. Then the walls of the town will collapse, and the people can charge straight into the town."*
- Leviticus 9:24 – *"Fire came out from the presence of the LORD and consumed the burnt offering and the fat portions on the altar. And when* all the people *saw it, they shouted for joy and fell face-down"* (NIV).
- First Chronicles 15:28 – *"So* all Israel *brought up the Ark of the LORD's Covenant with shouts of joy, the blowing of rams' horns and trumpets, the crashing of cymbals, and loud playing on harps and lyres."*
- Ezra 3:11 – *"With praise and thanksgiving they sang to the LORD: 'He is good; his love toward Israel endures forever.' And* all the people *gave a great shout of praise to the LORD, because the foundation of the house of the LORD was laid"* (NIV).
- Psalm 29:9 – *"The voice of the LORD twists mighty oaks and strips the forests bare. In his Temple* everyone *shouts, 'Glory!'"*

It cannot be ignored that none of these verses make room for the individual who doesn't feel comfortable shouting to God. Not even for the person who was raised in a non-shouting household. And there is no mention of accommodating those who are timid or shy. Everyone shouts. It's just part of the way God created us to respond to Him. It's part of the way we were wired to worship. It's part of our God-given nature. He desires nothing less. From each and every person He created. For His glory and for our benefit.

Singing

- Exodus 15:1 – *"Then Moses and* the people of Israel *sang this song to the* LORD: *'I will sing to the* LORD, *for he has triumphed gloriously; he has hurled both horse and rider into the sea.'"*
- Numbers 21:16–18 – *"From there the Israelites traveled to Beer, which is the well where the* LORD *said to Moses, 'Assemble the people, and I will give them water.' There* the Israelites *sang this song: 'Spring up, O well! Yes, sing its praises! Sing of this well, which princes dug, which great leaders hollowed out with their scepters and staffs.'"*

Dancing and Celebrating

- 2 Samuel 6:5 – *"David and* all Israel *were celebrating with* all their might *before the Lord, with castanets, harps, lyres, timbrels, sistrums, and cymbals"* (NIV).

It doesn't matter how you spin it. "All their might" clearly denotes doing something to the full extent. So, we can surmise these people weren't sweetly dancing like a bunch of cream puffs. They were full-on giving everything they had to celebrate the King of kings and Lord of lords. With great joy. Unabashedly. Unashamedly.

"Why, yes," you say, "that was part of their culture."

Right. So, what is culture?

As I mentioned in the introduction of this book, culture is roughly a summation of the long-term habits or rituals of a people group that have been established over a long period of time.

Culture is neither inherently good or bad. It just is. Culture is not deemed "acceptable" simply because it exists. No. If my culture conflicts with Kingdom culture at any point, it is wrong and must be overhauled.

Ironically, this is exactly what Jesus wants to do. Re-establish Kingdom culture in us. In His Church. Why? Because we have slowly drifted—over long periods of time—away from *His* culture. Either purposefully or accidentally. And by doing so, we have created our own culture—in rebellion to His culture.

Simply put, culture is whatever Jesus says it is. Period. If a particular culture has stood the test of time for eight hundred years, but it is not congruent with the culture of heaven, it has been wholly wrong for eight hundred years and must be upgraded. Likewise, if our culture has not made room for physical expression (or any other type of Biblical expression) in worship, it must change. As leaders, we must embrace and teach these important truths.

Bowing Down and Falling On Their Faces

- First Kings 18:38–39 – *"Immediately the fire of the LORD flashed down from heaven and burned up the young bull, the wood, the stones, and the dust. It even licked up all the water in the trench! And when* all the people *saw it, they fell face down on the ground and cried out, 'The LORD—he is God! Yes, the LORD is God!'"*
- Second Chronicles 20:18 – *"Then King Jehoshaphat bowed low with his face to the ground. And* all the people *of Judah and Jerusalem did the same, worshiping the LORD."*
- First Chronicles 29:20 – *"Then David said to the* whole assembly, *'Give praise to the LORD your God!' And* the entire assembly *praised the LORD, the God of their ancestors, and they bowed low and knelt before the LORD and the king."*
- Second Chronicles 7:3 – *"When* all the people *of Israel saw the fire coming down and the glorious presence of the LORD filling the Temple, they fell face down on the ground and worshiped and praised the LORD, saying, 'He is good! His faithful love endures forever!'"*

Take note, worship leaders and pastors. David actually told the people *how* to worship in 1 Chronicles 29:20, when he said, *"Give **praise** [Bârak] to the LORD your God!"* Ironically, I meet many young worship leaders who feel uncomfortable dictating the way in which others should worship God. I've even heard many tell their congregations, "We just want you to worship God however you feel led to do so." Yet this is not the way David led. He told the people exactly what was expected. Clearly and concisely. As a leader entrusted and empowered by God. And, amazingly, this helped everyone know exactly what was expected, so they could worship together fervently and rightly. As God intended.

Hands Lifted High

- Nehemiah 8:6 – *"Then Ezra praised the LORD, the great God, and all the people chanted, 'Amen! Amen!' as they lifted their hands. Then they bowed down and worshiped the LORD with their faces to the ground."*
- Psalm 67:3 – *"May the nations praise you, O God. Yes, may all the nations praise [Yâdâh] you."* [As we discovered, *Yâdâh* is the Hebrew word that means "to revere or worship with the hands. (Wringing, extending, waving.)"]
- Psalm 145:10 – *"All of your works will thank you, LORD, and your faithful followers will praise [Yâdâh] you."*

Are you a part of God's creation? Are you a part of the nations of the world? Are you a part of His faithful followers? Then God asks you to praise Him with your hands. Look, I'm sure it's possible—even likely—that the Israelites encountered commands to worship God in ways that didn't fit their natural personalities too. Like us. But, interestingly, the people in these Scriptures didn't seem to be sitting around calmly choosing how to worship God based on their feelings. They didn't seem to be pondering the latest worship trends to ascertain which expression best fit their culture. No. They simply responded in a moment—in the blink of an eye—nearly involuntarily.

God must have showed up so devastatingly that hitting the deck or crying out in praise was literally the only imaginable response. It's the same way we would throw our hands in the air if someone thrust a gun in our back. It's the same way we would run for our life if a giant grizzly came at us from thirty yards away. It's the same way we would burst into cheers if our son or daughter won their first Olympic gold medal. It's compulsory. Obligatory. Entirely unavoidable.

In these moments, we wouldn't need specific instruction on how to put our hands in the air, how to run from a grizzly, or how to cheer for our son or daughter. We would simply react. Fully. Impetuously. Instinctively. Just as all normal, sane people would.

It should be the same with our worship. When we are truly engaged with God—fully aware of who He is—we just can't sit quietly, uninspired. We are compelled to offer total, fitting praise together with all of God's people.

From Chapter 13

A DAUNTING ASSIGNMENT

I often provide challenging "assignments" for our worship leaders to help them grow in their worship leadership. One of these is an assignment I've been giving for eleven years now. It has proven to be fairly daunting (for some). It involves inviting our best worship teams to lead a single song for the entirety of our eighteen-minute worship set, something that helps them on many levels, but specifically as they learn to lead and flow in spontaneous worship.

One of my teams—the very first to receive this assignment—was not happy with my nice little extended worship challenge. They looked at me like a deer in the headlights. Had I lost my mind? How were they supposed to lead one song for eighteen minutes? They would look like fools, simply repeating the chorus or the bridge 121 times. (Remember, at this point, we were still defaulting to the all-too-common four-to-five-minutes-per-song rule.)

We discussed the situation intensely for a bit, and I remember leaving feeling frustrated and a bit deflated, feeling like very little of what I'd been trying to teach them was getting through.

Even so, realizing I probably should have worked with them a bit more on this idea, I went home and wrote an email with a template for how they could easily lead one song for eighteen minutes (without looking like fools). In fact, after listing the possibilities, it was clear that if they implemented everything on my list, they would easily be able to lead one song for thirty-five minutes (and would certainly be in trouble for going too long).

Here's the full list of items I gave them to consider for their "one song for eighteen minutes" worship set:

- Open with a call to worship (welcome, Scripture, prayer, teaching, spontaneous singing).
- Start by singing/teaching the chorus a couple times (especially if introducing a new song).
- Sing the first verse two times (instead of one time) with an instrumental section in between.
- Add an instrumental section or two throughout (let the instruments "prophesy").
- Share a teaching/doing moment in the middle somewhere (a Hebrew word of praise, etc.).
- Lead a spontaneous singing moment or two (soft and/or loud).
- Lead multiple bridges, ebbing and flowing dynamically and musically.
- Incorporate a longer-than-normal drums-only moment.
- Incorporate a moment of silence.
- Invite the congregation into a moment of prayer on a topic related to this song.
- Ask someone from the band or congregation to read a specific Scripture aloud.
- Allow space for the gifts of the Spirit within the body of Christ.

Here is the actual minute-by-minute sample set order I provided:

11:00 a.m.
1. Piano and pad vamp on chorus or intro (no click).
2. Leader welcomes everyone and begins with prayer or by saying something about the amazing invitation we have to come into God's presence.

3. Leader invites everyone to begin to lift their voices to praise God spontaneously (with singing and/or speaking) (band swells).

4. Leader leads out with a spontaneous prayer and/or spontaneous song.

5. Leader continues singing spontaneously, but *off* the microphone, encouraging the entire community to continue singing (let this go for a couple minutes and then invite everyone to "press in" or "step into the river" again if their singing begins to diminish).

11:04 a.m.

6. Leader sings the chorus or bridge a couple times with or without click.

11:06 a.m.

7. After teaching a repetitive section of the song with no click, the band smoothly transitions to the normal intro of the song with click.

8. Sing/play song with normal structure, possibly doing the first verse two times with a musical turn around between them (also, plan to do the bridge a few more times than usual).

9. At the end of the "normal" version of the song, the band swells and the leader sings the chorus again a couple times with or without click.

11:12 a.m.

10. Leader encourages everyone to sing a new song along with the chorus chord progression.

11. Let this go for a couple minutes again, encouraging them along the way and leading by example.

11:14 a.m.

12. Leader begins to sing the bridge again. This can start softly and continue for quite a while (maybe four or six times).

13. When it seems right, begin building slowly with the band, possibly building at least one bridge with normal chords, and then

one bridge with planned alternate chords (to provide newness as well as musical tension).

14. Important: Don't go into the chorus yet. Stay on the bridge chords and go big instrumentally with the band. (The leader should hold out a long/high note on the last word of the last big bridge note in order to signify to the band and the congregants that he is *not* planning to sing the bridge again, even though the band will continue to play the bridge chords instrumentally). Let the music carry things for one to two bridges (while the guitarist solos/*Zâmars* and the people respond in their own way, possibly with *Tehillâh*).

15. After one or two rockin' instrumental bridges, the leader can sing spontaneously through another bridge, but possibly along with alternate chords. Then consider building to a big stop on beat four as you go back into the chorus full out with the band.

11:18 a.m.

16. Sing a final chorus (or sing one and let the band play instrumentally one last time).

17. Hit the end big or, preferably (if time allows), begin bringing it down by going to the "intro/outro" vibe, still with click. Once on the intro/outro, the team can vamp on this for a while, singing spontaneously or letting the band carry things instrumentally. This could also be a good spot to say something to tie everything together; the Holy Spirit will quicken the leader with the right thing(s) to say.

11:20 a.m.

18. Turn off the click at some point in there, and bring things down, gradually moving into a slightly slower tempo.

19. If time allows, you could always sing the bridge or chorus one more time, pray, or just let the music play out.

20. Done.

Needless to say, my team completed their assignment of playing one song for eighteen minutes, and they killed it! They kept saying how surprised they were at how fast the time flew and by how little "meaningless" repetition it required.

Years later, our teams instinctively know we only plan one or two songs for our eighteen-minute chapel worship sets, and it rarely alarms them when I give them this assignment. Why? Because we've worked tirelessly to make spontaneous worship a part of our "normal" culture. This means our leaders and our worship community have now become much more accustomed to leading and singing spontaneous worship. Yet this has only happened because we painstakingly laid the groundwork of restructuring our culture over many months, one week at a time, one service at a time. Now it's your turn!

INDEX

Pick Up Jeff's first book,
Awakening Pure Worship,
on Amazon or at
jeffdeyo.com.

Listen to Jeff's latest music on Apple Music,
Spotify, or anywhere else music is streamed.

Worship Live

at North Central University

You can help others love God authentically by joining our NCU Worship Live worship teams.

Check out our newest singles, "Invading," "Adores," and "Constant" on Spotify, Apple Music, and Google Play, or view our powerful music videos on the North Central University YouTube page.

Visit **northcentral.edu/worshiplivecharts** to download the actual chord charts from beloved worship Live songs like "Breath of Heaven" and many more.

NORTH CENTRAL
UNIVERSITY

Grow in Your Leadership

Strengthen your calling as a worship leader by getting your undergrad or graduate degree.

Grow in your faith as you pursue your passion to praise God through spirit-filled worship. Our world-class music program, state-of-the-art facilities, and close bonds with local churches will provide you with connections and real-world experience.

Learn more about our Master of Arts in Strategic Leadership: Worship Arts Leadership program at **northcentral.edu/worship**

Learn more about our Worship Leading undergraduate degree at **northcentral.edu/worshipleading**

NORTH CENTRAL
UNIVERSITY